Ben McKelvey is the author or co-author of six books including the best-sellers *Songs of a War Boy* and *The Commando: The life and death of Cameron Baird VC, MG*. His books have won an Indie Book Award, a NiB Military History Award and have been shortlisted in the Victorian Premier's Literary Awards, Queensland Premier's Literary Awards, Australian Book Industry Awards, the National Biography Award and more. Ben Mckelvey has also worked as journalist in Sydney and abroad, and has been embedded with the ADF in Iraq and East Timor and has worked independently in Afghanistan, Syria and Iran.

Find
Fix
Finish

Ben
McKelvey

HarperCollins*Publishers*

HarperCollins*Publishers*

Australia • Brazil • Canada • France • Germany • Holland • India
Italy • Japan • Mexico • New Zealand • Poland • Spain • Sweden
Switzerland • United Kingdom • United States of America

HarperCollins acknowledges the Traditional Custodians
of the land upon which we live and work, and pays respect
to Elders past and present.

First published in Australia in 2022
by HarperCollins*Publishers* Australia Pty Limited
Gadigal Country
Level 13, 201 Elizabeth Street, Sydney NSW 2000
ABN 36 009 913 517
harpercollins.com.au

A catalogue record for this book is available from the National Library of Australia

ISBN 978 1 4607 6076 5 (paperback)
ISBN 978 1 4607 1398 3 (ebook)

Cover design by HarperCollins Design Studio
Cover image by William West/AFP via Getty Images
Typeset in Sabon LT Std by Kirby Jones
Printed and bound in Australia by McPherson's Printing Group

'Go tell to Sparta, thou who passest by,
that here, obedient to her laws, we lie'
– Epitaph on the destroyed Cenotaph of Thermopylae,
observed by Herodotus

The sound of drums is pleasant from a distance.
– Afghan proverb

Contents

List of Acronyms   xi

Prologue   1

The Opening   17

The Middlegame   151

The Endgame   313

Epilogue   376

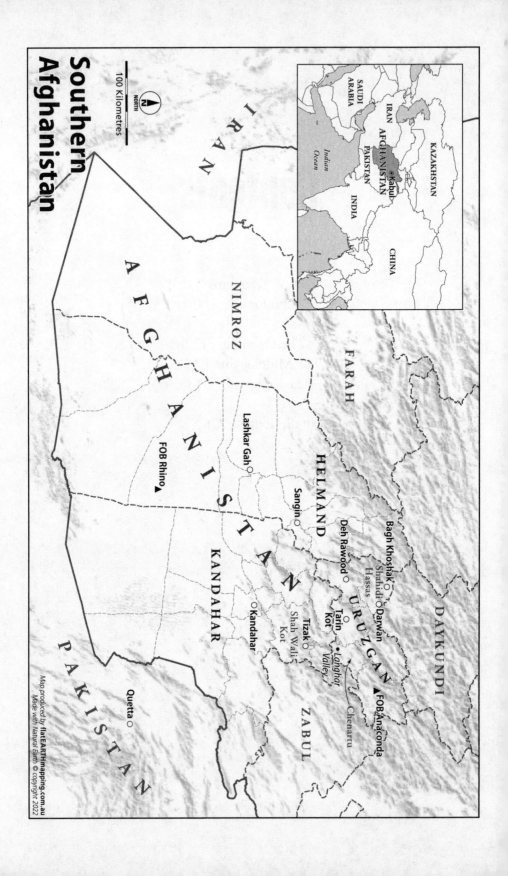

Southern Afghanistan

100 Kilometres

N
NORTH

IRAN

KAZAKHSTAN

SAUDI
ARABIA

IRAN

AFGHANISTAN

⊙Kabul

PAKISTAN

Indian
Ocean

INDIA

CHINA

IRAN

NIMROZ

A F G H A N I S T A N

FARAH

DAYKUNDI

LashKar Gah ○

FOB Rhino ▲

HELMAND

Sangin ○

Deh Rawood ○

Bagh Khoshak ○

Shahidi○Darwan
Hassas

URUZGAN

Tarin
Kot ●

KANDAHAR

Tizak ○

Shah Wali
Kot

Langhar
Valley

▲FOB Anaconda

Kandahar ○

ZABUL

Chenartu

Quetta ○

PAKISTAN

Map produced by flatEARTHmapping.com.au
Made with Natural Earth © copyright 2022

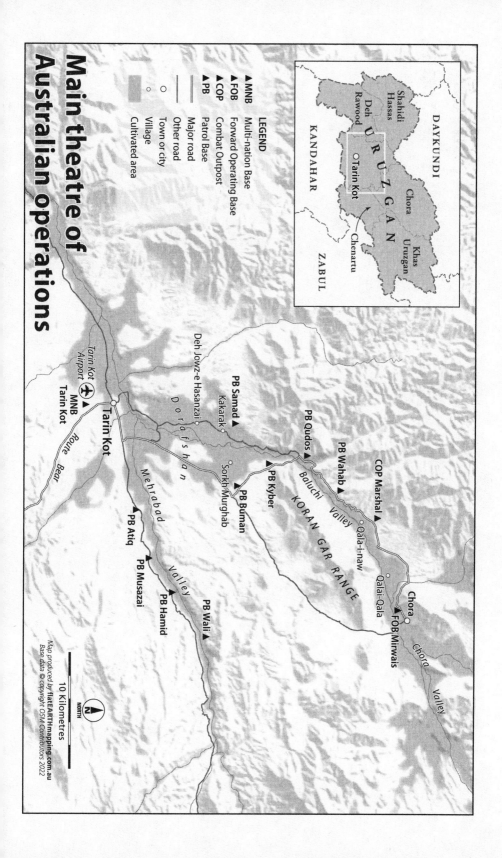

Main theatre of
Australian operations

LEGEND

▲ MNB   Multi-nation Base
▲ FOB   Forward Operating Base
▲ COP   Combat Outpost
▲ PB   Patrol Base

━━━ Major road
─── Other road
○ Town or city
○ Village
▢ Cultivated area

DAYKUNDI

Shahidi
Hassas

Deh
Rawood

U R U Z G A N

KANDAHAR

Chora
Khas
Uruzgan

○Tarin Kot

Chenarru

ZABUL

Tarin Kot
Airport ✈

MNB
Tarin Kot

▲ Tarin Kot

Rowre
Baer

Deh Jowz-e Hasanzai○

PB Samad ▲

Kakarak ○

D o r a f s h a n

Mehrabad

PB Qudos ▲

PB Wahab ▲

COP Marshall ▲

Baluchi Valley

Qala-i-naw ○

K O R A N   G A R   R A N G E

PB Kyber ▲

○ Sorkh Murghab

PB Buman ▲

Qalai-Qala ○

Chora ○

FOB Mirwais ▲

PB Atiq ▲

Valley

PB Musazai ▲

PB Hamid ▲

PB Wali ▲

Chora

Valley

10 Kilometres

N
NORTH

Map produced by flatEARTHmapping.com.au
Base data © copyright OSM contributors 2022

List of Acronyms

1CDO	1st Commando Regiment
2CDO	2nd Commando Regiment
3RAR	3rd Battalion, Royal Australian Regiment
4RAR	4th Battalion, Royal Australian Regiment
6RAR	6th Battalion, Royal Australian Regiment
ACAG	Afghan Combat Application Group
ACC	Australian Civilian Corps
ADF	Australian Defence Force
ADFIS	Australian Defence Force Investigative Service
AFP	Australian Federal Police
ANA	Afghan National Army
AIHRC	Afghan Independent Human Rights Commission
ASIS	Australian Secret Intelligence Service
ASLAV	Australian light armoured vehicle
AUSTINT	Australian Army Intelligence Corps
CDF	Chief of Defence Force (Australia)
CJSOTF-A	Combined Joint Special Operations Task Force – Afghanistan
CONOPS	concept of operations
COP	combat out-post
DEA	Drug Enforcement Administration
Delta	1st Special Forces Operational Detachment, aka Task Force Green

DEVGRU	Naval Special Warfare Development Group, aka SEAL Team 6, Task Force Blue
DFAT	Department of Foreign Affairs and Trade (Australia)
DSC	Distinguished Service Cross
EKIA	enemy killed in action
FATC	Fusion and Targeting Cell (Australian special forces intelligence)
FE	Force Element
FHT	Field HUMINT Team (Australian Army Intelligence Corps)
FOB	Forward Operating Base
HLZ	helicopter landing zone
HUMINT	human intelligence
IED	improvised explosive device
IGADF	Inspector-General of the ADF
IHL	international humanitarian law
IRR	Incident Response Regiment (Australian Army)
ISAF	International Security Assistance Force
ISI	Inter-Services Intelligence (Pakistan)
ISR	intelligence, surveillance and reconnaissance
JPEL	Joint Prioritised Effects Lists
JSOC	Joint Special Operations Command (US)
JTAC	Joint Terminal Attack Controller, service member who directs the action of combat aircraft
JTF	Joint Task Force
LRPV	long-range patrol vehicle
LZ	landing zone

MACV-SOG	Military Assistance Command, Vietnam – Studies and Observation Group
MTF-1	Mentoring Task Force One
MTF	Mentoring Task Forces (Australian)
NDS	National Directorate of Security (Afghanistan)
NSA	National Security Agency (US)
NSC	National Security Committee (Australia)
NVG	night-vision goggles
NZSAS	New Zealand Special Air Service
ODA	Operational Detachment A-team (US Special Forces)
OGA	other government agencies (US intelligence)
OTG	Special Operations Task Group
PRT	Provincial Reconstruction Team
PTSD	post-traumatic stress disorder
PUC	person under control
QRF	quick reaction force
RHIB	rigid-hull inflatable boat
RoE	rules of engagement
RPG	rocket-propelled grenade
RSM	Regimental Sergeant Major
RT-RG	Real Time Regional Gateway (intelligence data processing system)
RTF	Reconstruction Task Force
SASR	Special Air Service Regiment
SFTG	Special Forces Task Group (Australia)
SIGAR	Special Inspector General for Afghanistan Reconstruction
SOCAUST	Special Operations Command (Australia)
SOCC	Special Operations Command Centre

SOCOMD	Special Operations Command (Australian Army)
SOER	Special Operations Engineering Regiment
SOF	special operations forces
SOTG	Special Operations Task Group (Australian army)
SRV	special reconnaissance vehicles
TAG	Tactical Assault Group
TAO	Tailored Access Operations (intelligence-gathering technology)
TLO	Tribal Liaison Office
VC	Victoria Cross

Prologue

Winter 2011

PRIVATE SHANE HEALEY STOOD alone on the flight line, the large tarmacked area in the middle of Camp Holland, where all helicopter-borne Australian special forces missions started and ended. He was startled but exhilarated: in front of him was a mission, his very own. His own personal jackpot lay ahead.

Healey had helped to generate this target, as he had done many others before, and to get the target raised onto one of the Joint Prioritised Effects Lists, or JPEL (pronounced *jah-pel*). The prospective target was now a confirmed target – Objective Yeti Avlis – thanks to Healey, but it would also be his to process. This was an anomalous turn of events.

Healey was a squat, muscular Anglo-Indigenous soldier with bursting traps, an often-furrowed brow and extensive combat experience. He'd spent time in the Australian Navy and Army, and had field intelligence and combat experience working alongside the US military and the CIA in Iraq as a private contractor. He was not, however, one of the Australian Special Operations Task Group (SOTG) gunfighters. He was an intelligence analyst.

Healey didn't normally work on the rocky peaks or in the lush green belts of Uruzgan Province, in Afghanistan, like those in the Special Air Service Regiment (SASR) patrols or commando teams. He worked in one of the blast-proof and bulletproof rubber-mounted buildings in Camp Russell, Australia's special forces base within a base in the provincial capital of Tarin Kot. Healey usually worked at the Fusion and Targeting Cell, or FATC, the beating heart of Australia's special forces mission in Afghanistan.

The 'fusion' in FATC was the fusion of all the intelligence sources coming into the SOTG, which in 2011 included an incredible amount of satellite, drone and airborne imagery, and captured phone conversations, text messages, metadata and more. Also being fused was a huge array of human sources, cultivated across the province, country and region. Some were developed and run by the Australian Secret Intelligence Service (ASIS), but more came from the Field HUMINT (or human intelligence) Teams (FHT) of the Australian Army Intelligence Corps, known as AUSTINT.

After all that fusion came the targeting: finding and identifying the people who were going to be raised on the JPEL, the highly classified intra-coalition lists of people designated to be killed or captured.

In 2011, the processing of these JPEL targets was the primary task of the SASR. They had others tasks too, including mentoring Afghan forces, but having to fulfil these was almost a punishment or demotion. The SASR were the premier trigger-pullers within the Australian Defence Force (ADF). They liked to hunt and they wanted targets – they needed them, hungered for them. It was the role of the FATC to find these targets, and then help them be authorised for prosecution.

On that last day of February 2011, however, it wasn't to be the SASR prosecuting a target: it would be Shane Healey.

Rotors spun, engines roared and Blackhawks arrived on the flight line. Healey held up a sheet of paper to the US crew chief: 'Baluchi'. There was a nod of acknowledgement from a loadmaster inside the helicopter and Healey clambered aboard. Quickly they rose out of the military base, out of the secure airfield, out of the small provincial capital, and flew north-west, into the war.

The flight to Baluchi was only a few minutes, and yet Healey was flying over a blanket of complexity. The Blackhawk took him through the Tarin Kot bowl and then over the Dorafshan region to the Baluchi Valley. Below, pastoral land patched in rectangles of emerald, bottle and olive was alive with crops and villages. These green veins seemed to scythe through jagged and dead brown mountains where herders, smugglers and snipers plied their trade.

The distance between Tarin Kot and Baluchi was no further than between the SASR barracks in the beachside Perth suburb of Swanbourne and the CBD, yet dozens of tribes and sub-tribes were represented in the compounds Healey flew over, a knotted tangle of business interests, family feuds, ancient enmities and deep culture.

This tangle was the insurgency, and every man fighting with or against the Australians had his own reason to wield a weapon. This tangle was Afghanistan, for decades more a problem than a country, where most Afghans in the wild south knew no benefits of nationhood.

The SOTG was fighting not one nation but many. The Taliban, yes, but also tribes that had been wronged by Australia's local partners or the coalition, vengeful families who were bereaved, drug producers, truckers, some men who were paid, some men who were bored, and some whose motivations will never be understood by any Australian.

* * *

Throughout February 2011, Healey had been trying to answer the question of who was planting pressure-plate improvised explosive devices (IEDs) in the Chora and Baluchi valleys, north-east of Tarin Kot.

So far the Australians working in those areas – most of them regular Australian Army diggers attempting to train Afghan National Army soldiers – had been lucky, and the bombmakers unlucky. The devices had been discovered before detonation, or had detonated harmlessly. In a number of instances, the main explosives had been frozen inert, with only the primer detonating.

There were human sources suggesting that a man named Haji Hamidullah was laying bombs. There was confusion in the FATC, as they knew of multiple insurgents called Haji Hamidullah – including two brothers with roughly the same name. ('Haji' was an honorific title bestowed to those who had travelled to Mecca for the Hajj pilgrimage; the name Hamidullah meant 'all praise be to God'.)

After reviewing the intelligence and photographs of the discovered IEDs, Healey concluded that at least some of the bombs were being laid by the very large Haji Hamidullah who was estimated to weigh between 120 and 130 kilograms. He lived in Qala-i-Naw, a village that lay in the shadow of an Australian/Afghan combat outpost (COP) named Mashal, which sat just above the Baluchi Valley floor at the start of rocky incline.

Throughout the Australian war, Qala-i-Naw had been a wound that refused to heal. That small village, and another to the east of it named Kala Kala, were subject to constant Australian attention, thanks in no small part to many of the elders of those villages being the mortal enemies of Australia's preferred Afghan warlord, Matiullah Khan.

By day, the left hand of Australia's 'whole-of-government' effort might be reaching out to these villages, offering friendship, *shuras* (meetings with elders) and building projects. By night, the right hand – Australia's special forces – might be 'banging it in', blowing in doors, hunting targets and shooting anyone who fought back.

Liberal MP and former assistant defence minister Andrew Hastie, a former SASR troop commander, jokes: 'Blokes in Australia would say that they had real estate in Kala Kala ... gotta go and check out the portfolio.'

Multiple SASR operators would die in and around these villages, as would hundreds of Afghans. This is the area in which a number of war crimes are alleged to have been committed by Australian soldiers.

After a review of the available intelligence, and after conversations with the engineers and intelligence analyst attached to the 3rd Battalion Royal Australian Regiment (3RAR), which was manning COP Mashal, Shane Healey decided there was enough evidence to raise the large Haji Hamidullah of Qala-i-Naw on the JPEL.

All the available intelligence on him was compiled in a 'targeting pack'. This was sent, via the Australian Special Operation Task Group's intelligence officer, legal officer and commanding officer in Tarin Kot, to the US-led Special Operations Task Force South East in Kandahar. There, overnight, Haji Hamidullah became elevated on the JPEL and identified as Objective Yeti Avlis. In that moment, the legal protections afforded to Haji Hamidullah's person narrowed somewhat.

The JPELs were also known colloquially as the 'kill/capture lists', which referred to the rules of engagement that existed when Australian or international special forces (and only special forces) were prosecuting targets on that list. When hunting a JPEL objective, the Australians could kill their target without any attempt at capture, whether the target presented an immediate risk to the prosecuting forces or not.

After a JPEL target had passed 'green', referring to the time window in which the target could be attacked, a mission could be mounted against the target. This usually required three things: helicopters; an intelligence, surveillance and reconnaissance (ISR) craft, usually a drone; and a force element – the soldiers who would be doing the killing or capturing.

The Australian SOTG in Tarin Kot had three gunfighting force elements: Force Element Alpha (composed of soldiers from the SASR), Force Element Bravo (composed of soldiers from the 2nd Commando Regiment, or 2CDO) and Force Element Charlie (composed of soldiers from the reserve 1st Commando Regiment, or 1CDO, which was made up mostly of part-time soldiers).

When Objective Yeti Avlis was raised to the JPEL, Force Element Alpha were not yet in Afghanistan. Each winter, when the snow and bitter winds came and the fighting was lessened, Force Element Alpha and Force Element Bravo were withdrawn to Australia to rest, recover and retrain. This was when Force Element Charlie was inserted. In the quietest and coldest months of the year, there was a slowing of operational tempo but there was no pause.

As soon as Hamidullah was raised as Objective Yeti Avlis, Healey and others from the FATC briefed the Force Element Charlie leadership about the target.

'I said, "If you want him he's on a platter," but that wasn't sexy enough,' Healey explains. 'They wanted to go off and get in a gunfight.'

Objective Yeti Avlis was regularly seen in front of COP Mashal riding his motorbike alone and unarmed. He would be a very easy collar. This was not, however, what Force Element Charlie had in mind for their valuable 'air window', in which they had access to US helicopters. They were planning a mission against a JPEL target further up the insurgent food chain, designated Objective Slayer.

Charlie were planning on attacking Objective Slayer's 'historical activity zone' in Kandahar Province, meaning there was intelligence, either human or signals, that the insurgent had been known to frequent the area, but not necessarily recently. Analysts from the FATC had told the force element that they had signals intelligence indicating Objective Slayer was not in Afghanistan but in Pakistan, but Charlie were adamant that they would go to Kandahar, where a gunfight was far more likely.

While Force Element Charlie were in Kandahar, Healey was in the FATC. His phone rang: it was the intelligence analyst at COP Mashal. Haji Hamidullah was on their base, where a *shura* between the locals and Australian forces was being held. After much swearing, the FATC commander walked into the SOTG Operations Room and the operations officer gave him his orders: 'Grab your stuff – you're going. You're going to get your mate.'

Twenty minutes later, Healey's Blackhawk descended into COP Mashal, little more than a parking lot for armoured vehicles, protected by a perimeter of Hesco barriers and gun towers. Hamidullah, like everyone else in the *shura*, Australian or Afghan, watched the helicopter land and disgorge a single soldier, squat and strong like a bulldog, who charged at the Afghan giant as soon as he landed.

Healey, with an M4 carbine at the ready and a 9mm pistol strapped to his hip, closed the ground between himself and the

Afghan. He wondered what would happen when he met his target. Healey was an experienced martial artist, but was outweighed by Hamidullah by at least 30 kilograms.

Healey smashed his body into Hamidullah's at pace, and both men crashed hard onto the ground. The Afghan was flipped over and flex-cuffed, and blackout goggles and a hood were shoved over his head. He was dragged to the waiting helicopter.

Healey landed back in Tarin Kot with his heart still pounding in his chest. The helicopter was greeted by Australian Military Police, who took Hamidullah away for prisoner enrolment. After a confession was obtained during 'tactical questioning', Hamidullah was sent to the huge US detention facility at Bagram Air Base. The commanding officer of the SOTG then called 'jackpot', meaning a JPEL target had been sent off for long-term detention or killed.

Jackpots were the scoreboard of Australia's special forces war. In lieu of a front line to push and essential infrastructure to seize, the jackpot was the metric of success for the Australians. It was the pathway to medals, to promotions, to respect within the increasingly rancorous special forces community.

Objective Yeti Avlis was the first SOTG jackpot of the year, but Force Element Alpha would soon arrive back in country. When they did, the hunting season would start in earnest.

* * *

On 10 March 2011, Prime Minister Julia Gillard addressed the US Congress.

'From my discussions with your country's leaders in Washington, my meetings with our generals in Afghanistan and my time with our troops, this is my conclusion: I believe we have the right strategy in place, a resolute and courageous commander in General Petraeus, and the resources needed to deliver the strategy. I am cautiously encouraged by what I have seen,' she said.

In fact, as Prime Minister Gillard gave her speech, there was no 'right strategy', and no winning the war. By 2011, most astute observers already recognised this.

After the war, *The Washington Post* would win a court case giving the paper access to private correspondence within the US Special Inspector General for Afghan Reconstruction. These messages would show that senior US military officers and US diplomats knew by 2011 that the war would not be won.

Some Australians knew this too. Senior ADF officers had approached the Minister for Defence, Labor's Joel Fitzgibbon, telling him that 'we needed to find our way out of this thing'. As minister Fitzgibbon told me, he was attempting to 'not immerse ourselves further in the mire'.

Major General John Cantwell, the commander of all Australian forces in the Middle East and Afghanistan, thought to himself in 2011 that the Australian operation in Afghanistan was doing nothing but 'digging a well of misery'. When his second-in-command asked him why Australia was fighting in Afghanistan, he told his junior: 'We're here because we're freaking here.'

It was not all bad news coming out of Afghanistan, however. Australia's special forces had become increasingly adept at the type of warfare they were being asked to undertake, especially kill/capture missions. Coalition JPEL lists had been swelling, and those targets, as well as people around them, were being put to the sword at an incredible clip.

The ADF does not release the numbers of enemy killed (nor of civilians killed accidentally), but it's now believed that Australia's special forces war killed approximately 11,000 Afghans during the war in Afghanistan – roughly four times the number of Afghan soldiers who were trained or advised by the Australians' Mentoring Task Forces (MTF) and the SOTG throughout the war.

The manner and scope of the killing being done by the Australian SOTG was something the United States, our primary ally in the war, was exceptionally happy about. By 2011 the Australian special forces had killed many insurgents in Uruzgan Province and were now conducting missions in Helmand and Kandahar provinces as well, hunting insurgents who should, geographically speaking, have been the quarry of British or Canadian forces.

In June 2010, for instance, a small SASR element inserted into the Kandahar village of Tizak on a JPEL mission generated by the US 1st Special Forces Operational Detachment, aka Delta Force. They killed 76 people within hours, and ten of those killed on site were later designated as medium-value targets. A similar number of Afghans were believed to have been killed nearly simultaneously by Australian commandos a couple of valleys over.

The Battle of Tizak also generated the Australian war's biggest celebrity, a giant, hard-charging SASR corporal, a judge's son from Perth named Ben Roberts-Smith.

Just a few weeks before she spoke at the US Congress, Prime Minister Gillard attended the ceremony at which Corporal Ben Roberts-Smith had the Victoria Cross, the highest medal in Australia's honours and award system, pinned on his uniform. After the conferment, the Chief of Defence saluted Ben Roberts-Smith, not the other way round, as is the tradition of the VC.

At the ceremony, Prime Minister Gillard said Roberts-Smith's award 'honours the values and the discipline of a soldier; the marks of character acquired throughout a lifetime from family and school, mentors and mates; and the awareness of a greater tradition than that of his own, a greater tradition that binds all of us, a greater tradition of which he is now part, a tradition called ANZAC, and in awarding this VC today to Corporal Roberts-Smith, we are saying to him that he breathes that tradition anew'.

While addressing Congress, Prime Minister Gillard remembered her interactions with the Victoria Cross recipient. 'Corporal Ben Roberts-Smith is Australia's most recent Victoria Cross winner – our equivalent of your Medal of Honor,' she said. 'Ben is a veteran of five tours of Afghanistan and first went there in 2006. When we met recently, his words to me were compelling: "There are hard days ahead."'

Prime Minister Gillard had no idea how true these words would prove.

The JPEL was not the addition-by-subtraction tool US war planners had hoped it would be. It was changing the human terrain in unpredictable ways, not only in Uruzgan and Kandahar, but also in Canberra, Sydney and Perth.

* * *

Before the SASR came online in Afghanistan, Force Element Charlie were sent out to a trucking and shipping depot a short drive from their base to pick up another JPEL target: one of four brothers who owned and operated a logistics company in the Tarin Kot mercantile district nearby. The man was designated as Objective Heggitt. But regardless of the JPEL rules, the target – real name Hayat Ustad – was to be taken alive, primarily because he was the business partner of Australia's warlord, Matiullah Khan.

Officially, Matiullah was the head of something that looked like the Uruzgan transit police, but in reality he was something else altogether. Part viceroy, part mob boss, Matiullah was the most powerful man in Tarin Kot. His power and money had come from his control of Route Bear, the only real road in and out of Tarin Kot. Matiullah had put a toll on the road, and then built a militia – the Kandak Amniate Uruzgan, or KAU – to enforce his toll. In doing so, he had gone from being a taxi driver to a millionaire dozens of times over. Much of that money had been spent on the KAU, which kept the road secure, clear and profitable. A brutal and effective fighter, he was chosen to be a partner for Australian special forces in Afghanistan.

Everyone paid Matiullah's toll. If they didn't, there were consequences. When the Americans, Australians or Dutch didn't pay, the 'Taliban' would appear and attack convoys or lay IEDs on Matiullah's road. When Afghans didn't pay, they would be beaten or killed.

Hayat Ustad had once been caught shipping freight on Matiullah's road without paying and was severely beaten because of it. Indeed, Matiullah himself had beaten a permanent limp into Ustad. Afterwards, the pair had reconciled and had since forged a lucrative partnership.

Perhaps without Matiullah's knowledge, Hayat Ustad had started adding illicit cargo to his shipments. The FATC discerned that explosive componentry was being shipped into Uruzgan from Pakistan, using trucks from the logistics company owned by the Ustad brothers. They had identified Hayat Ustad as the culpable party, so he went into the JPEL pipeline, coming out as Objective Heggitt.

The SOTG had plans beyond killing Heggitt, however. An SOTG initiative known as the 'Rule of Law Cell' had helped raise an Afghan arrest warrant for him, which they planned to use to push Ustad through the Afghan court system. This was to be the first ever Afghan warrant generated with SOTG help. They would try to have Matiullah approve – and take credit for – the lawful execution of the warrant, which, they hoped, would lead to a courtroom conviction.

To that end, Shane Healey had been hinting to Haji Wali Jan, Matiullah's head of intelligence, during a daily morning intelligence meeting that the SOTG knew Ustad was working with the insurgency, and that they might one day grab him.

Sometime in March 2011, Force Element Charlie was sent to pick up Objective Heggitt, but they captured the wrong Ustad brother. Before that brother could be released and Hayat detained, the three remaining brothers, Dawood, Manan and Hayat Ustad, appeared at Camp Holland asking for the release of their innocent brother. The trio were invited to Camp Russell's *shura* room and a switch was planned.

Outside the room, the brothers were greeted by Healey, who had been tasked with positively identifying which brother they had a warrant for. Outside the door, soldiers from Force Element Charlie were waiting to grab Hayat after a signal was sent via the *shura* room's AV equipment.

The translated conversation between the Australian soldiers and the Afghan businessmen was conciliatory, and then even convivial. On behalf of the SOTG, Healey apologised for picking up their brother and, without explaining that Hayat was their target, offered to hand him back to them the next day. The

Afghans said they would return then, and Hayat offered Healey his phone number so that further mistakes might be avoided.

There was so much the FATC could do with Hayat Ustad's phone number. Open-source reporting suggests that Ustad's conversations could be monitored, all incoming and outgoing numbers could be captured, the phone's location could be tracked within a few metres, all data could be recorded, and the phone could be used as a listening device even when it was turned off.

A captured phone could be like the sword of Damocles hanging over an Afghan's head. Should a JPEL target use their phone, the target could go 'JPEL green' in the targeting system, meaning a mission could be launched against them and they could be designated a jackpot and legally killed. Should the target be captured, however, then further evidence must be found of their complicity in a crime before a jackpot could be called.

In 2012, then SASR Captain Andrew Hastie (now a federal politician) approached the commanding officer of the SASR, concerned that some patrols were choosing to kill Afghans suspected of being insurgents rather than capturing them, because the evidentiary standard for capture was much higher than for killing.

'You could launch on a target using a SIGINT trigger [for instance, a JPEL target using their phone] but you couldn't use that SIGINT trigger as a way of keeping them locked up for more than three days, and you had to find evidence, whether it be weapons, det[onation] cord, componentry,' a former SASR officer said.

This higher evidentiary standard for capture might also have created a killing incentive within SOTG command. The former officer notes that 'once we kept a JPEL count, you want to rack up the count, whether it's kill or capture'.

During the *shura* between Healey and the Ustad brothers, an on-the-fly decision was made to keep Hayat out in the field and on the intelligence hook. He had no idea he was a marked man – he had already promised to return to the camp the next day – but having compromised his phone, the Australian intelligence team might be able to explore more of the complicated insurgent web of which he was part. That web, it was known, included Australia's national priority target, insurgent commander Abdul Hai, designated as Objective Rapier.

Hayat Ustad walked away from the meeting a free man. He didn't know it, but he had started working for the Australians.

* * *

Friday, 29 April 2011 was a quiet day in the FATC, and in the Operations Centre. The SASR had relieved the reservists and had hit the ground running, killing and capturing a number of JPEL targets in the first month of their rotation. They were still beholden to the air window restrictions, however, and as 29 April was a day when they had no access to helicopters, the SOTG S2 (the senior SOTG intelligence officer) and S3 (the operations officer) were both away from Camp Russell.

In the afternoon, some of the intelligence staff in the FATC, including Shane Healey, went to the Camp Russell gym. When he got back to the FATC, he was met with shocked faces and anger.

'They fucking killed him, didn't they?' he asked a nearby soldier.

The soldier nodded.

Hayat Ustad had, by using his phone at his warehouse, turned JPEL 'green'. This status had been seen on a terminal being used by an SASR officer or patrol commander. A kill/capture mission was quickly assembled against Ustad, and an element of SASR operators rode over to the warehouse on their quadbikes (along with, according to local sources, armoured vehicle support). As Hayat Ustad sat down to have lunch with his uncle and some co-workers, he was gunned down.

'They were bored,' a source says. 'It's that simple. They were bored and they wanted to shoot someone.'

No one in the FATC cared that the Afghan facilitator had died – their job was often to condemn Afghans to death – but they did care about what the killing did to the strategic landscape. They had been gaining intelligence from Ustad and could, with the right prosecution at the right time, have brought Matiullah closer to the Afghan legal system, something Uruzgan desperately needed. Now Hayat Ustad was dead, with little advantage gained except on the JPEL's jackpot leaderboard (where Hayat's brother Manan Ustad would also end up, killed later as Objective Blanka).

The men and women working in the FATC considered themselves sculptors, shaping the battlespace with pressure, movements and cuts. As they saw it, Hayat Ustad's killing was not a means to anything greater, but an end.

The killing of Ustad had been duly authorised and so was legal, according to the 2011 rules of engagement binding the SOTG's JPEL missions, except perhaps for one thing: local and SOTG sources say that Ustad was not armed, and that, after the kill, the prosecuting SASR element placed a Makarov pistol on Ustad's chest before photographing his body.

On 30 April 2011, a press release was issued by the Department of Defence headlined 'Insurgent commander killed attempting to shoot Australian troops'. The release described the killing as a 'Afghan National Police-led operation in Tarin Kot' against a 'known insurgent leader', and declared that 'the operation was conducted with strict adherence to Australian rules of engagement'.

But had a 'throwdown' weapon been used? If so, why?

These questions can only be answered once we have understood Australia's special forces war in Afghanistan, where laws, rules, orders, ethics, incentives and morals combined in a giant ball of twisted twine, dyed in shades of grey.

* * *

In 2012, Ben Roberts-Smith flew back into Afghanistan. This rotation would be the last for the Victoria Cross recipient, but his first as an SASR patrol commander, a position he'd aspired to for his entire career.

He would now have battlefield independence like he'd never before experienced. According to a book authorised by the Special Operations Commander (Australia) – known as SOCAUST – Ben Roberts-Smith would have the most kills of any soldier on this rotation. For his work on this rotation, he would be awarded the Commendation for Distinguished Service, an honour normally reserved for senior officers. In his citation, Roberts-Smith's mentoring of the next generation of SASR operators was mentioned.

After this 2012 rotation, Roberts-Smith left the ADF for, eventually, a career in television management. He retired as the most decorated Australian soldier since the world wars, leaving behind an impressive legacy of medals – as well as an astonishing trail of animosity, resentment and rumour.

Some who had served with Ben Roberts-Smith were telling fellow members of the brotherhood of the SASR that the Victoria Cross recipient was an incompetent patrol commander, a bully and guilty of grievous misconduct. In 2018, these rumours were laid down in newsprint, first without naming Ben Roberts-Smith and then later outing him specifically. In 2020, the long-awaited Inspector-General of the Australian Defence Force's report on alleged war crimes in Afghanistan was released in a redacted form. The report found credible allegations of 39 murders, mostly of prisoners, placing responsibility on 25 soldiers. The vast majority of the alleged murders were committed in 2012.

The public face of the report was Chief of the Defence Force Angus Campbell, himself a former SASR officer, who told the media that ADF officers and investigators had been 'frustrated by outright deceit by those who knew the truth and, not infrequently, misguided resistance to inquiries and investigations by their superiors'. A 'bad apple' theory of military malfeasance was promoted, the idea that some rogue operators were misbehaving in a difficult but just war.

The only known alleged 'bad apple' was Ben Roberts-Smith (although neither he nor anyone else was named officially), and he became a lightning rod for news about the Inspector-General's report. Fresh allegations about Roberts-Smith began to be published in the press with metronomic regularity.

Roberts-Smith claimed compete innocence, and fought back, mounting a long and expensive (the legal costs of both sides are already estimated at $25 million) defamation case. With his Channel Seven billionaire boss Kerry Stokes backing him financially, Roberts-Smith hired two of Sydney's most prominent barristers to argue his case against the offending media outlets, primarily Nine Media (formerly Fairfax Media), publisher of newspapers *The Age* and *The Sydney Morning Herald*.

It was revealed during the trial that either Kerry Stokes or his company Australian Capital Equity was paying the legal costs of multiple SASR member appearing in the defamation trial who have been accused of war crimes including murder, and of a number of other witnesses appearing in support of Ben Roberts-Smith.

At the time of writing the trial is over but not been decided. No war crimes charges have yet been laid against the alleged perpetrators identified in the Inspector-General's report, that responsibility falling to a new statutory body called the Office of the Special Investigator, which is currently only funded through 2023.

Neither the defamation case nor the Inspector-General's report is a perfect historical torch that can shed light on the darkness that was Australia's special forces war in Afghanistan. And it must be remembered that, until a court of law determines otherwise, every Australian soldier and ex-soldier must be bestowed with the presumption of innocence when accused of any wrongdoing. But when we take the time to understand why and how Australia entered the fight, as well as where our forces fought, and how – then both the report and the trial suggest one thing: that Australia's sins in Afghanistan are not firewalled at the rank of sergeant.

The Opening

1

'To select people in the way we were ... and have them count coal trucks was just a complete waste of time'

IT WAS 29 AUGUST 2001, and powerful rigid-hull inflatable boats (RHIBs) carrying 45 SASR operators were scything through the warm Indian Ocean waves. They were moving towards a target: an Afghan target, the first of hundreds that would be prosecuted in the next 13 years.

The operators readied their weapons, checked comms and, in their heads, ran through the meticulously plotted action plans to storm the Norwegian freight ship ahead.

Meanwhile, in the extreme north of Afghanistan, close to the Tajik border, a two-man suicide bombing team moved closer to their target as a Saudi comrade in Washington DC purchased five tickets for American Airlines Flight 77 to Los Angeles.

The world was turning, and after three long decades of peace and peacekeeping, the SASR was going to war.

The men in the RHIBs were part of the SASR's Tactical Assault Group, or TAG, a sub-element within the regiment based on a capability developed by the British SAS to resolve domestic terrorism situations like building seizures, hostage taking and hijackings. The Australian SASR TAG teams have a particular emphasis on close-quarters marine battle, as many of the scenarios they train for involve the hijacking of oil platforms or large ships off the coast of Australia.

As Australia's foreign minister, Alexander Downer swapped calls with his Norwegian counterpart, Thorbjørn Jagland, about a Norwegian-flagged cargo ship not complying with Australian orders to sail away from Australian waters, the TAG element had been flown from Perth to Christmas Island, where it was transferred to HMAS *Manoora*, a Kanimbla-class transport ship following the rogue vessel. The Norwegian crew were told that if their ship did not comply with Australian orders, 'appropriate action' would follow.

When the ship moved closer to Australian waters, against orders, the TAG element was told to execute.

Before boarding their RHIBs, the SASR had examined the possible threat profiles. Peter Tinley, then the second-in-command (or 2IC) of the SASR boarding party and now a Western Australian MP, says one of these threat profiles suggested they may soon be involved in a fight.

'We thought there was a potential for our boarding to be opposed, but we had no particular information other than to cover every possible contingency,' said Tinley.

There was no suggestion that they were going to be resisted by the small Norwegian crew, but the large group of Afghans – a nationality with a warlike reputation, and likely to be numbering in the hundreds – were a different proposition.

As the Norwegian ship loomed larger on the horizon, the soldiers readied their Heckler & Koch submachine guns and grenades. Any resistance on the ship would be met with lethal force; the SASR doesn't shoot to wound.

Soon the ship became a wall of red metal, but to the delight of the SASR assault group, it was not a wall they would need to scale. A gangway had been lowered, from deck level to the waterline. The TAG operators knew this was no invitation to invasion: it simply indicated that the ship was expecting medical assistance, something the ship's captain had requested multiple times.

As the RHIB's drivers prepared to disgorge the TAG operators, the name of the ship could be discerned, written in white on its aft: TAMPA.

* * *

For decades preceding 9/11, the SASR had been rockstars in a time of rap. Throughout most of the 1970s, '80s and '90s, the acronym SAS had remained a catchword for high-octane military adventurism in Australia, but the reality had been quite different.

'When I was there, the SAS was pretty much looking for a role,' says Chris Roberts AM, CSC, the Commanding Officer of the SASR in the mid-1980s, and later Commander of Australian Special Forces. 'We were asking ourselves all the time: "How do we become a capability that would be useful?"'

The regiment had made its name during the Vietnam War, where they were dubbed the 'Ghosts of the Jungle' by the North Vietnamese Army, for their ability to disappear and reappear at will, but Roberts, a veteran of that war, believes the unit could have done far more.

'We did largely reconnaissance, and I have to say we did tactical reconnaissance, in which we supported the Task Force [1st Australian Task Force]. We also did harassing and a couple of raids – for example, I did a raid that destroyed a bridge,' says Roberts, who also notes that the regular army Task Force didn't really know how to utilise the special forces capability, which he believed could be far more offensive.

In the period of peace that followed, Roberts says the SASR became underutilised and unfocused. The SASR had developed one of the most stringent selection regimens in the world, comparable with (and borrowing from) British SAS techniques and procedures. They were selecting not only for extreme fitness, perseverance and a high capability for field and infantry skills, but also for a specific type of intelligence and even individuality, something not sought elsewhere in the ADF.

Roberts saw that the SASR could serve as a 'national mission unit', as did the United States Delta Force and the British SAS, with the regiment being a viable solution, in Australia or overseas, to any political problem that could potentially be delegated to men with guns.

Roberts and subsequent SASR commanding officer Jim Wallace AM, who also later became Commander of the Australian Special Forces, wanted the regiment to be able to put options on the table in Canberra whenever there was a problem. Some within the unit – although not Roberts or Wallace – even believed the SASR should sit outside the military chain of command altogether, reporting directly to the prime minister and cabinet, as some US special forces units do to the president.

'We really wanted to be the government's force of choice,' says Wallace. But for the 1980s and much of the 1990s, the SASR were likely barely thought of at all by senior government figures.

In the 1990s the doctrinal role of each Australian military unit became guided by a parliamentary report from civilian military expert Paul Dibb, issued to the Hawke government in 1986, and by a subsequent Defence White Paper, which suggested that the absolute priority for the ADF should be the defence of the Australian homeland. The report noted that Australia's special forces should concentrate on the surveillance and reconnaissance of Australia, and that 'other responsibilities ... should not be developed at further expense of its military responsibilities for surveillance and reconnaissance'.

'Personally, that didn't sit well with me,' says Chris Roberts. He thought the SASR had the capacity do so much more, and that its members had been hamstrung by 'jealous' regular army infantry commanders higher in the chain of command.

Orders were orders, however, and these local responsibilities meant the SASR spent a great deal of their time training in northern Australia, preparing for an Australian-based war that most thought would never happen.

'The regiment was dominated by this "defence of Australia" nonsense,' says Jim Wallace. 'I say "nonsense" because none of us ever thought we'd be fighting like that. To select people in the way we were and the quality of people we found and then to sit them on top of hills in the north of the Northern Territory and in the Kimberley District and have them count coal trucks was just a complete waste of time. I was certainly determined to have us ready for what the government actually wanted us to do.'

The only other role the special forces were allowed by the Dibb Report to develop was counterterrorism, a carve-out that made the SASR unique among almost all Australia's military assets, because they would essentially be operational all the time. The role meant the SASR was trained in, and funded for, a very different type of fighting.

'The real kick for SAS was the counterterrorism capability,' says Chris Roberts. 'I concentrated on the counterterrorism role, which had us training in close-quarters battle in urban areas or in buildings. That gave us a brand-new capability, which I think had a flow-on effect, all the way to Afghanistan.'

Jim Wallace had a similar concentration on counterterrorist fighting while he commanded the regiment, with 'black role' capabilities (counterterrorism) eventually seeping into 'green role' (land warfare) planning and improving capability.

Another undoubted benefit of the counterterrorism role for the SASR in the 1980s and '90s was that the TAG chain of command bypassed the army's Land Command, under which the SASR usually was housed, allowing it to make decisions about procurement, logistics, training and force structure without the need for external approval.

The SASR had agitated to be placed under their own command and not be beholden to the Land Command structure. In 1990 the first steps towards breaking free from Land Command were made when Headquarters Special Forces was established, with a view to Australia's special forces eventually having their own major general atop their own command, equal to the Fleet (Royal Australian Navy), Forces (Australian Army) and Air (Royal Australian Air Force) commands.

A number of developments in the 1990s considerably boosted the stock of Australia's wannabe command. A significant change was the ascension of the Liberal/National coalition government of John Howard in 1996. With that government came a more outward-looking security stance, compared to that of their Labor predecessors, a stance that only became more established as Australia's region went through a period of instability. In the late 1990s there were security breakdowns in Fiji, Cambodia and the Solomon Islands, but most concerning for the new government was the increasing political violence in Indonesia and Papua New Guinea.

In Indonesia the long-standing dictatorial and highly corrupt government of President Suharto was destabilised after the 1997 Asian currency crisis. As the Indonesian rupiah tumbled, independence movements were gaining traction in Timor-Leste and West Papua, and ethnic violence was increasing across the country. The human rights record and fraudulent economic behaviour of the Suharto government was under fresh scrutiny. Conditions were ripe in Indonesia for revolution.

Of particular concern for Prime Minister Howard was the former Australian colony of Papua New Guinea, and especially the North Solomons island of Bougainville, where an insurrection was in full bloom between ethnic separatists and Papua New Guinea's national forces, as well as private military contractors from the United Kingdom. Scenarios under which Australia needed to quickly project forces overseas were easily imagined by the Howard government, and it was clear that many of these scenarios could best (or only) be resolved by special forces.

Two structural reviews of the Australian military were undertaken, 'Army in the 21st Century' and 'Restructuring the Army', as developmental leaps in digitisation, automation, miniaturisation, aviation, communication and surveillance significantly changed how military power could be brought to bear. The reviews proposed a significant boost to Australia's special forces, both in resources and in size, one of the major recommendations being that Australia raise a second, full-time special forces gunfighting regiment alongside, but distinct from, the SASR (later becoming the 2nd Commando Regiment).

The SASR was designed to operate in small and often clandestine teams. This new commando regiment was to have a different structure, operating primarily in platoons, a force of 30 or so men. It would be used for overt operations, including the seizure of airfields, the establishment of beachheads and direct-action cordon activities.

The capability set of the new commando regiment was planned to be distinct from that of the SASR, but also complementary to it. In practice, however, there would be significant operational overlap, especially in Afghanistan, which fostered rivalry and, in many instances, hatred between the two gunfighting regiments.

In 1999 and 2000, Australia's special forces were in a period of change and also burgeoning utility. As both regiments prepared for Operation Gold, a major pre-Olympic counterterrorism preparedness mission, militia violence erupted in the tiny emerging nation of Timor-Leste and both were sent north.

Australia had agreed to lead an international force mandated by the United Nations to create stability and peace in Timor-Leste, but when it was estimated that Australia would need to deploy 5000 troops, the senior figures of the government were shocked to find that this was limit of what the ADF could deploy overseas.

Alexander Downer remembers: '[I was thinking,] "Well, that's alright, we can find five thousand troops, we've got many more than five thousand soldiers in the Australian Army." Well, as it turns out some of them do this, and some of them do that and they need to be rotated and so on, so five thousand is just about our limit. We were like: "What do you mean, five thousand is our limit?" You just don't know as a minister or prime minister. We, in 1999, had been really surprised by how limited the capability of the Australian Defence Force was.'

Downer says he and John Howard were also concerned about the lack of Australia's ability to force-project, as they had 'some old tub called the *Tobruk* and that's about it'. The Australian military had not been designed for use abroad. 'I thought, "Really, what the fuck? How can people have gone along with this crazy idea?"' says Downer. 'That's what people did, but that's not what I'd do, and it's not what we did do, Howard and I.'

After Timor-Leste, the government made a large investment to ensure the ADF was far more 'flexible and versatile'. According to Downer, the purchase of Boeing C-17 transport aircraft and the construction of landing helicopter dock amphibious assault ships were the result of the shock he and Howard felt when they realised how limited the ADF's ability was to project overseas.

Both Downer and Howard say the expansion of the special forces was also an effort to change the direction and capability of the ADF, including an ability to deploy overseas more readily.

Money poured into Australia's Special Operations Command (SOCOMD), and especially into the new special forces engineering unit, created to counter chemical, biological, nuclear, radiological and explosive threats during the Sydney Olympic Games. That unit became a fully-fledged regiment in 2002, named first as the Incident Response Regiment (IRR), then the Special Operations Engineer Regiment (SOER).

The Special Operations Combat Service Support Company (later the Special Operations Logistics Squadron) came online in 2003, allowing SOCOMD to deploy soldiers more quickly and operate more independently.

With the full-time gunfighting regiments, their own dedicated reserve force (the long-established 1st Commando Regiment), coupled with a dedicated special forces headquarters and a training and education centre, SOCOMD was becoming an 'army in a box', highly deployable and highly independent.

'They're almost an army within an army now,' says Jim Wallace, 'and when you have that, you can have a tendency to operate separately. That can be a problem.'

2

'If you go up, we will pull you down by your feet; if
you hide below, we will pull you up by your hair'

THE SASR OPERATORS STORMED up the gangplank of the *Tampa*
(except one, who shimmied up the anchor chain of the ship) and
burst onto the deck, guns level, safeties off, shouting instructions
at the hundreds of men, women and children in front of them.

'Lie down where you are!'

Many of those on the deck were already lying down, too weak,
too hungry or too sick to stand. Almost none spoke English, and
none of the soldiers spoke Hazaragi, the dialect of Dari spoken
most commonly by the people on the ship.

A teenager named Saed Ali Murad, who spoke some English,
approached one of the assault teams in an attempt to mediate.
Guns were levelled at him and he was shouted at. He couldn't
understand what was being asked of him. There was more
shouting and more guns on him. He lay down again.

Murad was scared. He knew these were Australian soldiers,
and that they were not supposed to kill unarmed people, but given
the way they had appeared – unexpectedly and with weapons
drawn, and yelling voices – he feared that his own short and
fraught life would soon come to an end.

Saed Ali Murad's journey to Australian territorial waters
had, like that of many of the 432 other people on the deck of the
Tampa, started in Afghanistan. Almost to a man, woman and
child, they were all running from the Taliban. Like most of those

on the ship, Murad was Hazara, a member of a minority ethnic group considered apostates by the Taliban. The Hazara people spoke a different language to most in the country and, more significantly, practised a different religion.

The Hazaras were Muslims like the Taliban, but they were part of the Shia sect, distinct from the Sunni sect, of which most Taliban were members. This sectarian difference is, in most places in the Islamic world and at most times, insignificant, but not in the Taliban's Afghanistan in 2001.

Seventeen years before the *Tampa* affair, Murad was born in a small village in the southern part of Ghazni Province, a few kilometres from the Uruzgan border. His village was part of what was called the 'Hazarajat', a large area in central Afghanistan spanning multiple provinces that was primarily populated by Hazaras and protected by their militia groups.

When Murad was born, the army of the USSR was nominally occupying the country. In reality, they controlled Kabul and a few other cities and towns, but in the countryside they were subject to constant attack by CIA- and Pakistani-supported *mujahedin*.

As Murad grew, Afghanistan changed. In 1989, the Soviet Red Army withdrew from the country, supporting from afar a communist puppet government under a Pashtun leader named Mohammad Najibullah.

The Pashtuns, Afghanistan's largest ethnic group and Pakistan's second-largest, have for hundreds of years, perhaps even thousands, been the most integral actors on Afghanistan's political and military stage, with a long history of wars against Afghanistan's other ethnic groups, other Pashtuns, the Soviet Union, Britain, the United States and even, according to many anthropologists, Alexander the Great and Genghis Khan (many Hazaras claim to be the descendants of Genghis Khan and his invading Mongol army).

After the Soviets left Afghanistan, Najibullah attempted to recant his communism and embrace Afghan and Islamic nationalism, but he was rejected by other Pashtun warlords and the *mujahedin*, who fought Najibullah's government forces and then each other. Throughout the 1990s a pall of general violent disorder descended over most parts of Afghanistan.

For Saed Ali Murad – who now holds a doctorate in international relations, and is a lecturer at an Australian university – these great events registered as the opening and closing of his school. 'Security on a local level was very much dependent on local actors, and communities had to negotiate with those local actors,' he says. 'Sometimes an armed group would establish security, and that meant stability and security, and generally they had no ideological opposition to schools.

'Sometimes there would be no security at all, and sometimes we'd go to school when there was fighting between two armed groups, with rockets flying overhead. That was part of life.'

Security for Hazaras was a local obligation. This was true of most ethnic, tribal and sub-tribal groups in most parts of Afghanistan, but it was especially true of Hazaras. With their distinctive Mongol and Turkic facial features and their unique dialect, they could not escape the terrible pogroms and massacres simply by blending into another community.

Murad's Hazara village lived next to a community of Pashtuns, and while the two communities were often at odds when it came to social issues like women's education, women's rights and medical practice, they mostly had a peaceful and functional relationship.

'There were limits to the relationship between the two groups – for instance, there are obviously no marriages between the groups – but we had business ties and, I would say, there was also friendship,' Murad says.

Regardless of the conviviality, the Hazara community felt safest when they lived under the protection of a strong and aligned Hazara militia. According to Murad, in the mid-1990s that sense of safety was lacking as the Hezbe Wahdat, the primary Hazara militia, suffered a series of battlefield defeats, and the borders of the Hazarajat started to crumble.

The Hazaras feared massacre, and they were far from the only ones. There was almost no law in Afghanistan in that period. The roads between cities and towns were often owned by armed militias, which constantly fought other militias for control. Raids into towns and cities were a regular occurrence; so too were punitive and arbitrary artillery bombardments.

Social services were few, death was ever-present and, as in most parts of Afghanistan, the law of the AK-47 was the only one that mattered.

It was in this climate that a group of Islamic scholars and religious students called the Taliban (literally 'students' or 'scholars') started emerging from Pakistan and southern Afghanistan.

This force was largely seen as a positive in Afghanistan, even by the Hazaras. The Taliban was predominantly a Pashtun force, yes, but the perception was that their Pashtun identity was subordinate to their moral identity, which they wore as a badge of honour.

When they first emerged, the group made pronouncements that they had not arrived for sectarian warfare, nor even Islamic cleansing, but to establish peace, law and order for all Afghans. They claimed they had no interest in governing themselves, instead saying they would create security and law and then install a national unity government, reinstating the Afghan king who had been deposed in 1973.

'They had a really romanticised image,' says Murad. 'They were just students who were fed up with the bloodshed and anarchy in the country. One of the metaphors that was used at the time was that they were "white angels".'

The Taliban took territory initially in the Pashtun-dominated south of Afghanistan, and there they cleared the roads of bandits and set up *sharia* courts in which land disputes and criminal claims would be heard; this was a hugely popular move. By 1995, the Taliban had unified most Pashtun militias under their white banner, and controlled most of the south of the country.

In 1996 they seized the multi-ethnic capital of Kabul and also the eastern city of Herat, populated mostly by non-Pashtun, Persian-speaking people. The manner of their capture of Kabul (among other atrocities, they indiscriminately shelled the city) and their brutal theocratic governance in Herat changed perceptions of the Taliban, and started to put fear into the hearts of the Hazara people.

Hazaras across Afghanistan rearmed, mirroring the efforts of ethnic-minority forces in the north, and many joined the larger anti-Taliban militias. The primary Hazara militia, Hezbe Wahdat, joined forces with what became the Northern Alliance in defence of Afghanistan's third-largest city, Mazar-i-Sharif. Mazar had largely been spared bloodshed throughout the 1980s and '90s thanks to the large community of ethnic Uzbeks, who welcomed the Soviet invasion and maintained a powerful militia throughout much of the 1990s.

In 1997, the pious, ethnically pure and completely ideological Taliban attacked the defenders of Mazar, who were multi-ethnic, multi-religious and religiously permissive (vodka and sex workers were known to be widely available in the city). In Mazar-i-Sharif, two visions of Afghanistan collided.

The Taliban initially suffered large losses in Mazar. Captured Taliban fighters were often tortured and killed, with Uzbek leader Abdul Rashid Dostum ordering much of the brutality. A siege of the city began, which was broken in August 1998 thanks, albeit tangentially, to a Saudi organiser and agitator named Osama bin Laden.

Bin Laden and his men had been fighting alongside the Taliban, and the Taliban had been given a fleet of vehicles and pallets of cash by the rulers of Saudi Arabia, who were trying to curry favour with the Taliban so that they would send Bin Laden back to Saudi. The Taliban took the money and used the vehicles to attack Mazar.

The alliance between the Uzbeks and the Hazaras in Mazar broke down quickly after the Taliban entered the city. The invaders installed their own governor, Abdul Manan Niazi, within days of entry. His first act as governor was to go from mosque to mosque giving fiery speeches about Afghanistan's ethnic minorities, especially Hazaras. He issued an edict that Hazaras would only be allowed to live in a Taliban-dominated Afghanistan if they recanted their religion and lived, as Niazi put it, as Muslims.

'Wherever you go we will catch you. If you go up, we will pull you down by your feet; if you hide below, we will pull you up by your hair,' Mullah Manan Niazi declared from Mazar's central mosque.

After his speeches, Taliban fighters went from door to door looking for Hazara men; when they were found, they were often dragged onto the street and slaughtered with a knife, as a halal butcher would. For a number of days after the killings, the Taliban refused requests from the families to bury these men, and their wives and children had to watch as their corpses were eaten by dogs. This was the start of a new Taliban policy with regard to Afghanistan's Hazaras.

'What the Taliban did was put an economic blockade around us, and I can remember this very well because we were all affected dramatically,' says Murad. 'They knew they could starve us instead of having to fight us. Where I was living, just a few kilometres away in the Pashtun areas a bag of rice might be 1000 Afghanis [A\$15], but where I was rice was 10,000 Afghanis [A\$150].'

One by one, the Hazara militias folded until the entire Hazarajat was surrendered to the Taliban.

'As soon as [the Taliban] came in, they closed the schools, and then they started going after people – first armed people and then NGOs [non-government organisations] and then any young people who had an education, and working their way down a long list,' says Murad. 'There hadn't been much hope before, but we had some. My brother and I thought perhaps peace would come and perhaps we could go to university and get a good job or something, but now there was no hope. There was only despair.'

As Murad came into his teenage years, he 'knew it would be torture or imprisonment or death for us, so eventually I left the area'. He fled to Kandahar. From Kandahar he arranged to be smuggled, under a blanket in the back of a ute, towards the Afghanistan–Pakistan border. Murad installed himself in the large Hazara community in Quetta, but there he was again a second-class citizen – in fact, a third-class citizen. While Pakistani Hazaras were persecuted by the majority Pashtun population, they at least had Pakistani citizenship, affording them basic education, healthcare and movement around the country and beyond.

Over his year in Quetta, Murad studied English and keenly watched the news, hoping for good news from the Hazarajat. There was no good news. The Taliban had cemented their hold on the country, with Pakistan, Saudi Arabia and some of the Gulf States recognising the organisation as the legitimate government of Afghanistan.

'Until then, Afghan Hazaras would not travel long distances,' Murad says. 'We would flee to Pakistan or Iran or perhaps even the Gulf States, but the hope is always to return. In 1999, after massacre upon massacre, it was obvious there was no prospect of going back.'

Things were hopeless in Afghanistan, and the swelling Hazara refugee population in Quetta, resented by the Pakistani Pashtun community, were subject to beatings and murder. Murad talked regularly with his father on the phone about what he could do next, until his father was taken by the Taliban and forced into hard labour.

'I never wanted to leave Afghanistan,' Murad says. 'All Hazaras want is to live in our area, our home, but there was just no path ahead for us.'

Except one: the smugglers' path.

* * *

Early on 23 August 2001, Saed Ali Murad arrived at a beach close to the Indonesian beachside resort of Pantai Pelabuhan Ratu, having spent months and his family's life savings to get there. Now the last leg of the journey was in front of him.

He and 432 other people – mostly men, but some women and children, mostly Hazaras but also a few Tajiks and Pashtun Afghans and Sri Lankans – were being crammed into the KV *Palapa*, a small wooden boat used primarily for short, inter-island Indonesian passage and fishing. A group of Indonesian people smugglers, whose number included uniformed police, filled every available inch of the boat with human cargo. Murad's knees had to be tucked under his chin for the journey ahead.

The Hazara people are not traditional seafarers. Most of those on the *Palapa* had never even seen a boat before and were panicked even in the short period when the boat was moving though calm waters, under broad sunlight.

The journey from the Indonesian port to Christmas Island, the Australian territory on which the group hoped to land, and there ask for legal protection under refugee statutes, was roughly 450 kilometres. The crew of the *Palapa* hoped to land after 36 hours of sailing.

After dawn on 24 August, it became apparent that the *Palapa* was not going to arrive at its destination after 36 hours, and perhaps not at all. Through the night, the sea had risen and roiled, and the boat's engine had been pushed to its limit as vomit and fear washed around the deck.

In the first morning light, a loud crack and a grinding noise could be heard, and then all became quiet. The boat's engine had worked loose from its fitting and destroyed itself. The *Palapa* was now adrift and, upon further inspection, was slowly sinking.

At this point the stricken boat was spotted by Australian authorities, and efforts were made by Australian representatives to have Indonesian naval or coastguard boats rescue the *Palapa*. When those efforts were ignored, a maritime message was sent out: all ships, all channels.

> Subject: Distress Relay. A 35-metre Indonesian type vessel with 80 plus persons on board adrift in the vicinity of 09.32.5 south 104.44 east ... vessel has SOS and HELP written on the roof. Vessels within 10 hours report best ETA and intentions to this station.

The call was answered by a huge Norwegian cargo ship transporting used machinery from Fremantle to Singapore. This was the MV *Tampa*.

When the ship sidled up next to the *Palapa*, Murad believed they had been saved – not only from the sea but from their wretched circumstances. He assumed that he and the other refugees would be transported to Australia, where they would be given medical assistance (a dozen of the group were unconscious, and many other were presenting serious medical issues) and then recognised as refugees.

'We had this high hope that we would by welcomed by the Australian government, not knowing at all about the politics,' he says.

The *Tampa*'s captain, Arne Rinnan, was in contact with Australian Search and Rescue (AusSAR), and late on 26 August he explained to the Australian officials that, with more than 400 passengers, many needing medical attention, and with lifeboats for only a couple of dozen passengers, he considered his ship no longer seaworthy. He planned to sail to the closest place where assistance might be rendered: Christmas Island.

AusSAR replied to Captain Rinnan that, as the master of his ship, this was his prerogative. He should hold a position offshore, where he would receive Australian customs officers.

Then the monumental decision was made not to allow the *Tampa* to access Australian waters.

In 2001, the Howard government was taking a beating in the media, night after night, over immigration policy. Although Australia's refugee intake was tiny in comparison to that of many countries around the world, there had been a significant uptick in the number of asylum seekers entering the country by boat. A controversial law proposing that asylum seekers who arrive by boat not have access to the Australian courts was making its way through the Senate, and detention centres in New South Wales and Western Australia, and on Christmas Island, were in the news regularly because of inmates' hunger strikes, riots and illness.

The press coverage in Australia was significant, and it seemed that the government was not in control of the issue. When the MV *Tampa* collected the refugees from the sinking KV *Palapa*, an opportunity for the government to take control appeared.

It was self-evident that the legal problems presented by refugees would be significantly reduced if those seeking asylum simply never made it to the territory on which Australia, under international law, would have to deal with them.

'We will decide who comes to this country and the circumstances in which they come,' Prime Minister Howard would later say.

Shortly after the government refused to allow the *Tampa* to dock at Christmas Island, polling and certain media commentary started to suggest that this stance was in fact a popular one. Diplomatic and legal challenges came, with most experts in international law (including those at the Wilhelmsen Lines Shipping Company, owner of the MV *Tampa*) believing that Captain Rinnan was within his legal rights to sail to Christmas Island, and that those rescued from the *Palapa* must be processed there as asylum seekers. Indonesia had steadfastly refused to accept the refugees, and by now it seemed it had no legal obligation to do so.

Australia held to its position of refusal, even denying Captain Rinnan's request that the sickest asylum seekers be moved to Christmas Island. Clearly the Australian government calculated that a backdown could be disastrous, with a federal election looming.

At 2 pm on 29 August, Rinnan chose to force the issue. He started to sail towards Australian territorial waters. Forty-five SASR operators nearby were loaded onto their RHIBs with orders to seize the boat, which they did easily.

On 3 September 2001, Saed Ali Murad and the other asylum seekers were transferred to HMAS *Manoora*, having remained on the deck of the seized *Tampa* for more than a week as the legal arguments raged in Australia. But the asylum seekers had gone from one limbo to another, and now they waited in the belly of the warship to find out where in the world they might be accepted after Australia said there was no chance any of them would be accepted there.

A little more than a week later, a young Australian sailor with whom Murad had become friendly beckoned him to come and see what was being shown on the crew's television screen.

'You probably want to see this,' the sailor said. 'I don't know ... maybe this might change things a bit for you guys.'

3

'What would you do if you got your hands on Bin Laden?'

NEAR THE END OF August 2001, two Belgian Arabs, Dahmane Abd al-Sattar and Bouraoui el-Ouaer, presented themselves to Northern Alliance guards on the front line between their group and the Taliban. The Belgians handed over letters of introduction from a British cleric named Yassir al-Sirri, who ran the Islamic Observation Centre in West London, and carried all the camera and sound equipment they would need to finish the documentary about the Northern Alliance they claimed to be working on.

The men were accepted and taken north to the town of Khvajeh Baha od Din, a pleasant, bucolic place in a green valley pressed up against the border with Tajikistan. This was the place where the Northern Alliance military command had been established.

The Belgians had a list of interview requests, but there was one man they wanted time with more than any other: military leader Ahmad Shah Massoud. The journalists were told to wait, so they waited. August became September. They spent time with two women, a French journalist and an American women's rights activist, who were also waiting for Massoud.

As the second week of September came, the purported documentarians became increasingly agitated. The men told their hosts they had a hard deadline – 9 September 2001 – which was only hours away. They told anyone who would listen that they needed an audience with General Massoud immediately. Their work would be incomplete without an interview with the greatest commander in recent Afghan military history.

* * *

Like most of Afghanistan's military leaders and warlords, the ethnic Tajik Ahmad Shah Massoud made his name fighting the Soviets. Having started the war with the Soviets as 27-year-old local commander in control of a strategically important mountain pass with fewer than 1000 fighters, Massoud ended the war as a 36-year-old regional commander in control of 13,000 fighters and a strategic mountain pass (nine times the Soviet Army mounted assaults on the Panjshir Valley and Massoud's men, and nine times they were repelled) and renowned throughout the country.

Massoud had arguably been the most effective of all of commanders throughout the Soviet War, and he had achieved that without some of the intelligence and equipment advantages being afforded to others, notably the Pashtun commanders with strong ties to Pakistan, which distributed most of the Saudi and US military aid and intelligence.

He was far from the only effective *mujahedin* commander, however. Across Afghanistan, almost all of the ethnic groups resisted the Soviet occupation, endlessly harassing the Soviets every time they left their bases. The Soviets tried to kill the country into submission, mercilessly bombing areas suspected of supporting the insurgency, but despite up to 2 million Afghans being killed, there was never a hint of submission. The Afghan tribes refused to break.

Also fighting in the war were the highly publicised but largely ineffective Arab brigades. After the Soviet invasion in 1979, the war in Afghanistan became a *cause célèbre* in the Muslim world, with the most senior clerical figures in Egypt and Saudi Arabia telling their flocks that young capable men with means had a religious obligation to fight against the atheist Russians.

Safe-harbour camps were established in Pakistan and in some parts of Afghanistan, paid for largely by the Gulf States and

Saudi Arabia, where Arabs could be trained for the fight ahead against the Soviets. Fundraisers were even held in Sydney and Melbourne to support the fight against the Soviets, and a handful of Australian Arabs were trained in Afghanistan and Pakistan and then fought against the Soviets.

Between 1982 and 1992, an estimated 35,000 Muslims from outside the 'Af-Pak' region fought in Afghanistan, and perhaps 60,000 more travelled to Pakistan to learn at *madrasahs*, or training camps. The most famous of these was Osama bin Mohammed bin Awad bin Laden, the millionaire 17th son of a billionaire father. Bin Laden senior grew up poor in Yemen, built a construction empire like no other in Saudi Arabia, and then died in 1967 after crashing his private plane into a mountain near the Saudi Arabia–Yemen border.

Osama bin Laden was neither a brilliant battlefield tactician like Massoud, nor a notable Islamic scholar like the leader of the Taliban, Mullah Mohammad Omar (*mullah* is an honorific religious title). He was intermittently rich, but also often unconnected to his family's wealth; even when he was connected, he took only a minority cut of the family income. He was tall and shy, and was often described as more follower than leader, but Bin Laden started his violent *jihadi* journey (*jihad* is an Islamic obligation and literally means 'struggle', usually a peaceful, internal struggle against ignorance) with near boundless ambition, and only became more audacious from there.

Like Ahmad Shah Massoud, the name Osama bin Laden was barely known at the start of the Soviet invasion of Afghanistan, but ten years later, as the Red Army withdrew, Bin Laden was famous in the Arab world and perhaps Saudi Arabia's most recognisable citizen, royal family members notwithstanding.

Bin Laden's war had been very different to Massoud's. Massoud had been a major impediment to the Soviet war effort; at times as many as 30,000 Soviet troops, supported by armour and helicopters, had been sent to try to clear Massoud and his force out of the Panjshir Valley. Osama bin Laden had no such battlefield résumé. His role had mostly been organisational, helping fund and transport Arabs who wanted to train and fight.

Bin Laden and the core of what would later become al-Qaeda ('The Base') had been involved in some minor military actions, primarily in the second half of the war, that made little strategic difference to the course of the conflict, but they were well publicised thanks in no small part to the efforts of journalist Jamal Khashoggi – a friend of Bin Laden who was later murdered under orders from Saudi crown prince Mohammed bin Salman – who wrote about his exploits for the Saudi media.

A modern myth has emerged that the CIA had funded and equipped Osama bin Laden and his Arab brigades in Afghanistan, and that this support was essential to the defeat of the Soviets, but the facts do not bear this out. CIA support to the Afghan *mujahedin* ran through a Pakistani pipeline, with Pakistan's Inter-Services Intelligence (ISI) agency arming and funding primarily Pashtun Afghans – people who would later either be aligned with or become the Taliban.

Many of the Arabs who travelled to Afghanistan during this period – especially government-connected Saudis and Gulf Arabs funded by petrodollars – were essentially war tourists. They often arrived with bags full of cash, trained, took some photographs and returned home in air-conditioned luxury, with a story to tell and the grace of Allah dusted over them. These posers and their friends, not the CIA or Pakistan, were the financial engine that drove the Arab brigades and, later, al-Qaeda.

When the Soviet Army withdrew from Afghanistan in 1989, it was clear that the war had been calamitous for Moscow. The Soviet dead (approximately 15,000) was a small number when compared to the Afghan dead, but the USSR's loss of prestige and power was significant. Yet President Mikhail Gorbachev claimed – as, it seems, is obligatory for foreign leaders announcing their defeat in Afghanistan – that the state of affairs was desirable, and that this was thanks to his troops:

Success of the policy of national reconciliation has already
made it possible to begin withdrawing Soviet troops
from portions of the Afghan territory. At present there
are no Soviet troops in 13 Afghan provinces – because
armed clashes have ceased there. The Afghans themselves
will decide the final status of their country among other
nations. Most often it is being said that the future peaceful
Afghanistan will be an independent, non-aligned and neutral
state. And now about our boys, our soldiers in Afghanistan.
They have been doing their duty honestly, performing acts
of self-denial and heroism. Our people profoundly respect
those who were called to serve in Afghanistan.

The truth was that many Afghans suffered horribly under the
Soviet yoke. The war had created Afghan monsters, and the civil
war that followed was undoubtedly all the bloodier because the
men prosecuting it were used to a battlefield in which the rape,
torture and massacre of civilians were commonplace tactics.

The Soviet Union itself had also been affected by the war, of
course, and this was reflected in Gorbachev's speech. 'Regional
conflicts are bleeding wounds which can result in gangrenous
growth on the body of mankind,' he noted.

It's an apt metaphor, as gangrene is rarely fatal if the patient is
otherwise healthy, but can kill those who are already seriously ill.
The fall of Soviet Union was not due to the war in Afghanistan,
but the war had been a minority contributor. Osama bin Laden
had not defeated the Soviets in Afghanistan, but his Arab
brigades had been a minority contributor. Regardless, Bin Laden
considered himself personally to be the vanquisher of the godless
army, or at least a vessel for the destructive will of Allah.

Osama bin Laden's focus shifted in the early 1990s to his
home country, Saudi Arabia, after Saddam Hussein and the Iraqi
Army invaded Kuwait. In the summer of 1991, Saddam's huge
army threatened the borders of the vast and wealthy Saudi state.
An energy crisis beckoned, and there was panic in both Riyadh
and Washington DC.

Bin Laden met with the Saudi royal family, offering his Arab brigades in defence of Saudi Arabia's borders and, of course, the cities of Mecca and Medina, the holiest places in the Muslim world. The fact that Bin Laden believed his lightly armed *mujahedin* could confront Saddam's forces with their armour, artillery and air support in the open desert spoke of his delusion.

Bin Laden's offer was motivated by two considerations. Increasingly, he saw himself as God's favourite vessel, and wished to personally defend the holy cities of his homeland, but he was also enraged by a royal plan to allow the United States to station huge numbers of troops on the border between Saudi Arabia and Iraq and Kuwait. Allowing thousands of armed *kafir*, or unbelievers, into the Holy Land was an affront against all Muslims, he thought, and against God himself.

The Saudi royals chose President George H.W. Bush over Osama bin Laden. More than half a million US troops were deployed to Saudi Arabia in Operation Desert Shield, with President Bush steadfastly promising to remove all US troops from Saudi Arabia when the confrontation with Iraq was over. This promise wasn't kept.

After Saddam's army was routed in the 1991 Gulf War, more than 5000 US troops stayed in the Holy Land, to the great offence of religious radicals like Osama bin Laden. His rhetoric against the Saudi royal family and the United States was not welcome in autocratic Saudi Arabia, and soon Bin Laden and his followers moved to Sudan, an impoverished East African country with an Islamist government and little regard for human rights.

From his base near Khartoum, Bin Laden built a private army, paying any Muslim man who wished to come and train in various types of guerrilla warfare and religious instruction a basic salary. He also poured large amounts of money into Sudanese businesses that were, by and large, failures, and when Bin Laden was cut out of the family business in 1994, his personal coffers started to dry up.

The pressure on Bin Laden and his group in Sudan rose steadily. He was no longer a source of seemingly inexhaustible funds for the Sudanese, and nor did he offer construction advice and assistance, as had been hoped. The Saudi government and the CIA petitioned the Sudanese government to silence and perhaps deport Bin Laden. After surviving an assassination attempt in 1996 by an unknown assailant, the Saudi *jihadi* decided to move his operation to perhaps the only place in the world where he might be welcome: Afghanistan.

After the Soviet retreat in Afghanistan, a communist puppet government had survived for a couple of years, staying in control only of small but populous parts of the country, before a ragtag army marched into Kabul and destroyed the last semblance of sovereignty. The fact that Kabul had fallen was no surprise; what was a surprise was that it hadn't been taken by Pashtun forces attacking from the south, but by a Tajik and Uzbek force from the north, led primarily by Ahmad Shah Massoud.

Massoud was a brilliant military commander, but no nationally focused politician. In the years that followed, a true and terrifying civil war took hold across the country, where the only law, justice and hope was that which one could arrange for oneself. In this patchwork of fiefdoms, micro-states and badlands, road banditry became a way of life and the promise of murder was constantly in the air. Until the Taliban emerged.

This force was a coalition of tribes and families, ostensibly driven by deep religious conviction but also funded by Pakistan, narco-barons (opium was and remains Afghanistan's primary export) and trucking magnates, who hoped for some kind of normalcy in Afghanistan and relatively free passage of goods through the Pashtun south. Pakistan also wished to help build a fighting force that might resist India's influence and power in Afghanistan, and perhaps also in contested Kashmir.

This force, the Taliban, was led primarily by men who had fought the Soviets and then the puppet communist government. They wanted peace – but that peace would seriously restrict the rights of women, even in the Afghan context; oppress or kill anyone who practised a religion other than theirs; and ban art, music, photography and many of modernity's benefits.

The group coalesced around the vision of Soviet War veteran Mullah Mohammad Omar who was famous for three traits above all others: his religious piety, his stubborn incorruptibility and his bravery in battle.

His vision, Mullah Omar claimed, was not metaphorical but literal: the Prophet had visited him in a dream, telling him to bring God's peace to Afghanistan. (Having suffered a serious head injury in the Battle of Jalalabad in 1989, it's possible that Mullah Omar experienced mental health issues.)

Omar built a senior leadership of men with backgrounds very similar to his own: Pashtun, pious and provincial. Few of the senior Taliban leadership had ever even visited a city until they took Kabul by force in 1996. Most hailed from Uruzgan, the small southern-central province that, in the next decade, Australia would be tasked with pacifying.

'We all knew each other – Mullah Omar, Ghous [Mullah Mohammad Ghous, the Taliban minister of foreign affairs and a childhood friend of future Afghan president Hamid Karzai], Mohammad Rabbani [second-in-charge of the Taliban] and myself – because we were all originally from Uruzgan Province and had fought together,' Mullah Hassan, once the governor of Kandahar and later a Taliban foreign minister, told an Afghan journalist.

'I moved back and forth from Quetta [in Pakistan] and attended madrassas there, but whenever we got together we would discuss the terrible plight of our people living under the bandits. We were people of the same opinions and we got on with each other very well, so it was easy to come to a decision to do something.'

The Taliban quickly became the de facto Pashtun force in Afghanistan, and eventually a strategic map of the Afghan civil war started to look less like a Jackson Pollock and more like a Mark Rothko. The rise of the Taliban was swift, but always incomplete. They seized Kabul in September 1996 and were recognised by Pakistan, Saudi Arabia and the United Arab Emirates as the legitimate rulers of the country, but northern leaders like Massoud resisted them, and they were also resisted in the Hazarajat.

On 18 May 1996, Osama bin Laden, his sons and the al-Qaeda leadership flew in an old Russian Tupolev aircraft from Sudan to the United Arab Emirates, and from there on to Afghanistan. Behind Bin Laden lay financial ruin: the Sudanese government had forced him to sell his businesses in that country for cents on the dollar. Ahead was an uncertain welcome.

* * *

The Taliban had not invited Bin Laden to Afghanistan, and when he arrived they sent a message to the Saudi government (which was providing them with arms) asking what they should do with him. The Saudis told them to keep him and, if they could, keep him quiet. But the Taliban leadership was split as to whether they should give shelter to Bin Laden and his group. Some thought these Arabs might be more pain than they were worth; others thought Bin Laden could perhaps fund and undertake desperately needed infrastructure projects in the ravaged country.

Ultimately, Bin Laden and al-Qaeda were allowed to stay, but with a warning. 'We don't want subversive actions to be launched here against other countries,' the acting Taliban information minister said when asked about the arrival of Bin Laden. 'In areas under Taliban control, there are no terrorists.'

A few months later, Bin Laden broke the Taliban's trust, issuing a statement titled 'The Declaration of War against the Americans Occupying the Two Holy Places'. In it he detailed his intention to attack the United States. This issuance was largely ignored by the Taliban, likely because they thought Bin Laden was just full of bluster. After all, he had yet to kill any Americans, and seemed to be no more than an angry dissident yelling at a superpower from the dusty maw of a central Asian cave.

From 1996, Osama bin Laden consolidated his power in Afghanistan. At the request of Mullah Omar, Bin Laden and his group moved to Kandahar, close to Omar's personal compound.

There, he once again invited rich Gulf Arabs to come and train in religious studies and violent *jihad*, and again it became a good source of income. Bin Laden also developed a personal relationship with Mullah Omar, one of the few Taliban who could speak some Arabic.

In 1998, an Egyptian doctor, Ayman al-Zawahiri – later Bin Laden's deputy and the group's organisational mastermind – arrived in Afghanistan, merging his own radical group, Egyptian Islamic Jihad, with al-Qaeda. Previously, Zawahiri had concentrated on attacking the Egyptian government and that country's dictator, Hosni Mubarak, but now he and Bin Laden had a considerably larger project: a war against America.

Bin Laden saw a war in Afghanistan as a possible means of achieving this end. If the United States could be drawn into the country, then a violent *jihad* could be conducted against it. If Soviet might had been bent and then broken in the valleys and mountains of Afghanistan, who was to say American might not also be conquered? Bin Laden and Zawahiri planned provocations.

Al-Qaeda's first successful operation in its war against America was a double truck bombing in East Africa on 7 August 1998. (The 1993 truck bombing of the World Trade Center in New York City was conducted by affiliates of the group, but not by al-Qaeda itself.) The attacks on US embassies in Dar es Salaam, Tanzania, and in Nairobi, Kenya, killed 224 and wounded 4000.

Almost all the dead and wounded were Africans, and many were Muslims, but some Americans had also been killed – and a military response was elicited. That was what Bin Laden very much desired. On 20 August, hundreds of millions of dollars' worth of US cruise missiles smashed into Sudan and Afghanistan. In Africa, a nightwatchman was killed and a pharmaceuticals factory was levelled. In Afghanistan, some militants, Pakistani government agents and civilians were killed, but it seems that no senior al-Qaeda members died.

The cruise missile attacks were a tactical failure, but they were also a strategic calamity, with Osama bin Laden seen, after the strikes, as a powerful resistance figure who had survived a storm of American fury. Reports also emerged that some of the cruise missiles hadn't exploded on impact, and had been sold by Bin Laden to the Chinese government for up to US$10 million. It's believed that Pakistan may have retrieved an unexploded Tomahawk cruise missile and reverse-engineered it to help create its own Babur cruise missile.

Two days after the missile attacks, US State Department official Michael Malinowski received a call from Afghanistan. It was Mullah Omar, complaining about the attacks and offering some advice. Such attacks were counterproductive for the United States, he said, as they only spurred further anti-American sentiment in Afghanistan and across the world. Mullah Omar suggested to Malinowski that perhaps President Bill Clinton should resign. The State Department official told the Taliban leader that was unlikely.

The cruise missile attacks became a wedge issue for the Taliban. Some of their number believed al-Qaeda and Bin Laden should be ejected from Afghanistan; others believed the cruise missile attacks made the US an enemy of the Taliban, and that it would be an affront to *Pashtunwali* (literally 'the way of the Pashtuns') to hand a friend over to an enemy.

Mullah Omar himself was personally challenged by the attacks. He had been proclaimed the protector of the Islamic faith by his supporters, and his image of staunch resolve would be seriously affected if he handed over a fellow Muslim, and such a popular one, to the unbelieving United States simply because of a few cruise missiles and a handful of deaths.

He summoned Bin Laden and expressed his concern about al-Qaeda's activities. Bin Laden told an *Al Jazeera* journalist that he cried in front of Mullah Omar, saying he would leave Afghanistan immediately if that was Mullah Omar's wish; he asked only that the Taliban harbour his wife and children and keep them safe. One of Mullah Omar's primary concerns was that Osama bin Laden threatened his supremacy in Afghanistan, but with the Saudi in tears, this must have seemed less of a concern.

In their meeting, Osama bin Laden gave Mullah Omar a personal *bay'ah*, or Islamic pledge of allegiance, in what was to prove a pivotal move. The *bay'ah* was the glue that kept al-Qaeda together, with all members being bound to Bin Laden by their own personal pledge, a contract that existed for life. Later, it would be significant that many Taliban commanders offered a *bay'ah* to Bin Laden. Mullah Omar knew that the offer from Bin Laden to become a supplicant for the first time in his life meant a great deal.

By the time Osama bin Laden's organisation struck US interests again, in October 2000, he and Mullah Omar were compatriots and friends, spending long afternoons together fishing at the Kandahar Dam. This October 2000 attack was a suicide boat strike against the USS *Cole*, a warship docked in the harbour of Aden, Yemen. Two suicide bombers died in the attack, as well as 17 US servicemen and women.

Although the attack resulted in devastating loss of life, and created images of American impotency as desperate efforts were made to stop the billion-dollar warship from sinking, there was little or no US response, largely because President Clinton was soon leaving office and there was little clarity as to who the new US commander in chief would be.

As the US courts fought over whether Republican George W. Bush or Democrat Al Gore had won the deciding state of Florida in the November 2000 presidential election, Bin Laden received unprecedented credit for his ability to strike the United States without a response. This hadn't been his plan, but his increasing fame in the months after the USS *Cole* attack generated millions of dollars for al-Qaeda's coffers and brought new recruits from across the Middle East and North Africa.

Another attack that had been in the planning stages for more than a year was now executed. The details of this plan had evolved over the years, but three elements had remained constant: it would create massive loss of life, it would use violent *jihadi* suicide bombers as its agents, and it would involve commercial airliners.

After the strike on the USS *Cole*, the details of this new attack started to settle. It would involve four commercial jets and 20 violent *jihadi*, mostly Saudis. These four jets would target three buildings: in New York a commercial site, and in Washington DC a military site and a political site.

This attack would be an atrocity that would undoubtedly wake the giant. There was hope that the United States would not come to Afghanistan but instead attack other Muslims in other lands. If the spark took hold, then retribution and reciprocity would be fuel for the violent *jihadi* fire. Al-Qaeda hoped for enough atrocities and death that the Islamic world would be riven in two. Good versus bad. Us versus them.

As the 'planes operation' progressed, another essential element of the plan emerged. Bin Laden and Zawahiri worried that even if the atrocity that they planned was a success, the Taliban might merely hand over the offending al-Qaeda members to the United States for criminal prosecution. This was an unlikely eventuality, they judged, but possible. And so the Arabs hoped to engender fraternity with the Afghans by removing a thorn in the Taliban side.

The Taliban had attempted, many times, to kill Ahmad Shah Massoud, as they saw his death as a means of splitting the Northern Alliance and creating smaller and more manageable opposition. Now al-Qaeda believed they could succeed where the Taliban had failed. Two European violent *jihadi*, born in Tunisia but with residential permits in Belgium, who had arrived in Afghanistan only a few months earlier to join al-Qaeda, were tasked with the mission.

They were sent back to Belgium using their own passports, and then, using stolen Belgian passports procured by al-Qaeda, they travelled to London to acquire a letter of introduction as well as camera and sound equipment. (The writer of that letter of introduction, Yassir al-Sirri, claims he knew nothing about the al-Qaeda agents' plans.) The pair travelled back to Afghanistan, received a bomb disguised as a battery pack and, on the border of Northern Alliance territory, presented themselves as documentary filmmakers.

The pair were welcomed in Khvajeh Baha od Din two full weeks before the 'planes operation' was to be executed. They were likely confident of fulfilling their mission before their deadline, but Massoud was a busy man and an elusive subject. As the days dragged by, the men were offered apologies and other interview subjects, but they were adamant that they must interview Massoud.

On 9 September 2001, the interview was finally approved when Massoud and a number of other senior Northern Alliance commanders appeared in Khvajeh Baha od Din. One of the documentarians suggested to his minder that perhaps he and all the commanders might take a group photograph together? He was told to hurry up and do his interview.

As the two men set up their equipment, they surreptitiously armed their bomb. Massoud sat in front of the camera, looking like a hybrid of Bob Marley and Ernesto 'Che' Guevara, rounding into middle age with a beard flecked with grey. Jauntily atop his head was his signature *pakol* wool cap. The camera was rolling but the interviewers were still playing with their equipment.

'Why are they taking so long to prepare the cameras?' They don't seem very professional.'

One of the interviewers changed the topic, asking Massoud a personal question: 'What would you do if you got your hands on Bin Laden?'

A wry smile crept across Massoud's face. Ahmad Shah Massoud had disliked Bin Laden even during the Soviet years, and was perhaps amused by the gap between what his answer must be and what his thoughts actually were. But he had no opportunity to answer. The bomb detonated, killing the interviewers and knocking Massoud unconscious. A few hours later, the Lion of Panjshir succumbed to his wounds.

The bombing of Ahmad Shah Massoud was the first recorded instance of suicide bombing in Afghan history. Throughout the Soviet War, the civil war that followed and the Taliban wars against local insurgents, no Afghan force had ever resorted to this tactic. Suicide bombing had been considered a shameful act in Afghanistan – and to be shamed was to be defeated. Now al-Qaeda had opened a tactical Pandora's box, and it remains open in Afghanistan to this day.

This threshold moment was largely forgotten, however, due to the monumental violence that came two days later to New York, Washington DC and Pennsylvania.

4

'We will stand by them, we will help them, we will support actions they take to properly retaliate in relation to these acts of bastardry'

AS A LEGAL DOCUMENT, the ANZUS Treaty, a security cooperation pact between Australia and the United States (New Zealand was a party to the treaty but all but withdrew in the 1980s because of its desire to keep US nuclear vessels out of its waters) means little. It is essentially a valueless contract.

Designed to build alliances against communist threats in the Pacific in the wake of World War II, the treaty speaks of each party being obliged to 'act to meet the common danger' when another signatory is threatened. That obligatory act could be purely diplomatic – and there is no enforcement mechanism that might hold the signatories to even that effort.

The hope for cooperation means something, however, and especially to Australia. As a large, resource-rich nation with a relatively small defence force and no nuclear deterrent, a great deal of Australian war gaming against hostile nations involves holding on long enough in the initial engagement for the Americans to interdict. This has been a cornerstone of the 'defence of Australia' policies. The ANZUS Treaty may be largely symbolic, but symbols can have power.

It was the symbolic power of ANZUS that brought Prime Minister John Howard to Washington DC in September 2001, and not July, the month in which the Australian prime minister traditionally visited the US president. The state visit had been delayed so that Prime Minister Howard and President George W. Bush could mark the 50-year anniversary of the ANZUS Treaty at an event on 10 September 2001.

Howard met Bush for the first time at that event, which was held at the Washington Navy Yard. Howard remembers being impressed by the spit and polish of the assembled US honour guard, and also by the direct and energetic manner of the president and his secretary of defense, Donald Rumsfeld.

When the ceremony ended, Bush offered Howard a lift back to the White House, where the formal discussions were to be conducted. According to Howard, the two Christian conservative leaders hit it off immediately. It was the start of a lifelong friendship that was cemented a little over a year later, Howard says, when they discussed the invasion of Iraq in 2003.

On the night of 10 September 2001, Howard dined with media baron Rupert Murdoch at a restaurant next to his hotel; the pair were intercepted by the press as they left. Howard wondered what the press would make of the meeting, and had some trepidation about the stories that might be printed in the papers the next day, Tuesday, 11 September 2001.

Howard rose early that day and took his famous daily constitutional through the streets of Washington DC. Under a cloudless sky, he walked down Constitution Avenue, past the Vietnam Veterans Memorial and the Lincoln Memorial, then back to the hotel so he could prepare for a 9 am press conference. It had been arranged so that Howard could speak about one of Australia's airlines, Ansett, which had gone into receivership, but he knew there would also be questions about the *Tampa* affair. An Australian civil liberties group had challenged, in court, the seizure of the MV *Tampa*, all but accusing the Australian government of piracy.

Shortly before the press conference was to start, press secretary Tony O'Leary interrupted Howard's preparations, telling him that a passenger plane had crashed into the North Tower of the World Trade Center in New York. Neither man considered the event anything but an accident until O'Leary interrupted Howard again, just before Howard was due to speak. Another plane had struck the South Tower of the World Trade Center. Howard surmised that this was an act of terrorism. He and O'Leary quickly prepared a brief statement, which the PM gave ahead of a short press conference, which still ended up being primarily about Ansett and the *Tampa*.

When the press conference came to end, Howard stepped down from the podium and was approached by a member of his Australian Federal Police (AFP) security detail, who told him that he'd heard a loud boom over his open radio channel to the US Secret Service. As staff opened the south-facing curtains, Prime Minister Howard saw smoke streaming towards the sky from the direction of the Pentagon. There was little doubt now that the United States would soon be going to war.

The US Secret Service told the Australian delegation that they must leave the hotel, and they were escorted to a bunker below the Australian Embassy, a couple of hundred metres from the White House. A grab bag of Australian businesspeople, military liaisons and politicians collected there, while Howard kept in contact with Acting Prime Minister John Anderson about the government's initial response to the attacks. In Australia, the AFP were sent to critical locations, and the intelligence agencies met and formulated briefings. The SASR's Tactical Assault Group was put on alert.

Initially, there was a fear that this was the first of a wave of attacks, and perhaps not only in the United States of America, but as the morning became afternoon, that seemed less likely. In the bunker, Howard dictated a letter expressing Australia's support for the United States, to be read out at a later news conference. 'We will stand by them, we will help them, we will support actions they take to properly retaliate in relation to these acts of bastardry,' the letter read, which also invoked the Pearl Harbor attacks of 1941, the event that had brought the United States into World War II.

On 12 September, Prime Minister Howard visited the US Congress as a mark of solidarity, and it was there, he says, that he started to sense the mood of the American populace and government. There was shock and pain and numbness, but something else too. There was rage.

Howard and the Australian ambassador to the United States, Michael Thawley, met later that day and discussed the attacks. Thawley told the PM that the US intelligence agencies believed al-Qaeda to be responsible, and perhaps also the Taliban Afghan government. Afghanistan would now almost certainly be a target nation, perhaps one of several. Thawley told Howard that Iraq, too, might be in the sights of the US military, not because they believed Iraq had been involved in these attacks, but because there were idealogues within the Bush administration who considered an uninvaded Iraq unfinished business, and they had been agitating for some time to depose Saddam Hussein.

Later that day, Howard and his entourage boarded Air Force Two, the plane of Vice President Dick Cheney, and flew to Hawaii. There they boarded a Qantas flight headed for Sydney. This was the first commercial flight out of US airspace since the 9/11 attacks. During the flight, Howard spoke to his trusted Minister for Foreign Affairs, Alexander Downer, about the possibility of invoking the ANZUS Treaty (subject to cabinet approval, which was unlikely to be refused).

Australia had never before invoked the ANZUS Treaty – neither in the lead-up to the wars in Korea and Vietnam, nor before the 1991 Gulf War. This would be an unprecedented event, indicating that whatever military action the United States chose as a response to the 9/11 attacks, Australia would pledge its support. Although not a binding action, it would be a significant gesture.

After brief discussions in Canberra, Howard and Downer fronted the press on 14 September and announced their decision. The Australian government would be invoking the ANZUS Treaty, even before any clarity existed about what the US response to the attacks might be.

The leader of the opposition Labor Party, Kim Beazley, had no choice but to support the action. Beazley and Labor had led in most national opinion polls until August, but the Howard government had enjoyed a surge of support in the wake of the *Tampa* affair. It seemed clear that national security would dominate the upcoming Australian federal election, and so it would be foolhardy and heartless for Labor to break now with the United States.

* * *

It was settled quickly within the US government that Afghanistan should be attacked imminently, but there were concerns that the lack of fixed targets there might mean the US forces could not mount as spectacular a response as its leaders desired.

President Bush asked for 'blue sky' responses to the 9/11 attacks. Donald Rumsfeld and General Tommy Franks – the head of United States Central Command – met to consider OPLAN 1003, a contingency plan developed in the 1990s for the invasion of Iraq.

Rumsfeld also assembled a slide presentation for President Bush detailing some outrageous potential 9/11 responses, including one slide that read 'Thinking Outside the Box: Poisoning Food Supply'. That shocked some in the US military establishment, and one adviser petitioned national security adviser Condoleezza Rice to intercept it before it could be shown to President Bush. She did so after confronting Secretary Rumsfeld. It was decided that a conventional invasion of Afghanistan would commence immediately, with any other potential US responses to 9/11 to be executed later.

Australia was preparing too. Less than a week after the invocation of the ANZUS Treaty, coveted RAAF P-3 Orion surveillance planes were scrambled to the US and British air base on the island of Diego Garcia in the Indian Ocean, where they would await orders. The SASR was ordered to prepare an element for deployment.

Air Chief Marshal Angus Houston, Australia's Chief of the Defence Force (CDF), was sent to the Persian Gulf, where he investigated which countries might allow Australia to stage SASR patrols, equipment and vehicles. Initially, representatives of Sultan

Qaboos bin Said of Oman were approached about the possibility of the Australians staging from Masirah Island. That overture was refused, but there was a warmer reception in Kuwait, where an SASR element would be welcomed, on the proviso that a couple of the SASR patrols stay in Kuwait to train that country's special forces.

Orders filtered down from government to the CDF to the Special Operations Commander Australia, and it was soon clear that the SASR would be making a meaningful contribution to the response under ANZUS. The details of what that contribution might be, and how it might be made, were up to them.

* * *

The only military command reporting directly to the US president was not going to be denied action in Afghanistan.

Joint Special Operations Command (or JSOC) was the inter-service command that oversaw the two 'tier one' special forces units: the US Army's 1st Special Forces Operational Detachment, known as Delta Force, and the Naval Special Warfare Development Group, commonly known as DEVGRU or SEAL Team 6.

Developed in the 1980s, these were the ultimate 'break in case of emergency' units, training for once-in-a-generation missions like the recovery of stolen nuclear weapons and the hunting of war criminals in a hostile country (something JSOC did in the former Yugoslavia). Their skill set didn't fit exactly with the planned invasion of Afghanistan, but that wasn't going to stop them from deploying.

Bush and Rumsfeld, as well as General Franks, the officer in charge of the invasion of Afghanistan, wanted JSOC incorporated into the initial attack plans, so the war planners attempted to find a 'behind-enemy-lines' target for them to hit. Eventually, three targets were shortlisted, which had been designated Objective Goat, Objective Gecko and Objective Rhino.

Objective Goat was a fertiliser factory that the CIA had been monitoring as a potential chemical weapons workshop being run by al-Qaeda. General Franks pushed hard for the site to be hit by JSOC, but the CIA decided, on balance, that it was probably just a fertiliser factory. (When the site was ultimately secured, this proved to be the case.) That left Objective Gecko and Objective Rhino. The former was a large, walled compound in Kandahar that had once been occupied by Mullah Omar, and the latter was a remote airfield south-east of Kandahar that had been used by the leaders of the United Arab Emirates and Saudi Arabia during hunting trips. The war planners hoped that the airfield might be established as the first US airhead in southern Afghanistan.

The usefulness of a JSOC attack on these objectives was questioned by intelligence professionals. It was highly unlikely that Mullah Omar or any Taliban leadership would be found at Gecko, they said, while Rhino was likely abandoned or maintained only by ground and maintenance staff. But both missions were approved regardless.

Objective Gecko was the first target hit, and it was seized without any resistance. The only shots fired were from an AC-130 gunship engaging a bus driving near the target. As figures tried to flee the bus, the gunship's weapons systems followed them – but the plane's optics found their targets were paired and holding hands. They were mothers and children. No enemy fighters were found at Gecko, nor was any actionable intelligence recovered.

DEVGRU were inserted to observe Objective Rhino before Delta Force, US Army Rangers and some combat cameramen assaulted the site. Footage of the assault was beamed directly back to a US Army psychological operations unit, which disseminated it to news organisations.

'Several of our men had been wounded, and many of the enemy had been killed,' Tommy Franks wrote of the assault on Rhino in his autobiography, *American Soldier*, but sources at the site said there was no resistance, and that the American wounded were from a hard helicopter landing and from US soldiers peppering themselves with their own fragmentation grenades. Two Army Rangers died as part of the operation, but those deaths occurred in a helicopter crash at a Pakistani staging area.

According to the official US military history, B-2 Stealth Bombers and AC-130 gunships hit Objective Rhino. A source who was at the site says approximately two dozen Afghans were killed during the assault; they were buried behind the air base. Objective Rhino became Forward Operating Base (FOB) Rhino, southern Afghanistan's first US airfield.

The first Americans flown into FOB Rhino were marines from the 1st Marine Expeditionary Brigade, commanded at the time by Colonel Jim 'Mad Dog' Mattis (later a four-star general, and then Secretary of Defense under President Donald Trump). Their task, according to Mattis, was to 'make sure the enemy didn't feel like they had any safe haven, to destroy their sense of security in southern Afghanistan, to isolate Kandahar from its lines of communication, and to move against Kandahar'. Joining them in this task (and arriving at FOB Rhino fewer than 48 hours after the first marines) was the Australian SASR element.

SASR commanding officer Gus Gilmore had been personally petitioning Colonel Mattis for his force to join the marines in Afghanistan. His argument was that while marines were good at a lot of things, they were not as adept at long-range patrols and special reconnaissance as the SASR. The US would have total aerial control, Gilmore reasoned, but there was nothing quite like having your actual eyes on a target.

Colonel Mattis liked this Australian officer, and was interested in what his force might be able to do. He told Gilmore he'd incorporate the SASR into his war planning, and then outlined exactly what he expected of those in his force. 'I don't want the enemy to ever fall asleep without feeling like the door can be kicked in and they're going to die,' Mattis said. 'I don't want them to find any refuge anywhere. They're to be hunted down and keep the pressure on them.'

Hunting was something the SASR would do enthusiastically, but not in the initial stages of the war. This would happen years later, primarily in the backwater southern province of Uruzgan, the place where a small American special forces element almost won the war in Afghanistan 20 years before it was lost.

5

'Fight the pagans all together as they fight you all together'

THERE IS NO TYPICAL SASR background, but there are some experiences that are true of many operators: a family with a history of Australian military service and generational patriotism; an upbringing of shooting and hunting; and also experience of childhood stress, struggle or trauma. Only the last of these was true of two-decade SASR veteran Matthew Bouillaut. His father was a Frenchman, his mother was a teacher and, growing up in Sydney, he didn't hunt or shoot. There was struggle, however.

According to Matthew Bouillaut, his father was self-indulgent and lacked drive as a young man in France. He was given some money by his family to go out into the world and find himself. In Darwin he found a wife. 'I don't think he had any positive male role models. I know he loved us but he wasn't what you'd call a good parent,' Bouillaut says of his father.

Bouillaut senior never settled into a career in Australia, and the family was supported wholly by Matthew's mother. He was still in primary school when his father developed a degenerative disease, one that took his life. As his father wasted away and his mother worked, Bouillaut half-heartedly trudged through schoolwork that was all means and no end. Then he started to perceive that there was a world beyond his childhood existence.

He first saw this world on television. As an 11-year-old in 1980, he watched men in black and carrying submachine guns abseil down a fancy-looking building in London, then smash through windows while English bobbies watched on in awe. He saw a huge flotilla of British warships leaving England to much fanfare and joy, en route to the Falkland Islands. He learned the story of a small group of soldiers who secreted themselves onto a western Falklands airfield, destroyed 11 Argentine planes on the ground and then fought their way back to a nearby British battleship.

'Do we have the SAS in Australia?' Bouillaut asked when an ADF career adviser came to his school. The adviser told him yes, they did, but that it was a very long and arduous road to be selected for that particular regiment.

Bouillaut quit school immediately, become a garbage collector and worked relentlessly on his fitness. At 16 years and nine months, the youngest age at which he could join, he went to infantry school and quickly passed selection to become a member of the 1st Commando Regiment. Then, in 1992, at the exceptionally young age of 23, Bouillaut earned his sandy beret: he had won his way into the SASR.

* * *

When a giant C-17 Globemaster bearing the first Aussie soldiers and equipment grumbled to a halt on FOB Rhino's desert runway in October 2001, Matthew Bouillaut was standing at the back of the plane. As the load door lowered, he was the first Australian to breathe the frigid Afghan air.

With a loaded weapon and pounding heart, he looked at this first southern airhead, which had last been used by Saudi falconers. US marines were dotted around the airstrip, many in dug-in positions, their heavy machine guns pointing outwards at a dark expanse of desert.

It was cold – much colder than the Australians had expected. It would be even colder soon as the short autumn became a long winter. In Perth there were soft seasonal curves, but here in the deserts of southern Afghanistan the weather turned corners. A few weeks earlier, when mission planning began, the tarmac of FOB Rhino was hitting 40 degrees, but now the windchill brought the temperature below zero.

The Australians found a place to set themselves up. As Bouillaut helped erect tents that had been used in the Vietnam War, he thought about the stark and frigid mountains in which he and his patrol would soon be fighting – the home ground of their enemy. Some trepidation seeped in, but it was so diluted by his sense of gratitude that he barely felt it.

This was what he'd wanted This was what they all wanted, every bloke who'd dragged his way through the SASR's gruelling 21-day selection course, and then through the equally difficult 18-month REO (reinforcement) cycle, in which a soldier had to learn all the shooting, driving, freefalling, hiding, navigating, hunting, exploding, engineering and strategising required to even start a career as an SASR operator. Every trooper throughout the chain of the SASR command who was beret-qualified had been trying to get into this fight for weeks, and now Bouillaut and the men of his patrol were here, cold but thankful.

Almost as soon as the planes hit the towers on 9/11, Bouillaut's phone started pinging. These were messages from his men and other patrol commanders sharing information and asking questions – the primary one being how they could get themselves into the fight that was undoubtedly coming.

No one knew what would happen or when, but they all resolved to be ready. Everyone spent more time at the barracks. Leave was cancelled, minor surgeries cancelled, men scrambled to regain professional currency. (SASR operators fall in and out of 'currency' all the time, as their requisite skills are updated almost constantly.) Within days it became apparent that the attacks on New York and Washington DC had originated in Afghanistan, and rumours abounded that an element would be going over.

'All any of us wanted to do was go to Afghanistan,' says Bouillaut. 'That created quite a bit of tension within the regiment.'

The SASR had three sabre (or fighting) squadrons, each of those squadrons broken up into three or four fighting troops, and those troops into four or five fighting patrols. Many believed that only one squadron would be sent on what could turn out to be a short trip. In September 2001, Bouillaut's 1 Squadron was transitioning out of a rotation as the 'green' or warfighting squadron; they were scheduled to become the 'black' or counterterrorism squadron as part of the Tactical Assault Group.

Would 1 Squadron stay 'green' and go to Afghanistan? Or would they become 'black' and stay in Australia? The men didn't know until they started receiving briefs about not only al-Qaeda but also the Taliban. The CIA started sending videos to the squadron of attacks executed by American backed *mujahedin* against Soviet troops in the 1980s.

Patrol commander Matt Bouillaut and his second-in-command, Blaine Diddams, the leadership group of their patrol Bravo 3, spent many evenings at Diddams' home drinking coffee, smoking cigarettes and watching those CIA videos over and over, trying to understand the terrain, the tactics and the battlefield in which they might soon be fighting.

Bouillaut arranged for his patrol to train at the Bindoon Defence Training Area an hour north of Perth, as well as ordering very long pack marches around metropolitan Perth, wearing their civilian clothes. In the cafes the patrol stopped at, onlookers sometimes stared at the group of men and their huge hiking backpacks. These onlookers would receive a smile and sometimes the explanation that the mates were preparing for a trekking holiday.

In October the call the men had been waiting for arrived. 1 Squadron was to deploy to a Kuwaiti air base and await further instructions. Some Land Rovers and long-range patrol vehicles (LRPVs) were coming with them, but not enough cars for all the patrols.

Bouillaut thought about the videos he'd watched at Blaine Diddams' house, and imagined himself on the battlefields of Afghanistan. When he pictured himself in a car, he saw hidden bombs and bullets flying in, from under bridges and from peaks above chokepoints. When thinking about being on foot, he saw himself atop those peaks, watching an unsuspecting enemy and in control of any engagements.

'I said to my guys, "Based on the Russian occupation and what we know so far, this is what I reckon. I think cars are an unnecessary bullet magnet in Afghanistan,"' says Bouillaut. 'I thought we'd be more deployable if we can go high into the mountains.' He therefore volunteered his patrol to be primarily a foot patrol.

There had been a scramble in the lead-up to deployment to equip the SASR element with appropriate communications equipment, weaponry and even intravenous prophylactic cover against chemical and biological weaponry. But there weren't appropriate jackets, sleeping bags, thermals or beanies in the military inventory. Before leaving Perth, an SASR quartermaster made the short drive from Campbell Barracks to an adventure retail shop in Cottesloe, and bought so much of its stock – everything he thought was needed – that he essentially closed the place down.

When the Australian patrols started projecting out of FOB Rhino, the soldiers were coldest in the open LRPVs. They found the temperatures far more bearable while climbing or dug in at an observation post. Bouillaut's foot patrol was best equipped for the conditions.

One of the first significant missions conducted by the Australians was a special reconnaissance operation, the type of mission for which, within the global special operations forces (SOF) community, the SASR were best known.

'Any American out doing reconnaissance is good for 48 hours, but we'll give you ten days, no worries,' says Bouillaut. 'That's why we have the selection we do.'

Bouillaut was told to report to one of the permanent structures at FOB Rhino, and there he found that a high-tech American command and control centre had been established. 'It was like something from Tom Clancy – dark with all the screens and that,' he says. In the room were marine officers and CIA agents, and on one screen was the satellite image of a village nearby, nestled in a valley. What the Americans wanted was for the Australians to put eyes on the 'US priority target' for as long as was needed. Eventually, the marines would come in and prosecute. This was exactly the type of thing Gus Gilmore and Jim Mattis had envisaged the SASR doing.

Two hours after the briefing, Bouillaut's patrol was loading quad bikes into two CH-53 Sea Stallion helicopters. After rolling off their landing zone wearing night-vision goggles (NVGs), they rode out of a blinding brownout and then into a landscape lit by a multitude of brilliant stars. This was the otherworldly Afghan countryside that so many Australians would experience in the years to come. A land of layered contours, seemingly empty but with the feeling that plotting eyes may be on you.

Bravo 3 cached their bikes and trekked silently to high ground above the compound they'd been sent to observe. Now they were the unseen eyes. For more than 24 hours, they observed what appeared to be normal Afghan life, until two Hilux trucks arrived with what looked a lot like the enemy: eight men, all armed, with rocket-propelled grenade (RPG) tubes stacked in the back of the trucks. Bouillaut silently called for his sniper and machine-gunner to place their weapons forward, and radioed for a bomber.

One of the trucks became bogged in front of Bravo 3's position, and the men from both trucks put down their weapons to free the vehicle. Bouillaut's men developed a plan in which one bomb could be dropped on the stuck truck, and then his patrol could clean up anyone who was still alive afterwards.

Bouillaut knew, however, that this target was not his to hit. He radioed back to the Australian command seeking approval for the attack, who relayed the message back to the US marines. A message came back: 'Let them go.'

'We watched them get their car out, they rolled off and that was that,' Bouillaut recalls.

The marines came in a day later, and as soon as they did, Bouillaut's patrol disappeared, back to FOB Rhino.

'The US had never used Australia in an op like that,' Bouillaut explains, 'and if we'd decided to shoot up a village and the main guy escaped, I don't reckon that would have been good.'

The mission had been a relatively easy 48 hours without a shot fired, but that successful special reconnaissance mission was a prelude for the hugely consequential mission that ended Bouillaut's rotation.

In December 2001, the SASR element moved from FOB Rhino to Kandahar Airfield, and there the patrols projected hundreds of kilometres out from Kandahar, with Bouillaut's team sometimes working as a mobile foot patrol and sometimes as part of a complete troop action, with the men in his patrol jumping on the back of the other vehicles.

The Australians were part of a huge intelligence effort to find Osama Bin Laden and the other al-Qaeda leadership. The US military's best guess was that Bin Laden was in the Pashtun south or the mountainous east, which abutted the ungoverned tribal regions of western Pakistan. The Taliban was a secondary concern throughout, in no small part because they appeared to have disappeared from the country. There were gunmen up and down the country, but they seemed not to be amassing to fight the invaders.

The Australians were given a wide remit, patrolling largely as they saw fit in what was primarily an intelligence-gathering exercise. They visited villages, talked with locals, and in some places set up medical clinics in the hope that information might emerge.

They were sometimes fired upon, and in many instances this was indirect fire issued after they left a village where they'd been warmly received. Most soldiers recognised these rounds for what they were: an expression of wounded pride and manly cultural obligation. The Australians were not here to fight the whole country, though, so as long as it was safe to do so, they largely ignored this 'annoyance fire'.

The cold was a constant hindrance for the vehicle patrols, with the men sometimes having to light fires under the fuel tanks of the LRPVs so the diesel didn't become a frozen gel. Often they slept with their water bottles so they had something unfrozen to drink when they woke. Another issue with the LRPVs was a lack of armour. They were excellent fighting vehicles, with superior mobility and visibility, but they afforded the occupants little protection from mines and IEDs – an issue that would later become persistent in Afghanistan and in Iraq.

The SASR greatly impressed US military planners. The length of time the Aussies stayed on patrol and out of trouble was unheard of. One patrol came back to base only after 52 consecutive days in the field. Then, early in 2002, the Australians suffered their first casualties.

First, north of Kandahar in January, an SASR corporal triggered an anti-personnel mine and lost his foot. Then, on 16 February 2002, an Australian LRPV drove into a minefield in the Kandahar River valley, triggering one of the estimated 5 million mines that had been left behind in Afghanistan by the Soviet Army.

A local man had attempted to alert the Australians to the danger they were in, but he was too late. An LRPV bearing Sergeant Andrew Russell and four colleagues drove over the mine. A US marine parachute rescue team dropped into the location to treat the wounded, but Sergeant Russell's injuries were too severe to survive. His was the regiment's first combat death since Vietnam. There was a small ceremony, then his body was repatriated to Australia, where he could be more fully grieved, and the work in Afghanistan continued.

* * *

In December 2001, US signals intelligence had identified that Osama bin Laden, as well as Ayman al-Zawahiri and al-Qaeda's most loyal fighters, were located in a mountainous cave complex in eastern Afghanistan called Tora Bora. Here, in the 1980s, the local *mujahedin* had escaped the fighting against the Soviets. The complex had a hydroelectric power system with ventilation and lighting that the CIA had helped fund and even build.

Tora Bora was located in a snowy area of difficult terrain, including mountain passes, cliffs and caves; to the east and south, passes into Pakistan were less than 50 kilometres away. No reliable maps of the area existed. This was the war; this was the reason the United States had come to Afghanistan.

A helicopter-borne assault against Tora Bora was discounted, as it was known that al-Qaeda and their supporters had anti-air weapons in the area, so a convoy of Hilux utes was sent into the area bearing two Delta teams, A1 and A3. They were to link up with an Afghan force led by a warlord whose allegiances were at best questionable, and together they would attack Bin Laden and his men.

US air power concentrated on the area for almost a week, dropping 1100 guided bombs and 500 'dumb' bombs, including the massive 5700-kilogram BLU-82 'Daisy Cutter' bomb, in the space of five days. Bin Laden feared that the terrible bombardment would result in his death, and on 14 December he wrote a will.

'Allah commended to us that when death approaches any of us that we make a bequest to parents and next of kin and to Muslims as a whole,' he wrote. 'Allah bears witness that the love of jihad and death in the cause of Allah has dominated my life and the verses of the sword permeated every cell in my heart, "and fight the pagans all together as they fight you all together". How many times did I wake up to find myself reciting this holy verse!'

As impressive as the bombardment was, it wasn't effective. Nor were the Afghan militia with whom the Delta operators were working. Bin Laden, Zawahiri and most of the al-Qaeda fighters escaped the area before any American on the ground even had a chance to fire a lethal shot.

'It was just over two months after 9/11, and for the most important mission to date our nation was relying on a bunch of AK-47-toting lawless bandits and fractious thugs,' Tom Greer, one of the Delta officers on the ground, told Sean Naylor for his book *Relentless Strike*.

As the Battle of Tora Bora was waged, plans were being drawn up for the Australian SASR element to return to Kuwait in preparation for the next phase of the war. There was an expectation that Tora Bora might be the final battle of this war, and that the coalition forces, including the SASR, might then move to Sudan, Yemen or Somalia, in pursuit of other al-Qaeda elements. But after the failure at Tora Bora, the Australians moved instead to Bagram Air Base, north of Kabul. There the SASR broke with the marines and joined the 10th Mountain Division for the largest battle of the war.

Reports came in of massing al-Qaeda fighters just 100 kilometres south of Tora Bora in Paktia Province. The area these fighters were reported to be was inhospitable at the best of times – and this was arguably one of the worst of times: in the depths of the Afghan winter, with snow driving down on impassable peaks above treacherous passes.

The SASR had proven to be one of the few forces, if not the only one, in the country that could operate in the mountainous border area on extended reconnaissance patrols, so they were sent in to survey the area.

It was a vehicle-mounted SASR patrol from C Troop working just 100 kilometres south of Tora Bora that observed a large group of al-Qaeda fighters with artillery pieces, armoured vehicles and heavy weapons. Of particular interest was a tall man who was observed to be travelling with bodyguards – on the enemy ICOM radio he was being referred to as 'the Sheik', an honorific that had been bestowed by the Afghan fighters on Osama bin Laden.

The fighters were seen in the Shah-i-Kot Valley, a pass between Afghanistan and a largely ungoverned part of Pakistan. It was another labyrinthine place where Afghan guerrillas had tormented invaders for more than 2000 years. Here Afghans had drawn interlopers, such as Alexander the Great, the Mongols, the British imperialists and the Soviets, to the valley floors and passes, where they would be killed by fighters lurking in hidden redoubts, goat tracks and bluffs.

The C Troop patrol was told to return to Bagram, which they did by night, when the temperatures were sometimes minus 30 degrees. The US military planned to mount a large-scale operation, having learned from their Tora Bora mistakes.

This was to be a 'hammer and anvil' helicopter assault: hundreds of US conventional soldiers would be inserted into the area, and would push the massed enemy fighters into a blocking force or into zones where they could be killed from the air, with bombs directed by teams situated in the peaks above the al-Qaeda and Taliban fighting positions.

'The US was on this post-9/11 roll,' says Matthew Bouillaut, 'and they basically killed as many people as they could in retaliation, but this was supposed to be the final flag-waving victory battle.'

This was to be called Operation Anaconda, and the US prey were to be squeezed to death as if by the carnivorous snake.

The Australian SASR officers were, of course, keen to be involved in the operation, as this would certainly be the meaningful contribution they had been ordered to make, but there were misgivings about the speed of the planning and the lack of intelligence. The Americans were anxious to destroy the al-Qaeda fighters in Afghanistan before they could melt away into Pakistan, where the Americans had no power to prosecute, but the war planners had little idea about the terrain into which the assault forces would be moving.

There would be no eyes on the ground before the helicopter assault, and the Australians believed that some special reconnaissance – their specialty – should be undertaken beforehand. Eventually, it was decided that the SASR would take on three roles in the battle to come.

The bulk of the SASR – all of the vehicle-mounted patrols – would be sent to the low, flat *dasht*, or desert, south-west of the Shah-i-Kot Valley, in a cut-off position designated 'AO Down Under'. If the enemy tried to escape through this position, the SASR were tasked with hunting them down and killing them.

The second role would fall to SASR operator Clint Palmer and signaller Martin 'Jock' Wallace, who were seconded to a US conventional force designated Task Force Rakkasan. Their main responsibility was to establish a communications bridge between the force in AO Down Under and the US force – most importantly so the two forces didn't end up shooting at each other.

The third role would be the most consequential, and thus the most desirable. One of the patrols was to secrete itself into a clandestine position atop one of the mountains where al-Qaeda fighters were believed to be; from there, they were to 'observe with the capability to interdict as required'. As Matthew Bouillaut explains, 'In special ops, that basically means do what you want.'

This would be a special forces task in a largely conventional battle. The infantry would do the fighting, the planes would do the bombing, and the special forces would be the reason the enemy drove themselves insane wondering how the infantry and planes knew what they knew.

Bouillaut, the commander of a patrol that had proven they could work independently of their vehicles and in the harshest conditions, was called in by his commanding officer and asked: 'What do you reckon an above-the-snowline patrol might look like?' The plum 'observe and interdict' job fell to his patrol, Bravo 3.

Bouillaut spent days afterwards with the SASR's mapping and graphics specialist, poring over a computer program called Intervisibility, which creates a terrain map from a particular perspective at a location and throws out red lines of sight on a 3D map at the prospective battlefield below. Bouillaut was seeking the best vantage point on the battlefield, but also somewhere the enemy wouldn't think could possibly be occupied.

'There was always the lazy, easy way to get somewhere, where you can get compromised, or the hard-as-fuck way,' says Bouillaut. 'That was our way.'

When Bouillaut found his position, the toughest part of the battle started: the waiting. A local warlord named Zia Lodin, who had given himself the title of 'general', had told the US forces that he could raise 450 men for the battle. With the Americans keen to build a force to whom they could hand over the country after they left, they pushed back the start of the operation so that Lodin's men could be armed and trained.

The Australians waited for the call to action, shivering at Afghanistan's biggest air base, built by Americans in the 1950s, then vastly rebuilt by the Soviets.

'It was like someone out of a *Saw* movie,' says Bouillaut of Bagram. 'Broken glass everywhere, and old and industrial. There were a lot of young Americans walking around with Bibles blessing people before the fight. It was fucked.'

With the Taliban seemingly routed and al-Qaeda located and amassed for destruction, few at Bagram in 2002 could have imagined the future of the base, which would undergo a multibillion-dollar expansion and refurbishment. Nor that, one day, the Americans would simply turn the power off and slip away into the night.

6

'We were meant to be representing the pinnacle of the Western military, and we were almost fucked so hard by these blokes'

THE ROCKET-PROPELLED GRENADE SEEMED to come towards Jock Wallace slowly. It didn't carve from left to right or right to left, as he'd seen before; it just went from being a dot to a spot and then, noticeably and obviously, an RPG round. In those frozen microseconds, it occurred to Jock to run, which he did, but instead of moving left or right, he ran straight, along the round's path. Of course it followed him.

'It was like that old joke about the Irishman running away from the train, along the tracks on a valley floor,' says Wallace. '"Why didn't you run up the hill, Paddy?" they'd ask. "Because I can run faster on the flat," he'd reply.'

The RPG was the first shot fired in anger by al-Qaeda in that area, but it had been preceded by a gunfight of sorts. Just a few minutes earlier, Wallace and Clint Palmer had spotted a group of armed men on high ground above. On further inspection, they saw that the men were waving colourful VS-17 emergency signal panels, denoting that they were friendlies. This was a DEVGRU team who, working with the CIA, had secreted themselves into the battlefield and were tracking an al-Qaeda element.

From their hidden position, the SEALs had been watching the men of Task Force (TF) Rakkasan move up the valley, closer and closer to a dug-in al-Qaeda force. The SEALs broke cover to warn their countrymen, and shortly afterwards the rattle of automatic weapons fire snapped across the valley. Many of the soldiers in TF Rakkasan had dropped to firing positions and opened up on the SEALs, assuming they were enemy.

'Me and Clint were kicking these cunts in the ribs, in the body armour, telling them to stop shooting,' says Wallace.

When the Americans did stop shooting there were a few precious moments of quiet before the first enemy RPG came in, wobbling, stabbing and effective. The enemy were now aware of both US forces.

That first RPG wended its way through the valley and towards Jock Wallace. It dipped just before it landed, smashing at the feet of a group of American officers in front of Wallace. The RPG didn't explode, but hissed and spat and scythed past the officers through the snow, tracking Wallace's footprints. As Jock Wallace leaped over the lip of a rocky rise, the round fizzed, spat once more and then sat inert and unexploded.

Jock's head popped up. There was another moment of silence before a DShK heavy machine gun opened up. Mortars started landing effectively, and small arms fire came into their position. The battle had begun.

TF Rakkasan had inserted very close to two villages, Marzak and Babkheel, and the locals rushed out to join the fight against the coalition. US intelligence estimate was that there were 150 to 200 al-Qaeda fighters in the area, but post-conflict reporting cited up to 1000 gunmen confronting the Americans. This was exactly the kind of thing Osama bin Laden had in mind when he planned his international attacks. The US military had been drawn into the very spot where the Soviet Army had twice been defeated, with enraged locals confronting and defeating the foreign devils.

The al-Qaeda fighters and the Afghans used the same anti-air tactics as they had against the Soviets, engaging fixed ZPU-1 and DShK positions and using their RPG-7 anti-tank rounds as flak, firing their rounds in the air knowing they would automatically detonate at 980 metres and create effective starburst rounds against helicopters. Two Apache helicopters took hits this way and had to return to base early in the battle.

Two US special forces teams, ODA 594 and ODA 372, were bringing Zia Lodin's men into the battle, but as their convoy approached the valley they were spotted by a US AC-130 gunship and attacked. A number of Afghans and an American warrant officer were killed.

This friendly-fire incident stymied a planned aerial assault that would precede the insertion of Zia Lodin's men, and when the friendly Afghans entered the valley, they did so without the protection they expected. General Zia's men took dozens of dead and wounded from mortar fire as soon as they entered the valley, and they quickly lost their desire for the fight, becoming combat-ineffective.

Meanwhile, TF Rakkasan was being hammered. Jock Wallace and Clint Palmer had wedged themselves into the only geographical feature on the valley floor that offered them some cover, a tiny rock fissure a few feet wide that the soldiers had dubbed Hell's Halfpipe. Rounds and mortars came in constantly. Inside the halfpipe, Jock Wallace dug himself a fighting hole using a pup knife, only leaving his hole to retrieve a wounded American soldier or to fire at an enemy position.

In one instance, an enemy mortar team 'walked' their rounds (watching their mortars explode and adjusting their attack vector accordingly) on to a 101st Airborne position, where Americans were trying to land their own mortar rounds. One enemy round flattened multiple US servicemen with shrapnel. Jock Wallace broke cover and dragged the injured Americans away from the zeroed position and into Hell's Halfpipe. There, he and Palmer gave the Americans emergency medical treatment.

Many of the al-Qaeda and local fighters realised that weapons like Wallace's M4 5.56mm rifle were ineffective at range. Wallace recalls a frustrating situation when an enemy fighter attacked him with a mortar, then stopped and smoked a cigarette, looking at Wallace as Wallace tried to shoot him. Wallace says he would have given his pinkie toe to swap his modern M4 for the old 7.62mm

SLR that the SASR carried in Vietnam. '[The M4 is] good for when you're driving round in cars and kicking in doors, but not so good when you're in a big fucking valley,' he says.

Also relatively ineffective were the bombs being dropped by the jets that were streaking in and out of the battlespace. These were regularly being directed by those on the valley floor, who often gave inaccurate or incomplete information to the pilots above. A huge amount of ordnance was being dropped around the besieged American position, but when the al-Qaeda and Afghan fighters realised it was being landed imprecisely, they moved closer and closer to their prey.

'We were nearly wiped out in the most embarrassing way possible,' says Wallace. 'It was so close to there being 82 dead bodies on the valley floor, five minutes into day one of this fucking thing.

'I can't even describe it in my own words. I can only feel it,' he says. 'We were meant to be representing the pinnacle of the Western military, and we were almost fucked so hard by these blokes.'

* * *

Matthew Bouillaut, Blaine Diddams and Bravo 3 were approved to insert into the battlefield on the first day of battle. That was the good news. The bad news was that there was a JSOC team hunting a 'high-value target' in their planned area of operations, so Bravo 3 was directed to another mountaintop position further south.

Bouillaut and his team inserted to a new staging point by way of an old Russian Mi-17 helicopter piloted by a civilian under the employ of the CIA, and then climbed to their new position, from which they could hear the battle but not see it. They watched B-52 bombers fly overhead and felt, underfoot, the explosions of the 2000-pound bombs, but they couldn't see the targets on the valley floor to the north. They couldn't see Jock Wallace, Clint Palmer or TF Rakkasan either, but they could hear every comms message as they reported more and more wounded.

On their radios, Bravo 3 also heard the 1 Squadron vehicle-mounted patrols begging to leave their positions and relieve TK Rakkasan and their mates. Each request was denied. Bouillaut also requested for Bravo 3 to be allowed to trek down and engage the force besieging TF Rakkasan. They too were told to stay put.

Bravo 3 spent a cold and frustrating night in their nest listening to the sounds of a battle in which they were desperate to take part. Later, they were relieved to hear that Clint Palmer and Jock Wallace were extracted unharmed.

Two forces of nature saved the men of TF Rakkasan: the fall of night and AC-130U Spooky gunships. With attack helicopters fearful of the al-Qaeda anti-air positions, and with fast-moving jets having difficulties targeting a moving enemy, the AC-130 gunship, with its ability to loiter, proved invaluable in stopping a massacre of US soldiers. Two AC-130s above the Shah-i-Kot Valley put consistent cannon fire around the Americans and the Australian pair throughout the afternoon, keeping at bay the al-Qaeda and Afghan fighters who were looking to overrun the coalition position.

As the sun set, the AC-130s kept up that fire as a helicopter mission was mounted to extract the broken element; under the cover of night, the whole element was extracted without loss of life. Thirty-five American soldiers had been wounded, however, many seriously. It had not been the massacre Osama bin Laden had dreamed of when planning the 9/11 attacks, but for the Saudi this was certainly a promising start.

* * *

As one potential disaster was resolved for the US military, another beckoned. Two DEVGRU teams attempted to insert atop Takur Ghar mountain, a peak overlooking the south of the battlefield.

The teams were supposed to have been inserted deep in the night some distance from the peak, and from there move tactically to their position before dawn, but their launch time was repeatedly pushed back. When they finally boarded their Chinooks, it was decided the only way they could get to their positions before sunrise was to fly straight there to the peak.

An overwatch flight showed no enemy activity at the planned landing zone, but when the Chinook came in to land it was immediately engaged from multiple positions. Two RPG rounds smashed into the helicopter, and heavy machine-gun rounds tore through the fuselage. The stricken Chinook managed to limp away to the valley floor, but not before DEVGRU petty officer Neil Roberts was blown out of the back of the helicopter.

Another DEVGRU team was sent in to recover Roberts. They too were attacked, by fighters in a prepared bunker. A quick reaction force (QRF) was dispatched, but one of the helicopters flying the men in was destroyed by enemy fire, resulting in multiple casualties.

The coalition's planners needed to resolve the increasingly complex fight at Takur Ghar, but they also needed to try to win this battle. US forces were still attempting to push the enemy to the south, where they could be met with aerial bombardment, but they needed to secure elevated positions from which those aerial attacks would be orchestrated.

Matthew Bouillaut received a page from command and read it with a laugh.

'Hey, boys, guess where they want us? That fucking spot I spent days figuring out was the best spot.'

They moved to a spot where a helicopter could extract them and were dropped on a low ridge at the back end of the valley, from where they could hike to their originally planned position. Attached to the patrol was Jim, a US Air Force JTAC (joint terminal attack controller – a specially trained military member who can embed with a combat element and liaise between that element and planes and drones above). Bouillaut asked him if he could get a Predator drone on their position, and they used the drone to check the ground ahead as they moved. Using intelligence, surveillance and reconnaissance (or ISR) platforms in this way would soon be standard procedure for special operations missions, but in 2002 this was groundbreaking for the Australians.

'You're clear for 1000 metres,' said Jim.

They climbed 1000 metres through a stark, rocky cathedral.

'You're clear for 1000 metres,' said Jim.

They climbed another 1000 metres as the snow started to build.

'You're clear for 1000 metres,' said Jim.

And so on for nine hours through the night, as the report of gunships and bombers echoed down the valley. When Bravo 3 summitted the mountain, the men lay down on their packs, exhausted. The moment they did, a vibration, then a tremble and a strong tremor ran through their bodies, before it suddenly stopped. It had been an earthquake, its epicentre a few hundreds of kilometres north. This was a strange time in Afghanistan.

From their elevated position, Bravo 3 could see they were now in a perfect spot, just south of where the al-Qaeda positions were dug in. Further south, special forces teams from Turkey, Germany, Norway, New Zealand and Denmark, designated as Task Force K-Bar, had been set up on peaks above where the Americans thought the al-Qaeda and Taliban fighters might flee, but the enemy had chosen to stay in their fighting positions in the valley, which meant Bravo 3 was the only patrol with consistent sight of the enemy.

Bravo 3 now split their patrol in two, with Diddams arranging patrolling, sentries and protection of their position so that Bouillaut and the JTAC Jim could concentrate on bringing in ordnance. Over the next 12 days, Bravo 3 brought in ordnance from 'everything with wings, rotors and guns'. Hour by hour, day by day, more and more of the US air was handed over to the Australians.

On their first day in their new position, Bravo 3 supported the battle at Takur Ghar, with Bouillaut watching an enemy fighter directing a .50-calibre machine gun on the downed QRF helicopter, and a US Navy jet missing the man by 50 metres. Via the JTAC, Bouillaut contacted the pilot, telling him to wheel around and add 50 metres to his vector.

'The bomb landed right on him. I watched [the enemy fighter] disappear in a flash,' says Bouillaut.

The mission was planned to last for three days and they had packed for five. After two days it was obvious that they would be useful in their position for much longer than that. The patrol halved their rations, and later would halve rations again.

Jim and Bouillaut could see that the B-52 bombers were largely dropping ordnance in open fields, away from where the enemy were, or where the enemy were likely to be. The pair were eventually given control of the full suite of American air being used, with all kinds of aircraft checking in from bases across the region and beyond. There were F-class US Navy jets coming in from three aircraft carriers in the Arabian Sea, Super Cobra and Apache helicopters from Bagram, AC-130 gunships coming in from Oman, and even B-1 and B-2 Stealth Bombers flying all the way from the United States. Jim had created a communications link between all of them and Matthew Bouillaut.

The pair even established a link to the US command in Saudi Arabia, where the US B-52s were stationed, who in turn connected the pair to the incoming bombers. For the B-52s, Bouillaut put together 'map-to-ground appreciations' and converted them into 'designated mean points of impact', which are essentially coordinates that can be punched into the US Joint Direct Attack Munition (JDAM) system that guides bombs.

From their position, Bouillaut and Jim could see the enemy supply and infiltration and exfiltration positions, or where they were likely to be, so they directed the B-52 ordnance onto those positions, which had the effect of bolting many of the enemy to their current positions. They even had A-10 Warthog attack aircraft checking in from Kuwait, where they were stationed primarily as a defence against Saddam Hussein's tanks.

'They were never going to use the A-10 in Afghanistan because of the depleted uranium, but after the helicopters had been shot down [at Takur Ghar] and [Americans] were killed they went, "Fuck it, the gloves are off,"' Bouillaut says.

Depleted uranium (DU) is an immensely dense metal like tungsten, but far cheaper to procure for the US military, as it is a byproduct of nuclear power generation. DU rounds are typically used against tanks and armour, and are known to shed toxic particles that persist for years. Numerous studies have linked DU use with dramatic jumps in childhood cancers and genetic defects in areas where US forces have used those rounds.

During the battle, Bouillaut was contacted by an Australian operations officer and asked to tally all the airstrikes they had ordered.

'You're fucking joking, mate,' he replied. They had ordered literally hundreds of strikes.

Bouillaut and Jim had access to so many air assets over such a long period of time that they ended up using the assets in new ways. One procedure was something that Bouillaut and Jim called 'perching', in which, when they had an AC-130 wheeling onto the battlefield, they were creating targets with a CIA Predator drone and sending them on before the AC-130 optics could find targets themselves.

Later, Jim would be summoned to the CIA headquarters in Langley, Virginia, to meet with the agency's heads and debrief them about how their drones had been used in a conventional battle. Bouillaut was asked to give an address at a symposium in America on this practice and his experiences in the Shah-i-Kot Valley.

'This was the pinnacle of special operations,' says Bouillaut. 'I'd never even seen an AC-130 before, let alone worked with one.'

After 12 days, the valley was clear of enemy positions and fighters, and the men of Bravo 3 were relieved by another special forces patrol in case there was mopping up to do. In a particularly trying battlespace, amid the freezing peaks and valleys of Afghanistan in winter, they'd been the eyes and ears for the forces below and above them. They'd killed America's enemies, al-Qaeda fighters who had come to Afghanistan to prosecute Bin Laden's global violent *jihad*. Very few other coalition soldiers who served in Afghanistan could make that claim.

The SASR had been told to make a meaningful contribution to the response under ANZUS, and they'd found a way to do so.

The element moved to back to the extraction point and flew back to Bagram, where they met up with the rest of 1 Squadron. After finding some crates of cigarettes and bottles of Johnnie Walker whisky, the SASR men smoked, drank and decompressed in a huge Russian-built hangar.

When the Australian SASR element returned to Perth, they received a hero's welcome, led by Prime Minister Howard himself. Matthew Bouillaut would be later awarded the Distinguished Service Cross, an honour for command and leadership, while Jock Wallace would be awarded the Medal of Gallantry, which recognises acts of bravery in hazardous conditions. Their commander, Rowan Tink, would be awarded the Bronze Star, an American medal that can also be awarded to foreign soldiers and civilians for meritorious service when fighting alongside American forces.

Bouillaut says that, at the time, he thought Operation Anaconda would be the peak of his career, and that it would mark the end of the war in Afghanistan. He was wrong on both counts. War in Iraq beckoned, and the war in Afghanistan had only just begun.

Al-Qaeda's leadership and their odious ideology atomised, metastasised and migrated to Pakistan, the Middle East and North Africa. Some Taliban fighters also fled to Pakistan, but no further. These men were Afghans, and they had only Afghan ambitions.

One of the latter was Mullah Saif-ur-Rehman Mansoor, a son of the famed *mujahedin* commander Maulvi Nasrullah Mansoor. Saif was young and hungry for fame when the Americans came to his valley, Shah-i-Kot. He fought the apostates, killed Americans, destroyed their helicopters and fled to the tribal areas of Pakistan as something of a folk hero. There, fighters would collect around him.

The Taliban were a husk of a force in 2002, and the Australian and American war in Afghanistan could have ended after Operation Anaconda. But in the ruins of places like Shah-i-Kot, the embers of the Taliban were allowed to become a conflagration.

* * *

The SASR were lauded by the US military after Operation Anaconda, but not so some of America's European allies. The US military publication *Stars and Stripes* singled out the United Kingdom's Royal Marines as malingerers, saying it was 'disappointing' that they were sent out to hunt al-Qaeda and Taliban fighters and had come back empty-handed. The British response was that there hadn't been anyone appropriate to kill.

The US military were also disappointed with Germany's special forces, the Kommando Spezialkräfte (KSK), who were part of Operation Anaconda but refused to hand prisoners over to the Americans, over fears those prisoners may be executed. In the German current affairs magazine *Stern*, some KSK officers complained about the conduct of the Americans; one detailed an instance when a KSK position was compromised by a herd of goats and a goatherd. The Germans moved their position and were then pilloried by the Americans for not killing the goatherd. 'The images of ... torture in Iraqi prisons did not surprise me,' one KSK officer was quoted as saying.

In the wake of Operation Anaconda, a series of war crimes were alleged to have been committed after the body of DEVGRU member Neil Roberts was retrieved from Takur Ghar. Roberts' head had been partially removed after a failed beheading. Despite the body being in a gruesome state, all of Roberts' teammates from Red Squadron were told to spend time with their mutilated friend directly after the battle. It's alleged that Red Squadron subsequently conducted a series of wanton killings of Afghans, also allegedly mutilating corpses. This theme of brutal criminality followed Red Squadron, and some other DEVGRU units as well, as they were deployed in Afghanistan and Iraq. Many of these crimes were uncovered by US investigative reporter Matthew Cole.

Cole's investigation and others, including one by *The New York Times*, have reported that Red Squadron operators, who wear a Native American warrior as their insignia, have sometimes been known to carry custom-made 14-inch hatchets into battle, and have used them to commit war crimes, including scalpings. There have also been many reports of the commanding officer of Red Squadron demanding that their young soldiers start their careers with 'blood on their hatchets'.

According to Cole, some soldiers from DEVGRU's Blue Squadron, whose insignia is a pirate, were imitating crimes from a book that glorified the actions of Nazi soldiers, and were using custom-made knives to skin their enemies. A Blue Squadron operator also allegedly beheaded an Afghan in Helmand Province after his team leader asked for a 'head on a platter'. DEVGRU were also reported to have 'canoed' a number of Afghans and Iraqis, meaning they would execute a victim by striking them on a specific spot on the forehead with their hatchets, so their head opened up like a canoe.

None of the alleged crimes of DEVGRU have been comprehensively investigated and the unit maintains significant cachet within the United States military, as well as within segments of the Australian military.

7

'We could never kill them all anyway'

IN 2001, DOCTRINALLY AND culturally, the units of JSOC and those of the US Army Special Forces – colloquially known as the Green Berets – were worlds apart. Delta and DEVGRU were famed as last-resort door-kickers with a penchant for raw brutality, but the Green Berets were known as warrior diplomats and fighting anthropologists. With their motto *De oppresso liber* – commonly understood as 'to liberate the oppressed' – the Green Berets were a force trained to empower and organise local forces against a common foe, using their 12-man Operational Detachment Alphas (or ODAs), also known as A Teams.

ODAs are designed to be an agitating force behind enemy lines, not only with their force of arms but with their ability to encourage uprisings and build local resistance. To that end they are trained in psychology, diplomacy and languages.

During the initial aerial invasion of Afghanistan, a number of ODAs were sent into Northern Alliance–controlled areas to connect with Ahmad Shah Massoud's now leaderless men and other elements. Their aim was to bring the fight to Kabul. These northern ODAs fought a series of well-publicised actions alongside warlords and Northern Alliance generals.

The actions of one A Team, ODA 595, became the subject of the Chris Hemsworth film *12 Strong*. But it was another A Team, ODA 574, that inserted into the south of Afghanistan and conducted what could have been the most integral mission of the entire war. This mission might have ended the war with the Taliban, and perhaps ended the Taliban itself, but that possibility was undone by American hubris and bloodlust.

ODA 574 was commanded by Captain Jason Amerine, a lean and thoughtful Hawaiian-born soldier with a bachelor's degree in Arabic. On 11 September 2001 Amerine was already in Central Asia. He and his ODA were training local paratroopers out of a Kazakh air base close to the Russian border, but after the attacks in New York, Washington and Pennsylvania, he was ordered to make his way to an air base in Jacobabad, in central Pakistan, and await orders.

There he was told they would be inserting into south-eastern Afghanistan, where they would link up with Abdul Haq, a famed *mujahedin* warlord who was on the payroll of the CIA. Haq was best known for his brutality, and for his skill in fighting on horseback despite the loss of one of his feet. Amerine was to help develop a force that could create a 'southern front', much like the Northern Alliance.

'The stated mission was to destroy military targets and render Afghanistan unusable for al-Qaeda, but for all the ODA team leaders it quickly became apparent that the mission was to do whatever the local warlord wanted to do,' says Amerine.

In preparation for his meeting with Haq, Amerine had arranged a welcome gift: whiskey and the traditional ODA gift of a 'BFK' (big fucking knife). Before he could meet the warlord, however, Haq had, against the wishes of his CIA handlers, rushed unaided into Afghanistan, where he had quickly been captured and then executed.

Soon another mission fell to ODA 574. This too was a mission of facilitation, assisting another Pashtun leader, but their partner this time was not a warlord. They would be partnering with a man from a noble family close to the royal lineage. Named Hamid Karzai, he had supported and funded the Taliban during their ascension to power, but eventually fell afoul of the group and fled to Pakistan, and then to Europe.

After being given the Karzai mission, Amerine and his team

were moved away from the Pakistani base to a suburban CIA safehouse. In the wake of the 9/11 attacks, Pakistan had made extraordinary and very public concessions to the United States, but the coalition forces never wholly trusted the Pakistani military. Jason Amerine first met Hamid Karzai as they both went into the safehouse's bathroom.

'We had a polite hello. I was surprised; he spoke English as well as you and I do,' says Amerine. 'He reminded me of Ben Kingsley in [the film] *Gandhi*. We all really liked him straightaway.'

Karzai was no Abdul Haq. He was slight and bald, and wore a clipped beard. He dressed in Afghan clothes but had an English manner. He was the head of his tribe, the Popalzai Durrani, a powerful Pashtun group, especially in southern Afghanistan, with lineage tracing back to Ahmad Shah Durrani, known as the founder of modern Afghanistan. Karzai had not fought to gain his title: he had ascended after his father was assassinated by the Taliban in 1999.

So Karzai had powerful blood, but he was a statesman, not a warrior. He was a man who fundraised during the Soviet War while obtaining a postgraduate degree in international relations. He was also someone who had contacts within the CIA, and after 9/11 he was assigned a case officer from the CIA's paramilitary arm, the Special Activities Division. This was Greg Vogle, now a legendary figure in the US clandestine services. On Hamid Karzai's shoulders the CIA placed a heavy burden of hope.

This was an essential mission. In the north of the country, the CIA had a ready-made proxy force in the Northern Alliance, a coalition that held strong despite the killing of Ahmad Shah Massoud. With the help of US intelligence and air assets, they would undoubtedly take Kabul. In the south, however, there was no ready-made proxy force to fight the Taliban. There were tribal warlords and there was the Taliban – and that was all.

The American hope was that a tribal coalition could be built around Hamid Karzai, and that, as the head of that coalition, he might be accepted as an appropriate leader of the new Afghanistan. But there was a problem. Afghans knew Karzai as a man of talk, not action, and a history of violence had become an essential part of any Afghan political CV.

Vogle, the CIA and Karzai himself knew that the invasion represented a once-in-a-lifetime opportunity. Indeed, such was Karzai's impatience to get into Afghanistan after 9/11 that he had nearly been killed.

In the second week of October 2001, shortly after the Americans started bombing the few fixed Taliban positions that existed in the south of Afghanistan, Karzai and a handful of bodyguards and advisers dressed as peasants, loaded their motorcycles and rode from Pakistan, through Kandahar and into Uruzgan. With bricks of US dollars supplied by the CIA, they planned to foment insurrection. Capture by the Taliban would mean nothing less than death, but Karzai and his group avoided detection and managed to meet with some of Uruzgan's most senior tribal elders in Deh Rawood, east of Tarin Kot.

The Taliban were nominally in control of Uruzgan Province, but they maintained no garrison there and their standing force in Tarin Kot had been built though franchising and deputising. Such was the Taliban way. The real power structure in Uruzgan was tribal, and while no single tribe would be able to revolt against the Taliban, it was conceivable that a few of the larger tribes could create a coalition that could seize power. Hamid Karzai was convinced that he could orchestrate the necessary tribal alliance.

At the base of this alliance was another Popalzai leader, Jan Mohammad, a man who would become the most consequential figure in Uruzgan in the post-invasion years. 'JMK' (the K came from the honorific title Khan), as the US and Australian special forces came to know him, was illiterate and foul-mouthed, sexually abusive (with the brunt of his rapacious lust often being borne by boys) and not particularly adherent to his Islamic faith. He was, however, an effective and brutal leader with a history of rule in Uruzgan.

During the Soviet occupation, JMK had been the commander of two major *mujahedin* groups, and in the years between the Soviets and the Taliban he had thrived. With a strong local militia,

Jan Mohammad sat atop a vast crime syndicate during the civil war years, involved in drug production and smuggling as well as kidnapping and road banditry and tolling. Men like him were the reason the populace greeted the Taliban with a resigned sigh in the mid-1990s.

The Taliban had installed Jan Mohammad as the governor of the province, but after a while, sick of his malfeasance and double dealing, they arrested him and transported him to a prison where they sentenced him to death. When Hamid Karzai entered Uruzgan in October 2001, JMK was languishing in a prison in Kandahar city. Karzai was sure that Kandahar would soon fall, and that the prisoners in its jail would be slaughtered as a result.

Karzai feared Jan Mohammad's death for two reasons. One was that he needed him to generate support in Uruzgan, but another was the genuine feeling Karzai had for Jan Mohammad, whom some described as like an older brother or father figure to Karzai.

The Karzai family had some political power when they lived in Kabul, where Hamid's father, Abdul Ahad Karzai, served as deputy speaker of the National Assembly under Afghanistan's last king, Mohammed Zahir Shah. Hamid Karzai himself served for a time as deputy foreign minister, but the Karzai family always understood how power was expressed in the wild south, where the family's tribal roots and authority lay.

Abdul Ahad Karzai had a strong relationship with a number of *mujahedin* and warlords, but probably none so important and strong as the one he developed with Jan Mohammad. Abdul would often tell Hamid that, should he be killed, the younger man must observe and obey Jan Mohammad. Abdul Ahad Karzai was assassinated by two men aligned to the Taliban in 1999. As Hamid Karzai rushed into Uruzgan while US aeroplanes pounded Kabul, he surely remembered his father's words.

With his motorcycles and bags of money, Karzai and his aides travelled to Deh Rawood to confer with other Popalzai powerbrokers, Haji Zahir Aka, Malem Rahmatullah and Sher Mohammad. He also courted the leaders of other powerful tribes and families, including Rozi Khan and Haji Zaher Khan from the Barakzai tribe. Karzai tried to convince these men to join him in an assault against Uruzgan's provincial capital, Tarin Kot, but the local leaders were almost uniformly sceptical that the bookish Karzai could accomplish this. Karzai explained to all of them the power of the United States, and the enduring rage that would surely come to their province. Some told him that if that were the case, they would like to see it.

Karzai's first mission attempting to seize Uruzgan lasted a week. He was constantly harried by Taliban-aligned fighters, and once had to call for a weapons resupply after a depleting gunfight. Then, surrounded by Taliban and close to being overrun, Karzai had to call for a DEVGRU team to insert and ferry him back to Pakistan.

Despite this failure, neither Karzai nor the CIA was put off. A new insertion was planned immediately, and this time the CIA requested that Karzai be supported by an ODA. When Jason Amerine met with Vogle and Karzai, Karzai explained that he wanted to reinsert into Uruzgan almost immediately, with an attack on Tarin Kot to follow swiftly.

'Uruzgan is the heart of the Taliban movement,' Karzai told Amerine. 'Liberating Tarin Kot will strike a demoralizing blow against the Taliban. If they can't control Uruzgan, their credibility will unravel ... if we take Tarin Kot, we rip the heart out of the Taliban.'

Karzai believed all this must be done immediately, however, as the imminent execution of Jan Mohammad could be a way to activate Popalzai tribesmen in Uruzgan. Using those men as the ground fighting force, he felt sure he could take Tarin Kot, then Kandahar, and then the country.

'He honestly thought perhaps this whole thing may be able to be done bloodlessly,' says Amerine. 'He thought an uprising in Tarin Kot could happen, and then the Taliban could start considering [surrender] terms.'

Karzai believed that most of those fighting with the Taliban had greater fealty to their tribal, ethnic and religious identity than to their Taliban commanders. If the men who stood against him could retain their tribal, ethnic and religious dignity in a post-Taliban Afghanistan, he argued, they could happily live without being a Talib.

Colonel John Mulholland, the commander of the combined US Special Forces in Afghanistan, designated Task Force Dagger, was sceptical. Even with abundant air support, a 12-man ODA simply didn't have enough firepower to take a town like Tarin Kot of up to 60,000 people. Mulholland relayed to Amerine that the mission wasn't to be undertaken unless Karzai's force totalled at least 300 guerrillas.

Karzai swore that he would have the men once he was in Uruzgan. Deals had been done, he promised Amerine, and a number of tribal militias would join him once he got to Uruzgan.

This view was strengthened on 12 November, when Karzai received a call from Mullah Omar's personal secretary, who asked about his immediate plans and his plans for the future. Karzai saw this as a very good sign: Mullah Omar and other senior Taliban were apparently trying to use Karzai as an intermediary to negotiate a surrender.

Amerine and Karzai discussed the possibility of a conditional surrender, in which the Taliban might be allowed to just melt away. Karzai thought that would be a preferable outcome to war. 'We could never kill them all anyway,' he told Amerine.

On 13 November, Captain Amerine requested insertion of his ODA without the guarantee of a guerrilla force waiting for them. The request moved up the chain of command, and later that day – perhaps because the US leadership had realised that the Tarin Kot airfield was one of the few places in southern Afghanistan where they could create an airhead – the mission was approved.

Early on the morning of 14 November 2001, with dawn still a few hours away, Amerine, his ODA, Greg Vogle, Hamid Karzai and three Afghan bodyguards loaded up into two MH-53 Pave Low helicopters and left Jacobabad. From there they flew to another Pakistani airfield close to the Afghan border, where the group transferred into five modified Blackhawk helicopters from the US Special Operations Aviation Regiment (SOAR) for the insertion into Afghanistan.

As they climbed aboard, Amerine noticed a company of US Rangers facing out at the darkness, offering perimeter security. Pakistan was ostensibly a friendly country, and yet Rangers were needed there to ensure safety. Amerine wondered what role Pakistan might play in the years to come.

8

'The United States is not inclined to negotiate surrenders'

THE SOAR BLACKHAWKS FLEW fast and low over jagged mountaintops, over empty desert and over small but lush farming belts. Outsiders coming into Uruzgan have often noted an apparent inverse relationship between the amount of fighting that happens there and the number of reasons there are to fight. Uruzgan has opium, but not like the lush pink fields in Helmand; nor is it a trucking centre, like Kandahar. There's no coal or copper mining, no jewels or gold, as there is in the north of the country. There are few roads that seem worth fighting over, except the patchy strip of bitumen between Tarin Kot and Kandahar.

An Uruzgani will tell you, however, that they fight not because they have so much but because they have so little. Most people in the province are farmers, and many at a subsistence level only, growing their maize, potatoes, rice and fruit in emerald strips of arable land between brutal hills and mountains of shale and rock. These green belts are life itself. Management of water, of land, of migrant workers and fertilisers and trucks, is an existential endeavour. Federal governments have only a patchy history of exerting any control in Uruzgan, and there is little record of unified provincial control. In Uruzgan, tribal and traditional law reigns. Disputes are settled according to conventions established over many generations; these are well known to locals but often unfathomable to outsiders.

The concept of *Pashtunwali*, a code of living that existed in Afghanistan even before the arrival of Islam, is especially strong in Uruzgan. Its three tenets – *tora*, or courage; *melmestia* and *nanwati*, or hospitality and asylum; and *badal*, or revenge – are built not only into tribal law but into the very psyche of many Pashtuns in Uruzgan.

The physical and human terrain of Uruzgan was as complex as anywhere in the world, and Jason Amerine spent his time in Pakistan learning as much as he could about it. Even so, when the Blackhawks left him atop a jagged and naked mountain a few kilometres north of Tarin Kot, he felt like he had landed on another planet, or in another time.

The insurgent group trekked down the shale slope, eventually watching the first sun of the day creep over lush fields of apricot and poppy below. At the base of the mountain they rested at a small complex of mud-brick buildings owned by a tribal elder named Haji Badhur. This was to be their base of operations, somewhere Amerine thought they might set themselves up for days and perhaps weeks as Karzai collected his forces.

Weapons drops were called in, with crates of AK-47 rifles, PKM machine guns, ammunition and RPGs floating down to their location. Locally, word of the bounty spread quickly. Farmers arrived by the dozen, and were given weapons in exchange for their promise that they would join the imminent assault against Tarin Kot.

After two days in Haji Badhur's cove, Karzai told Amerine that he had heard of a revolt in Tarin Kot. The Taliban governor had been dragged onto the street and killed, and his bodyguards had fled the town. Karzai believed the tide had turned and the people had rebelled. He wanted to march on Tarin Kot immediately.

'Okay, now we're really fucked,' Amerine thought to himself.

The plan had been to develop a tribal alliance built around Karzai and, using that force, to occupy the plains around Tarin Kot, then squeeze out the Taliban. Currently, Amerine had only 20 to 30 armed Afghans with him, mostly Popalzai. That was far too few, Amerine felt, to take the provincial capital. Yet the ODA was here to facilitate Hamid Karzai, and if he wished to march on Tarin Kot, that's what they would do.

A small caravan of Hilux trucks and horses laden with weapons and men made their way down into a mountain pass and into the Tarin Kot bowl: a flat land, roughly oblong, about 20 kilometres across, in the middle of which lay the town itself.

The group entered the town and found it a dusty clutch of abandoned adobe buildings, mud-built walls and dirt streets that weren't sleepy but petrified. Karzai warned Amerine that gunfire may come from the town soon, but that it would be celebratory.

Yet there was no gunfire, no celebration. There was nothing. Only a few people could be seen outside, and just a handful of motorbikes and animals broke the silence of the morning. It was Ramadan, which perhaps contributed to the quiet, but it wasn't just that. There was fear in the air.

Karzai, with Greg Vogle, moved into the governor's mansion, and they invited any tribal leaders of the uprising to join him in breaking the day's Ramadan fast. Amerine moved into an empty building next door and ordered his team to set up a command and control centre, from where they could establish a communications link-up with Task Force Dagger.

The day had been warm, but this was an area of seasonal extremes, and a November sunset brought with it the promise of bitter winter. Amerine was invited to join Karzai in a celebratory meal, and in the governor's compound he arrived to the smell of spiced meat, vegetables and naan bread. Before the food could be served, though, Karzai received a call from Kandahar: a Taliban force, he learned, perhaps hundreds, perhaps thousands of men, was leaving the city – and heading not west to Pakistan but north towards Tarin Kot. The Taliban were coming to retake the town.

Also relayed to Karzai was the fact that the fighting force was led by Afghans, but for the most part they were Pakistani. Karzai knew what this meant. Afghan Taliban might refuse to kill those aligned with their own tribe or family, but Pakistani Taliban would have no such compunctions. This force was coming to inflict a massacre.

This was the eventuality that Amerine had feared. It was the reason he and Vogle had stressed to Karzai that they would need 300 fighting men before taking Tarin Kot. The ODA could bring in a significant amount of air power, but could only use it on the plains and passes around the town. They also needed manned fighting positions in the town, from which to repel any Taliban who slipped through the bombardment, and also to resist any locals who might decide to fight with the enemy.

Amerine rushed back to his command centre and started making preparations. Karzai's intelligence suggested the convoy would arrive at dawn, which gave them a window of a few hours to come up with a plan of action.

At about 1.30 am, Amerine's combat controller, Tech Sergeant Alex Yoshimoto, advised his captain that an FA-18 patrolling above them had spotted a convoy of eight vehicles driving quickly towards the Uruzgan border. Was this the Taliban advance party? A recon force? Or was it just a large family coming home from a wedding? What was the pattern of life in this part of the world? Was it normal for people to be driving around in convoys at 1.30 am?

Amerine had no idea, but he was the commander on the ground so he had strike approval. 'Smoke 'em,' Amerine said to Yoshimoto. A few moments later the F-18 relayed back that five of the vehicles had been destroyed and all those inside them killed. Three of the cars had escaped.

It's not known who these people were, but they weren't the Taliban force coming from Kandahar. That convoy was much larger – it was later estimated to be nearly 1000 men – and travelled in a mix of armoured personnel carriers, flatbed trucks, technical vehicles with fixed machine guns and Hilux utes. They were not spotted by any American air assets, but were already on their way to Tarin Kot when the airstrikes happened around 2 am. The Taliban force was commanded by four men, including a senior Taliban fighter who had contacts inside Tarin Kot. He knew the size of Karzai's force and was confident of victory.

The Tarin Kot bowl was framed by soaring, jagged peaks to the west and north, broken by a northern pass leading to the

Baluchi and Chora valleys. To the south, about 20 kilometres from the town, was another mountain range broken by a pass that led south towards Kandahar. These two passes – north to Dorafshan, the Baluchi Valley and the Chora Valley, and south to Kandahar – would be defining areas in the Australian war to come.

Amerine knew the Taliban vehicles would emerge from the southern pass, which meant the plain between the ridgeline and the town could be his killing ground. He must get all available American air assets routed into Uruzgan at the right time, and place his combat controller, Yoshimoto, in a position where he could direct bombs onto the attacking force.

At 4 am Karzai presented for battle at Amerine's command centre. He had with him no more than 20 lightly armed fighters. Amerine asked Karzai to join him on a hillock south of the town, where they had a clear line of sight to the plain and all the way to the mountain pass. With the ODA and Karzai's men positioned, they waited for dawn, and when the ridgeline separated itself from the dark sky, Amerine received word that the first Taliban vehicle had arrived on the plain.

* * *

'Is that a … BTR?' Amerine's weapons sergeant asked, seeing a boxy armoured vehicle bouncing into sight.

Both Amerine and his sergeant held binoculars to their faces.

'That is, no shit, a fucking BTR,' the sergeant continued.

It was. A Bronyetransportyor-80, the ubiquitous armoured personnel carrier of the Soviet Union, a throwback from the Cold War rumbling towards Tarin Kot. An F-18 let two bombs fly. The first missed the target but the second bomb smashed into the vehicle, punching through it and leaving a hole in the desert. All the men inside were killed instantly.

Amerine watched as dozens of vehicles spilled onto the plain. The Taliban force arranged themselves into three columns, and Amerine's team issued tasks for the F-18s and F-14 Tomcats (which were in their final months of service). 'Put it all on the centre column for now,' Amerine relayed to the 30 or so pilots flying above them.

. The Taliban now saw what real American rage looked like. Vehicles started exploding, limbs and metal spewed out of the explosions, men rolled out of twisted vehicles as they burned to death. This was nothing like a Soviet attack, in which helicopters or tanks brought fire from a visible distance. This was another type of devilry altogether.

Still, it was a dangerous moment for Karzai's insurgent forces. The first wave of jets were largely depleted of bombs, and Taliban vehicles were still streaming towards Tarin Kot. A second wave of jets were coming but they were precious minutes away.

The jets above offered gun runs, which would bring their 20mm Gatling guns to bear but could also expose them to ground fire. The offer was accepted. If the Talibs reached the town, even only in small numbers, Karzai and his handful of men, who had fled back to the town during the bombardment, could easily be overrun.

The Talibs saw the enemy with their own eyes for the first time. Jets streaked into sight, their noses or wings ablaze. A deadly report came and trucks were shredded and men dismembered by 20mm rounds. One Taliban commander watched a supply truck next to him take a barrage, with metal, flesh and burning flatbread scattering behind the destroyed vehicle. Then the shock of the 500-pound bombs came. The second wave of jets had arrived.

The Talibs ordered a general retreat. The intact vehicles tried to turn and flee, but destroyed vehicles blocked their path. It was a turkey shoot for the pilots, who racked up combat kill after combat kill. From the hillock where Amerine was operating, he was momentarily panicked as he heard automatic gunfire behind him. He feared that a Taliban force had punched through the fire and reached the town. It was no Taliban force but the men from Tarin Kot. They had come out of their homes to see the future – a future that surely did not include the Taliban. They knew it would do them no favours to have remained on the sidelines during the Battle of Tarin Kot.

By the time the last bomb was dropped, the sun was high, but it sat pale and weak in a sky stained by smoke and dust. The story of the battle was written on the plain in a language that even the largely illiterate Afghans could understand: the Americans were incredibly powerful, and therefore Hamid Karzai was incredibly powerful.

Anand Gopal's book *No Good Men Among the Living* tells the story of a Taliban commander who fled the battle. This man abandoned his vehicle and trekked out of the Tarin Kot basin, hoping to find his Taliban comrades so they might regroup. But he met none, so he returned to his tribe, who had previously supported the Taliban. In his village he was mocked by men on the street for now being unarmed. One man told him the war was over and it was time to go home to his wife and his farm. The man did just that.

After the battle a new Afghan guerrilla group from Deh Rawood, commanded by a man named Bari Gul, arrived to join Karzai. Some Afghans told Jason Amerine that this new group was formerly part of the Taliban and that Bari Gul had previously been a Taliban commander. Amerine challenged Karzai about these new guerrillas. Karzai said these men were pragmatists, and that their arrival was a good omen.

'Could be Taliban or against the Taliban; it does not matter. God, family and tribe are what matters,' Karzai said to Amerine.

A day after the battle for Tarin Kot, Task Force Dagger requested a battle damage assessment (BDA), so half of ODA 574 went out to the killing field alongside a new Afghan guerrilla group from Deh Rawood commanded by Bari Gul.

Bari Gul and Amerine took photographs of the destruction. It had only been a day, but Amerine saw piles of rocks where men had died – makeshift graves – and vehicles already stripped of useful parts. Weapons had been taken too, and usable clothing. All that remained was what was burned, broken and useless.

Some Afghans had rushed out of the town to kill the invaders; others had rushed out to bury them. Both groups had likely scavenged. The area was alive with people and varied interests, and the power dynamics in the Tarin Kot bowl were in violent flux.

'In some ways this is the moment that Karzai's plan went to shit,' Amerine says. 'He never thought we'd have to kill so many people, and even the townsfolk in Tarin Kot were uncomfortable with the level of carnage. The people in the town supported us but the people in the outlying villages didn't like that we'd slaughtered so many Pashtuns, and they weren't going to join us.'

Men like Bari Gul were now asserting local control, and excluding their tribal enemies. More crates of AK-47, PMK rifles and RPG-9 rocket launchers were air-dropped into Tarin Kot and distributed by Karzai, Bali Gul and other tribal leaders. For days after the battle, Amerine and his ODA stayed alert in Tarin Kot, waiting for a Taliban counterattack. Every so often Amerine was sent intel about vehicles making their way north from Kandahar Province, potentially to Tarin Kot.

Many times Amerine spoke to Karzai about whether to clear the jets hot for attack or not, depending on the very limited information available. Karzai couldn't identify on a map which villages would likely be friendly and which hostile. Amerine authorised 54 vehicle kills and refused 12. Once a large camp of people spotted by an F-18 on patrol was also offered up as a target. Some of the men in the group were armed; the pilot suspected a Taliban force. After some deliberation, the target was refused due to its location and composition. It later became clear that this was a family group fleeing the bombing.

'This notion of fighting from a distance and fighting with airstrikes, it didn't sit well with me,' says Amerine. 'It almost promoted the promiscuous use of military power.'

* * *

As the southern front was being established in Uruzgan, Hamid Karzai became a notable figure, not only in Afghanistan but across the world. The credit for the victory on the plains of Tarin Kot had fallen to Karzai, and his satellite phone was running hot. He was taking calls from media outlets, but also from his half-brother Ahmed Wali Karzai, who was travelling to Bonn, Germany, to attend an international conference organised by US Secretary of State Colin Powell to discuss the composition of a post-Taliban government in Afghanistan.

Hamid Karzai was now in pole position for national leadership. He was a Pashtun leader with military experience, acceptable to the CIA and the United States, and he presented well. Task Force Dagger had assumed that it would take ODA 574 weeks to get to Tarin Kot and months to build up a tribal force big enough to take Kandahar, but things had moved far more quickly. It seemed Karzai was approaching a tipping point. He had finally built his force of 300 guerrillas in Tarin Kot, and emissaries of many of the southern tribes who had previously aligned with the Taliban were now calling or arriving in person, promising that they would stand aside in the fighting to come. These deals were often sealed over bricks of US dollars.

Karzai also received calls from senior Taliban commanders and officials, who wished to discuss the terms under which they might surrender. One such call came from Abdul Ghani Baradar, then considered to be Mullah Omar's second-in-command, and today one of the leaders of Afghanistan.

Amerine's task was evolving as a result. 'Our job was now to get Hamid to Kandahar and force the Taliban to surrender,' he says. As ODA 574, Karzai and his guerrilla force were preparing to convoy south, Amerine was ordered to prepare for the insertion of his battalion headquarters: a 15-man command-and-control element with a lieutenant colonel in charge and operators from Delta as security.

Karzai didn't want an additional American force with him, as he thought it important that the force marching on Kandahar be seen as Afghan, not American. He asked Amerine to send a message saying that 'ODA 574 is doctrinally capable of conducting operations without additional personnel at this time'. The message fell on deaf ears. Pave Low helicopters inserted, and Lieutenant Colonel James Fox, callsign Rambo 85, assumed command responsibility. He also assumed the role of Hamid Karzai's official US military liaison.

With Amerine and his ODA 574 in front of the convoy and Rambo 85 behind it, Karzai's ad hoc forces, including Bari Gul and his men, worked their way along the road towards Kandahar. In this group was an illiterate Popalzai taxi driver named Matiullah. As the convoy moved ahead, they were sometimes met by surrendering men: Taliban foot soldiers who had abandoned their positions and were travelling back to their villages. Two such men greeted Karzai and told him that his group would soon be met by a large, hostile force, who were gathering at a *madrasah* ahead of them.

A US bomber flew over the area, but its optics simply revealed a mass of people and vehicles like 'grazing sheep', as one of the pilots described it. Amerine asked Karzai if he was sure about this intelligence, worried that it may be an instance of tribal score-settling, but Karzai said he thought it best to proceed with the bombing.

Rambo 85 had left Captain Amerine in battlefield control, so the decision was his. This was Karzai's country now and he wanted the group destroyed, so Amerine cleared the bombers hot to bomb. As they heard over the radio that the planes were coming in, Amerine stood above a ridge and waited for the blasts, which would be many kilometres away. The explosions came as pale orange pulses rising over the mountains.

How many people had died? And who exactly had been killed? Jason Amerine would never know. It was his practice to write brief thoughts down each day in a journal, and at the end of this day he penned just four words: 'death on the horizon'.

* * *

The convoy had so far moved through Uruzgan unopposed, but they finally met resistance across the border in northern Kandahar Province – close to the place where, eight years later, Ben Roberts-Smith would be involved in an action that would see him awarded the Victoria Cross. The US/Afghan convoy had by now split in two, with ODA 574, Bari Gul and half of the Afghan fighters in front as a spearhead force, and Rambo 85, Hamid Karzai and the rest of the guerrillas a few kilometres behind as a reserve force.

When ODA 574 approached a bridge near Shah Wali Kot, they did so slowly, as they could see white Taliban flags fluttering in the wind from the rooftops around the bridge. Before they crossed the bridge, a barrage of machine-gun fire and RPGs erupted from multiple positions. The ODA set up defensive positions, but before Amerine could create a plan of action, Bari Gul and his men rushed across the bridge and into the town, firing from the hip.

Amerine had not yet seen such martial gusto from an Afghan force, and he wondered whether tribal animus was motivating Bari Gul and his men. ODA 574 supported their Afghan partners as best they could, but Amerine was put off by how often Bari Gul asked for buildings to be destroyed from the air, pointing at farmhouses, schools and mosques – places from which they had not received fire – and then extending his fingers and wiggling them, as though to indicate bombs floating down through the air.

One of Amerine's men was shot through the neck and a number of the Afghan guerrillas were killed, but Taliban reinforcements were kept away from the area by a circling AC-130 gunship. The bridge was won after a day and a half of fighting. Behind the ODA, Hamid Karzai, protected by his Delta bodyguard and alongside Rambo 85, was contributing to the Bonn conference in absentia.

Things were moving quickly on the ground in Afghanistan: Kabul had fallen, Kandahar was within sight, and the Americans and Europeans were keen to install an interim leader of the country. Three candidates had emerged as frontrunners: Mohammed Zahir Shah, the 87-year-old former king of Afghanistan who had been exiled in the 1970s; Burhanuddin Rabbani, a well-respected ethnically Tajik Islamic philosopher; and Hamid Karzai, who had been championed throughout by the CIA and was represented at the conference by his half-brother Ahmed Wali Karzai.

South of Shah Wali Kot, another conference was underway. At a guesthouse in Kandahar city, Mullah Omar had called a *shura* of his senior commanders to discuss what to do when Kandahar fell to the Americans, as they now knew it would. Mullah Omar spoke passionately about the invasion, seeing the incursion of apostates in these Pashtun lands as an affront to their honour. He asked his commanders to take their men into the mountains, build tribal support and start an insurgency, as the *mujahedin* had done to combat the Soviets.

A handful of commanders wanted to continue the fight, but most thought it would better to make terms and go back to their homes. After conversations with Hamid Karzai, many believed that the Americans would leave Afghanistan, that Islamic law would be maintained in the country, and that former Taliban adherents would be left alone.

A Taliban spokesperson, likely Abdul Ghani Baradar, called Hamid Karzai and asked if he would receive a peace delegation from Kandahar at his position. Karzai agreed, and he and Rambo 85 moved up to ODA 574's position in Shah Wali Kot in preparation for the delegation.

On 5 December, Jason Amerine sought out the headquarters assistant operations officer from Rambo 85, a friend he had served with in Panama, to discuss how the two callsigns could safely progress into Kandahar together. As the men walked and spoke, they were both shocked when they saw the flash and then the boom of a 500-pound bomb on a ridgeline just across the river. There hadn't been a shot fired in anger in 15 hours, and Amerine thought it unlikely that the Taliban would attack while Karzai was waiting to receive their peace delegation.

Amerine jogged over to Rambo 85's command post, situated in a commandeered building.

'What's going on, sir?' he asked a major who was part of Colonel Mulholland's staff.

'I'm orienting my staff, Captain' the major said. 'Engaging Taliban positions on the ridge.'

They had seen some men on the other side of the river, but these men had shown no hostile intent. After the bombing, the men on the ridge had fled into a cave, and the major called for bombs to destroy it. A special warfare airman, part of Rambo 85, borrowed a laser designator called a Viper from the battalion's weather specialist, zeroed the coordinates for the cave and relayed that information to a pair of F-18 pilots above. The jets dropped six bombs but none of them hit the cave; some landed hundreds of metres away. The airman was confused, as were the soldiers watching. These were uncharacteristic misses, and the airman suspected a Viper calibration failure was the issue.

The F-18s went off station and a B-52 Stratofortress checked in, listing its available weapons for Rambo 85 below. One of the available bombs was a 2000-pound JDAM, a very powerful weapon that can guide itself by means of grid coordinates. The airman went through the process of recalibrating the Viper and again lasered the cave as the target position – but somehow he accidentally and tragically gave their own building as the bomb's target.

This was the first instance of a JDAM bomb ever being dropped in a US close-support mission. At the time, the protocols required to avoid friendly fire were sorely lacking. Amerine remembers walking away from the major, but then only a little of what happened next.

He remembers seeing a man brushing his teeth. He remembers seeing a couple of Afghans chatting. He remembers a flash. He remembers black smoke and chemicals. As Jason Amerine slowly came to, his first coherent thought was that a Taliban mortar must have landed nearby. But he quickly surmised that this rain of rock, paper, cloth and human flesh around him couldn't possibly be the result of a mortar strike.

Amerine dragged himself to his feet, but fell again immediately. Rubbing his left thigh, he found shrapnel wounds and blood soaking his pants. He dragged himself to where the bomb had landed, and there saw a smashed compound and an amorphous lump of bodies covered by fine dust. He saw a severed leg and an arm; a whole head and part of another head – Bari Gul's face detached from his skull.

Two of his ODA 574 were dead, and another US intelligence officer had also been killed. Around 50 friendly Afghans had been killed too. All Amerine's men had suffered injuries, from compound fractures and puncture wounds to burns and traumatic brain injuries. All had to be medically evacuated.

'How did this happen, Jason?' Hamid Karzai asked Amerine. By sheer luck, Karzai had not been killed. He had been injured, but not significantly, and would be able to continue on to Kandahar.

Amerine didn't know what to say. There was nothing to say. The bombing just was, and the dead were just dead. All of the men of ODA 574 walked or were carried onto a Pave Low and left Afghanistan, never to return.

Only a few minutes after the blast, while the body parts were still being collected, Karzai's satellite phone rang. It was the BBC reporter Lyse Doucet.

'What's your reaction to being named prime minister?' she asked.

In Bonn, the conference delegates had settled on an interim leader of the country, and that leader was Hamid Karzai.

* * *

Later that day, a Taliban peace delegation of some of the most senior figures in the movement, including defence minister Mullah Obaidullah Akhund and chief of staff Tayyab Agha, arrived to intreat with Hamid Karzai. They offered terms of peace that, in later years, the Americans could only dream of.

The Taliban were willing to disband, denounce terrorism and give up most of their arms. In return, they asked that their fighters and commander be allowed to melt away to their families and tribes, with no further prosecution. They also requested that some former Taliban commanders might enter the government. Karzai said this might be possible, but this was likely an overreach of his new powers. Karzai also explained that there would be no possibility of an amnesty for Bin Laden and his al-Qaeda fighters, and the Taliban delegation said they understood and accepted that.

Karzai considered this an acceptable agreement, but said he could not approve the deal unilaterally. He would have to discuss it with representatives of the US government. He did ask for one thing that he wanted the delegation to attend to immediately, as a gesture of good faith: his friend Jan Mohammad should be freed.

The negotiations with the Taliban continued, with a major sticking point being an amnesty for senior Taliban, including Mullah Omar. By the time the forces with Karzai arrived in Kandahar, no agreement had been settled, and many of the Taliban commanders had disappeared. It was reported later that Mullah Omar drew up a document breaking the *bay'ah* or pledge of faith between him and his men, and allowing all his deputies, clerks, commanders and soldiers to surrender, should they choose to. He also issued documents that transferred all Taliban assets, including weapons and vehicles, to tribal leaders.

Mullah Omar reportedly drove away from the city on a Honda motorcycle and disappeared into the mountains east of Kandahar, likely on his way to Pakistan. (There have been persistent rumours, however, that Mullah Omar lived out much of the rest of his life in a village in Uruzgan Province.)

Hamid Karzai says he stressed to the United States that the war must end in some kind of political settlement, and that there be no attempt to eradicate the Afghan enemy. Even the CIA took that line, and suggested to the White House the idea of creating a 'Taliban for Karzai' government faction, which would serve as a powerful piece of propaganda marking a division between al-Qaeda and the Taliban, and as a way of unifying the Pashtuns.

The idea was presented to Vice President Dick Cheney, who flatly rejected it. Secretary of Defense Donald Rumsfeld and a number of influential senior White House officials were also vehemently against a political settlement with the Taliban so soon after the 9/11 attacks. They saw little reason to negotiate with Mullah Omar's forces either, as they seemed to have been completely routed.

'The United States is not inclined to negotiate surrenders, nor are we in a position with relatively small numbers of forces on the ground to accept prisoners,' Secretary Rumsfeld said at a press conference in November 2001.

At the same press conference, there were questions of what the war would look like after the fall of Kandahar. It also became clear that manhunting was on Rumsfeld's agenda.

'The United States of America has to deal with those enemies ... and certainly special forces would play a role and a significant role,' he said. 'People can hide in caves for long periods, and this will take time.'

9

'Have a nice day. From Damage, Inc.'

ANAND GOPAL'S BOOK *No Good Men Among the Living* tells the story of what happened to Jan Mohammad in the hours after Hamid Karzai's meeting with the Taliban.

The warlord heard an ancient, heavy bolt on the door of his cell slide open. He thought it could mean just one thing: it was time for him to die. With a guard on either side of him, he was walked out of the darkness of his cell and into the brilliant light of the prison's courtyard. After his eyes adjusted, he was surprised to see a man he knew to be a senior Taliban official standing with the prison warden. The warden unlocked the manacles that bound Jan Mohammad's hands. This didn't look like an execution.

'Is this a joke?' Jan Mohammad asked.

'I hope you'll forgive us for what we did to you,' the official said, explaining that he had arranged for a car and driver so Jan Mohammad could meet his friend Hamid Karzai at his camp to the north.

When Karzai saw his old friend, usually fat and gregarious but now skinny and covered in sores, he cried. From the camp, Jan Mohammad drove to Tarin Kot, raised more men from his tribe and joined Karzai for the march on Kandahar. Anand Gopal later asked the Popalzai leader what he most wanted after being freed from jail in Kandahar.

'I wanted revenge,' he replied.

After Karzai installed himself as president in Kabul, he reinstalled Jan Mohammad as the governor of Uruzgan Province. Karzai also established similar figures as governors of the provinces around Uruzgan. Notorious narco-baron Sher Mohammad Akhundzada became governor of Helmand to the east, while Gul Agha Sherzai, who was well known as a rapist and paedophile, became the governor of Kandahar. Alongside Hamid Karzai's brother, Ahmed Wali Karzai, these governors worked as an organised crime syndicate, independently but also collaboratively trafficking drugs, extorting and running businesses, and crushing opposition.

All these men built up strong relationships with the CIA and the US special forces, offering the tantalising promise of counterterrorism cooperation and often using US forces to target their rivals. In Uruzgan, Jan Mohammad offered to lease some land just south of Tarin Kot to the US special forces so they might have a permanent counterterrorism presence in the province (the land was not owned by Jan Mohammad, but he leased it regardless).

This land, just south of Tarin Kot, would became FOB Ripley, later FOB Davis, then Camp Holland and the Multi National Base Tarin Kot. This would also be the site of Camp Russell, the home of the Australian Special Operations Task Group in Afghanistan.

* * *

As soon as he was installed as governor of Uruzgan, Jan Mohammad sent out allies to the ten district centres across the province so they could assume control as district governors on his behalf. One of these men, an elder named Abdul Qudus, was sent to Khas Uruzgan, a population centre 100 kilometres north-west of Tarin Kot. In this district Jan Mohammad had little tribal sway, with the Popalzai representing less than 1 per cent of the population.

When Abdul Qudus arrived in Khas Uruzgan, he found another man already installed in the governor's residence, someone who had been chosen by the tribal elders of the area. This man, named Tawlidar Yunis, claimed that he and a police chief named Malek Rauf, also tribally elected, were the legitimate administrators of the district.

Abdul Qudus was in a pickle. Although he was the governor's official representative in Khas Uruzgan, there was little he could do to remove Tawlidar Yunis. Abdul Qudus and his men requisitioned a schoolhouse close to the governor's residence, and a stand-off began.

Both groups petitioned President Karzai, to whom they pledged their allegiance. Both men claimed legitimacy through their anti-Taliban bona fides, Abdul Qudus through his connection with Jan Mohammad and Tawlidar Yunis as a former *mujahedin* commander who had refused to accept Taliban power when it came, had lost his position and status, and had spent the Taliban years as a janitor. Karzai knew better than to wade into intractable tribal politics at a district level, so he told the men to sort it out among themselves.

Meanwhile, Tayyab Agha, Mullah Omar's chief of staff who had met with Hamid Karzai on the road to Kandahar and asked about a general Taliban surrender, arrived in Khas Uruzgan, with Agha Jan Motasim, a former Taliban finance minister, and Mohammad Abbas Akhund, a former Taliban health minister. All three men had ancestral links to Khas Uruzgan, and all three hoped to be integrated back into the community. But they were confused: to whom should they surrender? The three reportedly hid in a nearby home, waiting for the stand-off to resolve itself. And on the night of 23 January, it was resolved – in the worst way imaginable.

With cold wind and scattering snow whipping around the streets, there was an explosion at the school where Abdul Qudus and his men were. The bodyguards of JMK's man saw fighters pouring through the gates of the school, their faces masked and their rifles raised. A gunfight began. Meanwhile, just down the road, Tawlidar Yunis's bodyguards, rugged up and chatting, were also attacked, with the gate to their compound swinging open and armed men pouring in. A gunfight began in that location too.

The shooting ended in both locations after 30 minutes. Helicopters swooped down onto the street to take away the assailants, along with 26 prisoners. There was a brief moment of quiet before the cannon of an AC-130 started pounding both sites, igniting weapons caches and sparking fires.

The locals of Khas Uruzgan waited until dawn before stepping into what had been a schoolhouse and a district governor's compound. Both buildings had been destroyed, and in the ruins they found 21 people dead. A number of those killed were found handcuffed to their beds. These men and boys included Abdul Qudus. A calling card was found in the rubble. It bore an American flag and a handwritten message: 'Have a nice day. From Damage, Inc.'

It's not known what intelligence preceded this raid, but it's likely that someone who wanted Abdul Qudus or Tawlidar Yunis out of the picture had told US forces that either the governor's compound or the schoolhouse was an al-Qaeda hideout. The location had been designated AQ-048 by the US and, as it was monitored, they expanded the mission to incorporate the other compound, as they had seen armed men coming in and out of it.

A mission against the compound was assigned to the US Special Forces Group at Kandahar Airport, as the Australian SASR were patrolling in preparation for Operation Anaconda. A special reconnaissance mission was attempted, hoping to put eyes on the target before the raid, but was aborted because of inclement weather. The raid proceeded regardless.

Immediately after the raid, Secretary Rumsfeld claimed the US forces had struck against an al-Qaeda target. Later, General Richard Myers of the US Air Force, the chairman of the Joint Chiefs of Staff, said: 'Once the compound was raided, we found it was mostly of a Taliban nature.' In the months that followed, the US finally admitted that the people they had killed were neither al-Qaeda nor Taliban, with Secretary Rumsfeld conceding that the mission had been 'untidy'. Afterwards, the US military released the prisoners captured during the raid. It's been reported that at least one of those prisoners had been tortured in Kandahar.

More than a year after the mission, US Master Sergeant Anthony Pryor was awarded the Silver Star, one of the highest American battlefield honours, for killing four men in the governor's compound, including one, he said, in hand-to-hand combat. In an article posted on the US Army's website in 2011, Pryor said: 'This isn't a story about one guy. It's a story about the whole company instead of an award on the chest. If the guys hadn't done what they were supposed to do, [the mission] would've been a huge failure.' The article makes no mention of the fact that the raid killed 21 men who had pledged themselves to the US-backed government.

Jan Mohammad was furious when he heard about the Khas Uruzgan raid, but he also recognised that he'd been presented with an opportunity. His Popalzai advocate had been killed in Khas Uruzgan, but so too had his tribal rivals. Jan Mohammad used the raid as a cautionary tale, explaining that unfortunate incidents like these would be less likely if all of the Uruzgan districts fell into line and acquiesced to his wants.

'As you know, Afghanistan is a country of tribes,' he told a journalist.

> We have many tribes in Kandahar and Uruzgan, and they
> have some enmity among them dating back many years.
> The foreigners don't understand this. I know the situation
> in Uruzgan. It is my home. I grew up there and fought
> there against the Russians. I know every tribe and I am
> famous there. The Americans don't know these things,
> and people use them to create internal problems. I told
> the Americans that they should consult with me. I can tell
> them where to go and which areas are important. I can
> protect my people and also defeat terrorism.

In the six months after the raid, there were two more high-profile instances of accidental killings in Uruzgan: the first was in May 2002, when US special forces were given bad intelligence and killed five farmers in Shahidi Hassas; and then, a few weeks later, a US AC-130 and a B-52 attacked a group near Deh Rawood, killing 48 people, including a number of women and children. One of the planes had reported incoming fire, which was later understood to be celebratory gunfire at a wedding. The planes in the area had been hunting Abdul Ghani Baradar.

'There cannot be the use of that kind of firepower and not be mistakes,' said Rumsfeld. 'It is going to happen.'

After the killings, religious leaders in Deh Rawood said their flock now had a religious obligation to take revenge on the Americans. Mullah Baradar and Tayyab Agha, as well as two compatriots, all escaped to Pakistan in 2002, where they become significant leaders of the insurgency.

Tayyab Agha became the head of the Taliban's political office in Doha, Qatar, and Baradar the head of the 'Quetta Shura' – essentially the command-and-control centre of the insurgency.

In 2021, after settling terms with President Trump's negotiators a year earlier and paving the way for Taliban control of Afghanistan, Abdul Ghani Baradar was named one of *Time* magazine's 100 most influential people of the year, alongside Elon Musk, Alexei Navalny and Lil Nas X.

10

'An industrial-scale counter-terrorism killing machine'

IN MARCH 2003, THE United States, alongside three minor military partners – the United Kingdom, Poland and Australia – invaded Iraq. Shortly after the bombing and the Bradley Fighting Vehicles came to Iraq, mobile telephony also arrived.

Before the invasion there were 800,000 fixed telephone nodes in the country, servicing its 26 million people. During the invasion, most of those nodes fell inert, with much of Iraq's communications infrastructure having been destroyed by the US forces. Saddam Hussein had banned mobile phones in his country, so all Iraqis were, for a time, uncontactable.

There were abundant commercial opportunities in Iraq after the invasion, but few were more fertile than in the field of mobile telephony. The industry was being heavily subsidised by the United States, but it also flourished because of massive demand. New mobile phone towers went up nearly every day in 2004, and handsets couldn't be imported fast enough. For a period, there were 100,000 new subscribers to an Iraqi mobile phone network a day.

When the insurgency in Iraq developed, the mobile network would be an essential tool for both sides of the fight: the insurgents would use their Nokia phones to coordinate attacks and as triggers for roadside bombs, while the US and British special forces used increasingly sophisticated hacking equipment so that enemy and civilian mobile phones could become tracking and listening devices. And in 2004, one man sat right at the confluence of mobile telephony and the Iraqi insurgency: a 26-year-old Pennsylvanian named Nick Berg.

Berg was a communications tower repairman. Having worked as a freelancer in Kenya and Uganda, he thought he would try his luck in Iraq, but instead of finding a contract in the United States and then being ushered along a relatively safe path, Berg flew himself to Iraq and moved from city to city, from cheap hotel to cheap hotel, trying to find work.

He was grabbed by the Iraqi police in Mosul and detained for his own good. After being released, he travelled to Baghdad, where he was kidnapped in May – either directly by a radical Sunni Islamic group, or by a criminal group before being sold to the violent *jihadis*. After a short and highly publicised incarceration, a video of Berg's beheading was posted on a Malaysian website and spread across the world.

It is a repulsive video, but also a vision of the future. For the first time, a man was publicly executed while wearing an orange jumpsuit, reportedly as a response to imagery coming out of Camp X-Ray at Guantanamo Bay, and at the prison at Abu Ghraib, both US-run facilities where the detainees wore orange.

Berg's killing was widely attributed to al-Qaeda, but it was not the al-Qaeda of Osama bin Laden. This was the al-Qaeda of Abu Musab al-Zarqawi, a Jordanian who had fought and trained in Afghanistan, and had some contact with Osama bin Laden and Ayman al-Zawahiri, but was not beholden to their group. To whom Zarqawi was beholden and what relationship he had with any transnational violent *jihadi* group are still points of contention.

Zarqawi lived for a time in Afghanistan at the tail end of the Soviet era, and conflicting reports say that he either fought in battles in eastern Afghanistan as part of the Arab brigades or covered the war for a jihadist publication. After Afghanistan, he spent time in a Jordanian jail, and was tortured there, before being released as part of a general amnesty ordered by the Jordanian king. He returned to Afghanistan after the American invasion and was injured, either in an airstrike or by shooting. He recovered in Iran and then, by 2003, was in Iraq, where he became a leading figure in one of many resistance groups.

By the time Nick Berg was executed, Zarqawi was well known to the United States. In 2003, Secretary of State Colin Powell gave a speech at the United Nations in support of a resolution justifying the war the Bush administration was poised to commence. It later became infamous, so full was it of falsehoods, assumptions, and discounted and debunked intelligence claims.

In his speech, Powell dedicated many paragraphs to Zarqawi, making the Jordanian central to a single, complete story about al-Qaeda, 9/11, Osama bin Laden, weapons of mass destruction, transnational terrorism, regional domination and Saddam Hussein. Powell claimed that this integral figure was at the heart of a 'sinister nexus between Iraq and the al-Qaida terrorist network' – as though he were some kind of Forrest Gump of early millennial terrorism.

It's likely no such nexus existed, and even if it did, it was certainly weaker than the nexus between al-Qaeda and US allies like Pakistan and Saudi Arabia. Furthermore, although Zarqawi had been trained by al-Qaeda in Afghanistan – and that was no exclusive claim in the jihadist world – there was no love lost between the al-Qaeda leadership and Zarqawi by the time the United States invaded Afghanistan. Musab al-Zarqawi and Osama bin Laden had significant ideological differences.

Put simply, Zarqawi had far more extreme views on *takfir*, a practice in which a Muslim may be excommunicated from the faith. This, in Zarqawi's mind, allowed him to kill other Muslims with impunity, something Bin Laden was wary of doing. It was this belief that allowed Zarqawi to help instigate and then exacerbate the monumental sectarian violence that racked Iraq in 2005 and threatened to tear the country apart.

When Nick Berg was executed in May 2004, it behove both the US military and Zarqawi to further the narrative that Zarqawi was all that Powell had said he was. For Zarqawi, the

American interest gave him the appearance of power and influence he didn't actually have yet, putting him above an increasingly crowded Iraqi violent *jihadi* market looking for local and foreign support and men. For the United States, and especially for the Bush administration, who had sworn that Saddam Hussein had harboured weapons of mass destruction and yet had found none, Zarqawi was now the justification for a war that was starting to go to shit. After Berg's execution, the hunt for Musab al-Zarqawi brought focus to an unfocused war.

A US$25 million bounty was placed on the Jordanian's head, and an incredible amount of military assets were dedicated to the special forces missions trying to find Zarqawi, often at the expense of the 'landowning' conventional military forces that were trying to bring security to Iraqi neighbourhoods.

For better and for worse, this hunt and those that followed would change the way special forces across the world operate. The perceived success of early Iraqi manhunts would contribute to the 'addition by way of subtraction' counterterrorism strategy of lethal tactical raiding, airstrikes and drone strikes that would be deployed across the globe.

Throughout the war in Iraq, JSOC's fighting unit migrated from being what many called a 'National Mission Unit' – highly skilled but barely ever used – to a high-tempo command, hitting not only targets like Zarqawi and Bin Laden, but more than 10,000 other people of varying importance. In Iraq, JSOC became, according to John Nagl, a military liaison to the US Department of Defense, 'an almost industrial-scale counter-terrorism killing machine'.

Sean Naylor, an American journalist who has written extensively about JSOC, called the command the 'Ferrari in the garage' before 9/11; afterwards it became the everyday ride. It was no less powerful, but had significant wear and tear.

The 'Ferrari in the garage' was also how some in the US military described the Al Muthanna Task Group in 2005, the Australian military force situated in a largely peaceful part of Iraq that was dedicated to reconstruction and doing almost no fighting. There were many in Canberra, political and military, close to the decision not to be involved in the intense fighting in Baghdad, Fallujah and elsewhere, who were thankful that Australia hadn't been drawn into the morally compromising and tactically difficult urban fighting in Iraq.

Another group, however, believed that Australia's military honour had been damaged by the decision for our military to sit out this intense period of combat instigated by our closest allies. Many of those people believed that the low-cost, low-danger, high-impact way to not be duly dishonoured was to deploy Australia's special forces into Iraq.

Although SASR's 1 Squadron had been part of the invading force in 2003 – punching into the western desert from Jordan at the outset of the war, hunting SCUD missiles, destroying a relay station, gunfighting with Saddam's soldiers and seizing the Al Asad Air Base, later a major base of operations for coalition forces against ISIS – the SASR men were largely removed before the manhunting phase of the war. Some operators remained in Baghdad, for the protection of the embassy, but they were not tasked as an offensive force.

The only Australian special forces operators involved in this first Iraqi manhunt (Australian special forces would be engaged significantly in Iraq ten years later, hunting ISIS targets) were private contractors who had left the Special Operations Command and those who had been seconded to British or US special forces. One man in this latter category was Matt Bouillaut, who commanded one of the hunting patrols.

The hunt for Zarqawi, his network of former Ba'ath Party figures and any individual the United States wanted off the battlefield was largely tasked to JSOC, which, in Iraq, was divided in two: the DEVGRU teams were designated as Task Force Blue, while the Delta teams were designated as Task Force Green. There was also a third kinetic task force: Task Force Black. This was constituted of soldiers from the British Army's Special Air Service (SAS) and from the Special Boat Service (SBS), the Royal Navy's gunfighting contribution to the UK Special Forces Group operating out of Baghdad.

The SAS and the SBS had more manhunting experience than JSOC, but in a drastically different environment. Embedded into the DNA of the modern SAS and SBS was their service in Northern Ireland, when they'd operated against the Irish Republican Army (IRA) during the 1970s and '80s. In that period, the British special forces' in-house intelligence service, known as 14 Intelligence Company or 'the Det', became legendary.

In Northern Ireland, the Det ran complicated human intelligence operations, developing a spy network of often disgruntled members or those motivated by greed. They also ran imaginative, long-lasting deceptions, such as the Four Square Laundry Service, a business run by the Det that cleaned shirts, pants and jocks in contested areas, but that also tested them for gunpowder and explosive residue. Another business secretly run by the Det in a contested area was a massage parlour, used for leverage and loose conversation.

The Det was effective, but its members could only analyse so many pairs of undies and listen in on so many conversations between an IRA member and the masseuse giving him relief. JSOC had its own internal intelligence apparatus, known as the Intelligence Support Activity (it was also tagged 'the Army of Northern Virginia'), but it, like the Det, had limited capacity.

In Iraq, and then in Afghanistan, Pakistan, Yemen, Somalia and Syria, JSOC and ancillary special forces, US and international, developed far greater ambitions than an internal intelligence service could possibly hope to service. Among others, the CIA and the National Security Agency (NSA) – known as 'other government agencies', or OGA – became significant players in the giant global manhunt that was eventually named the Global War on Terror.

* * *

During the invasion of Afghanistan, JSOC didn't do missions for the CIA and the CIA didn't directly supply intelligence to JSOC, but immediately afterwards JSOC was providing ground support for a new aerial armed platform that the CIA was trialling. This was the Predator drone, which only recently had been fitted with AGM-114 Hellfire missiles. Operating quietly and with a lurk time of more than 24 hours, the Predator killed without announcement, and did so without the need for combat search and rescue (C-SAR) contingencies, something all manned aircraft required. The Predator and its more modern variant, the Reaper (also known as the Predator B) became favourites of the US military, and especially JSOC, which used them for killing but also for intelligence, surveillance and reconnaissance (ISR).

In October and November 2001, Predators destroyed at least one vehicle each night on the orders of JSOC troops. These vehicles were often seen trying to flee Afghanistan for Pakistan, and usually anyone inside the vehicle was killed. This was a situation of mutual advantage for JSOC and the CIA, but it wasn't true cooperation. The agency and the command didn't truly share intelligence or targeting lists at the start of the war in Afghanistan, despite a relationship between US special forces and OGA that extended all the way back to the 1960s and that was rekindled in the wake of 9/11.

Special forces had paired with the CIA in Vietnam and then, controversially, in Laos and Cambodia as part of the Military Assistance Command, Vietnam – Studies and Observation Group (MACV-SOG). The US special forces and the CIA also worked cooperatively in Central America in the 1980s as part of a program called 'Quail Shooter' that supported anti-communist death squads.

In both instances, the coupling enabled US special forces to expand the legal powers of their shooters by 'sheep dipping' them as temporary CIA agents, who have extra authority under US law to conduct covert international operations.

All US military legal authority is sanctioned under Title 10 of the Code of Laws of the United States, which generally prohibits the US military, including JSOC, from conducting covert international operations. The CIA's legal authority, however, is sanctioned under Title 50 of the US Code, which confers different powers, including the ability to operate covertly in foreign countries. In the case of MACV-SOG in South-East Asia, and in the Quail Shooter program in Central America, JSOC personnel were thus given a fig leaf of legality for their covert operations in countries with which the United States was not at war.

In the Australian context, the relationship between the special forces and the Australian Secret Intelligence Service (ASIS) is opaque. During the 1970s and '80s, the 1st Commando Regiment had a cooperative relationship with ASIS, sharing training facilities and expertise on Victoria's Swan Island. Since 2005, Swan Island has been the home of the SASR's undeclared 4 Squadron, which undertakes 'grey role' unconventional intelligence and military tasks with ASIS. They have operated in a number of countries where there is no declaration of war, and could only legally have done so either with the approval of the countries they were operating in, or by using an Australian legal process akin to 'sheep dipping'.

When JSOC started working collaboratively with OGA in Iraq and then all over the world, their cooperation was not about Title 50 rights and sheep dipping, but about intelligence.

In Iraq, the United States was about to start collecting every single phone conversation and every text message, and geolocating every mobile phone user in the country. As more Iraqis signed up for mobile phones, more intelligence was gathered – but that vast trove of information needed to be turned into targets, and JSOC was unable to do that alone.

Much as Amazon was at the time learning how to industrialise book selling, JSOC was learning to industrialise manhunting – but they couldn't have done so without the help of the NSA, the CIA and 'other government agencies'.

'It is a covert but deadly game of Marco Polo'

'IT TAKES A NETWORK to beat a network,' says General Stanley McChrystal, who was in command of the US Joint Special Operations Task Force in 2003, and who became the commander of JSOC from 2003 to 2008. When did General McChrystal say that? All the time.

Network thinking was a large part of McChrystal's strategic outlook, which spread throughout Iraq and then later Afghanistan. When McChrystal came to Iraq, he says, there were two networks he needed to understand and shape if he wanted to kill Musab al-Zarqawi: the enemy's and his own.

Not beholden to the military chain of command, and taking orders directly from the President of United States of America – with little oversight – JSOC had for decades operated apart from not only the US military but also much of the US government. This meant that JSOC was often viewed with wariness by other US military and intelligence organs. JSOC was highly secretive, rarely sharing plans, tactics or equipment, so it was rarely the beneficiary of generosity from other intelligence-gathering bodies.

That changed after 2003, when General McChrystal went to the CIA headquarters in Langley, hat in hand, to ask for help finding a one-legged Afghan man whom JSOC was hunting near Khost, in the east of Afghanistan. With help of CIA intelligence or a CIA asset, his soldiers ultimately got their man – and souvenired his prosthetic leg, a breach of the Law of Armed Conflict that Australia's SASR soldiers would repeat some years later.

After that successful start, JSOC courted greater cooperation between themselves, the CIA and the NSA, America's premier intelligence agency concerned with signals intelligence. JSOC requested secondments from old-head interrogators, analysts, and geopolitical and language specialists, but also software engineers, mathematicians, and systems and network analysts. The NSA helped JSOC incorporate a number of technology elements into its manhunting efforts in Iraq and Afghanistan, the most consequential of which was capturing of communications, and especially mobile phone intercepts.

Geolocating mobile phones for the purposes of targeting was something JSOC had done before, most famously when Delta operators, working with the Colombian military, found and helped kill the drug kingpin Pablo Escobar in 1993 as he spoke to his son for too long on his mobile phone.

JSOC soon found, however, that hunting people in Iraq was quite different from hunting them in Colombia. The original assumption had been that the Zarqawi network could be destroyed in the way one might an organised crime cartel or a military unit: each soldier would be linked to his commanding officer, who would in turn be linked to his commanding officer, all the way up to the primary target. But as JSOC raided and gained more intelligence in Iraq, that assumption didn't seem to bear out.

'By habit, we started mapping the organisation in a traditional military structure, with tiers and rows,' Stanley McChrystal wrote in his 2011 memoir, *Team of Teams*, of the hunt for Musab al-Zarqawi. 'At the top was Zarqawi, below him a cascade of lieutenants and foot soldiers but the closer we looked, the more the model didn't hold.'

McChrystal wrote that he had found 'constellations' of fighters, with links not through hierarchy but through reputation and family connection. In 2004, McChrystal was dedicated to a decapitation strategy in the fight against al-Qaeda in Iraq, launching missions against the stars shining brightly in these constellations, but his deputy, General Michael Flynn, was agitating for an expansion of operations, arguing that the insurgent 'constellations' could not be destroyed by taking out just high-level insurgents: they also needed to kill the secondary and tertiary leaders. The truth was that JSOC and other US military units didn't understand how Iraqi networks like Zarqawi's worked, nor their motivations and hierarchies.

The NSA, who were secretly capturing all mobile phone signals traffic in Iraq, were tasked with identifying targets and networks for prosecuting forces like JSOC. Initially, all of those terabytes of information had to be personally filtered by NSA analysts in the United States, and the conclusions passed back to JSOC before they were given to US operators on the ground. The intelligence lag time was regularly days. Some NSA information was being turned into actionable intelligence, but US military commanders, including General McChrystal, knew that far more could be done, and far more quickly.

A deluge of technicians and analysts from the NSA's Cryptologic Services Group were deployed on the ground in Iraq to support JSOC, and a huge amount of resources was directed to streamlining the pipeline through which the intelligence flowed. One of the most consequential and successful programs was the creation of the highly secret Real Time Regional Gateway (RT-RG) and RT-10 computer networks.

The result of a project headed by technician Dr James Heath, an ideological right-hand man of the NSA chief, General Keith Alexander, the RT-RG and RT-10 were systems designed to process and order the massive amounts of intelligence, including all mobile phone traffic, in a way that could be actioned immediately in country, by special forces commanders and their staff.

Using both human and AI elements, the RT-RG and RT-10 systems could help generate targets, suggest network connections and produce lists of people, houses and areas of interest. Speaking to *The Wall Street Journal* in 2013, an unidentified source familiar with the system described it as 'literally being able to predict the future'. It's not known whether the RT-RG or the RT-10 were used in 'signature strikes', a controversial practice in which the US military killed unknown people because of their pattern of life and relationships with other people in a network, but it's likely.

In an internal NSA presentation, on a page titled 'RT10 in Baghdad', Dr Heath described the system as a 'near-real-time data and advanced analytical tools provided to in-country units [to] enable tactical decisions', and also claimed it would 'enable find-fix-finish operations'.

This last detail referenced a special forces targeting doctrine. 'Find' is the identification and location of a target, even if that location may be too broad to launch a mission against it yet. 'Fix' denotes the creation of a precise location for that target, in a time-sensitive window, allowing a mission to be launched against the target. 'Finish' is the mission during which the target is killed or captured, be it a direct-action raid or a drone strike or airstrike.

The NSA has also developed complementary tactical equipment that could be used by operators prosecuting these 'find-fix-finish' missions. This includes material that amateur cryptographic circles have been investigating since the Edward Snowden information dump unveiled a catalogue for NSA 'Tailored Access Operations' (TAO) equipment that could be on-sold to approved buyers. This included the Typhon system, which was, according to the NSA, a 'Network-in-a-Box (NIB), which includes all the necessary architecture to support Mobile Station call processing and SMS messaging in a stand-alone chassis with a pre-provisioning capability'. Essentially, this means that soldiers in the field (or a drone) can imitate a mobile phone tower, capturing the phone's output in real time, turning on its microphone when desired and also creating a ten-figure grid reference for the phone's location, accurate to within a metre.

This system was used in concert with a piece of equipment called the 'Waterwitch', which the NSA described as 'finishing tool' to be used in the 'last mile' of 'find, fix, finish' (or F3) missions. This piece of equipment could be carried by a soldier, likely a signaller or electronic warfare operator, who might be part of a special forces team, and could direct the team to the exact location of a specific mobile phone using a liquid ink display that could be handheld or arm-mounted.

Often, ownership of a mobile phone was considered identification, and many targets of kill/capture missions were hit because of the phone they carried. It's known that this TAO equipment was used by the Australian SASR and other Australian special forces elements in Afghanistan, and were especially useful in JPEL missions.

Mick Lehmann, a former intelligence colonel in the ADF who played a significant role in Australia's intelligence apparatus on the ground in Afghanistan and in Canberra from 2007 to 2014, spoke about Australia's special forces use of this equipment in Afghanistan in an ANU paper titled 'Niche Wars':

> Mobile telephones can be located when an emitter is used
> to mimic a mobile telephone tower, convincing a target
> phone to connect through it. If the emitter itself is mobile,
> then triangulation can occur as the platform moves and
> measures the targets phone's signal strength. It is a covert
> but deadly game of 'Marco Polo'.

For the ADF, the Australian Signals Directorate (ASD) and other agencies, obtaining this post-9/11 equipment and software was undoubtedly a driving factor in Australia's enthusiastic engagement in the fight in Afghanistan. Australia is a member of the Five Eyes intelligence compact (with the United States, the United Kingdom, Canada and New Zealand) and could through that channel gain access to some of the NSA's most sensitive systems, but these would not be shared automatically.

Technology transfer was an unstated but undoubtedly sought-after war aim of Australia's in Afghanistan, especially in the later years of the war.

* * *

Musab al-Zarqawi was killed in an airstrike on 7 June 2006 after his spiritual adviser, Abu Abdul Rahman, inadvertently led JSOC to a safehouse about 50 kilometres north of Baghdad. That same night, 14 other buildings were also attacked, chosen because Abu Abdul Rahman had also visited them, leaving a SIGINT trace everywhere he went. President Bush personally called General McChrystal to congratulate him on the killing of Zarqawi.

From mid-2006 to mid-2007, about 40,000 Iraq civilians had been killed, while the US military had suffered roughly 1200 dead and 8400 injured. Then, in August 2007, the level of violence started to drop precipitously. The reduction was credited to a troop surge, increasing US forces from 130,000 to 165,000, and to counterinsurgency strategies, including the kill/capture program championed by JSOC. But most military historians and strategists now have a different and less US-centric view of why the violence in Iraq lessened.

An insurgency had been boiling in Iraq, but also a sectarian civil war between Sunni groups such as Zarqawi's and many Shi'ite groups, some backed by Iran. There were also intra-sect rifts developing within the Sunni tribes, especially in the violent Anbar Province, and splits developed between the *jihadi* groups fighting the US military, such as Zarqawi's, and the tribes that had accepted US money and formed a loose coalition called the 'Sons of Iraq'. By mid-2007, the Shi'ite groups had largely triumphed in their fight, and the Sons of Iraq in theirs.

The net effect of kill/capture in Iraq is not established. Insurgent groups such as Zarqawi's were undoubtedly affected by RT-RG targeting and JSOC raids, but it seems that, in many instances, it was the old heads with poor operational security who were killed or captured, and they were replaced by younger, more radical fighters who knew to stay away from mobile phones. The effect to which raiding, killing and detention contributed to radicalisation is not known, but the practices of the US military certainly created strange violent *jihadi* bedfellows.

One notable instance was at Camp Bucca, one of the US prisons where widespread prisoner abuse happened. This was where Abu Muslim al-Turkmani, a former colonel in Saddam Hussein's army, and Haji Bakr, a colonel in Saddam's intelligence service, met radical theologist Ibrahim Awad Ibrahim al-Badri. The trio seemed unlikely collaborators but were unified in their hatred of the occupying force and in their desire to unify the sectarian fight, and so found common cause and helped start a new, extreme *jihadi* group. Ibrahim Awad Ibrahim al-Badri later changed his name to Abu Bakr al-Baghdadi; the group the men created became ISIS.

In 2007, however, the American nightmare in Iraq seemed to be coming to an end, and McChrystal and JSOC were getting some of the credit. In 2007, kill/capture missions were in vogue. Night raids were in vogue too, and the career of General McChrystal was soaring. After a period as the Director of the Joint Staff, McChrystal was given his fourth star, raising him to the highest rank of the US military. On 10 June 2009 he assumed command of the International Security Assistance Force (ISAF) in Afghanistan. This put him in command of all international forces in Afghanistan, including the Australian special forces.

Before 9/11, JSOC had been a rarely used command of 1800 people. By 2013, there were 25,000 people in the command, and they had been allowed to run multiple, massive, lethal campaigns across the world without much oversight. It's not known exactly how many kill/capture missions were launched in Iraq and Afghanistan, but a top-secret NSA briefing about the RT-RG network contained a slide explaining that in 2011, in Afghanistan alone, the coalition launched 2270 special forces kill/capture operations from RT-RG intelligence processing, and that these missions had resulted in 6534 killings.

These missions were conducted by JSOC and what the Australian military strategist David Kilcullen describes as 'fungible SOF', meaning other nations' special forces units that could target and execute in Afghanistan as JSOC units could. And that, by 2011, included the Australian SASR.

* * *

General Peter Cosgrove was wary of aimless, bloody American military messes, perhaps because he'd seen one at first hand.

As a young infantry officer in 1969, then Lieutenant Cosgrove led multiple assaults against enemy bunker systems in Vietnam resulting in significant casualties. In his first public engagement as Australia's new Chief of Defence in 2002, General Cosgrove said it had been a mistake for Australia to be involved in a war in which some 15,381 young Australian men had been conscripted for service, 1479 of whom were injured or killed, while thousands more suffered mental injuries.

This was a notable admission for two reasons. Firstly, no Australian general had ever publicly admitted that the Vietnam War was a mistake. Secondly, Cosgrove's speech was given at a time when there was a great amount of public debate over whether the Australian military should be involved at all in any invasion of Iraq. In his speech to the National Press Club, Cosgrove also noted that regardless of any Australian military member's feelings, they were legally and honour bound to do the lawful bidding of their government.

In 2003 General Cosgrove facilitated Australia's role in the invasion of Iraq and also the removal of those invading Australian forces. In 2004 he advised the government not to recommit to Iraq in a fighting capacity, and was resolute in his position that the ADF's post-invasion commitment to Iraq should primarily be in the form of naval and air support, logistics and training.

As the months passed in 2004 and 2005, this seemed increasingly prescient advice. Not only was there increasing violence in Iraq, but new stories of rendition and 'black sites' (prisons where the US had no legal responsibility) were regularly revealed in the American and Australian press. The public learned that detainees in Iraq and beyond had been physically abused, and sometimes even anally raped, by CIA agents and US military personnel.

It's been reported that many of the people interrogating Iraqis had no training and were using techniques they had seen in movies and on television. A specific claim was that many of the abuses suffered by Iraqis had been shown previously on the television show 24, in what has been termed 'Jack Bauer syndrome'. This prompted senior US military officials to meet with the producers of the show and ask them to scale back the scenes of torture.

The ADF was caught up in one of these torture scandals when one of its legal officers, Major George O'Kane, who had been seconded to the US military and was working at Abu Ghraib prison, told his Australian and US superiors that some prisoners were being hidden from the International Committee of the Red Cross, a violation of the Geneva Convention. An Australian Senate inquiry attempted to look at O'Kane's role in Abu Ghraib in late May 2004, but the Department of Defence banned O'Kane from attending, telling the Senate he was too junior an officer to participate.

Earlier that month, General Cosgrove had written to Defence Minister Robert Hill in an official minute classified 'secret': 'Recent media expose of Iraqi PW [prisoner of war] treatment has created a negative environment and any realise [sic] of further information regarding PW/detainee involvement by Australia would escalate the situation.'

* * *

In April 2005, a small ADF battlegroup was sent into Iraq, but they worked in the quiet governorate of Al Muthanna, in the south of Iraq, protecting a Japanese reconstruction element. When the Japanese force left, the Australian troops relocated to Tallil Air Base, outside the city of Nasiriyah, where there was relative peace. These Australian soldiers did very little fighting, and none was killed. For many this seemed to be the perfect non-participatory form of participation in what was an unpopular war.

Many within the ADF were unhappy, however, believing that Australian military honour had been diminished. Also unhappy about the ADF's bloodless role was the Pentagon. Australia's defence minister met with General David Petraeus, by then the commander of all international forces in Iraq, and asked about Australia's military commitment in Iraq.

'Those trainers you sent us last month were excellent. Thank you,' said Petraeus.

The minister left the meeting believing that the American general was happy with Australia's contribution, until one of his military advisers explained that when a wartime general thanks a politician for a non-combat element, he's about as happy as he would be if someone had taken a shit in his hat. The alliance brownie points that Australia had earned during the invasions of Afghanistan and Iraq was disappearing with every passing day.

As 2004 came to an end and 2005 began, another persistent backchannel request started to filter through from Washington DC to Canberra: the United States would like Australia to recommit to Afghanistan. The message was unmistakeable: *You guys have a Ferrari and you won't let it out of the garage.*

On 3 July 2005, Peter Cosgrove retired from the army. He was one of the last, if not the last, full-time serving Australian soldiers who had seen combat in Vietnam.

* * *

Until 2005, there were few Australians with manhunting experience. One was Matt Bouillaut, who had been seconded, by way of the SASR's exchange program, to the British SBS, and deployed to Iraq as part of Task Force Black. There, he served as a patrol commander.

Bouillaut was given a list of names with intelligence packets relating to targets' suspected location, movements and behaviours, and his task was to ensure the target was killed or captured. This was similar to the role SASR patrol commanders had undertaken in Afghanistan. The targets were varied, from a Turkish businessman coming to do business with insurgents, to Ba'athists and leaders of al-Qaeda in Iraq (sometimes known as AQI).

One of Bouillaut's targets was even on the very first Iraqi kill/capture list, the infamous deck of playing cards that was handed out to invading forces showing the names and locations of senior Ba'athists who were to be sought out. That target, Saddam's right-hand man, Izzat Ibrahim al-Douri, escaped detection until 2015, but dozens of others were killed or captured by Task Force Black in some of the war's most high-octane missions.

Using Little Bird helicopters to drop through the night into what were often urban locations, clearing buildings, finding targets, then taking the bad guy off the chessboard – these missions were the antithesis of the surveillance and reconnaissance missions that the SASR had been known for.

'We were sometimes doing four missions a night ... you have a heightened level of awareness and it's a good feeling,' says Bouillaut. 'When it's gone your way, which it does nine times out of ten, and you're taking your body armour off, stowing your guns, you're like: "Fuck, how good was that?"'

One time Bouillaut was ordered to leave Iraq and go to Hereford, the home of the British SAS, to run a night-fighting course. When the course was pushed back, keeping Bouillaut in the UK, he says he felt a deep sense of missing out. For special forces operators, men who are selected for a strong tendency towards action, these types of manhunting missions became habit-forming.

'Is it addictive? No doubt,' he says.

12

'We are all dead, we have no more honour. We'd
prefer death to this humiliation'

IT WAS APRIL 2004, and Lieutenant Colonel Asad Khan of the 1st
Battalion 6th Marines had been left with shit duty. While there
were 140,000 US soldiers fighting in Iraq, supported by hundreds
of planes, helicopters and armour, Asad was one of only 10,000
US soldiers in Afghanistan, and one of only 5000 outside Kabul.

According to Washington DC, the war in Afghanistan was
over. Donald Rumsfeld had visited Kabul a few months earlier,
saying that he and Hamid Karzai 'have concluded we're at a point
where we clearly have moved from major combat activity to a
period of stability and stabilization and reconstruction activities.
The bulk of this country today is permissive, it's secure.'

Of course, Uruzgan was neither permissive nor secure. A few
weeks before Khan's marines landed, on 26 March 2004, the
United States received its first documentary evidence that the
Taliban were planning a military resurgence. An Omega team
(a hybrid CIA and 'sheep-dipped' DEVGRU element) hunting
in eastern Afghanistan and Pakistan had discovered a strategy
document formulated by the Taliban in Pakistan, which was being
circulated to some tribal leaders across Afghanistan. It related
to the first Afghan presidential election, mandated by the Bonn
agreement, which was scheduled for later in the year. The Taliban
had no standing army with which to attack Afghanistan, so they
would attempt to disrupt and discredit the election, then try to

siphon off parts of the populace who could feel disenfranchised by the elections and left out of the governmental process.

The United States itself would go to the polls in November 2004, and with the Iraq War going badly, the last thing the Bush administration needed was a blood-drenched, ineffectual and inconclusive election in Afghanistan – especially after the administration had said that Afghanistan was 'permissive and secure'.

General David Barno, the head of Combined Forces Command Afghanistan, and the Afghan-American diplomat Zalmay Khalilzad were tasked by President Bush with ensuring that the elections were uneventful. To that end, a number of warlords who showed little interest in bending to Kabul's authority, including Abdul Rashid Dostum, Mohammed Fahim, Ismail Khan and Gul Agha Sherzai, were compelled, with carrot and stick, to endorse the elections. In Dostum's case, General Barno even sent a B-1 bomber to conduct a low-altitude flyover at his home by way of a threat.

The 22nd Marine Expeditionary Unit (MEU) was sent to Uruzgan to secure the population and disarm and confront insurgents who might attempt to disrupt the election. With them was independent Australian video journalist Carmela Baranowska, who was embedded with Asad Khan and his marines.

'I will go fucking spastic on every fucking one of you,' Khan yelled at his marines in one of Baranowska's videos, smashing his fist into a soldier's chest. 'You better fucking wake up, you better get some fucking intensity. This is serious fucking business!'

Khan's closest significant support was in Kandahar, a whole province away, and he had only limited air support and medevac assistance. The intelligence apparatus available to the American special forces in Iraq was also largely unavailable to him. Having been born in Pakistan, Khan spoke some Urdu and Pashto, but he was a stranger in a strange land. What he did have, however, was the support of the local governor, Jan Mohammad.

Khan's marines were relying heavily on Jan Mohammad and his men for intelligence as to where they might find Taliban sympathisers and weapons that might be used to disrupt the presidential election. Jan Mohammad personally led raids with Khan and his men against his own tribal enemies in the Tarin Kot bowl, Dorafshan, the Baluchi Valley and the Mehrabad Valley.

Baranowska's footage shows Khan and his marines and Jan Mohammad and his men arriving at a village called Musazai in the Mehrabad Valley, directly east of Tarin Kot. Jan Mohammad bellows at a clutch of compounds, yelling for everyone in the village to hand their arms over to him immediately.

'I fuck his wife's vagina, whatever type of person he is,' Jan Mohammad hollers in Pashto at the villagers. 'Isn't it true that I, as governor, have come to you before? If those things are found here again, I swear I'll set fire to your houses.'

After the speech, Colonel Khan's marines started kicking in doors and pulling people out of their homes, going from house to house searching for weapons and ammunition. In one of the houses they found some soft-focus photographs of some local boys in traditional dress. The photographs were handed to Jan Mohammad.

'Aren't they heavenly creatures?' What beautiful boys they are,' he says, staring at the photographs. 'They're more beautiful than ten women.'

Jan Mohammad was notorious for the rape of boys and young men. A local teenager named Janan had been detained in one of the village sweeps and was taken to Jan Mohammad, who accused the teen of being part of the Taliban. Janan denied the accusation.

'I stick my penis in your head,' Jan Mohammad says to Janan. 'Tell the colonel we'll take him along with us and for a few nights he will keep us entertained,' he says to a translator. 'He'll do his thing with us and we'll see.'

After another raid, Khan observed a field of poppies later to become heroin. One of Jan Mohammad's men had given himself the title of 'provincial agriculture minister', and Khan told the man, through a translator, that he didn't see any agriculture, and he thought the 'minister' was doing a shitty job.

'Tell him I may have been less responsible in agriculture, but I've been clever in this war,' the man replied to the translator.

'When we're done with the war on terrorism, we start the war on drugs. You're not going to be our friends anymore,' one of Khan's marines chimed in.

The marines left Uruzgan in July 2004, and an official history of the 22nd Marine Expeditionary Unit (MEU) says the group searched 175 villages, seizing 2502 weapons and 75,000 pieces of ordnance. An official marine record of the operation says 100 Afghans were killed, with the marines suffering only one foot injury. In the same record, an Afghan villager is quoted as saying of the marines: 'Wherever they go they create death; they are death walkers.'

General David Barno said: 'Never in the history of Operation Enduring Freedom has there been an offensive operation like the one the 22nd MEU conducted. Never have we been this successful. You have made history here.' Another US military leader, Admiral Eric Olson, said: 'Never again can [the Taliban] use [Uruzgan] as a sanctuary.'

After being embedded for three weeks with Khan's unit, Baranowska was sent back to Kandahar, but returned to Uruzgan independently, visiting one of the villages that had been raided by the MEU and Jan Mohammad. She interviewed a father and son, both of whom claimed to have been taken to Kandahar Airfield and there penetrated anally, likely as part of an induction search.

'They tied my hands and then they put me in a container,' said a man named Noor Mohammad Lala. 'They removed my clothes. I pleaded through an interpreter that it was against Islam. "Don't make me stand here, naked." But they said no.

'I said, "For the sake of Allah and the Koran, don't do this." They said, "You can't get away." They took my clothes, I couldn't do anything. I was told to look up and put my hands on the container. I couldn't see behind me, but someone was fingering me. Some of them were pulling my testicles.'

Another village elder said he and the others taken to Kandahar could no longer live honourable lives, something of utmost importance to Pashtun people. 'We are all dead, we have no more honour. We'd prefer death to this humiliation,' he said.

* * *

The Afghan presidential election was held on 9 October 2004, and while there was not the widespread violence that was feared, the election was not a success. There was a substantial amount of vote rigging and fraud, as Hamid Karzai was returned as the president of the country. After the election, it was essentially business as usual – which for many Afghans, especially poor, rural people in places like Uruzgan, was bad news.

With the American invasion had come a promise of change: of a government that would bring security and justice and services like electricity, roads and efficient water capture and distribution – the latter was a significant concern in rural Afghanistan, and the root of many tribal disputes. Three years later, that promise had not been realised. Roughly 5 per cent of people in Afghanistan had access to the electricity grid at the end of 2004, no new roads had been built in rural areas since the invasion. No extra effort had been made to solve the water capture issues either.

Security and justice in rural areas of Afghanistan were, in fact, worse than they had been during the rule of the Taliban. The United States decided not to dedicate resources to building the Afghan National Police until 2005, so that task was left to the government of Germany. In an assessment from the German Federal Foreign Office and Federal Ministry of the Interior, there were just 17 people dedicated to that task nationwide in 2004 – in a country of 40 million. It was in these conditions that the Taliban started to return to Afghanistan, and to Uruzgan.

'People think that the Americans and later the Australians were seen as the oppressors and invaders from the beginning, but that wasn't the impression I got at all,' says Pieter Van (not his real name), a Dutch diplomat and academic who worked for aid agencies in Afghanistan during the Taliban era and then worked for the European Union and Dutch governments. 'They were ready to accept anyone, and even any religion, if you would just bring us peace.'

Pieter Van, who lived in Uruzgan and met with most of the tribal leaders in the province from 2002, says there was a period in which all the people of Afghanistan, even the conservative tribes of rural Uruzgan, would have accepted quasi-American rule. Yet he found that calloused enmity against the Americans, Hamid Karzai and Jan Mohammad grew month by month, with the most common grievance being questions of justice.

'People were exhausted [in 2002]. There's an incredible amount of pragmatism [in Afghanistan]. If they win, they win and as long as you leave them alone, they leave you alone but only if people weren't personally targeted,' Van says.

People were targeted, however, all across the south. In Uruzgan, Jan Mohammad 'would report his rivals to the Americans as al-Qaeda and there would be raids on their houses or their houses would be bombed', according to Van.

Some of the loudest grievances voiced, Van says, were over the Americans' 'intrusion into women's boxes' during raids, a phrase that in Pashto can mean rape, but can also literally mean opening a box of belongings. There is no linguistic distinction, Van says, as both transgressions are an equal affront to a woman's honour.

According to Van, the United States' disastrous poppy eradication programs of 2004 and 2005 also furthered the rise of the insurgency. With the US military stretched in Iraq, these programs were handed over to private American military contractors, who often subcontracted the work to warlords friendly with Kabul, most of whom who had their own drug interests. Overall, in 2004 and 2005, there was no appreciable decline in opium production, the cut in production in 'enemy' poppy fields being offset by the surging rise of production in 'friendly' poppy fields.

For the those in the disenfranchised 'enemy' communities, a large amount of debt was created. Farmers and suppliers defaulted on loans and, fearing starvation or attack by a creditor, fled to Pakistan. There these men often joined the reconstituting Taliban across the border.

The Taliban were not strong in 2004, but with the border between Pakistan and Afghanistan unsecured, the United States and the new Afghan government unwilling or unable to provide security, federal ministries weak and corrupt, and provincial governments compromised by warlords and narco-barons, the citizenry in Afghanistan and abroad began reconsidering them as potential national leaders.

Given the options of a strong federal government offering improvements in amenities, security and justice on the one hand, and the Taliban on the other, most rural Afghans would have chosen the former. Only that wasn't what was being offered. What was being offered was a weak federal government that, in Uruzgan, most people only experienced in the form of Jan Mohammad and his men. At least the Taliban would offer a familiar form of justice.

The Taliban were also being reconsidered in the power centres of parts of the Islamic world, like Saudi Arabia, the Gulf States and Pakistan. Only three years after the 9/11 attacks, the Taliban were officially the enemy of any United States ally, but, as the long view and regional dynamics had to be considered as well, an increasing amount of unofficial support for the Taliban was being established.

For those who only flew into Kabul and toured that city and its fringes, Afghanistan looked like any other developing country with some security issues. But in the view of those who understood Afghanistan and the martial nature of the people involved, the conditions were ripe for the reignition of war. Much of the rural populace in particular was increasingly sympathetic to the Taliban.

Following the national vote on October 2004, Hamid Karzai had become the elected president of Afghanistan. But soon a nickname emerged, one that captured his government's inability to project power in the thousands of valleys, mountains and desert villages of Afghanistan. Hamid Karzai wasn't 'the President of Afghanistan' but 'the Mayor of Kabul'.

13

'"Who are we?" ... They say this is a corrupt government'

IT WAS MARCH 2004 and three Australians pulled their four-wheel drive to the side of the road just outside Kabul. They started walking up a hill, and a group of armed Afghans, who had parked nearby, created a loose cordon around them, with AK-47 rifles slung over their shoulders.

There were only four Australians working in an official capacity in Afghanistan at this time. One was a military officer maintaining a desk within the heavily fortified and exclusionary green zone in Kabul; these three men were the others. The trio trudged up the hill, leaving behind the patchwork fields of Parwan Province as they made their way to an open-air *shura* pavilion at the hill's peak.

In the pavilion the Australians were greeted by more than a dozen armed militiamen and the leader of a militia group. The man, who was in his thirties and had spent more than half his life fighting the Russians, the warlords and then the Taliban, introduced himself and proudly showed them six scars that had once been gunshot wounds – his résumé.

One of the Australians asked the man how his life had been since the Taliban were displaced in 2001.

'I had been fighting a long time, and now everyone is coming back,' the man replied. 'Many people left during the war when we were fighting, and many have gotten educations. I wish them well, but now they think they can tell us what to do?'

Their conversation was being interpreted by a man who was exactly the type of person the militia leader was talking about. This was Mahmoud Saikal, an Afghan who left the country during the Soviet occupation and established himself in Australia, where he completed degrees at the universities of Sydney and Canberra, and at Deakin University in Melbourne. Saikal would later become Afghanistan's ambassador to the United Nations.

'The aid did not get to us, the contracts did not get to us and we have no jobs,' the militia leader said. 'But we have guns,' he continued, brandishing his AK-47.

'Let me ask you something,' the man then said. 'You have four sons and a war starts; one son stays and fights and he lives; one son stays and fights and he dies; one son leaves and comes back when the war is over; and one son leaves and never comes back. Which son do you love?'

The three Australians waited for the man to answer his own question but he did not. He wanted an answer.

One of the Australians, strong-featured with greying hair at his temples, was Alan Griffin, then the federal member for Bruce, a Melbourne electorate that was home to many of the Afghan sons who had left during the Soviet occupation or the civil war and never returned. Griffin vacillated, saying that sons can be loved equally, as each has his own qualities and virtues.

The other Anglo-Australian, a bespectacled man with blond hair atop a round face, interjected. 'It's not that simple,' said Kevin Rudd, then the Labor opposition's shadow minister for foreign affairs.

'It *is* that simple,' the militia leader replied, steely-eyed. 'You will love me.'

In Afghanistan familial love, like everything else worthwhile, is earned at the business end of rifle. The man was trying to explain to the future prime minister of Australia that, regardless of first-world reconstruction fantasies that can be believed in Kabul and surrounds, Afghanistan was still a violent and unyielding place where pragmatism, tribalism and warlord rule reigned.

This was a message that Kevin Rudd may not have fully understood.

* * *

Rudd and Griffin had flown to Afghanistan via commercial routes from Sydney, using their parliamentary study budget. They stayed in the country for just three days. The pair met with a series of Karzai acolytes, and didn't venture out of the relative safety of Kabul and surrounding areas. While in Afghanistan, Rudd was interviewed for ABC Radio by Mark Colvin, who asked about Rudd's position on Australia's military commitment in Iraq.

Rudd had strong opinions about the post-9/11 wars, and liked to consider himself an expert on them. In the lead-up to the invasion of Iraq, Rudd had travelled to Britain to review what was then being called the 'Blair dossier', a collated and somewhat fabricated intelligence product that made the argument for war in Iraq and now had done fact-finding in Afghanistan.

Rudd knew a fine line had to be trodden when talking about Australia's commitment to the unpopular war in Iraq. With the ADF being ensconced in a solidly Shi'ite and largely safe area of southern Iraq, and working almost exclusively on reconstruction projects, Rudd saw no reason for Australian troops to leave the country. But he was not the leader of his party. The Labor leader, Mark Latham, wanted Australian troops out of Iraq by Christmas.

'Our international obligations to provide for the security stabilisation of Iraq changes at the point at which an interim Iraqi government is established as of 1 July [2004],' Rudd said. 'And our position is this, we will then re-evaluate our security contribution as a party to Iraq, once that event occurs, and judge it on the basis of what the United Nations is saying at the time and the security circumstances in Iraq at the time.'

The point of this word salad was essentially to punt the problem down the road. Wait and see.

Colvin also asked Rudd about Afghanistan, a subject far easier to talk about. 'Front and centre for Australia's national security is the war against terrorism ... the war against terrorism still continues here in Afghanistan,' Rudd said.

In 2004, the United States lost 52 soldiers in Afghanistan, against the 849 that had been killed in Iraq in the same period. Afghanistan was not only seen as the good war, it was understood by those who didn't really understand the war as the easy war and the safe war.

Just a couple of weeks before Griffin and Rudd's trip to Kabul, ten bombs had torn apart commuter trains in Madrid, killing 193 people and injuring or maiming another 2000. In 2002, a car and suicide bombing in Bali, Indonesia, had killed 202 people, 88 of them Australians, and injured hundreds more. The Bali bombings had rocked Australians to the core. They were an attack on the Balinese, whom Islamic radicals saw as apostates and intruders on their land, but it was also a direct attack against Australians, the bombs having been set off at a nightclub frequented by Australian holiday-makers.

A week later Rudd was interviewed on the ABC's Radio National, and he was even more supportive of a new military investment in Afghanistan, this time toeing the Labor Party line that Australian troops should be out of Iraq by Christmas.

'Frankly, we see priorities lying for Australia's troop commitments elsewhere,' Rudd said of Iraq. 'And I just would emphasise the point – last week I was in Afghanistan. That is the front line in the global war against terrorism. That's where Osama bin Laden is. That's where al-Qaeda is. That's where the Taliban still are.'

In fact, Osama bin Laden was almost certainly in Pakistan in 2004, with the bulk of the al-Qaeda fighters. Most senior Taliban leaders were also in Pakistan.

Days after their trip, both Griffin and Rudd stood in the Australian parliament and made speeches advocating a further Australian military commitment in Afghanistan. Both men called for Australia to commit a Provincial Reconstruction Team (PRT), having observed the New Zealand PRT operating in the peaceful Bamyan Province, which was within the 'Mayor of Kabul's' protection catchment. Both men hoped that Australia might operate in the way the New Zealanders were. But this would not be the fate of Australia's soldiers.

* * *

In June 2004, Prime Minister John Howard was in Washington DC, his fourth visit since September 2001. It was unusual for an Australian prime minister to visit the United States with such frequency, but the relationship between Prime Minister Howard and President Bush was also unusual.

The men seemed strange bedfellows: the American a gregarious former hellraiser and dynastic shooting star, and the Australian a bookish former lawyer. They were bonded, however, through their extant Christian beliefs, and through war. In public they sometimes took the posture of a naval captain and his executive officer, with everyone else having the option of being in their boat or being in the water.

There was a threat to that relationship in June 2004, however. In fact, there were two. In October 2004, Australia would have a federal election, and then a few weeks later the United States would hold its presidential election. It looked like both would go down to the wire.

For both the prime minister and the president, then, the press conference held on the White House lawn was a campaign event. Foreign policy, especially the increasingly calamitous Iraq War, was emerging as a significant wedge issue in the US election, and having a staunch international ally who was supportive of the war standing alongside Bush played well for him. The war in Iraq was a non-issue in the Australian election, but counterterrorism and a general sense of 'us versus them' was undoubtedly a tool in Howard's election toolbox – and a strong, fraternal relationship with the US president always played well for Australian prime ministers.

At the press conference, President Bush was asked by a journalist from *The Australian* newspaper what he thought about Mark Latham's intention to withdraw Australian troops from Iraq by Christmas, should the Labor Party win power. President Bush replied that it would be 'disastrous'.

'It would embolden the enemy, who believe that they can shake our will. See, they want to kill innocent life, because they think the Western world, and the free world, is weak.'

In his book *The Latham Diaries*, Mark Latham wrote this about the incident: 'I will win the election and if not, what the people are saying is that they don't mind being an American colony under Howard. That's a nation not worth leading.'

In the lead-up to the election, Latham attempted to dance to a relatively complicated tune when talking about national security. He argued that asylum seeker policy didn't relate to terrorism, and that terrorism was often a policing issue, not necessarily a military one. He also said that the war in Iraq wasn't only a distraction from the struggle against terrorism, but animating potential terrorists.

AFP commissioner Mick Keelty created a headache for Prime Minister Howard when he made a similar statement on *60 Minutes* in the wake of the Madrid train attacks. 'The reality is, if this turns out to be Islamic extremists responsible for the bombing in Spain, it's ... likely to be linked to the position that Spain and other allies took on issues such as Iraq,' Keelty said.

Howard's national security two-step was danced to far simpler music. He was purely with the Americans, claiming to see the War on Terror in the way President Bush did: it encompassed Iraq, Afghanistan, local and international policing, asylum seekers, maritime borders and legal challenges. All of it.

Mark Latham lost the 2004 election in a landslide, and a less than a month later President Bush was comfortably returned to the White House. There seemed to be a soft electoral mandate in the United States for the foreign wars to continue, and Howard knew that as long as there weren't a large number of Australian soldiers coming home in body bags, Australia's national security policy could largely be what he and Alexander Downer – known to some in the Liberal Party as 'the team' – wanted it to be.

After the election victories, the United States started applying backchannel pressure to the Howard government, and to the ADF chiefs in Canberra, asking that Australia recommit to Afghanistan. These conversations hadn't yet risen to the level of official talks, but were far enough along that US Deputy Secretary of State Richard Armitage was having regular conversations with Downer about what a new Australian commitment to Afghanistan might look like. Australia was being asked to contribute to a PRT, despite reconstruction in a warlike environment not being something the Australian military was really built to do.

There were also conversations about the redeployment of Australia's special forces, a capability that, Downer says, in the wake of previous post-9/11 deployment had become a 'USP', or unique selling proposition, in negotiations with the Americans. Australia's 'army in a box' were now far more versatile and could deploy faster and in larger numbers than in the wake of 9/11, but the government wanted to ensure that any special forces deployment be time-limited.

This was, in part, due to concerns that special forces might be needed closer to home, with Downer citing concerns about Indonesia and Fiji, and John Howard about Papua New Guinea (many SASR troopers at this time were still learning Indonesian and Tok Pisin as part of their training), but there was also a fear of 'mission creep'. As an old Afghan maxim went, 'It's easy to march an army into Afghanistan, but you must first consider how you will march them out.'

* * *

As a clean-shaven ethnic Tajik (and former confidant of Ahmad Shah Massoud), Amrullah Saleh was not comfortable in the wild Pashtun south. Yet when the 34-year-old flew to Kandahar in 2004 and then drove around a number of southern provinces, including Uruzgan, to meet with Pashtun warlords, former *mujahedin* commanders and poppy producers, he did so knowing he would be relatively safe.

There were men in Uruzgan who would have happily killed the Tajik, but during his tour of the south, Saleh was protected by a cloak of *melmestia*, the *Pashtunwali* principal of hospitality. The northerner had asked to meet these men, and offered them money for their time. When they agreed, he became an invited guest and could not be harmed.

Saleh had travelled south as the head of the National Directorate of Security (NDS), Afghanistan's answer to the CIA, which was in fact funded and trained by the CIA. A former Northern Alliance intelligence chief, Saleh was one of the few effective parts of the Karzai government. In his first week as the head of the NDS, he'd found 38,000 'ghost salaries' and got rid of them.

Early in his tenure at the NDS, Saleh wanted to see for himself what was happening in the south of the country. Through NDS contacts and friends he arranged to meet with some of the armed agitators in the south. Many told him the same story: they had been sidelined, maligned or ignored by the men whom Karzai had installed as governors and heads of police. Some had been hunted by the Americans, and in some instances their families and allies had been attacked. Some of these tribal leaders had sought allies and support, others relief or mediation from a dispute, tribal or familial, over land, water or honour.

In Uruzgan, Saleh found that two tribal groups were of primary concern. The first was the Ghilzai, a large Pashtun tribe that had been largely maligned by the other Pashtuns in Afghanistan since the 18th century; their number included many of the senior Taliban, including Mullah Omar. The second group was the Nurzai, another Pashtun tribe whom Popalzai leaders such as Jan Mohammad considered inherently inferior. These two groups represented more than 30 per cent of the population of Uruzgan.

This was a sizeable group from which an insurgency could be built, but Saleh found the problem to be even greater than that. Many of the other, larger tribes such as the Barakzai and Achekzai, which had supported the government and would not openly support the Taliban, were being white-anted by certain families and clans who were enemies of Jan Mohammad. These tribes too might potentially support an insurgency. Along with the Ghilzai and Nurzai, this group represented more than 70 per cent of the population in Uruzgan.

In the south, Amrullah Saleh found, the Taliban didn't have much by way of physical presence – garrisoned buildings, standing forces or fluttering flags – but he realised that unseen support was building. Also concerning was evidence of Taliban coordination and strategy.

Even while in government, the Taliban had been as much the expression of an idea as a structurally organised entity. Now it seemed some kind of strategic coherence was coming into Afghanistan from across the border in Pakistan. Saleh believed the United States' relationship with Pakistan was not what the Americans thought it was. Pakistan appeared to be playing both sides of the conflict, accepting financial and military support from the Americans, while also harbouring and perhaps supplying the Taliban.

Pakistan flatly denied Saleh's claims, with President Pervez Musharraf calling the suggestion 'absurd'. Karzai, who in any case refused to acknowledge there was organised resistance to his government at all, largely accepted this denial.

Much of this Taliban coherence seemed to be coming from the Pakistani province of Balochistan, and from the Balochi capital, Quetta, which was only 140 kilometres from the Afghan border, and not much more than that again to Tarin Kot. In Quetta, senior Taliban had been supported and sheltered by Pakistan's secret intelligence agency, Inter-Services Intelligence. ISI support for the Taliban had not been consistent after 2001; the intelligence agency has assumed American domination of Afghanistan after 9/11, but following the US invasion of Iraq they feared a waning of US interests in Afghanistan and a rise in Indian influence in Kabul. Pakistan already shared a hostile border with India to its east, where the two states were in a nuclear stare-down. The nightmare scenario for Pakistan was to have a hostile, Indian-influenced western border too.

In Quetta, the ISI likely helped the Taliban set up their permanent war council, known as the Quetta Shura. This was a group of senior clerics, including Mullah Abdul Ghani Baradar, who would decide strategy in Afghanistan. In 2005, this included bringing into the ideological fold those left behind by the Afghan government, and reinstalling their rough version of Islamic justice that had been popular at the height of the civil war.

Initially, this justice came in the form of night letters and assassinations, but later the Taliban brought in a complete shadow justice system, with mullahs moving from town to town holding *sharia* courts, making binding rulings over land, water and marriage disputes, as well as judgements on capital crimes such as murders, kidnappings and apostasy. Also adjudicated upon was the crime of supporting the government.

The Quetta Shura had decided to embrace poppy and opium production. In 2001, the Taliban had banned the crop, creating an international heroin supply crisis. (At that time, Afghanistan grew more than 90 per cent of the world's illicit poppies; it now grows more than 95 per cent.) The difference now was that they needed to stimulate a wartime economy and ingratiate themselves with narco-barons.

Upon his return to Kabul, Amrullah Saleh delivered a damning report to President Karzai, writing that the Taliban insurgency had great momentum, on the back of surging popular support. '"Who are we?" A lot of people in the villages of Zabul, Helmand, Kandahar, and Uruzgan have a simple answer to this question. They say this is a corrupt government,' the report stated.

Saleh's analysis was echoed in reports from British, Italian and Dutch academics and intelligence professionals, who had bravely spent months in some of the most remote parts of Uruzgan, Helmand and Kandahar doing fieldwork at the behest of their governments, which were considering committing troops.

President Karzai was enraged by Saleh's findings; he was particularly unhappy about the use of the word 'insurgency'. He told his head of intelligence never to use that word again. There were policing problems in southern Afghanistan, Karzai acknowledged, but surely nothing that constituted an insurgency.

Saleh replied candidly: he believed the insurgency was already entrenched in the southern provinces of Zabul, Helmand, Kandahar and Uruzgan. And if something wasn't done about that, the Taliban flag might be flying in some cities in Afghanistan as soon as 2009.

The Middlegame

14

'I just hope they make a decision soon, before all
the easy places are gone'

IN A DEFT MOVE of branding and necessity, the United States began internationalising the war in Afghanistan from 2004. Since the invasion, the war had been commanded by ISAF, the International Security Assistance Force, but until August 2003 ISAF had been commanded by US generals and was constituted almost exclusively of US troops. That month, NATO assumed control of ISAF, and by mid-2004 soldiers from Canada, Germany, Spain, Romania and New Zealand were committed to Afghanistan.

This internationalisation, and the fact that NATO forces were operating largely without fighting – in 2005 they were operating almost exclusively in the quiet north, where President Karzai maintained control – put further pressure on Australia to recommit its support. If the militaries of Romania, Spain and New Zealand were safely operating in Afghanistan, surely Australia could do the same.

In early 2005, Secretary General of NATO Jaap de Hoop Scheffer came to Australia – the first such visit in the organisation's history – and in Canberra he petitioned the government to join the fray in Afghanistan. After the visit, Defence Minister Robert Hill tabled a proposal to the federal cabinet's National Security Committee (NSC), arguing for Australia to commit to a PRT in Afghanistan. This proposal had been written by General Peter Cosgrove and other senior officials at the Department of Defence in Russell, Canberra, and suggested sending military engineers and conventional force protection to Afghanistan, without any special forces.

But in the NSC, Howard and Downer decided that Australia's commitment should, initially, be of special forces, for which Howard had particular regard for after the *Tampa* incident, Operation Anaconda and the operations in Iraq. After that exploratory special forces mission, a PRT could potentially follow later.

The submission was sent back to Cosgrove, who liaised with SOCAUST Major General Mike Hindmarsh to prepare a special forces submission for NSC approval. This initial proposal was for a 45-person special forces element, tasked with largely ancillary operations – but before the proposal could be finished and sent to government, General Cosgrove's three-year term as Chief of Defence ended, and he retired.

The proposal was handed over to the incoming Chief of Defence, Air Chief Marshal Angus Houston, and by the time it reached the NSC, a larger contingent – primarily of SASR shooters – had been recommended. Meanwhile, triangular deliberations between Canberra, Washington and Brussels had started as to where in Afghanistan the Australian forces might deploy. In Canberra, these deliberations involved politicians, academics, members of the Afghan diaspora and senior military officials.

Some in Canberra wanted Australia to work in the north of the country, close to Kabul, where most of the militias were aligned with the government and there was little violence. Some in the military saw this as a mistake: little honour and few alliance brownie points would be earned there, especially in the wake of our quiet time in Iraq. SOCOMD wanted its soldiers to be used for more than force protection in a quiet province. While recommendations were made, ultimately the decision would be in the hands of John Howard, Alexander Downer and Robert Hill.

One person who was involved in these meetings (and who does not wish to be named) walked out of one of these pre-

Afghanistan meetings with Air Chief Marshal Houston, who was frustrated by the deliberations. This person asked Houston where he thought his troops would end up. 'I don't know,' Houston replied. 'I just hope they make a decision soon, before all the easy places are gone.'

Meanwhile, Deputy Special Operations Commander Brigadier Tim McOwan and SASR Commander Lieutenant Colonel James McMahon had been sent to the United States to meet with JSOC head General Stanley McChrystal. The American general asked the two Australians what expertise their operators could contribute, and the officers told him they would bring skills in surveillance and reconnaissance, with all associated medical and intelligence apparatus.

This was a good match for JSOC. While their forces were doing direct-action missions in Iraq, in Afghanistan they were also working with the CIA and US Army Rangers as they tried to find al-Qaeda's leaders in the mountainous region between Afghanistan and Pakistan. They had set up listening devices and engaged local sources, and were already running clandestine missions in the area, with the aim of directing a local force, named the Afghan Combat Application Group (ACAG), in pursuit of al-Qaeda targets. (As it turned out, JSOC and ACAG fought primarily against insurgents and local warlords; it would later be alleged that JSOC forces perpetrated a number of war crimes in border region.)

McChrystal saw great benefit in SASR participation in this mission, and the two Australians relayed his views to Canberra. A message was sent back to them that the SASR would not be working with JSOC in the border region, because Canberra was not comfortable with the Australians operating in Pakistan. After receiving that communication, McOwan and McMahon flew on to a Kandahar airfield, where they met with the commanders of the Combined Joint Special Operations Task Force – Afghanistan (CJSOTF-A).

ISAF was assuming security responsibility for the southern Afghan provinces from the Americans; this was part of a four-stage plan in which ISAF was to assume power by quadrants. They had already taken responsibility for the peaceful north and west, and now they would be attempting to control the Pashtun south and the eastern areas abutting Pakistan.

Canadian and British forces were about to insert into southern Afghanistan. The British SAS had been sent into Helmand to survey the province in preparation for the British Army to assume control of the province from the Americans. (The survey found that the province was peaceful, as it was flushed with reconstruction and opium money and under the thumb of a dominant warlord, and therefore should be largely left alone.) The Canadian military, meanwhile, were about to assume control of Kandahar Province from the United States. In between Helmand and Kandahar was Uruzgan Province, where the Americans were establishing a PRT but wished to hand over control to a partner.

From Kandahar, McOwan and McMahon were flown 120 kilometres to FOB Davis. This flight took them over the site where Jason Amerine's ODA 594 had been bombed and where Hamid Karzai was offered a Taliban surrender, over what would soon be Matiullah Khan's road, and over the valley where Ben Roberts-Smith would earn his Victoria Cross.

As they neared Tarin Kot, the Australian pair watched US door gunners firing their Miniguns at who-knows-what. As the sound of high-velocity rounds hammered their ears and muzzle-flash filled their eyes, the Australians must have thought that perhaps the state of affairs in Uruzgan Province wasn't exactly what Canberra thought it to be.

* * *

If it was decided that if the Australian SASR were going to end up in Uruzgan, they would have restart their mission in Afghanistan with some good old-fashioned eyes-on patrols and 'ground-truthing'. Ninety-five soldiers from SASR's 2 Squadron were inserted into FOB Davis in Tarin Kot, alongside 56 commandos and six special forces engineers. Their role was to assess the enemy's strength and find areas that might have been infiltrated by the Taliban, and so might be in use as safe havens or travel hubs.

Intelligence in Uruzgan was thin on the ground, but two areas were identified as possible Taliban enclaves. The first were the passes towards the district of Gizab, a green island of life in an ocean of rock and dust in Daykundi Province, just north of Uruzgan. The second was Shahidi Hassas, an area in the extreme north-west of Uruzgan where farmers, many of them cultivating poppies, clung to a bottle-green river. Gizab had traditionally been a Hazara area, but recently had been taken over by Pashtun and specifically Ghilzai tribespeople. Shahidi Hassas had traditionally been an area settled by Nurzai tribespeople, but there was also a strong Ghilzai presence.

The Australians were to undertake two concurrent vehicle-mounted missions in their ground-truthing mission, both missions involving LRPVs laden with heavy weapons and motorbikes driving for weeks on barely there tracks, sometimes through graveyards of Soviet armour. The Australians drove past dead men hanging from trees, or lying on the ground with their heads next to them. These deaths, they learned, were sometimes the result of tribal feuds, but in many instances rough justice had been dealt to men who had been summarily convicted of crimes such as theft and murder, but also of supporting government engineering programs or of teaching women and girls how to read.

An assessment of the province had found that, in 2005, no child in Shahidi Hassas was in school, and no sick person had any immediate access to modern medical treatment. This was a place where there was essentially no government presence. Here, the SASR were nothing less than aliens. Little cultural ground was shared between the Australians and the people of Shahidi Hassas. Little except an understanding of warfare.

On 22 September 2005, the SASR's Shahidi Hassas element, while patrolling in the Khod Valley, started to sense an ambush coming. This was the first Australian incursion into Uruzgan, and the soldiers didn't yet understand the area's patterns of life, but as they approached the village of Bagh Khoshak they could feel the impending attack. The six-car convoy of LRPVs, augmented by Suzuki DR dirt bikes and a clutch of Afghan National Army soldiers, were clearly not welcome.

In the Khod Valley, a local leader had been arrested and then sent back to Tarin Kot. A signaller attached to the SASR element had reported a spike of ICOM radio and phone traffic. The soldiers saw an abandoned construction site with tools left unattended. There was electricity in the air.

The Australians approached a chokepoint, known to both locals and foreigners as the ideal spot for an ambush. Some of the Australians dismounted from their vehicles and scanned the trees, adobe-style buildings and peaks around them. Hidden around them were what Australian commanders would later call 'anti-coalition militia', or ACM, and what the Aussie shooters called 'shitcunts'.

These people were the enemy. Perhaps in their ranks there were Taliban professionals, perhaps Taliban sympathisers, perhaps locals aggrieved by the US special forces or Jan Mohammad. Perhaps some were following their brothers or fathers. The motivations of the enemy are not a concern when the bullets start flying.

The first incoming shots were fully automatic and at close range: a stream of 7.62mm rounds flying into the convoy, smashing into cars and men. One Afghan soldier was killed instantly, the rounds puncturing the body of an LRPV. A bullet smashed into the earmuffs of an Australian non-commissioned officer, knocking them off his head. The Australians returned fire, killing the man who had jumped out and started the ambush. As the Australians ran for their heavy weapons, an RPG round smashed into the grille of one of the LRPVs without detonating, and AK-47 rounds shredded one of the vehicle's seats.

More than a dozen enemy had appeared from near and far, bringing RPK light machine guns, AK-47s and RPG-9s to bear on the Australians; the RPG munition was used as starburst rounds from a distance, just as it had been during Operation Anaconda. At least one Australian sustained a fragmentation wound.

The heavy weapons the Australians were using were more effective, their FN MAG machine guns, MK-19 grenade launchers and M3 Carl Gustaf recoilless rifles turning the tide on the attack. The last weapon – simply 'the Gustaf', in Australian military parlance – was developed as an anti-tank weapon but became a favourite anti-personnel weapon among Australian special forces in Afghanistan throughout the conflict.

The fighting was intense, but one soldier involved says that the overwhelming firepower the Australians carried into their vehicles decided the day. The Australians took the ascendency even before the US Apache gunships arrived and started destroying enemy positions. A large number of Afghans were left dead, while the Australians suffered only minor wounds.

When the element returned to FOB Davis days later, they were greeted by a number of their superiors and Defence Minister Robert Hill, who had flown in unannounced to see, at first hand, what the reality was on the ground in southern Afghanistan. That reality was evident in the men and their cars just returned: vehicles had been perforated by bullets and grenades, while uniforms were caked in mud and in some instances blood.

Hill declined to be interviewed for this book, but it has been reported that he was shocked by what he saw in Tarin Kot. Although he'd hoped Australia's commitment to Afghanistan would primarily be post-conflict reconstruction, that was not what he saw at FOB Davis in 2005.

By the time 2 Squadron returned to Perth from their rotation, Robert Hill had given up the defence portfolio and retired from politics altogether. Speculation was rife that there had been friction between Hill and the leadership duo of Howard and Downer, and in particular that the two South Australians, Downer and Hill, didn't see eye to eye on national security. It was reported that Hill, a former barrister, hadn't agreed with the conduct of the US military in Iraq.

Hill was tight-lipped about his departure from politics, and shortly afterwards he was awarded one of the most coveted diplomatic positions available: a stint in New York as Australia's ambassador to the United Nations. At the time of Hill's departure, the Australian media speculated about how Australia's commitment to Iraq may have factored into his decision to leave politics, but few if any speculated about the influence of Australia's second commitment to Afghanistan.

Hill has said little about Australia's military commitment to Afghanistan since leaving politics, but he did contribute a few paragraphs to an edited volume about Iraq and Afghanistan that was published by the Australian National University in 2020, writing:

> With its 'can do' attitude, the military sometimes
> overestimates what it is able to achieve. It is for the
> politicians to set the mission parameters, and they should
> be realistic in assessing what is for the military and what
> requires other elements. The challenge is to get the right
> mix. I do not think the international community invested
> enough in nation-building in Afghanistan. But if they had,
> it still might not have worked.

It's not known whether this was an opinion formed from the clay of hindsight, or an idea that clanged around in the South Australian senator's head as he stood in the middle of FOB Davis, with blast walls around him and a murderous warlord by his side, welcoming Australia's battered elite soldiers back from what he might have thought was someone else's fight. Perhaps Hill saw the winding and blood-drenched road ahead. If he did, he didn't inform the incoming defence minister, Dr Brendan Nelson, who says he received no handover from Hill. Indeed, Nelson has said he did not hear from Hill in the first three months of his tenure.

* * *

'As far as I could see it was musical chairs, and the music stopped and we got Uruzgan, in the middle of southern central

Afghanistan,' says Brendan Nelson of Australia's decision to commit to Uruzgan.

John Howard and Alexander Downer were also asked about the decision to place Australia's military in Uruzgan and not another province, but both said decision-making at that level was left to the Chief of Defence. 'Those sorts of things were very much based on military advice,' Howard says.

David Kilcullen, a former lieutenant colonel in the ADF who was seconded to the US Department of Defense and became a leading adviser to the US and Australian governments on counterterrorism, counterinsurgency and Afghanistan, says of the decision: 'They [the ADF] wanted to pick a place that was more central to the effort and more kinetic than just Bamyan and Panjshir [in the north of Afghanistan] or something, but they also wanted one that would primarily be about building Afghan capability ... not primarily having to fight every day to maintain themselves. They were looking for a happy medium and they got the worst of both worlds.'

ISAF was assuming responsibility of Uruzgan in 2006 from the United States. As a smaller province nestled between the provinces for which Canada and the United Kingdom would assume military responsibility, Uruzgan made a kind of sense as the place where Australia would make its military commitment. The United States and ISAF hoped that the ADF would assume control of the province, installing a general officer and sending Australian aircraft, but there was neither political not military appetite for that kind of holistic commitment. Australia would only commit to being a minor partner in any province. In part that decision was made because Australia's special forces were to be committed on strictly time-limited bases.

'We made that very clear,' says Howard. 'We would commit specialty forces at the sharp end, but ... we would not be involved in any long peacekeeping pacification.'

The plan was to have Australia's special forces committed for a maximum of 12 months, creating the conditions from which Australia's military engineers could work. NATO was in discussions with the Dutch government about the Netherlands assuming control in Uruzgan, with Australia and the United States augmenting their forces. A soft commitment came to NATO and the United States in 2005 from Prime Minster Jan Peter Balkenende, but he could not commit forces to Afghanistan in the frictionless way the Australian government could.

Balkenende sat atop a conservative multi-party coalition in the Netherlands, and relied on a razor-thin majority for his authority to govern. While he and the leaders of the other large parties in the coalition wanted to accede to NATO's request, at least one of the minor parties was demurring.

The Dutch already had experience as the lead of a PRT, working in Baghlan, north of Kabul, from 2004 to 2006. They had concentrated on education and the reconstitution of the province's dairy industry, opening a cheese factory. They had suffered no casualties and had done very little fighting. They knew, however, that Uruzgan would be a different proposition, as throughout 2005 and into 2006 the Dutch had employed civilian contractors to survey the human terrain.

While Australia's special forces were already fighting in Uruzgan – working under, as Howard describes it, 'operational control of United States forces' – the Dutch parliament was still debating whether they should involve themselves in the province at all. In a mild panic, NATO Secretary General Jaap de Hoop Scheffer and UN Secretary General Kofi Annan visited The Hague as debate raged both in the Dutch media and in the national assembly.

'The United Nations and local leaders say this new mission is very desirable and feasible, but we do not want a policy based just on good intentions,' said Bert Koenders of the Labour Party, which opposed the deployment. 'Southern Afghanistan is too dangerous for naivety.'

'In the area where Dutch forces are engaged in reconstruction, there must be no airstrikes ... An airstrike against civilian targets contravenes international law,' another lawmaker said.

The surging Dutch Socialist Party was even more adamant. 'Our party has not supported any mission in Afghanistan,' said leader Harry van Bommel. 'You lose any credibility if you try to fight a war and keep peace in a country simultaneously. In Afghanistan, military action does not curb terrorism, it nurtures terrorism ... all we are is a subcontractor.'

Eventually the Balkenende coalition held and a Dutch mission to Uruzgan was approved, but one with guardrails. The Dutch parliament demanded transparency and a strict respect for human rights and international law with regard to prisoner treatment and transfers. The Dutch were wary of the American way of doing things in Afghanistan, and wanted to be part of a European command structure, not a US command structure.

'There will be a demarcation between Operation Enduring Freedom and ISAF, and Operation Enduring Freedom will only be engaged where needed for direct operations against identified terrorists,' said Dutch defence minister Henk Kamp. 'This must involve clearly identified exceptional cases. A commanding officer in ISAF will be "doublehatted" in the chain of command of both missions' operations; there will be no risk of hiding behind a lack of knowledge or authority.'

John Howard, Alexander Downer and new CDF Angus Houston all had serious concerns about this NATO-led, largely European mission, and were worried that Australian and Dutch military goals and methodologies in Uruzgan might not be aligned.

'They didn't want to do any work that was dangerous,' says Downer. 'I went to The Hague and met with the prime minister and their chief of defence, General [Dick] Berlijn ... at my level we had no problems but militarily there were questions about their remit, like all the non-British European militaries, I suppose.'

After six months, Australia's first special forces element in Uruzgan rotated back to Australia and was replaced by a mirror force, with most of the gunfighters coming from SASR's 1 Squadron. This force arrived in Uruzgan in January 2006 and would work through the winter until May, when the Afghan fighting season began again. The soldiers of this rotation saw no fighting of the scope of the battle in Bagh Khoshak, but that is not to say the Australians didn't get a sense of the danger emerging in the province.

On 5 January, shortly after they arrived in Tarin Kot, a massive suicide bombing rocked the provincial capital, killing ten and injuring as many as 50. According to the Taliban, the target was 'American officials': the detonation happened just a few hundred metres away from the heavily protected US ambassador to Afghanistan, Ronald Neumann, who was in Uruzgan visiting Jan Mohammad and US forces. Witnesses say, however, that the suicide bomber seemingly made no attempt to attack American forces; instead, he gravitated towards a group of men and children who were crowding around to watch a dogfight, and then detonated himself.

This was part of a nascent trend in Afghanistan, only a few months old. There were only two suicide bombings in Afghanistan in 2002, and just three in 2003, but the January 2006 suicide bombing in Tarin Kot was one of 77 such attacks that year. The number and efficacy of suicide bombings in Afghanistan would only increase from there.

'Suicide assailants in Afghanistan and their supporters seem to be mobilized by a number of grievances,' stated a United Nations Assistance Mission in Afghanistan report on the rise of suicide bombing. 'These include a sense of occupation, anger over civilian casualties, and affronts to their national, family, and personal senses of honour and dignity that are perpetrated in the conduct of counterinsurgency operations.'

Also driving the surge was the Quetta Shura, which, having seen the relative success of suicide attacks against Western forces in Iraq, created a religious framework for such attacks: it became accepted among many Pashtuns that the *istihadiyeen* (suicide bombers) were martyrs like any other honourable fighter, and therefore eligible for entry into *jannah* (heaven). There is also some evidence that technical know-how made its way from Iraq to Afghanistan, helping create increasingly sophisticated suicide bombings but also car bombs and improvised explosive devices. The parameters of the David and Goliath fight that was coming to southern Afghanistan were being set, with new tactics being developed on both sides.

In April 2006, a 'medium value target' – designated Objective Rockport on a national-level JPEL – was discovered in Shahidi Hassas, where the SASR were patrolling. Objective Rockford was shaped into an ambush by US artillery, and then killed by operators from SASR's B Troop.

This was likely the first time an Australian element had hunted and killed an enemy combatant named on a kill/capture list since SASR patrols attached to Provincial Reconnaissance Units in Vietnam had killed Viet Cong operatives and sympathisers as part of the CIA's vicious and controversial assassination program known as Phoenix. But Objective Rockford was to be the first of many Australian JPEL killings.

Also in April 2006, Prime Minister Jan Balkenende of the Netherlands was in Canberra for a whistlestop visit to talk to Downer and Howard about Dutch/Australian cooperation. He was surprised when the Australian journalists at a press conference asked him no questions about Afghanistan, instead focusing on Indonesia and climate change. Just two months later, Australian and Dutch special forces soldiers would be engaged in some of the heaviest fighting of the war.

15

'I think I might be busy tonight'

WITH A SHOCK OF red hair, white-walker blue eyes and a stellar military record, Mark Smethurst was already a notable officer within the ADF before he went to Afghanistan to do a crucial job at a crucial time. The son of one of the first SASR commanding officers, Major General Neville Smethurst, Mark Smethurst came to Uruzgan with a service history that included time as an SASR squadron commander, commander of Australia's commando regiment and deputy commander of Australia's special forces in Iraq.

In Uruzgan he would be the commanding officer of the Australian Special Forces Task Group (SFTG) for the third and final special forces rotation in Afghanistan. It comprised an SASR squadron minus and a commando company group minus (fewer shooters than normally in a squadron and company, but including the full headquarters complement) – roughly 200 shooters – tasked with fighting what it was hoped would be Australia's first and last major battles in Uruzgan.

The ground-truthing special forces mission was ending, with Australia's Javelin missiles, Gustafs and almost all the SASR and commando gunfighters leaving Uruzgan, to be replaced by the bulldozers, cement mixers and engineers of Australia's first Reconstruction Task Force (RTF), who would work with the Dutch-led Provincial Reconstruction Team. The PRT was to create roads, schools, medical clinics, courts and police stations, with the aim of destroying any need for and support for the insurgency. To safely allow that transition, a final clearance in Uruzgan was planned, part of a wider ISAF offensive action conducted by US, British, Canadian and Dutch forces that was designed to break the back of the developing insurgency.

After two rotations, the Australians had developed a much better understanding of all the places where resistance to the PRT would come. Given the time and resources available, they were not going to be able to fight in every contested area and pacify Uruzgan. Mark Smethurst knew that. The SFTG would have to be deliberate and incisive with their missions and clearance.

About 25 kilometres north-north-east of Tarin Kot was the town of Chora, and between the provincial capital and the town was a series of villages, compound clusters and farms being fed by a river and tributaries. This pastoral land was dispersed in the Tarin Kot bowl, and then through the area known as Dorafshan, narrowing at the mouth of the Baluchi Valley that then led into the Chora Valley and Chora town. This area was just a small part of Uruzgan, but it was here that Australia's RTF would concentrate their efforts. Their aim was to build a series of police checkpoints between Tarin Kot and Chora, and to establish a safe route, on a paved road, through the area. From a zone of security and prosperity between Tarin Kot and Chora, the PRT might then be able to spread their influence across the wider province.

'Why did we spend so much time in Chora and Baluchi? Because it was relatively close,' Smethurst explains. 'That's what the conventional forces would be able to manage.'

A large-scale clearance mission of those areas was to be undertaken, preceded by a number of smaller missions. Some were to be kill/capture missions, removing from the battlefield those men around whom the resistance might coalesce. Some were existing JPEL targets, but others were discovered and elevated to the JPEL by a new Australian intelligence apparatus, pioneered under Mark Smethurst's command: the Fusion Analysis and Targeting Cell or FATC. This was where intelligence would come in and targets would come out, with increasingly sophistication and decreasing friction.

'This is something I'm very proud of, and it became a model throughout [Australia's time in Uruzgan],' says Smethurst. 'I won't say where we got the intelligence from, but we matured the process because of Iraq. That was the first time we used collection capabilities that we normally wouldn't have on the ground with us. Those lessons were learned from our coalition partners.'

With a clearer intelligence picture, Mark Smethurst found that the area up to Chora was a target-rich environment, but Australia's SFTG was a small element, with negligible ISR and air-support assets – only the helicopters required to get in and out of target locations, and weapons-enabled Predator drones or AC-130 gunships that could lurk and give support to the assaulting force. The SFTG lacked the ability to 'service' all its targets.

Mark Smethurst found that the best way to confront this problem was by working multilaterally, and he sent some targets on to the special forces coalition commanders in Kandahar or Kabul. 'I could have targets approved if they reached a threshold, but what you wanted was to have them approved a high level,' he says. 'The higher level with the right justification, then you got assets assigned.'

The 'higher level' was placing Australia's target on a national-level (US-managed) JPEL list, then marrying Australian intelligence and shooters with assets assigned to service that list.

At the beginning of 2005, American military reporting cited Chora as one of the safest parts of Uruzgan, but by the middle of 2006 the area was no longer a place from which the provincial government had much control of or support. Chora had been one of the places where Hamid Karzai had been sheltered in October 2001 – by Achakzai leader Abdul Khaleq and Barakzai leader Rozi Khan. Both men had since been, in one way or another, marginalised or attacked by Jan Mohammad.

The Achakzai and Barakzai still voiced public support for the Karzai government, but support for the insurgency in Chora built steadily through 2005 and 2006, as it did in much of Uruzgan.

By 2006 the insurgency was no longer just a force of whispered decrees, night letters and assassinations. Considerable tribal support had been built, and in places like Chora, weaponry, plans and commanders had been brought in for pitched battles against the local government and massing infidels. This was a period of hubris for the insurgents, and one in which they would learn a painful lesson about the nature of asymmetrical warfare against a modern enemy.

Before the fighting started in Chora, however, the Australian special forces were active in an area that would prove a deadly headache throughout the war. It was a place where the deaths of Australians and Afghans are closely scrutinised and discussed to this day.

This was Dorafshan, the plain that led into the mouth of the Baluchi Valley only ten or so kilometres from Tarin Kot. With no district centre, no identifiable leader and five distinct tribal groupings, Dorafshan was home to great animosity – against Jan Mohammad, against locals and against outsiders. In the years to come, Dorafshan would receive outsized attention from the Australian military, in reconstruction projects (including the construction of a hospital, a medical centre and a number of schools) but also in vicious and bloody special forces raids.

* * *

Spots on this SFTG rotation – planned as Australia's last – were like payload weight on a space mission: only essentials need apply. Canberra had imposed a hard cap on the numbers allowed on this last special forces rotation, and this meant that every time a support staff member was committed to Uruzgan, the commander in Tarin Kot had one less shooter to send out on operations. Even with the establishment of the FATC, every 'green lanyard' analyst from the intelligence corps or liaison officer from the Australian Signals Directorate (then known as the Defence Signals Directorate) had to be approved by the CDF himself, ensuring a critical mass of gunfighters was maintained. If a job could be done by a local, or by someone back in Australia, then that was how it would be.

This meant that on rotation three there were no Australian cooks in Tarin Kot, and no full-time psychologists either. There was, however, a chaplain. Reverend Rob Sutherland would cater to the spiritual needs of all Australian soldiers in Afghanistan – in Kandahar and in Kabul – but his work was primarily in Uruzgan, where he maintained a prayer room in an abandoned patrol tower and led Bible study classes.

Uruzgan was where snipers came back from action, having seen, down their scopes, the effects of the rounds they fired. Uruzgan was where Australian commandos and SASR operators had killed women as they ferried mortars to enemy fighting positions, and old men and boys who were relaying Australian positions to enemy fighters via ICOM radios. Reverend Sutherland was in the country because these experiences were hard to atone for or reconcile spiritually over the phone, but also to perform a duty he hoped he'd never have to: the repatriation of a fallen Australian soldier.

In the very early morning of 10 June 2006, atop the control tower of the rudimentary airstrip, Reverend Sutherland feared that the day when he must fulfil his darkest task had arrived. A short, helicopter-borne mission lasting no more than half an hour had been planned against a Dorafshan village in which a local doctor had been elevated to the JPEL. The target had been designated as Objective Nile, and the Australians had been cleared for a kill/capture mission.

When two Australian Chinook helicopters from the 5th Aviation Regiment – callsigns Patriot 46 and 47 – flew to Dorafshan, the expectation of casualties was low, but when they landed in the dark and a rattle of explosions and gunfire started – far more than expected – the likelihood of friendly wounded or dead grew.

Patriot 46 and 47 returned to Tarin Kot and the sound of gunfire settled. Nothing could be heard in the control tower except the steady drone of an AC-130 wheeling around the force waiting to be picked up. The coalition owned the night, with their NVGs affording them a distinct tactical advantage over the insurgents, but everyone knew that when the two 25-tonne aircraft returned, the enemy would have a target.

Reverend Sutherland watched the rotors of the Australian helicopters slowly turning as they waited for the call from the assaulting force to bring them home. Just before 3 am, the Chinooks' engines spooled up, and he watched as the helicopters cut a line towards their target, which was only minutes away.

'We could see the engines almost all the way to the target,' says Reverend Sutherland. 'The moment they landed, the whole sky lit up.'

Explosions, gunfire, RPGs and tracers cut through the sky like laser beams, and the deathly heartbeat of an AC-130 cannon was felt as it pounded targets below. Reverend Sutherland could see and hear it all from his position atop the airfield. This was just the start of fight that would grind through the night until dawn. A forlorn thought emerged in his mind: *I think I might be busy tonight.*

* * *

Intelligence placed Objective Nile at the village of Sorkh Morghab, east of the Dorafshan River, and roughly halfway between Tarin Kot and the entrance to the Baluchi Valley. The intelligence package given to the assaulting force suggested that their target would be protected by a small coterie of bodyguards, perhaps three or four armed men.

With the SASR patrols tasked elsewhere, some on reconnaissance and surveillance missions in the mountains above the Baluchi or Chora valleys in preparation for the clearance proper, the assaulting force for this an otherwise largely Australian mission was to be an element of Canadian Special Forces, with two Australians embedded as liaison officers, as well as a CIA paramilitary officer and an element of greenhorn Afghan National Army commandos.

A French Mirage fighter jet flew over the area before the assault, and its optic sensors saw nothing out of the ordinary. The Australian Chinooks, accompanied by two Dutch Apache attack helicopters, took off and headed towards the target location, which was marked by a giant green beam crashing through the night onto the ground ahead. This was an immensely powerful infrared laser being projected by an AC-130, able to be seen only by those wearing NVGs. The locals in the Tarin Kot bowl saw nothing, but for the pilots of Patriot 46 and Patriot 47 it looked like the hand of god – which was what the soldiers called the light.

Also seeing the hand of god was a 30-man element from the 4th Battalion, Royal Australian Regiment (4RAR, later the 2nd Commando Regiment), in three armoured Bushmasters piloted by drivers from the 6th Battalion (6RAR), and in four open Land Rover special reconnaissance vehicles (SRVs). This Australian element, sitting two kilometres south-west of where the laser beam was landing, was the quick reaction force, or QRF – a cavalry to be called in should the strike force need reinforcement.

On approach, the two Dutch Apaches reported an open helicopter landing zone (HLZ), and Patriot 46 and 47 came in to land. A message from the AC-130 crackled over the Chinooks' comms: 'Negative. The HLZs are hot, you have guys all over the place.'

It was too late. The Chinook door gunners started firing their Miniguns blindly into the dusty brownout that had been created by the wash of the rotors, and the Canadian shooters piled out into a situation of zero visibility, each soldier holding the man in front so they didn't become separated. As the Chinooks took off and wheeled back to Tarin Kot, a gunfight began.

The assault force used explosive charges to breach the compound where they expected to find Objective Nile and quickly killed him, but soon afterwards they were attacked by at least a dozen gunmen. The AC-130 then reported more than 100 fighters coming from all directions. The assault force had flown into a *shura* of resistance commanders, and now those men and their bodyguards were fighting the coalition forces. It seemed that a large number of local men had woken and also had joined the fight. When one of the inexperienced Afghan commandos was killed and a number were injured, as well as an American who was mentoring the Afghans, the Australian QRF was beckoned urgently.

Doctrinally, the role of the QRF, and of the Australian commandos, was to overwhelm, but they would be 30 men against at least five times that. They joined the battle well before they reached the Canadians, with many locals taking pot shots at them as they tried to reach the assault force. The Australians may have been outnumbered – a rare occurrence in this war – but they were not outgunned. As they drove towards the Canadians, bullets pinged in at the Australians vehicles, but missiles, grenades and machine-gun fire poured out.

As the assault force garrisoned the compound and waited for the Australian commandos to fight their way to them, the AC-130 smashed ground targets around them, with the plane's hand of god dancing around though the dark, before settling on targets. One Australian described the plane's 105mm cannon as thunder and lightning – the boom of the weapon above being heard before the terrible impact on the ground.

When the commandos reached the Canadian compound, they created, with ordnance, a landing zone from which the assault force could extract. There was a lull in the fighting and Patriot 46 and Patriot 47 were called back to remove the assault force. The Canadians destroyed the house that they had garrisoned, then ran towards the incoming Australian helicopters though a cordon of Australian commandos.

At Patriot 46 and 47 approached, machine-gun and rifle fire and RPG rounds poured into the landing zone. The insurgents had been waiting. The commandos returned and suppressed that fire with heavier weapons, using their distinct advantage of night-vision optics. The commandos successfully covered the extraction as the Australian helicopters flew back to FOB Graceland (also known as Camp Gecko), the home of the Canadian Special Forces in Kandahar, without incident.

But the mission was far from over. There were still 30 Australians in seven vehicles left in a maelstrom. The Australians intercepted a conversation between an Afghan commander and his men, calmly telling them to kill most of the foreigners, but also to capture a few.

In a straight line it was little more than a 20-minute bush-bash back to Tarin Kot, but it took the commandos hours to return. They made their way through a labyrinth of dirt roads and compounds, resolving ambush after ambush, with the enemy fighters leapfrogging ahead of the Australians on motorbikes and setting up machine-gun posts from which they could attack.

Throughout the fight, the AC-130, with an Australian commando plans officer aboard, gave intelligence updates and offered fire support, as did the Apache gunships. Eventually the AC-130 announced it was 'Winchester' – meaning every piece of ammunition on the plane had been expended – and the plane was replaced by a US Air Force B-1 Lancer, which smashed 500-pound bombs into the Tarin Kot bowl ahead of the Australians.

At around 7.45 am, the Australian commando element limped back into their base, Reverend Rob greeting them at the gate of Camp Russell – the start of a tradition. Both the vehicles and the men bore the signs of battle: one Bushmaster had been disabled by enemy fire and was being 'skull-dragged' back in, while many other vehicles were bullet-scarred, inside and out, and blackened and dented from impacts and blasts. Some of the vehicles would never be the same, but the men were all alive, having killed approximately 150 Afghans.

The Australian commandos had acted with extreme valour and utility in resolving an incredibly dangerous situation without any Australian casualties – but had the mission been a success? For the commandos and for SOCOMD it undoubtedly had been. The commandos had been largely sidelined in Iraq, and so were untested in battle. Now they had introduced themselves to Afghanistan and to the coalition as a force whose training, equipment, composition and mettle was well suited to battle there.

For the SFTG, too, the mission was considered a military

success. Their task was to kill or capture an insurgent commander and he was dead. Many other insurgents had presented themselves for elimination too, without needing to be hunted. But in the larger calculus of the war, and within the overall mission of ISAF, had the operation been a net positive?

Bitter fighting had taken place in the Tarin Kot bowl, planes had been used to strike targets, houses were smashed to bits with 500-pound bombs. All of this, of course, affected what the military call the 'human terrain'. Perhaps another people in another place can be pounded into submission and subjugation – but, as history suggests, not the Pashtuns.

* * *

In 2009, David Kilcullen published a book titled *The Accidental Guerrilla*. One of its central premises was that when fighting a big insurgent war, such as those in Afghanistan or Iraq, one must try not to be drawn into smaller wars against or between tribes, factions or families. Fighting the enemy is an essential part of a counterinsurgency campaign, but to make inessential enemies is to court defeat.

Kilcullen describes a patrol undertaken by US special forces in Uruzgan outside the Tarin Kot bowl just a month before the mission against Objective Nile. One American died and seven others were injured in a coordinated attack using heavy weapons, mortars and dug-in sniper positions. Also attacking the Americans were farmers who were working in fields nearby, who dropped their tools and ran home, in some instances five kilometres, to pick up their weapons and join the fight. In interviews later, some of the farmers said they had neither affiliation with nor affection for the Taliban and were 'generally well disposed to the Americans', but honour dictated that they join the fight against the outsiders.

For some Pashtuns, the call of honour was strong when hearing the sound of guns, but far stronger when their family members or their homes had been attacked. Had the prosecution of Objective Nile taken fighters off the battlefield, or inspired more to join it?

16

'I saw things in Afghanistan and I did things in Afghanistan ... that I'm not proud of, and I live with that'

THEY WERE WAITING FOR Ben Roberts-Smith, talking, stamping their feet and blowing into their hands. The tools of their trade were slung over their shoulders or were in their hands – not at attention but ready for when their target arrived. When he approached them, he was unmissable. As the television executive saw them, he didn't drop his head, as many arriving in court do. He strode tall, eyes ahead, a foot taller than many of those who massed around him, and seemingly a foot wider at the chest too.

They rushed at him, photographers and cameramen, journalists from print, radio, television and online outlets. They knew their target would give no meaningful comment, but they needed a grab nonetheless. They needed vision for their stories about the opening arguments in what was the Australian defamation trial of the century.

It was 2021, and since the cessation of Australia's special forces war in Afghanistan, a series of media reports by Nine Media through Fairfax newspapers had been printed, posted, published and broadcast that alleged immense wrongdoing by the former SASR corporal and Victoria Cross recipient Ben Roberts-Smith. He claimed that these reports were false and defamatory, and had brought the matter to trial. He would therefore be the first witness called.

The image of Australia's most famous soldier standing in front of a Federal Court judge would be dramatic. Regardless of whether one considered Roberts-Smith a hero for confronting those whom he described as 'bullies', or a murderer finally about to be exposed (albeit in a civil court), it would be a day of unmissable drama.

I ducked into the Federal Court as Ben Roberts-Smith was slowed by the media pack on the street, moved through security and stepped into the lift that would take me up to court 18D. As the doors closed, a large hand with an expensive watch stopped them. Ben Roberts-Smith entered the lift and breathed in and out deliberately. This would be the first courtroom engagement of a very long campaign.

There is surely no operator like Ben Roberts-Smith. For a start, his height and bulk are unusual for role that requires the endurance of a long-distance runner, but his background is also unusual. His father, Len Roberts-Smith, was a Justice of the Supreme Court of Western Australia and had a long and celebrated career in the Army Reserve, eventually earning the rank of major general as he became the Judge Advocate General (JAG) of the ADF, making him the most senior person in Australia's military justice system. Ben was educated at Hale School, an exclusive Anglican private school in Perth, as was his brother Sam, now a famous opera singer.

It's perhaps not surprising that Roberts-Smith joined the military after leaving school: 'few institutions in this country's history can boast an armed services involvement such as that of Hale School', according to the Old Haleians Association. The vast number of Old Haleians who join the Australian military do so as officers, but Ben Roberts-Smith joined as an enlisted soldier and was posted to a rifle company.

As a soldier, Roberts-Smith saw 17 years of full-time service – seven as part of 3RAR, and the rest in the SASR. He left full-time service as a corporal, a relatively junior rank for someone with the experience he garnered. It seems, however, that Roberts-Smith knew exactly the career he wanted in the military, and he attained it. He was often in the midst of the action, and sometimes acted with disregard for his own safety.

After leaving the military in 2013, Roberts-Smith completed an MBA and became an executive at the Seven Network, taking leave from his job as the general manager of Seven Television Queensland in 2021 as he prepared for the defamation trial.

Ben Roberts-Smith would appear in the witness box to present his grievances and explain the loss of reputation and income he claimed to have experienced. The aim was to set a baseline from which a monetary reckoning could be built, should the opposing side be unable to establish the truth of their claims. Afghan and Australian witnesses would follow, with the expectation being that 21 current and former SASR operators would give testimony. Some of those men were the sources for the critical stories about Roberts-Smith that were published in the Australia media.

Roberts-Smith's primary legal team, veteran defamation lawyer Bruce McClintock SC and Arthur Moses SC (the latter was then known as the boyfriend of former New South Wales premier Gladys Berejiklian), would accuse these sources of lying, and also of cowardice, ineptitude and jealousy. They would claim a large and coordinated smear campaign was mounted against Ben Roberts-Smith, one that started with rumours, then progressed to media interviews and, finally, to perjury.

'This is a case of courage, devotion to duty, self-sacrifice and, perhaps most important of all, surpassing skill in soldiering on one hand,' said McClintock in his opening address. 'On the other hand, it's a case about dishonest journalism, corrosive jealousy, cowardice and lies ... led by bitter people, jealous of [Ben Roberts-Smith's] courage and success, aided by credulous journalists.'

The barristers representing Nine Media (formerly Fairfax Media) – primarily Nicholas Owens SC, who was known in legal circles for acting on large property matters – would allege in return that all of the reporting published about Ben Roberts-Smith was true and accurate, and that it told a story of bloodlust, self-aggrandisement and cover-up.

Both stories would largely focus on 2012, when the bulk of Roberts-Smith's and Australia's war crimes were alleged to have

Green Beret captain Jason Amerine (far right), with his A-Team ODA 594 and Hamid Karzai (centre, dark lungi) on 3 December 2001. After seizing Tarin Kot in Uruzgan and killing hundreds of Taliban repelling a counter-offensive, the Taliban leadership offered Karzai a peace deal. It was a deal acceptable to Karzai, who had then become interim leader of Afghanistan, but not to the US administration.

The SASR patrol Bravo 3 returning from Operation Anaconda, one of the largest battles of the war in Afghanistan, in 2002. Patrol commander Matthew Bouillaut (far right) was awarded the Distinguished Service Cross for his role and was later part of the shadowy Task Force Black in Iraq. His 2IC Blaine Diddums (far left) was killed in Uruzgan in 2012 while conducting a JPEL mission in the Chora Valley.

In 2001, Mattiulah (later Mattiulah Khan) fought alongside Jason Amerine and his A-Team in the Battle of Tarin Kot. Then he was then a poor and illiterate taxi driver, but later became a brutal millionaire militia leader, and Australia's primary special forces partner, earning the moniker 'Australia's Warlord'. *US Navy / Jacob Dillon*

An Electronic Warfare Operator brandishes two weapons during operations in Afghanistan on the last SOTG rotation. These EWO's were at the heart of JPEL operations, often locating targets through their mobile telephone signals in what former ADF intelligence colonel Mick Lehmann has described as a 'covert but deadly game of Marco Polo.'

A JPEL target designated Objective Brick being questioned by an Australian SOTG member. It was closely guarded secret that the rules of engagement allowed Australian special forces to kill JPEL targets without attempt at capture. Some soldiers believed they had on obligation to attempt capture if they could, others did not.

Former SASR captain and now Liberal MP Andrew Hastie (right) campaigning with former prime minister John Howard. Mr Hastie thought the JPEL rules of engagement may have incentivised killing over capture in Afghanistan as: 'You could launch on a target using a SIGINT trigger [for instance, a JPEL target using their phone] but you couldn't use that SIGINT trigger as a way of keeping them locked.' *Newspix / Justin Benson-Cooper*

Caches of weapons were often discovered during special forces operations, as was the case in the attack on the Whiskey 108 compound. Here an Australian soldier holds out an AK-47 variant, one of many weapons recovered from a tunnel discovered at Whiskey 108 in a village in Dorafshan. This image is from a tranche of evidence used in the defamation case brought by Ben Roberts-Smith against Nine Media.

Australian ASLAV and Bushmaster vehicles patrol a village in the Mehrabad Valley. This area was home to tribes who had historical enmity with the warlord partners of the Australian and US military. After the ousting of the Taliban in 2001 and 2002, these tribes were marginalised or attacked and many of those tribes joined the insurgency. The Mehrabad Valley was an area of particular interest for Australia's commando regiment. *Nine Fairfax / Angela Wylie*

Mark Wales, then a captain in SASR, was deeply sceptical of the kill/capture program, saying that it created dangerous incentives, depleted the SASR operationally and morally, and was not creating the outcomes that were wanted. 'All I knew was that there would be no line drawn under the JPEL,' he said.

Major-General Cantwell, then commanding officer of all Australian military in Afghanistan, speaks to the opposition leader Tony Abbott in Afghanistan in October 2010. Cantwell became disillusioned with the war, saying all the Australian mission was doing was 'digging a well of misery.' *Newspix / Gary Ramage*

Then Defence Minister Joel Fitzgibbon flanked by Chief of Defence Angus Houston and Deputy Prime Mister Julia Gillard at the funeral of SOTG member Brett Till. Fitzgibbon often struggled with lack of transparency from the ADF and after he got a handle on the war he believed his first job as minister was to make sure we 'not immerse ourselves further into the [Afghan] mire.' *Newspix / Sam Mooy*

A compound in Uruzgan, designated by the coalition as Whiskey 108, that was bombed (inset) and then raided by the SASR. This was where, it was alleged by Nine Media, that Ben Roberts-Smith was involved in two murders, including a victim with a prosthetic leg. Roberts-Smith claimed that the man was killed legally and that he had believed the man may have been JPEL Target Objective Xiphoid, a local bombmaker.

In 2006, General Stanley McChyrstal assumed command of the elite US Joint Special Operations Command or JSOC, and turned the command into what Dr John Nagl describes as an 'almost industrial-scale counterterrorism killing machine.' The Australian special forces took many processes and technologies from General McChrystal's command. *US Navy / Mark O'Donald*

Ben Roberts-Smith was invited to Buckingham Palace in 2011, as much of his troop was in Western Australia training for what would be a highly controversial deployment. 'In general terms, as a monarch, she was very happy with our progress, and that's something I'll pass on to the lads when I get home,' Roberts-Smith told the media. *Anthony Devlin / AFP via Getty Images*

The only Australian civilian casualty of the war in Afghanistan, David Savage, was tasked with stabilisation in the Chora Valley close to Tarin Kot. Stabilisation and reconstruction were designed to be a carrot to the JPEL stick but Savage says money was spent haphazardly and may have furthered the insurgency. Savage was blown up by a child suicide bomber in 2012, leaving him a paraplegic.

Operators from SASR's 2 Squadron in Afghanistan with some members of their local partner force. In November 2020, and in response to the IGADF report about alleged war crimes in Afghanistan, it was announced that this squadron would be taken off the Army's order of battle and soldiers would be re-tasked as the bulk of murder allegations centred around the actions of this squadron.

occurred. But the stories started in 2006, during Roberts-Smith's first tour of Afghanistan, just before the killing of Objective Nile.

* * *

Ben Roberts-Smith was part of a five-man SASR patrol commanded by a British SBS NCO on secondment designated Kilo-2. In June 2006, the patrol was tasked with secreting into the mountains above the Baluchi and Chora valleys in preparation for a coalition assault below.

Kilo-2 was to establish an elevated bird's-nest position and stay concealed. From there, the patrol would observe the 'pattern of life', attempting to discern civilians from combatants, and identify potential enemy positions and weapons. When the assault started, Kilo-2 would coordinate airstrikes; a JTAC had been added to the patrol for that endeavour. In many ways Kilo-2's mission would, ideally, be similar to the one Matthew Bouillaut and his patrol had conducted in Shah-i-Kot four years earlier.

In the afternoon of the last day of May 2006, a troop-sized SASR element made its way north in vehicles through the Tarin Kot bowl to the desert east of Baluchi, and at last light the convoy dropped off Kilo-2 at the base of a mountain called Koran Ghar. For ten hours through the night, each man climbed with a pack weighing 50 to 60 kilograms to the patrol's lying-up position, a relatively flat area with steep drop-offs on either side from which they could see the town of Chora and the Chora pass below. With seven days' worth of supplies, the element was tasked with staying clandestine for the duration of the patrol, and supporting any engagement below.

On 1 June there was intense fighting below them. The rest of the SASR troop, K Troop, and the supporting Australian commandos fought alongside Dutch Korps Commandotroepen and the Afghan National Army against entrenched militia throughout the day. Unlike in later engagements, when the militia would disappear in the face of overwhelming force, this insurgent force dug in, using pre-established fighting positions and attempting to remain in control of the valley. The militia were being devastated, but offered strong resistance. A number of Afghan army personnel were killed. Some Australians were injured, including the SASR's Sergeant Andrew Cave, who was seriously wounded after an RPG round exploded above his head.

During the fight, Kilo-2's observation post directed Dutch Apache attack helicopters and a number of US aircraft, including A-10 Warthogs, against enemy positions, especially those where Afghan recoilless rifles and mortars were found. K Troop withdrew, with what one soldier described as a 'bit of a bloody nose'.

On 2 June, an unarmed Afghan boy, described in court as 'looking about 14 or 15 years of age', appeared in front of Kilo-2's observation post on a goat track, wearing a traditional waistcoat and *pakol* cap. He was seen by two operators, who watched the boy walk out of sight, but a minute later he reappeared, retracing his steps as he walked away from the observation post. He was carrying a small bag he hadn't been seen carrying earlier. They decided the boy hadn't seen them, and sent a message to the lying-up position nearby, saying that a local boy had walked past.

Two soldiers from the lying-up position, Matthew Locke and Ben Roberts-Smith, then found the boy and killed him.

A patrol commander's situation report, admitted into evidence, said this:

ACM [anti-coalition militia] MEMBER APPEARED TO BE AGGRESSIVELY PATROLING, BOTH HANDS ON WEAPON, READY TO FIRE. LOST SIGHT OF ACM MEMBER IN DEAD GROUND. K22 & K25 [Locke's and Roberts-Smith's callsigns] DISPATCHED AND NEUTRALISED ACM MEMBER.

When talking with a researcher at the Australian War Memorial, Ben Roberts-Smith said two males were discovered atop Koran Ghar, and that he and Locke, the second-in-command of Kilo-2, 'hunted them down and got rid of them'. It's agreed by all now, however, that there was only one male and that he was unarmed; Ben Roberts-Smith said he likely confused that killing with another incident. No explanation has been offered for the patrol commander's inaccurate report.

What is in question now, however, is whether the boy needed to be killed, regardless of whether he was an enemy 'spotter' or not. Temporally, this was the first point of contention in Roberts-Smith defamation trial.

Patrols like Kilo-2 were given discretionary powers to decide who might or might not be a 'spotter' – that is, an individual who was relaying information about Australian positions to the enemy – so that is not at issue. But whether it was the correct tactical decision for Kilo-2 to break cover, kill the boy and potentially expose their own position was and remains a contested one within the patrol and regiment.

Bullets from Matthew Locke's M4 hit the boy first, and then rounds from Ben Roberts-Smith's SR-25 sniper rifle. Both weapons were suppressed, meaning they made less noise than an unsuppressed weapon, but there is no such thing as a silent gun, and the shots that killed the boy rang out across the mountaintop and through the valley. A decision was made to leave the boy's body in the open, and the patrol went to '100 per cent stand to', waiting for an attack from an alerted enemy. None came – until, a few hours after the boy was killed, voices were heard to the east or north of Kilo-2's position.

Armed men were observed and a fight ensued. One Afghan was killed by Locke, and another escaped. Locke gave chase and then, on a jutting ridgeline, the two men exchanged gunfire at close range. This is not an ideal scenario for the SASR, which historically has been a force that prefers to kill from a distance or with the element of surprise. Although Locke was likely a far superior marksman with a superior weapon, close-quarters battle undoubtedly evened the contest.

Ben Roberts-Smith brought his sniper rifle to bear against some other Afghans. At one point another Australian soldier fired his Para Minimi machine gun at what he believed to be enemy.

After a few rounds this soldier, the most junior in the patrol, had a gun stoppage. After resolving that stoppage, he had another. He had forgotten to bring gun oil, essential for his machine gun to work at full efficiency.

Under the broad afternoon sun, Afghans were drawn to the mountaintop fight. Gunfights raged in multiple directions at Kilo-2's position, and the Australians were slowly but surely surrounded as they adopted an 'all round defence' posture. 'Danger close' gun runs were requested around their position, meaning the planes would be firing very close to their friendly forces.

A-10 Warthogs – warplanes that have been described as a giant gun with a plane wrapped around it – were brought on station. Soon the screaming-fart sound of 30mm Avenger cannons filled the valley, smashing 3900 heavy rounds a minute just beyond Kilo-2. The Warthogs then left the engagement to attend to a Canadian gun run request elsewhere.

The enemy were still close. They could be heard. If Kilo-2 were overrun, they would receive no mercy; the craggy peak of Koran Ghar would undoubtedly be the grave of every man in the patrol. If they survived until sunset, they would likely escape, their NVGs giving them a sense the enemy would lack. Throughout the day, Kilo-2 had trouble connecting themselves with the larger SASR force in the valley below, and also with the command and control element in Tarin Kot, but late in the afternoon they managed to pass a message on: 'Zero Alpha ... in close contact requesting immediate air support. Without air, we may not be able to hold this position.'

In Tarin Kot and at Bagram Air Base, Australian officers petitioned for Kilo-2 to be reprioritised. The A-10 Warthogs were taken away from the Canadian engagement and to the battle atop Koran Ghar. With Warthogs patrolling above and the sun waning, Kilo-2 gained the initiative again. That night an AC-130, on station in preparation for the assault, scanned the mountaintop for Kilo-2 and saw no movement around them, so Kilo-2 went to '50 per cent stand to'.

Through the night, they provided overwatch for an American night assault below and, in shifts, some of the soldiers slept, including the junior soldier who had forgotten to bring gun oil. In court, Ben Roberts-Smith has said this man suffered a night terror atop Koran Ghar, waving his machine gun in a near-fugue state and shouting, 'Friendly, friendly!' This allegation was contested by that soldier in court.

Just before dawn's light, the patrol put their packs on and left the way they'd come. Kilo-2 slipped away to join the larger force, physically together but now a patrol deeply riven.

'The task for the mission was to observe and surveil ... not to become decisively engaged,' said one of the operators on the mission while giving evidence in the trial. 'That was to be avoided at all costs, because it then affects your ability to complete your larger mission.'

Later, the junior soldier who forgot the gun oil – who is still in the SASR and now holds the rank of sergeant – said in court that Ben Roberts-Smith bailed him up after the patrol and told him that if his performance didn't improve, he was 'going to get a bullet in the back of the head'. He said he believed that this was not a euphemistic threat, but a literal one.

Back in the hermetic confines of a Sydney courtroom, Nicholas Owens SC asked Ben Roberts-Smith why there was so much inconsistent reporting about the mission at Koran Ghar, a mission for which Roberts-Smith was awarded a medal for bravery.

'You did not want the Australian public to find out you'd won a medal for shooting an unarmed teenager?' asked Owens.

'Not only do I find that a disgusting comment, it's completely false,' Roberts-Smith fired back. 'I saw things in Afghanistan and I did things in Afghanistan like having to engage adolescents that I'm not proud of and I live with that. I accept that and that is a trauma I've lived with.'

Perhaps Roberts-Smith found the comment disgusting, but it was far from the most extreme allegation that had been made. In court 18D, there was a lot of ground to cover and a lot of war still to come.

* * *

One evening after attending the trial, I was interviewing Alexander Downer. He was in Kensington, London, and I in Sydney. He was aware the trial was happening but wasn't following it. We spoke about some of the specifics and the circumstances around the trial.

'There's a part of me – a part, not the whole part – that reminds people that this is war,' Downer says. 'You put the army into these situations, not aid workers. You send them heavily armed and heavily trained. Mainly men, young men … I can understand how they can be a little bit trigger-happy. I cut them a lot of slack.

'Don't send the SAS in if you're worried they're going to kill someone,' Downer laughs. 'Of course they're going to kill someone. They're *trained* to kill someone.'

* * *

Operation Perth, as the large Australian clearance through to Chora was designated, began 72 hours after Kilo-2 left Koran Ghan. It was a massive operation combining conventional and unconventional warfighting.

During the day, the Australian commandos and their coalition partners would fight through villages in traditional clearance operations, and then at night the SASR would sneak into compounds of interest, punch holes in the compound walls and 'service' JPEL targets.

It's estimated that between 200 and 400 Afghans were killed during Operation Perth, which was part of a much larger coalition action across the south called Operation Mountain Thrust. At least 1000 Afghans were killed in this larger operation, but likely more. More than 100 friendly Afghan soldiers were killed, along with 24 American and six British soldiers. The Australian SFTG suffered 11 injuries.

Much of the Australian fighting in the Chora and Baluchi valley was believed to be against local fighters, but there was evidence that a contingent of enemy fighters had come from outside the region, the province and even the country. There had been an influx of auxiliary Taliban fighters before the fight, and it seems some of the outsiders who had been killed had been targeted by locals such as the Barakzai militia and tribal leader Rozi Khan, who had led a resistance against the insurgents in Chora.

In August, the handover between SFTG officers and the RTF officers began. By September, the bulk of the SFTG left Afghanistan, most of the FATC going with them. Some of their last intercepts between Quetta and Uruzgan were buoying for the Australians: the Taliban commanders in Pakistan were urging their ground commanders to continue the fight, but those commanders were saying they could not.

Though the job was far from done, Mark Smethurst was somewhat satisfied. The strategy had been to smash a hole through the resistance up through to Chora, which they hoped the conventional army could help fill with Afghan government services. They had smashed that hole, and killed many Afghans designated as key insurgent leaders. Furthermore, through three special forces rotations, the Australians had suffered no fatalities.

* * *

In the period after the removal of the SFTG and after Mountain Thrust, Afghans across the south of the country returned to war-racked villages to rebuild homes, bury fathers and sons and prepare for winter. For the coalition and Afghan government, this was the time to consolidate the opportunities afforded by the fighting – but they were not seized. As winter took hold in the Chora and Baluchi valleys, insurgent groups bloodlessly started to assume control again.

In November, John Howard, Alexander Downer, Brendan Nelson and Governor-General Michael Jeffery – a former commanding officer of the SASR himself – visited Holsworthy Barracks, home of Australia's commandos, to award a Star of Gallantry, a medal for bravery second only to the Victoria Cross, to the sergeant in command of the bullet- and RPG-strafed vehicle that led the way in the fight back to Tarin Kot after Objective Nile was killed.

A similar ceremony was also undertaken at Campbell Barracks in Perth, home of the SASR, in which three operators were awarded the Medal of Gallantry and one the Commendation of Gallantry. Medals of Gallantry were awarded to Matthew Locke and Ben Roberts-Smith for their actions at Koran Ghar, and their citations were read out during the ceremony.

These citations were one of the few ways the civilian leadership could gain an understanding of what soldiers were experiencing in Afghanistan. Brendan Nelson says he found one of them particularly affecting, and he read three it times:

> On the 2nd June, the Observation Post had become the focus of the Anti-Coalition Militia force and repeated attempts to locate and surround the position ensued. In one particular incident the Militia attempted to outflank the Observation Post. Lance Corporal Roberts-Smith was part of a two man team tasked to move out of their relatively secure Observation Post in order to locate and neutralize the Militia and regain the initiative. This task was successfully achieved.

* * *

After Ben Roberts-Smith left the stand in courtroom 18D, he was replaced by Dr Brendan Nelson – considerably shorter, wearing a fine suit, with his clipped grey hair combed back and a black facemask, which he removed before giving his evidence.

The former leader of the federal Liberal Party appeared not as an expert or material witness, but as a character witness in support of Ben Roberts-Smith. Dr Nelson was at times emotional on the stand as he spoke about newspaper articles that he clearly thought were not in the public interest. His praise of Ben Roberts-Smith was not so much glowing as nuclear-powered, calling the former soldier 'one of the greatest Australians'.

'Ben Roberts-Smith, VC, MG was the most respected, admired and revered Australian soldier in the last half-century,' Dr Nelson said on the stand. 'Men and women … would want to be with him, to shake his hand, perhaps to have a photograph. In some cases at the Australian War Memorial, I saw people fall into his arms, very emotionally describing their experiences.'

Dr Nelson's evidence primarily related not to his time as defence minister, but in his later role as director of the Australian War Memorial, a position in which he shared a boss with Ben Roberts-Smith. In the organisational chart of the Australian War Memorial, Dr Nelson reported to the Council Chair of the Australian War Memorial, Seven West Media owner Kerry Stokes. When Ben Roberts-Smith became the general manager of Seven Queensland, the former soldier also reported to Kerry Stokes, who happened to be covering the considerable legal costs accrued by Roberts-Smith in bringing this defamation case to trial. (There is no suggestion that Dr Nelson would represent himself any way in court but truly and honestly.)

Dr Nelson left his position at the Australian War Memorial in 2020 to take up a role as the president of Boeing's Australia, New Zealand and South Pacific division, which makes, in roughly equal measure by way of revenue, commercial aviation products and defence-related products. I interviewed Nelson as he sat at his work desk, behind which was a bookcase packed with military memorabilia: Australian Army slouch hats from years gone by, caps worn by Australian special forces operators in Afghanistan, replica medals for bravery. There were also large and small replica Boeing planes, among them one small passenger plane and seven larger military planes, including some of those that had roared over Uruzgan in support of Australian troops.

We talked almost exclusively about his time as Australia's defence minister, but we did briefly touch on the defamation trial. While watching Dr Nelson's testimony, I had seen how invested he was in the case: he was one of the few senior people in the military/civilian apparatus to have defended Roberts-Smith continuously and publicly. Only a small part of the evidence that

Dr Nelson gave related to the truth of the allegations that the newspapers had published; mostly it was about Roberts-Smith's inspiring feats of arms.

I wondered whether Dr Nelson's opinion of Roberts-Smith was formed solely from his knowledge of these feats of arms, regardless of any potential moral or criminal transgressions. As the interview came to an end, I asked Dr Nelson whether, if it were proven beyond any doubt that Roberts-Smith had committed the war crimes of which he had been accused, his opinion of Roberts-Smith would change.

Dr Nelson's answer was uncharacteristically quick and flat.

'No.'

Then he continued: 'There are many Australian soldiers alive because of his courage and what he did. If he has done something wrong in terms of the rules of armed engagement in Afghanistan, then that becomes a part of this story, but it doesn't change my opinion of him, nor my support of him.'

17

'The Americans wanted us to do the dirty work ...
we were prepared to do it'

'WE WERE GETTING ADVICE from the special forces ... going,
"You're all going to die. You're just going to be shot at and you're
all going to die."' This was how Major Clare O'Neill of the
Reconstruction Task Force describes her arrival in Uruzgan in a
documentary series made by the ABC.

When the RTF arrived in Uruzgan for a handover from
the special forces, neither group could quite believe what was
happening. In the places where, only a few weeks before, the SASR
and Australia's commandos (not to mention AC-130 gunships
and B-1 bombers) had all but emptied their ammunition at fixed
fighting positions and company-sized enemy elements, now
a group of engineers were going to attempt to deploy tractors,
bulldozers and shovels.

A tiny contingent of SASR would stay to help with intelligence
gathering, but they could do little by way of clearance, force
protection or kill/capture. In one of their first missions, the
RTF attempted to build two police checkpoints in Dorafshan.
The Afghan security force manned the checkpoints for less than
two days before abandoning them, and when armoured vehicles
returned to the police checkpoints, they found the buildings
destroyed and burned.

'The more we went on and the more we learned, the more
we appreciated just how little we understood that society,' says

O'Neill. In the eyes of the people she was trying to help, she recalls, she could see a plaintive request: 'Just leave. You're going to do more harm than good.'

* * *

For the first five months of his tenure as defence minister, Brendan Nelson believed that, should anything happen in the places where Australian soldiers were deployed that required ministerial attention or knowledge, someone from the Russell Offices, the administrative home of the ADF, would contact him. Then, on 21 June 2006, he was disavowed of that belief.

On that day a security detachment of Australian soldiers in Baghdad was conducting a mission to the offices of the Iraqi trade minister in preparation for an Australian diplomatic visit. Iraqi officials say they weren't told of the visit, but when they saw the Australian armoured vehicles arriving they attempted to clear traffic for their guests, sending the trade minister's bodyguards to do the job. Mistaking the bodyguards for insurgents, the Australians started shooting. Three bodyguards sustained gunshot wounds and one died.

Nelson wasn't notified of the event when it happened, and only learned about it hours later, via a US media report. Shocked, Nelson called his defence liaison and was surprised to find that Russell was refusing to supply him with any information about the attack even after he requested it.

'I'm the minister, trying to get that information, but I'm in my office watching CNN and I'm seeing the carnage in Baghdad on my TV screen, and I remember asking defence leadership: "Why is it I can get this information from television … but I can't get this from my own department?"'

Nelson says he knew the ADF was 'highly protective of giving any information to the public', and far less transparent than allies like the United States, but he didn't know that this lack of transparency would also extend to him, the responsible minister.

In the organisational structure of the Australian military, both the secretary of the Department of Defence (a civilian) and the Chief of Defence report to the minister and are subordinate, and yet Australian defence ministers have often found it difficult to get full transparency from the ADF. This is partly because the government's role within the Australian defence structure is usually restricted to authorisation and empowerment, not execution.

'Once our government, our executive, makes a decision that war needed to be fought, we hand it over to the military with the objective we think [is justified, and then] we let them go and do it,' says Nelson.

The government does have discretionary power over military decisions, although it's unusual for it to use that authority. One time Nelson did wish to exercise his discretionary power was regarding the military's assessment that Australia's special forces should be removed from Uruzgan after three rotations.

Time limitations of the special forces deployments were an essential part of the agreement John Howard and Alexander Downer had made with the Americans after Chief of Defence Angus Houston explained that the Australian special forces simply couldn't maintain an ongoing large kinetic deployment overseas without being stretched, changed or degraded. Nelson, however, believed that the Australian special forces should go back into Uruzgan, and it seems he found supporters in the uniformed ranks.

'I arranged to see [SOCAUST] Mike Hindmarsh,' Nelson explains. 'I said, "Are you supportive of this idea? Isn't this like weed control? You need to keep weeds under control, you need to maintain it." I unsuccessfully tried to convince Howard and Downer that we should keep the special forces there. I was fairly forward-leaning on that [but] my view didn't prevail.'

A series of factors eventually resulted in that decision being reversed. Operation Mountain Thrust had not had the desired effect. NDS head Amrullah Saleh met the NATO commanders in September 2006 and explained that there were still four provinces in Afghanistan in imminent danger of falling to the insurgency: Helmand, Farah, Zabul and Uruzgan.

Saleh said that, according to his intelligence assessment, Uruzgan was being used as a safe haven and for rest, recovery and medical treatment by the Taliban, and that his agency estimated there were still more than 60 armed groups in the province supporting the insurgency. The Dutch were now entrenched in Uruzgan, but the Americans had concerns about the focus of the Dutch efforts there, and about how their forces were prosecuting the war.

A leaked diplomatic cable to Secretary of State Condoleezza Rice from one of her staff in preparation for the arrival in Washington DC of the Dutch foreign minister, Ben Bot, was candid about the tenuous relationship between the Bush administration and the Dutch: 'The current [Dutch] government's close ties to the U. S. have not been without cost to the coalition government or to Bot personally.' The cable claimed this was primarily because of US war policies such as the rendition and torture of detainees. The cable praised the Dutch military for 'killing the enemy' in Uruzgan, but said that 'the Dutch continue to place a higher emphasis on "hearts and minds" reconstruction efforts than on the hunt for terrorists – combat missions have been largely reactive instead of proactive'.

While the Dutch military were perhaps capable and also willing to conduct offensive missions and to prosecute JPEL targets, it could have been politically damaging for the Dutch government if it was publicised that such missions were being undertaken by its military. Brendan Nelson says of the Dutch in Uruzgan that 'they were hesitant to do the things that we thought ... needed to be done, and they were reticent to conduct kinetic operation[s], including hunting high-value targets [who] needed to be captured or killed'.

'The Americans wanted us to do the dirty work,' says Nelson. 'We were ... I was about to say "happy", but that's not quite the right word. We were prepared to do it because we could do it and we would do it.'

As the Dutch tried to keep at arm's length from the American military and intelligence machine, Canberra was trying embrace it, and that attempt at closeness may have been another reason for special forces reinsertion in Afghanistan. In the wake of Australia's commitment to the invasion of Iraq, President Bush had signed a directive, supported by Donald Rumsfeld and acting CIA director John McLaughlin, that laws preventing foreign powers from seeing highly classified intelligence would no longer apply to Australia when that intelligence related to counterterrorism or combat operations.

In the wake of that directive, Australian intelligence agencies and the military had found that the order was not being respected, and a large amount of US intelligence marked 'NOFORN' (no foreign eyes) was still being withheld from Australian agencies. In some instances, this was even intelligence that had been collected by Australia.

Britain was in a similar situation. They were the only other nation authorised to receive NOFORN intelligence, and yet the British military found a great deal of it was out of bounds for them. US journalist Bob Woodward noted in his book *State of Denial* that even the British pilots flying certain American warplanes weren't allowed to read parts of the classified pilot manuals.

John Howard petitioned Bush directly to bring the directive into full effect, and even made a public statement criticising the US military and intelligence agencies. 'There is always a degree of inter-agency jealousy about anybody having access to these things, even very close allies, and it did take a lot of pushing,' Howard notes.

Australia did eventually gain access to an array of intelligence products previously denied to it. Australian defence and intelligence organisations were given further access to SIPRNet, an intelligence product repository described as a secret internet inside the internet, and also far more sensitive material and capabilities. It's not known whether the reinsertion of Australia's special forces into Uruzgan was a chit that Australia used to trade for intelligence products and technological upgrades, but it is known that Australia's special forces and intelligence agencies used some of the most sensitive US intelligence material in JPEL operations, including satellite imagery and SIGINT capabilities and equipment.

John Howard announced on 10 April 2007 that the Australian special forces would soon be reinserting into Uruzgan so they would be active before the 2007 fighting season. He also stated that this would be another strictly time-limited deployment, with Australia scheduled to leave in 2009. The special forces reinserted into Afghanistan as a reassembled entity now known as the Special Operations Task Group (SOTG), which was to be larger than the SFTG and comprised two distinct and independent combat entities: Force Element Alpha, the SASR; and Force Element Bravo, Australia's commandos, a force now battle-hardened and, for the first time, deployed into Afghanistan with their own officer in charge.

* * *

When assuming control of Uruzgan, the Dutch created a whole-of-government-body command element combining their military and civilian efforts, then titled Task Force Uruzgan. This entity was controlled by a 'duumvir', meaning that two people would be in charge together – one a Dutch colonel, and the other a senior Dutch diplomat. In the Dutch system, the diplomat, who reported to Dutch government, would not be subordinate to the colonel; and the colonel, who reported to the Dutch military, would not be subordinate to the diplomat. The system was designed to ensure maximum transparency and military–civilian coordination, and it reflected the way the Dutch saw the conflict.

The Dutch assumed an ethnographic focus in Uruzgan. They planned to attempt to create tribal balance, using what was being called an 'inkblot plan'. They would try to secure a handful of population centres; build public services, roads and governance; and establish influence and security in those areas. They would attempt to do this in Tarin Kot and then in tribal areas that had been neglected or marginalised.

In May 2006, the Dutch established the Tribal Liaison Office in Uruzgan, from which ethnographers and anthropologists would attempt to understand the war from a local perspective, in order to advise both the duumvir and The Hague. Most working in this office had worked in Afghanistan previously, including some before the 2001 invasion.

One of the most significant recommendations from the Dutch civilians was that Jan Mohammad be removed from his position as governor of Uruzgan and even moved away from the province altogether. There were complaints from the US special forces who had partnered with Jan Mohammad, and from Hamid Karzai, but for the Dutch it became a non-negotiable.

Speaking to author Anand Gopal, Jan Mohammad had much to say about this Dutch demand:

> The Dutch actually support the Taliban. I've got all the evidence. It's a well-known fact among certain people. You see they want to destroy our country so they can fund the Taliban. They and the ISI work together. The Dutch are weak, not like the Americans ... The rest want to bend us over and fuck us.

Jan Mohammad was given an advisory role in Kabul, lucrative but disempowering. From the capital he cast a long and agitating shadow, but he was no longer the most significant figure in Uruzgan. A new governor from out of the province, Abdul Hakim Munib, was installed as governor, but – as a leaked US diplomatic cable noted – he 'likely acted as a net detractor in the security of Uruzgan'.

That November 2006 cable, sent to US and European intelligence agencies, explained that Munib had been given money from a NATO discretionary fund to build a militia loyal to the government, but that force was nowhere near as large as NATO had expected it to be, and it had spent no time fighting the Taliban. Instead, it was found, the militia had probably been behind attacks against American and coalition convoys, and the looting of the Tarin Kot bazaar.

Munib was removed from power in 2007, but at that point local power in Uruzgan was running through another man, who never aspired to the governorship – a fact that said more about the power of the governorship than the ambitions of the man. This new powerbroker was young, brutal, provincial but also very smart. With the help of the US and Australian special force, he became one of the few province-level powerbrokers in the country under 50 years of age. This man was Jan Mohammad's second nephew, Matiullah.

On 11 September 2001 Matiullah was an illiterate taxi driver. He lived in Tarin Kot but spent his days driving passengers and materials between that town and Kandahar, on the main route in and out of the province, his security on the route then assured by the Taliban. In 2001 he had no money, no power and not much of a future, until the tectonic shift of the invasion arrived.

When he was in his mid-twenties (Matiullah's age was not known, possibly even to himself), Matiullah fought alongside Jason Amerine in the Battle of Tarin Kot, and afterwards became the commanding officer of a *kandak* (a roughly company-sized element) within the 593rd Brigade of the Afghan Military Forces, based in Uruzgan.

In 2003, a national disarmament, demobilisation and remobilisation of the Afghan Military Forces (which was seen as working for minority interests) was ordered by President Karzai under ISAF insistence. Three of the four *kandaks* from the 593rd Brigade were disbanded and incorporated into the new Afghan National Army, but the fourth, Matiullah's *kandak*, rebranded itself as the Kandak Amniate Uruzgan (KAU), or the Uruzgan Highway Police. As a police unit, they were immune from demobilisation.

The KAU concentrated on the one and only trucking route between Tarin Kot and Kandahar, but security was only assured if you paid Matiullah's toll, which, for trucks ferrying supplies to the ever-expanding military base at Tarin Kot, was estimated between US$1000 and US$1500 per truck. If the toll was not paid, attack was likely. Who exactly was committing those attacks was a point of contention, but for the coalition it was simply cheaper and easier to pay.

As the commander of the KAU, Matiullah amassed money, power and blood-drenched reputation, as well as the suffix 'Khan', or king, a title given to someone with great influence. More Marlo Stanfield than Michael Corleone, Matiullah Khan had little interest in official titles, little desire to affect politics in Kabul and no intention of absconding to Dubai with a stacked bank account. All he wanted was Uruzgan in his grasp – for himself, his family and his tribe, the Popalzai.

Because Matiullah reinforced the power systems developed by Jan Mohammad (and was also known for torture and murder), the Dutch refused to work with him. But the American special forces embraced Matiullah Khan – or MK, as he was known – as he was renowned as a Taliban killer.

When the Australian SOTG came to Uruzgan, they also embraced Matiullah as their partner, building their compound next to his and sending his men in to fight alongside Australian forces. Eventually, Matiullah would be known as 'Australia's warlord', with millions, if not tens of millions, of Australian taxpayers' dollars ending up in his coffers and funding his militia.

* * *

The missions of Task Force Uruzgan and the Australian special forces in Uruzgan were, if not at odds, at least discordant. While ISAF was ostensibly in charge of the war, and the Dutch were the senior ISAF partner in Uruzgan, the Australian special forces often worked under the worldwide US counterterrorism banner of 'Operation Enduring Freedom'. This meant the Australians were not only taking orders from outside Task Force Uruzgan, but sometimes the Dutch were not even authorised to know the details of the SOTG's missions or its JPEL targets.

'There was a chronic issue in Uruzgan, and that was that there were two groups of people doing two very different things,' says a Dutch diplomat who was part of Task Force Uruzgan for the duration of the Dutch commitment there, and who still works in the Dutch government. 'Our philosophy was to convince the groups that were currently hostile to the government to come into the fold, and I think perhaps the Australian special forces were ... well, perhaps not as concerned with that.'

Killing became the primary wedge issue between the Dutch and the Australian special forces. The Dutch policy in Uruzgan was to attempt to isolate the Taliban or anti-coalition militia by bringing into the governmental fold as many tribal groups as possible. The SOTG was a front-foot force, often taking its lead from the United States, with one of Force Element Alpha's primary roles being 'counter-leadership'. In this role they were sometimes 'servicing' JPEL targets whom the Dutch were actively trying to bring in from the cold.

A consistent complaint by some Australian military is that the Dutch fundamentally misunderstood the character of the war in Uruzgan, and that a more offensive strategy was required for success. This is a view Alexander Downer shares.

'[The Dutch] would cower in Tarin Kot in the base there, teaching the locals woodwork, while our SAS were in a separate part of the base suppressing the enemy,' Downer says. 'If you don't want anyone to get hurt, don't send your army into a combat zone. Don't be a dickhead. Think, THINK. Think it through, I used to say as foreign minister.'

* * *

The Taliban mounted a large offensive campaign in Uruzgan in June 2007. On 15 June, representatives of Task Force Uruzgan were leaving a women's education event at a girls' school in Tarin Kot that the Dutch were funding; a car laden with explosives smashed into one of the Dutch armoured vehicles and exploded. One Dutch soldier was killed, and three more were severely injured. Eleven nearby Afghan children were also killed.

This was the start of a significant offensive that involved the torture, murder and mutilation of dozens of people who supported the government in Uruzgan and their families, in the Baluchi Valley and Chora. These acts of brutality were coupled with the overrun of three police checkpoints and an attempted overrun of the government administration centre in Chora, known as the White Compound. The Taliban were eventually defeated in Chora thanks to overwhelming air power and the large local militia that formed to support the Dutch, led again by Rozi Khan. At least 100 people were killed in the three-day battle in Chora, primarily Afghan combatants but also many dozens of civilians and one Dutch soldier.

While Task Force Uruzgan was concentrating its reconstruction efforts in Chora, Tarin Kot and the western town of Deh Rawood, the Australian special forces were sent out to test the waters in the further reaches of the province. An Australian commando company, assembled in a large, heavily armed vehicle convoy, punched into the Mehrabad Valley, east of Tarin Kot. This was an area where a large number of Ghilzai lived, including an influential commander and enemy of Jan Mohammad named Mullah Shafiq, who initially supported the government but had shifted towards the insurgency.

Joining the commandos were aerial intelligence platforms, either planes or drones, and also electronic warfare operators, or 'bears', who would operate listening devices that could capture signals intelligence, either mobile phone or radio intercepts. From those intercepts they would try to put together a picture of the insurgency and generate JPEL targets.

The Australians were not welcomed in the Mehrabad Valley, and there were gunfights daily. After their mission there, the commando element moved north, where intelligence suggested some of those who had organised the Chora attack might be found. Here they pushed all the way into the edges of the Hazarajat, crossing the border between Pashtun lands and those tilled by the Hazara, the persecuted minority group who had made up the bulk of the asylum seekers rescued by the *Tampa*.

During these 2007 operations, the SASR were often recording patterns of life and doing reconnaissance and surveillance, while their 'little brothers', the commandos, were doing the bulk of the gunfighting. This was not a state of affairs that was agreeable to all of the Perth operators. The rotation was considered a success, however, judged by the intelligence gathered and the JPEL targets prosecuted – and the fact that no Australian soldiers were killed. There were incidents, though: some were moments of ill-discipline and others of alleged criminality.

A 2020 report by the Assistant Inspector-General of the ADF (IGADF), Paul Brereton, following his inquiry into alleged war crimes, found that there was credible evidence suggesting that during this rotation one or more Australian special forces personnel was involved in the murder of an Afghan who was a 'person under control', or PUC, essentially a prisoner. This was the first such SOTG allegation the IGADF had found. (One previous SFTG incident was found credible: a 2006 incident in which unnamed special forces soldiers 'killed an unidentified male person, who was unarmed', which was then 'wilfully misreported ... as an engagement with an armed insurgent'.)

It was also in this period that an infamous photograph was taken showing an SASR patrol, out on operations, flying a large Nazi flag, red with a white circle, inside which was a swastika in black. Some former operators and officers I spoke to about the flag think this display meant little: it was just a dark joke made while conducting a dark duty. Others have a different view. During interviews, it was noted that a soldier either believes in the authority and power of flags or not, and if you assign any meaning to the Australian flag on your shoulder, then you must also assign meaning to a swastika, especially if you choose to raise it while on operations.

One of the most startling aspects of that incident is that, according to sources, one of SOCOMD's best-regarded officers (then working as a major commanding Australia's commandos) was in the photograph; he was reportedly unhappy that the SASR patrol commander was flying the flag, but was apparently unable to stop him. This patrol commander was a sergeant, outranked by the officer by some measure, and yet he assumed he could commit what was clearly a sanctionable act with impunity. That SOCOMD officer is now a brigadier.

18

'We were like, "Fuck it, these people are all against us"'

IN THE AUTUMN OF 2007, Australians started dying in Uruzgan. The first death was a cavalryman serving as part of the RTF. Trooper David 'Poppy' Pearce had been driving in an Australian light armoured vehicle (or ASLAV) back to Tarin Kot, near Dorafshan. His vehicle hit an IED and he was killed. Force Element Alpha and Force Element Bravo would each also lose a soldier.

In September 2007, the Chora Valley was, yet again, falling under insurgent control. After the battle in Chora in June, the Dutch forces had largely left control of the area to Afghan police and military, and those local elements had been unable to stop insurgents taking over. As the SOTG's rotation five came into Uruzgan, they knew one of their first jobs would be to support yet another large-scale clearance of the Chora, this time named Operation Spin Ghar. The main assaulting force would be British, and would include the Gurkha Regiment, the famed British-Nepalese fighting force.

A 2 Squadron SASR element was tasked with a number of close-target reconnaissance roles supporting a larger conventional force, which meant they would sneak into the valley before the clearance and report on what they saw: how many enemy soldiers there were, where they were and what weapons they had. This was a traditional combat role for the regiment, and through the nights before the clearance, E Troop's four combat patrols would secrete into Chora and report back.

On 21 October, three armed men almost bumped into one of the E Troop patrols, so, at a distance of just two metres, the Australians killed them. On 23 October, Sergeant Matthew Locke, one of E Troop's patrol commanders and a man who had already won the Medal for Gallantry in the peaks above Chora, actually entered a number of empty dugout enemy fighting positions. He measured them with his rifle, before returning to base and creating wire-frame diagrams of the position on his computer, which were then sent to the clearing force.

* * *

The commanding officer of these E Troop patrols was a 26-year-old captain named Mark Wales. SASR officers, like their men, are often formidable figures, and that was true of Wales, who stood six-foot-three and had muscular bulk comparable to any operator. Within the SASR, however, officers do not have the automatic standing and influence they enjoy in other regiments.

With officers coming in and out of the regiment, the corporals and sergeants of the SASR, especially those commanding patrols and those with combat experience, were the powerbase of the regiment. With six combat rotations having been undertaken in Afghanistan, some non-commissioned officers, or NCOs, were on their fourth rotation, and these more experienced and battle-hardened NCOs were developing influence that went beyond their rank. Every officer coming into the SASR knew his fate was in the hands of his soldiers, and especially his NCOs, which included Koran Ghar veteran Matthew Locke.

'If you lost trust of the team, were rejected by them, you could suffer a career-ending removal in combat,' says Mark Wales, who notes that he considered himself lucky in 2007 to have had patrol commanders he trusted.

'Fuck knows why you're painting that – you'll be in the office while we run the clearance,' Matthew Locke told Wales as the officer applied green paint to his M4 rifle in preparation for the start of Operation Spin Ghar.

Wales considered this a good interaction, a healthy one. Matthew Locke, the most senior of his patrol commanders, was joking with his captain, who had already patrolled with him and his patrol in Chora and Baluchi a few nights earlier.

Wales would be leading his men in a battle for the first time. He had no combat experience, he'd never fired his weapon at the enemy and, like so many soldiers, he wondered what his response to combat would be. He desperately hoped that the fight was in him. There's no more shameful trait in an officer than letting his men down under fire.

On the evening of 24 October 2007 E Troop blasted AC/DC and Metallica as they painted their faces and prepped their weapons. Wales had asked his patrol commanders what to take into battle. An extra jacket? Yes – the nights are cold and the troop might be forced to be static. Extra ammunition and gold-top grenades? Yep, that's essential weight. Kevlar body armour plates?

'Green roles, no requirement,' said Locke, referring to the part of the valley they would be operating in. They would be in the valley itself, among the fields and homes, crops and livestock, not in the barren *dasht*, where Locke thought them more likely to catch a bullet.

The troop assembled for a group photograph before driving to where their mission would start.

By dawn, they were to have secured a location between Baluchi and Chora where helicopters could land and the Gurkhas could insert. After leaving their vehicles, the four patrols, their troop commander, a signaller and a combat dog moved silently under cover of night through Baluchi fields rich with crops. All was still and silent, except for the faint hum of an MQ-9 Reaper drone, underslung with a camera and Hellfire missiles, watching them from above.

By 4.30 am the Australians had found their objective, an open area they had identified in advance as an HLZ. They marked the area with infrared strobe lights, cleared any impediments for the helicopters and watched for enemy activity. Soon the aircraft arrived, disgorging stout, fierce Gurkha fighters who would push up en masse towards the blocking force further in the valley. So far the mission had been uneventful.

By 6 am, E Troop had done its job; now the men had options. They could go back to Tarin Kot and wait for a new task, they could wait here and observe, or they could push up towards the blocking position and see what action they might get involved in. One of Mark Wales's patrol sergeants, a British soldier on exchange from the SBS, wanted to return to base. Matthew Locke wanted to push up to the blocking force. The man with the Medal for Gallantry broke the tie and Wales ordered the patrols north.

For about half an hour they walked, in the morning sun, through carefully tended fields of apricot, walnut, marijuana and poppy as aqueducts dribbled here and there. E Troop came across a field of corn that abutted a river. This was bad ground, tactically. The corn was high and unkempt, somewhere fighters could hide. The river was an obstacle. A thought went through Wales's mind: *This is a good place for an ambush.* The handful of insurgents hiding in the corn felt the same way.

The Australians watched a man, woman and child walk away from them, and Wales says the air somehow hummed, before PKM machine-gun rounds smashed through the cold morning air. The Australians dropped down and fired back through the corn. There was a rattle of incoming and outgoing fire, and the *thunk* of Wales's gold-top grenades. Explosions rang out, and leaves and bark from eucalyptus trees floated down on the Australians.

Wales received a call over the radio: 'Man down – there's a man down.' He thought a man in his patrol was announcing an enemy killed in action. He was not – it was one of his. Wales rushed to the casualty, as did many of the men in the troop. Matthew Locke had been shot and was unconscious. The medic working on him announced that he was not breathing – and that he was 'pri 1'. A priority-one casualty meant that, unless he received medical assistance within an hour, his injury would kill him.

Enemy fire poured in at the cluster of Australians crowded around Locke. This had become a golden opportunity for the enemy. More Afghans moved through the corn, closer to the Australians. More grenades were fired in an attempt to create a barrier. Fewer than 30 metres now separated the two sets of fighters. Wales ordered a rear passage of lines, meaning that his teams would fold out behind the position he was holding and they would pass the casualty backwards, away from the fighting.

Before they moved Locke, the men watched the medic perform a combat tracheotomy on him. The medic inserted a breathing tube into the patrol commander's neck and blew into the tube as a another soldier leaned in to do chest compressions. Wales could see it in both men's eyes: they were losing their mate. A large volume of enemy fire smashed around them.

Sean McCarthy, the troop's signaller – who would be killed a year later, also in the Baluchi Valley – now stood and started to pin a large orange marker panel to a tree just beyond their position. The enemy concentrated their fire on him, but he finished his work and dropped back down to relative safety. Now the friendly eyes above them could see that everything beyond that orange marker was enemy, and could be attacked.

From an overwatch position, close to where Ben Roberts-Smith and Kilo-2 had secreted themselves a year earlier, explosive, armour-piercing .50-calibre sniper rounds flew towards the corn and the enemy. One Afghan fighter was spotted in the riverbed – he was killed by the Australian snipers. Another came to help him – he was killed too. Two more Afghans came to help and were also killed. A British Apache helicopter arrived; escort for the medevac helicopter coming to collect Locke. The Apache helicopter started laying down cannon fire, and then fired missiles at Afghans who were spotted attempting to flank the HLZ.

With the cacophony of death beyond them, Wales and his troop managed to load Locke onto a helicopter, but it was too late. In a few hours' time, the unit's padre, wearing his pressed dress uniform, would arrive at the home in which lived Matthew Locke's wife and 13-year-old son.

After a sombre ramp ceremony, in which Locke's body was loaded on a transport plane for repatriation to Australia, E Troop enjoyed a less sombre wake at the SASR bar on base known as the Fat Lady's Arms. They celebrated their recently killed friend as though he were there with them, drinking, smoking cigars and laughing. Someone had sourced the gun camera footage from the British Apache which had supported the medevac helicopter that removed Matt Locke from Chora. They cheered heartily as they watched Afghan fighters disappear in the explosions of Hellfire missiles, as many as five men at a time. They cheered as the helicopter's cannon tore limbs and heads from the enemy.

Mark Wales cheered too. He had hoped to stay a dispassionate officer in the field, but had very quickly developed a hatred for the Afghans who'd killed this respected comrade under his command.

'After Matt was killed, we were basically like, "Most of these areas are going to be bad,"' says Wales. 'The Australian Army had done peacekeeping for so long and we had an innocent-before-proven-guilty mindset, and then after that we were like, "Fuck it, these people are all against us."'

* * *

Two days after Matthew Locke's death, E Troop was sent out again on a new and flashy type of mission, one that would later become the primary activity of the SASR in Afghanistan: manhunting.

Australia's priority target, then and for many years to come, would be the JPEL target designated Objective Rapier (the convention for some years would be for Australian targets to be given weapon names as codenames), a bombmaker and Taliban commander who regularly hopped between Pakistan and Afghanistan. This man was believed to have been involved in the death of David 'Poppy' Pierce.

Speculation would become rampant within later SOTG rotations that the target of Objective Rapier was actually the work of many insurgents, rolled into one JPEL file, but in 2007 the focus was on an insurgent named Abdul Hai.

Mark Wales and E troop were to move to Hai's 'historical activity zone' in the Mehrabad Valley. During the day, they would set up vehicle checkpoints, attempting to provoke conversation on enemy phones and radios. By night they would look to follow each signal's activity to their target. Eventually they traced a phone to a compound where they were sure they'd find Abdul Hai. They planned a night raid, moving the vehicles to a position a few kilometres from the target, from where the assault teams would storm the compound.

Abdul Hai would soon become known to the Australians as a consummate professional: he limited his phone and radio interactions, switched phones regularly, moved from place to place, was careful not to create a predictable pattern of activity, and also ensured strong perimeter security. It was this last measure that derailed E Troop's first attempt to scratch Objective Rapier off the JPEL.

The operators drove towards their target with soldiers piled into and on top of open vehicles to minimise the sound they were making. Mark Wales watched the lead vehicle launch into the air in a ball of flame. Large dark pieces of debris started to land heavily on the ground, and Wales swore he saw a leg, but when they set up a perimeter and started to account for the damage, there were no dead. Three were injured, but none dismembered.

Everything forward of the LRPV's firewall had been obliterated, but behind it the men were somewhat sheltered. The Australian injuries ranged from severe burns to a shattered leg, but all the men would survive. Wales was instantly presented with a pressing tactical issue. His troop was visible and static in an unfriendly and populated area whose residents had now awoken. Things became even more pressing when they intercepted radio transmissions that said they were about to be rocketed.

'We were exceptionally rough on the locals when they approached us,' Wales says. 'We separated them and held a group as human shields. I would have never done that normally, but in those circumstances it was entirely appropriate.'

This action was in contravention of international humanitarian law, and Wales surprised even himself with his own actions. But there was the law and there was survival. He was amazed by how far his moral compass had shifted in such a small amount of time.

'Basically, I was like, "If I don't disconnect my emotions with how we deal with this population, we're not going to survive,"' he says.

Later in the rotation, Wales would lead his troop on a mission with the British into the adjacent Helmand Province, and there they had happened upon a large group of militia fighters, which they devastated with rockets, machine guns and finally two 500-pound bombs launched from a Reaper drone hovering overhead. The Afghans were torn apart, limbs and heads separated from torn and mangled bodies. To most it was the stuff of horror, but to Wales it work well done.

'It felt good to PUNISH THOSE CUNTS,' he wrote in his diary that night.

This would only be the first of many trips to Afghanistan for Wales, and yet his world had already changed. Nightmares started to penetrate his mind; a post-traumatic stress disorder (PTSD) diagnosis was not far away. His understanding of universal human rights and compassion had eroded.

'That was after one [combat] tour,' he observes. 'I think the average number of tours was five and a half, and some did as many as eight. It doesn't take a genius to know what you're going to be like after doing that many tours. Your sense of what's normal is going to be totally skewed.'

* * *

By 2007, the entire Australian commando regiment had been qualified in advanced close-quarters battle, an initiative undertaken by the then regimental commanding officer, Mark Smethurst. This was a significant upskilling, meaning that all four commando companies were able to engage in the urban warfare and building clearance that was a requirement of service in the TAGs – but it also meant the commandos were ready to undertake a different and more independent role in Afghanistan.

Mitchell McAlister, a former commando from Force Element Bravo, writing on the international special forces blog SOFREP. com, says that when they came to Afghanistan in 2007 there had been a 'paradigm to shift [for the commandos] from primarily vehicle-based patrols and QRF operations to a more offensive deliberate action strike role'.

The basic unit of the commandos was the team, and this was slightly larger than an SASR patrol. These teams were constituted into a platoon, and the platoons into companies; again, both were larger than SASR troops and squadrons. This meant they were built for larger engagements, and they were generally more offensively minded than the SASR and were able to bring more firepower to bear.

The Bravo men were younger and less experienced than their SASR compatriots, but they were exceptionally well trained, and very hungry for a fight. In 2007, a fight was something they were tasked with generating. As McAlister explained it:

> Essentially we would drive our convoy into areas known
> to be infested with insurgents in order to generate some
> kind of a response, and then generate a counter response.
> The company, ready to put their new skills to good use,
> would implement the obligatory two am 'hard knock'
> keeping Afghan door and hinge makers in business all over
> Uruzgan province.

These vehicle patrols, initially into the Mehrabad Valley, were often multi-week affairs, with the soldiers living out of their vehicles and at night hitting what were known as 'compounds of interest'. The actions of the era were defined by 'dry holes', with teams or platoons of commandos smashing their way into compounds, often to find nothing but terrified or aggravated locals. The danger was omnipresent, however, and the insurgents were there, in the shadows. This fact was proven starkly on 23 November 2007, a month after Matthew Locke's death.

Bravo Company had been in the middle of a vehicle patrol into the Mehrabad Valley when intelligence came in that a JPEL target named Mullah Baz Mohammad, thought to be a shadow Taliban governor, was to stop overnight at a compound cluster relatively close to their location. This compound was in Chenartu, a district where the government only had control of the northern third, in which the Popalzai primarily lived. This northern area was patrolled by a 150-person paramilitary/militia force, paid for by the government but acting predominantly for tribal interests.

Some villages in the southern part of Chenartu had welcomed insurgents at least partially to offset this northern threat, but as was often the case, it was not an instance of one tribal area strictly supporting the government and another strictly supporting the insurgency.

'Of course, we have Popalzai within the insurgency ranks, as much as we have many of our tribesmen working for the Government; no one knows what will happen in the future,' a Popalzai tribal elder had once told a Dutch ethnographer.

As the Australian commandos made their way to their Chenartu target, signals intelligence was received that Mullah Baz Mohammad was not at the compound cluster, but a decision was made to make the assault anyway. At 11 pm the commando vehicles were harboured some kilometres from their target compound, and the soldiers walked through the night towards their fight.

Just shy of the village, the company split, so they could assault the linked compounds simultaneously from two different entry points. As one young commando was making his way to his point of entry, he heard a sound behind him. He turned and saw, in the shimmering green of his NVGs, the enemy.

'Black *dishdash*, *shemagh* wrapped around his head, big black beard and AK ... we'd been in plenty of contacts but this was the first time I'd been face-to-face with one of them,' he says. 'I was thinking: *Fuck, he might have the drop on me here ...*'

The Afghan, too, had seen something in the dark. Local and foreigner rushed to bring their rifles to bear – but before either could fire, the Afghan was killed by a flanking commando. Another Afghan nearby was also shot and killed.

For the men of the other commando team, who were attempting to gain entry into the compound a few dozen metres away using a crowbar, the tactical situation had changed. The element of surprise was ebbing away with every passing second. When they popped the compound door open, the Australians were met immediately with machine-gun fire.

A 26-year-old commando named Luke Worsley took rounds to the head and was killed instantly. In a hail of machine-gun fire, another young commando, Cameron Baird – who would be awarded a Medal of Gallantry for his actions – ran into the compound and started throwing grenades and firing at the internal windows. The other commandos followed behind and a room-to-room gunfight ensued. Up to 18 Afghans were killed, including six members of the Daad family: three men, one woman, a teenage girl and a baby, killed by a fragmentation grenade.

The commandos had to make a slow fighting retreat back to their vehicles as the locals took pot shots at them. Six commandos carried Worsley's body in a long reverse march back to the vehicles, and a Reaper drone monitored their progress, firing its Hellfire missiles at any locals who approached. Later, the Chenartu district chief said that there had been Taliban in the compound but that the Daad family were not Taliban; they were just unable to refuse insurgent impositions. The ADF have said they gathered intelligence linking the Daad family to the insurgency.

This raid had been a threshold moment for the commandos. It had brough the regiment's first combat death, but it was also known within the regiment as a night of pride, and a sign of their growing competency.

After the end of their vehicle patrol, the commandos piled into their Padre's plywood hut in Tarin Kot for their own wake. The young soldiers were sad but ebullient, emotional and exhausted. They drank heavily and bared buried thoughts. Someone produced a guitar and Cameron Baird stood on a table and drunkenly but passionately smashed out 'Good Riddance (Time of Your Life)' by Green Day.

Almost to a man, they loved their job and assaults like this. All of the attendant death was part of the job. In fact, it *was* the job. Some of the commandos and SASR members left SOCOMD after this tour, but most couldn't wait to get back to Afghanistan.

Luke Worsley and Matthew Locke were dead, but their friends felt very much alive. Combat was destructive but, as Matthew Bouillaut had found two years earlier in Iraq, it was also addictive.

19

'WHO RUNS DEFENCE?'

IT'S CHRISTMAS 2007 AND winter winds whip through the Chora and Baluchi valleys. In Tarin Kot preparations are being made for the 'surprise' arrival of the prime minister – a new prime minister, as a month earlier John Howard had lost not only government, but also his own parliamentary seat of Bennelong. Nationally, the election had been a rout. The Labor Party was assuming government and its leader, Kevin Rudd, the prime ministership.

Throughout the 2007 election campaign, the post-9/11 wars were not discussed much. While Rudd had sometimes used the failure of the war in Iraq as a stick with which to beat Howard, he was careful not to make the same anti-American mistakes his predecessor and internecine foe, Mark Latham made. When mentioning Iraq, the bad war, Rudd would often also mention Afghanistan, the good war, the necessary war.

Rudd came into office having made four national security promises. Three were to maintain the high levels of defence spending established by John Howard, and to maintain the military and counterterrorism alliances that had been established in the wake of the 9/11 attacks. The fourth was that the ADF would leave Iraq, but in doing so Rudd would reaffirm the ADF's commitment in Afghanistan.

The Americans were losing a 500-soldier battlegroup in Iraq, but they had convinced the incoming Australian government to leave all their other assets and soldiers based in Iraq. They had also earned a further and enduring commitment to Afghanistan.

A leaked US diplomatic cable, issued three days after the Labor win, speculated about Rudd's cabinet, noting that the 'micromanaging' Rudd would appoint inexperienced lawyer Stephen Smith as foreign minister, but in practice 'the real foreign minister will be Kevin Rudd'. Only weeks after winning the election, Rudd was in Afghanistan (without Smith), forging ahead with a new commitment to the war.

Before visiting Tarin Kot, Rudd stopped in Kabul to meet with Hamid Karzai. In his speech at Tarin Kot, Rudd said: 'One of the messages I delivered to His Excellency the President is that Australia is here in Afghanistan for a long haul.'

* * *

In Canberra's ministries, projects and missions were being handed over. Howard's people were giving way to Rudd's appointees. John Howard says he had no conversations with Kevin Rudd about the war in Afghanistan, however, and at the Department of Foreign Affairs and Trade, the incoming minister, Stephen Smith, sought no handover briefing from Alexander Downer (because, as Downer puts it, 'he thought I was a dickhead'). Things were a little different at the Department of Defence, though.

Former tradie Joel Fitzgibbon was the incoming defence minister, taking over from a friend in Brendan Nelson. Even though the pair were political adversaries, Nelson had made sure that the shadow defence minister received briefings from the Chief of Defence and updates on foreign deployments, especially Afghanistan. As he departed the portfolio, Nelson gave Fitzgibbon some advice: 'Do not be captured by Russell.' Defence works for the government, but, Nelson warned Fitzgibbon, senior ADF officers and the Department of Defence will also have their own agenda, and sometimes it's difficult for a minister to discern what those agendas are.

Just two weeks into the job as defence minister, Fitzgibbon travelled to Edinburgh to meet with the defence ministers and leaders of the eight nations fighting in the south of Afghanistan. Three days before the meeting, Prime Minister Gordon Brown of the United Kingdom gave a public update on the war.

'Let me make it clear at the outset that as part of a coalition we are winning the battle against the Taliban insurgency,' Brown stated. 'We are isolating and eliminating the leadership of the Taliban, we are not negotiating with them.'

Fitzgibbon had believed that Australia's military efforts in Afghanistan were part of a larger American and (to a lesser extent) British strategy to win the war, and that this strategy was aiming at victory. This was not the case. 'I thought I knew about Afghanistan, but it turns out I knew very little,' Fitzgibbon says. 'I was shocked when I became the minister and got more transparent and deeper briefings.'

After sitting down with people like David Kilcullen and Defence Intelligence Organisation head Maurie McNarn, Fitzgibbon realised progress hadn't been made towards victory, thanks largely to macro problems that were simply not being addressed. These included the open border with Pakistan, the weakness of the Afghan government forces and the problem of the opium poppy – which was funding the insurgency, but the eradication of which would be highly destabilising. Then there was the Karzai government, entrenched in Kabul but weak in many other places, and with many of the men he'd put in positions of power as corrupt as a hard drive at the bottom of the ocean.

One example that stuck with Fitzgibbon was that if an Afghan had their bike stolen in Uruzgan, the Taliban were more likely than the police to get it returned.

Briefings from SOCOMD were more positive, however, and stated that counter-leadership missions were forging ahead with increasing success. 'It was explained to me that if you were going to kill this insurgency, you have to cut off the head. I never had any difficulty with [JPEL],' says Fitzgibbon. 'They were fighting an enemy that didn't wear a uniform and didn't adhere to any rules whatsoever, so they had to have maximum capacity to conduct their missions and protect themselves.'

One former senior Australian special operations officer, who was part of one briefing the minister received, says a disservice was done in both the manner and the content of the briefings. According to this officer, one particular briefing given to Fitzgibbon that was simplistic and values-based, and ascribed traits to the enemy that that were also common among Australia's allies. 'It was so "good guys versus bad guys", I thought he was going to start laughing,' the officer said. 'He lapped it up.'

A consistent issue throughout the war was the quality of information making its way from the battlefields of Afghanistan and from Russell to civilian decision-makers like Fitzgibbon. Some within the ADF did try to cut though the informational process and explain the reality of the conflict in Afghanistan to one of the few people who could do anything about it.

'Very privately, some uniform guys made it very, very clear they were concerned about the lack of strategy and mission objective,' says Fitzgibbon. 'While they never said it explicitly, it was implicit that we needed to find our way out of this thing.'

* * *

Although a great deal of SOTG activity was concentrated in the Tarin Kot bowl, Chora and Baluchi and east through the Mehrabad Valley, the SASR were authorised to hunt JPEL targets to the limits of Uruzgan Province. In August 2008, a target codenamed Objective Sabre had been tracked to an Achakzai tribal area close to the Khas Uruzgan district centre (where, in 2002, US special forces had accidentally killed not one district governor but two).

For the SOTG, killing JPEL targets with a drone was an option, but a legal officer says the approval process was far more time-consuming than launching a direct action using the SASR or the commandos, so the latter was almost always the preference.

An SASR element was to be sent to FOB Anaconda, a Green Beret outpost just to the west of Khas Uruzgan. The FOB and the tiny district centre were the only areas in the district that had been secured; beyond, insurgents roamed with near impunity.

The US special forces operating in the area had built up little rapport with the locals, a common complaint being that armed insurgents would come to houses or villages, demand food and shelter, and leave behind a SIGINT trace. These houses or villages would then become 'compounds of interest', and were liable to be targeted by the Americans in airstrikes or night raids.

When the SASR arrived at Anaconda – a small base on a hill above a large, green agricultural area of paddies and fields dubbed 'Mortaritaville' for the sheer amount of mortar rounds, both incoming and outgoing – intelligence was collected that the target was not in Khas Uruzgan, but in Pakistan. It was decided nevertheless that the Australians would stay in Khas Uruzgan and conduct some missions with the US special forces, who were attempting to gain traction in the valleys nearby.

A plan was developed: US Humvees would enter one of the valleys in which they were attacked each time they entered, after I Troop's patrols had secreted themselves above the valley and set up sniper hides. The vehicles would be bait and the SASR would be the trap in what was colloquially known a 'tethered goat mission'.

At midday, three men carrying weapons were spotted by one of the SASR patrols in the target valley. Australian snipers killed all three. The bodies were left in the open in the hope that others would come to retrieve them. A Toyota Hilux arrived with six armed men, and they were all killed by the Australians too. The Australians waited and watched the nine dead men, and yet another van arrived. The Afghans who spilled out were killed as they emerged, but the Australian fire stopped when they saw a woman trying to escape the vehicle.

The survivors disappeared, and when US and Afghan soldiers did a battle damage assessment, they found a dead baby amid the carnage. To their great relief, it was discovered that the baby had not died recently. Possibly one of the vehicles was transporting the child to a funeral.

The mission was considered a success, and it would be emulated three days later – even though it would overlap with the start of Ramadan, the Islamic holy month in which offensive actions generally lessened. This action would result in one of the largest Australian battles of the war to date – and the awarding of a Victoria Cross, the highest award for valour in the Australian military award system.

In the early hours of 2 September, four SASR patrols moved a few kilometres east of Anaconda and set themselves up in hidden sniper positions. At dawn, five vehicles driven by US, Australian and Afghan soldiers moved towards their position – bait in another snipers' trap. Again, in the middle of the day, armed men were spotted and killed. Before nightfall, it was decided to move the convoy back to FOB Anaconda. As the convoy moved away, they were met by a large ambush.

Approximately 150 fighters had amassed to attack the convoy, which included fewer than 40 coalition shooters. The convoy was attacked and then, after moving a few hundred metres attacked again. Over more than two hours, the vehicles, sometimes moving at walking pace due to disabled vehicles and casualties, worked their way back to FOB Anaconda. Casualties mounted, minute by minute. Dutch Apache helicopters wheeled above, but infuriated the Australians and Americans when they failed to fly low enough to identify and attack the enemy.

One American soldier was shot in the head and killed; another was wounded. Nine Australian soldiers were wounded, with one patrol commander peppered with shrapnel from an RPG. He was also shot twice on separate occasions, and bullets hit his hat and the ejection port of his weapon as he was firing it.

An Australian explosive-detection dog named Sarbi bolted after the shockwave of an RPG rocked one of the Humvees; incredibly, the Labrador/Newfoundland was found again more than a year later by an American serviceman. She became one of two celebrities created during the battle. The other was a softly spoken, redheaded SASR trooper, a man who had rare universal respect from his special forces peers.

Mark Donaldson was awarded the first Victoria Cross since Vietnam for his action of arms, moving outside his vehicle and suppressing enemy fire time and time again with heavy weapons and his rifle, and primarily for saving the life of an Afghan interpreter, who had been blown up by an RPG and thrown from a US Humvee, then accidentally left behind. Donaldson ran 80 metres under accurate fire to pick up the interpreter, who had significant head injuries, and carry him back to the convoy and away from an undoubted fate.

The next day the battle was covered by most Australian newspapers, with Kevin Rudd appearing at the Australian War Memorial announcing the engagement and saying the SASR was 'taking the fight to this enemy for all of us'. Then opposition leader Brendan Nelson also made an official statement: 'I join with the Prime Minister in ensuring that the political will and resolve of this parliament will remain as it has ever been to see this through.'

Brigadier Brian Dawson, Director-General of Defence Public Affairs, announced rudimentary details about the engagement to the press, refusing even to say where the battle had happened. Later, more information about Sarbi was given to the media, and Mark Donaldson was named publicly in preparation for him to be awarded the Victoria Cross (an honour he accepted only on the proviso that he could continue deploying to Afghanistan).

Even though it was of little strategic importance, and indeed an engagement that could be considered a defeat, the Battle of Khas Uruzgan was, for a time, the best known action of the Australian war in Afghanistan. Donaldson became the Australian face of the war, and not for taking life but for saving it.

The battle was not, however, even the most important the SASR had that month. In mid-September, soldiers of I Troop shot and killed Rozi Khan, the Barakzai leader who was one of Uruzgan's most effective anti-Taliban leaders and a Dutch ally. Khan had fought against the Russians, alongside Jason Amerine at the Battle of Tarin Kot, and had more than once activated his militia to fight alongside the Dutch against insurgents in Chora. As the leader of the Barakzai tribe across Uruzgan and a broker in the Barakzai/

Achakzai power block (representing more than 40 per cent of the province's population), Khan was important in checking the surging power of Uruzgan's Popalzai powerbrokers, men like Jan Mohammad and Matiullah Khan. Then he was shot dead.

On the night of 17 September, Rozi Kahn was in his home village, Sarshakhli, five kilometres north of Tarin Kot, when he received a panicked phone call from an ally: tribal enemies were coming to kill him. There were a few hundred Barakzai families in the area, but beyond was a potpourri of families, tribes and motivations, and Uruzgan had recently suffered a spate of tribal assassinations. Rozi Khan gathered a small group of armed men to find these assassins before they found him.

He and his men saw some armed figures. This was an SASR patrol in the area, according to SOCOMD, hunting JPEL target Objective Musket. SOCOMD said that Rozi Khan fired first; Khan's eldest son, Daoud Mohammad, who was with his father when he was killed, said it was the Australians.

At the time, the Dutch were making some inroads with their tribal balance strategy, and successfully keeping the Barakzai and Achakzai away from the insurgency. Uruzgan's new governor, Asadullah Khan, had also built a significant relationship with Rozi Khan, in part to bring him into the governmental fold, but also to enhance the governor's own power in the province, to the detriment of Matiullah's power. Now Rozi Khan was dead.

An open revolt of the local Barakzai (and possibly also the Achakzai) would have been a disaster, and a significant diplomatic effort was quickly undertaken by the Dutch to pacify the Barakzai. An undisclosed amount of blood money was paid by the ADF, and the 20-something Daoud Mohammad, now became Daoud Khan, who was also shot at by the SASR, was installed as the Uruzgan leader of the tribe.

The people who benefited most from the killing of Rozi Khan were Matiullah and Jan Mohammad, so there was speculation in Uruzgan and externally that the Australians had unwittingly been used in the killing of Rozi Khan. It's highly unlikely that the SASR killed Rozi Khan at the direct behest of Matiullah or Jan

Mohammad – but that isn't the only way they could have put him in Australian gunsights.

Regardless of how Rozi Khan came to be killed, the leader of a major tribal group in Uruzgan had been gunned down in the night, in his home village, by Australian soldiers. When asked about this incident, Joel Fitzgibbon, Australia's Minister for Defence at the time, did not remember ever being briefed about this killing.

* * *

The Australian special forces operating in Afghanistan worked under a series of rules of engagement (RoE), which stipulated the circumstances under which they could and couldn't kill enemy combatants and collateral Afghans. Those RoE changed depending on where they were operating, who they were working with and what type of mission they were undertaking, and they were also adapted in light of migrating enemy techniques, tactics and procedures. All those RoE are still classified, but all necessarily adhered to international humanitarian law, or what the military call the Law of Armed Conflict (LoAC).

The term 'international humanitarian law' (IHL) refers to a set of international laws based on a series of post–World War II treaties, including the Geneva Convention, and a series of unwritten customs that were investigated and codified during the Nuremberg trials of Nazi war criminals. The primary role of IHL is to protect innocent civilians in a war zone, and it largely imagines conflict between two uniformed forces. But there is a framework for conflict between uniformed combatants and civilian insurgents.

Simply put, in a conflict between uniformed combatants and civilian insurgents, the people who may be targeted are those who are 'directly participating in hostilities' (DPH). In Afghanistan and especially Uruzgan, that left a huge amount of scope.

Alexander Downer says that he, John Howard and Robert Hill personally signed off on Australia's initial RoE for Afghanistan, but his memory of those rules doesn't comport with what was allowed on the ground.

'I think the rules of engagement said you can shoot someone in self-defence,' says Downer. But he doesn't think they would have allowed Australian forces to be involved in targeted killings. 'I'm confident we weren't shooting unarmed people. Quite apart from anything else, there's the issue of political self-preservation,' says Downer.

There were a number of instances in which Australian special forces were allowed to target and kill unarmed people, including spotters, Afghans fleeing compounds (known as 'squirters'), Afghans travelling with a legitimate target and considered to be acceptable as collateral damage deaths, and also in kill/capture missions targeting JPEL-designated insurgents.

In 2012, Major General Gus Gilmore, then SOCAUST, gave a rare interview to *The Sydney Morning Herald* about kill/capture missions, saying that they were a fabrication created by the media, and that Australian special forces actually conducted 'deliberate detention' missions that sometimes required lethal force.

The facts do not seem to bear this out.

Statewatch, a not-for-profit organisation that monitors civil liberties in the European Union, sighted one of the JPEL lists and found a redacted designation on some of the targets that, it was later confirmed, meant 'kill only'. In a few instances a JPEL target was designated 'capture only', but largely the decision to kill or capture was at the discretion of the military forces prosecuting the strike, who were not legally obliged to attempt capture of their targets.

In 2020, a public inquiry in New Zealand looked at the conduct of the New Zealand Special Air Service in its prosecution of a JPEL target, and its involvement in the killing of number of people, including a toddler. The legality of killing JPEL targets without any attempt at capture was also investigated.

Dapo Akande, Professor of Public International Law and co-director of the Oxford Institute for Ethics, Law and Armed Conflict at Oxford University, made a submission to the inquiry saying:

> States have refrained from elucidating a specific principle
> about the act of targeting of combatants when such
> targeting is not necessary. It would seem that this silence is
> not accidental.
>
> The view may be taken that [International
> Humanitarian Law] has already determined the range
> of persons against whom lethal force may be used and
> this determination is already based on ground of military
> necessity. Therefore, no further and more specific restraints
> exist with regard to who is subject to lethal force.

This view essentially holds that once a person is designated as a target on the JPEL, they can – within the timeframe that considers them to be directly participating in hostilities – be killed within the law without any attempt at capture. Professor Akande further noted that the JPEL could be considered a targeted killing program.

A number of former Australian soldiers and officers say that the preference was usually to kill rather than capture for a number of reasons, including the poor and porous Afghan justice system.

When I asked John Howard about the JPEL and the RoE allowing the killing of unarmed people, it seemed that he wasn't familiar with the term JPEL. But he said this of the potential for Australian forces to be conducting targeted killings: 'I obviously accept responsibility for the rules of engagement that was agreed upon in the time I was prime minister. What they mean in certain circumstances? I'm not going to answer that question. I understand the sort of war we were involved in. I understand the necessity for fairly direct and decisive measures to be taken.'

The IGADF report into alleged war crimes says that the RoE are directives to the ADF from the CDF 'in consultation with government'. It also states that 'the number and scope of ROE applicable at any given time changed as ROE were merged, amended, and new ROE issued'.

Alexander Downer does not remember being given updated RoE to approve during his time in government. Joel Fitzgibbon, minister of defence from December 2007 until June 2009, says he was never given updated RoE to approve either.

* * *

Fitzgibbon visited Uruzgan twice as defence minister, and in on both occasions he asked to be taken beyond Tarin Kot. He was rebuffed each time. When the minister came back to Canberra, he reported on his trips.

'When I stood up in parliament and said positive things about what we were doing, I meant it,' says Fitzgibbon. 'You have to believe it. Was there scepticism in the back of my mind? Yes, there was.'

Looming on the horizon in Uruzgan in 2009 was an uncertain year ahead. The Dutch parliament had only approved the nation's military deployment in Uruzgan until 2010, and, unlike Australia's commitment, any extension would need to be debated and then approved or rejected by the Dutch parliament. The United States wanted Australia to assume control of the province should the Dutch leave, which would mean bringing to bear a significantly larger force. Fitzgibbon was adamant that Australia would not be assuming primacy.

'It was very clear we didn't have the capacity, nor did we have the will to do so,' says Fitzgibbon. 'It was clear to everyone privately that there was no winning this. The first job was to not immerse ourselves further in the mire.

'The strategic plans that we did have were at best confused, and despite what was being done by the boys on the ground, from an Australian government perspective, we were really only there out of alliance commitment. I had a realisation we were just marking time [in Afghanistan]. The boys [soldiers] weren't, but as a government we were.'

According to a confidential cable sent from the US Embassy in Canberra to the US Secretary of State in March 2009, the Australian Defence apparatus was fighting with Fitzgibbon over Afghanistan. It was also noted that an alliance commitment to the United States was the number one priority of Kevin Rudd's government, and that it was possible that Fitzgibbon's strong relationship with US Secretary of Defence was keeping him safe in his ministry.

'Fitzgibbon has been able to engage with his U. S. counterpart, Secretary [Robert] Gates, in support of his administration's number one priority: the U. S. Alliance,' the cable read under a subheading that read: 'WHO RUNS DEFENCE'.

The cable noted that 'Fitzgibbon has clashed with Defence' over a number of issues, including transparency in Afghanistan and Defence's stonewalling of the Australian media. It included a quote from Brendan Nelson that read: 'I think it's fair to say that at times the uniformed side of Defence finds it difficult to respond to directives that come from civilians in the form of the government and minister of the day … There is no doubt that you had to keep testing information to confirm its accuracy.'

Later that month, media reports emerged that Defence had directed the Defence Signals Directorate (later the Australian Signals Directorate) to hack Fitzgibbon's phone and computer systems. Allegations were also levelled at Defence that some of Fitzgibbon's personal information, having been obtained illegally, was then leaked to the media. It was reported that Fitzgibbon's relationship with a wealthy Chinese-born family friend was the reason for the alleged illegal hacking.

For the three months after the hacking allegations were made, Fitzgibbon was forced to defend himself against a number of allegations of improper behaviour, including that this Chinese family friend had paid for him to travel to China, and that the minister hadn't declared the travel as a gift. Eventually, in early June 2009, Fitzgibbon became the first Rudd minister to resign his ministry, for failing to declare travel gifts and 'not fully complying with the ministerial code of conduct'.

An investigation of the hacking allegations was called for, and, after an internal review, the Department of Defence cleared itself of any wrongdoing. Meanwhile, General Stanley McChrystal assumed command of ISAF and the war in Afghanistan rolled on.

20

'There were a lot of operators who took great
pleasure from hunting and killing people'

EARNING YOUR WAY TO the SASR headquarters, Campbell
Barracks in Perth, via selection and the reinforcement cycle is a
significant achievement, but being posted there is too. Even more
so in a time of war. Being part of the support staff of the SASR
can be the pinnacle of a military career, especially during a period
when the SASR are in combat.

Whatever the role – doctor, physio, IT expert, mechanic –
this is what you are trained and paid to do, and there is immense
satisfaction to be had when you are able to do so. Which is not to
say that a posting to Campbell Barracks during a time of war is
enjoyable. Most, in fact, say it is not.

'It was a highly aggressive and assertive culture, and a long
fucking way away from comfortable,' says Lieutenant Colonel
Mark Mathieson, who conducted eight SOTG deployments and
served as the SASR unit psychologist.

'From a psychological perspective, it was extremely tribal,'
says Mathieson of the SASR culture. 'There were people who
wouldn't sit on the same side of the mess with each other. Officers
were no different. There were officers that fucking hated each
other, so there was a normalisation of that culture.'

Mathieson had no problem with the lack of comfort. No one
joined the SASR and expected to be comfortable, but he became
increasingly concerned that the 'kill or be killed' attitude of the

regiment was bleeding from the battlefield back to the barracks. Grievances often developed in Afghanistan. Bullying was rife, with junior soldiers sometimes being beaten and belittled by more senior soldiers. Many of the soldiers considered not only support staff but the rest of Defence and the civilian apparatus as being of lesser importance.

According to Mathieson, threats were common within the regiment. Some involved impediments to another soldier's career, but others were physical, ranging from assault to death.

'You can't have a unit that's all about violence and not have threats of violence as a form of influence,' he says. 'Sometimes very subtly and sometimes not, and as you went up the hierarchy of rank people generally became more subtle.'

He says this 'Lord of the Flies' culture was embedded into the regiment even before Afghanistan, but was often not considered an issue as long as everyone was effective in doing the job. When Mathieson came to the unit, however, there was some confusion about exactly what the job should be.

The long-range reconnaissance mould in which the SASR had historically been cast was being destroyed, in part because of technological advances in drones and optics, but also because of how the post-9/11 wars were being prosecuted. An exceptional number of raids, direct actions and compound assaults were carried out in Iraq and Afghanistan. Many at SOCOMD believed this work was best left to the commandos, and that the SASR operators should not become blunt instruments of this type.

'There was a lot of talk within the unit about how the SASR had lost a bit of direction,' says Mathieson. 'It was already seen [that] the commandos were taking many of the heavy-hitting roles and they were getting lots of kudos [at SOCOMD] for coming up to speed so quickly.'

There was a desire within SOCOMD for the SASR to become a unit of warrior-spies, working closely with organisations like ASIS and the ASD on clandestine missions in the region and beyond. 'There was almost this panic about finding this new role. I was told to contribute to [building] a model that would help select those people,' says Mathieson. 'They wanted me to [build selection criteria] for these guys who could be spies, but it was completely different to the commando mindset.'

This model was sometimes at odds with the ideal candidate for the type of warfighting that was being undertaken in Afghanistan. That operator was 'aggressive, assertive ... somewhat narcissistic', and enjoyed conflict.

'There's a term we use in psychology called "sensation seeking", and these are people who are driven to seek sensation, as conflict is a form of sensation,' says Mathieson, citing another selection criterion. 'If a sensation seeker hates someone, they hate them with a passion, so you have to manage that.'

This warfighting personality was at odds with what was needed, should the SASR transition to a more clandestine role.

'You don't want the gregarious commando [for that role],' Mathieson explains. 'You want a bloke that's full-on bland and perceived as a failure in his everyday life. You don't want the 110-kilo monster, you want a weedy, middle-aged, balding guy.'

This problem with this selection transition was that, in Afghanistan, the SASR desperately needed more assertive, aggressive sensation seekers. The SASR's obligation in Afghanistan was to red-line the regiment. With one squadron deployed in Afghanistan at all times, all the warfighting operators in the unit were either deployed, preparing for a future deployment or recovering from the last one. With injuries common and operators required to complete a raft of courses to stay current, there was a constant struggle to keep the squadrons fully staffed. New operators were always desperately needed.

Afghanistan created a tension over the future of the SASR. Many believed it should distance itself from the upskilled infantry and direct-action roles the unit had taken on in Afghanistan – but this was the type of work the Americans were asking Australia to do, and whoever did this work was going to get the 'pats on the head'.

'The [2nd Commando Regiment was] getting new facilities, new gear,' says Mathieson. 'There was a lot of anxiety about the funding. Within the unit there were a lot of discussions about how we retain, or perhaps even regain, that force-of-choice mantle within the minds of the politicians. You can't underestimate the power of decision-making and how it relates to budget.'

The US military leaders wanted the SASR conducting kill/ capture missions in Afghanistan, and many influential figures within the regiment also wanted to do that. The Australian government generally just wanted SOCOMD to do whatever the United States wanted. Mark Mathieson left SOCOMD in 2011, but says that by then, as far as he could tell, nothing had come of this effort at a selection and focus pivot.

* * *

Many people tried to investigate who was being killed in Afghanistan and why over the course of the war, but few had the access to forces and territory of Australian lawyer Philip Alston. As a United Nations special rapporteur on extrajudicial, summary or arbitrary executions, Alston – who had grown up and studied in Australia but then moved to the United States, where he had worked as the co-chair of the Center for Human Rights and Global Justice at New York University – was able to open doors that were firmly closed to almost everyone else in the world.

ISAF had been established under the authority of the United Nations Security Council Resolution 1386, and that meant the UN had some ability to scrutinise the conduct of those prosecuting the war, including the United States. By 2009, conflict deaths and civilian deaths were on the rise in Afghanistan, and Alston was engaged by the United Nations to 'investigate how and why these killings are happening, and to formulate recommendations directed at reducing civilian casualties, however or by whomever they are caused'.

Alston and his team prepared as well as they could in New York, before travelling across Afghanistan to investigate. Their work took them from Kabul to the provinces of Parwan, Kunar, Nangarhar, Kandahar, Helmand and Jowzjan. Alston focused on civilian-on-civilian murder and indiscriminate targeting by all the forces in Afghanistan, including the Taliban, but also investigated a raft of what looked like assassinations or summary executions by Western or Afghan government aligned forces.

His team recognised that targeted killing could be a legal part of a modern military campaign (something that is contested, Alston notes), but regardless looked at approvals, intelligence, missions and civilian involvement, and how they related to the US and international justice systems, and the evolving Afghan justice system.

Having neither the time nor the resources to investigate all the targeted killings happening in Afghanistan, Alston decided to focus on a selection of incidents – one of which was the killing of two brothers, one a shopkeeper and the other a poultry butcher, who had been living in the outskirts of Kandahar city.

Over six months, the brothers, Abdul Habib and Mohammad Ali, were the subject of three night raids. In each instance they were hooded and shackled and taken away for interrogation; one time they were held for a month. Neither brother was ever charged with a crime, nor were they informed of what they were suspected of doing. Abdul Habib was told not to tell anyone about his detention, and was threatened with violence if he did. Regardless, he approached the Afghan Independent Human Rights Commission (AIHRC), saying neither he nor his brother were involved in the insurgency, and that he feared for their lives.

A few weeks later, at about 1.30 am, their house was cordoned off by Afghan soldiers, then a group of what looked like American soldiers smashed through the door and scaled the walls of their home. In front of their families, both men were shot dead. The brothers had no weapons, and witnesses said they had offered no resistance.

ISAF was required to give Alston and his team unfettered access to its personnel and files, and this resulted in interviews being conducted with its most senior commanders, the commanding officers of the regional commands and the most senior Afghan officials, including President Hamid Karzai and NDS head

Amrullah Saleh (who, Alston later found, was tapping his phone). Alston found it exceptionally difficult to gain clarity on the Kandahar raid, but discovered that the coalition and the United States were maintaining at least six JPEL or kill/capture lists.

'If you challenge people who are drawing up these lists, they say ... "No, no, no, we never put anyone on without verification, and we even try to get triple verification," and yet there were so many cases like the chicken butchers of Kandahar ... that the only conclusion to be made was that it was some business rival who put them on the list,' says Alston.

Eventually, it was found that it was CIA paramilitary agents who had stormed the house and killed the brothers. Alston attempted to discover what evidence might justify the killings, and tried to link the brothers to the insurgency, but he could find no connection.

'There were many cases that were subsequently tracked down, but there was no justification for putting people on these lists,' Alston says. 'To confidently say that someone ... is taking an active part of hostilities – you'd like to see the evidence.' Alston claims he was never allowed to review the evidence used to place a target on a JPEL.

In his report, Alston wrote about the impenetrable intelligence and approvals process of kill/capture, seeing it as a regression to the bad old days of the Cold War, when the United States was supporting or, in some instances, running its own death squads around the world without any oversight. Alston expanded upon his thoughts in the *Harvard National Security Journal*: 'From the perspective of both domestic and international law, the practice of secret killings conducted outside conventional combat settings, undertaken on an institutionalized and systematic basis, and with extremely limited if any verifiable external accountability, is a deeply disturbing and regressive one.'

Alston also found that many Afghans had been killed accidentally in night raids, as rural Afghans would likely 'fire on anyone, including troops, breaking down the compound's door at night'.

Something on which Alston didn't report – and the most depressing aspect of his work in Afghanistan – was just how disconnected the military effort and programs like JPEL were from actual peace, or winning the war. The enemy could be constantly killed in JPEL raids, but to what end? Apparently, to create space for an Afghan government and military partners that, Alston says, were often more predatory and destructive than the enemy.

'I had all these meetings with people where everything they were saying was such obvious bullshit,' says Alston. 'The Taliban offered security on their terms, which was obviously problematic, but they would offer social services. They would be providing food or healthcare and resolving divorces and other disputes. If you had those problems and called in the government, they would most likely shake you down. Compared to the warlords, you would be better off under a Taliban-run village system, because at least there would be systems and some predictability in place. It was obviously not a value system you wanted, but in the short term, and keeping your life going, it was pretty straightforward.'

According to Alston, in those places where night raids and JPEL prosecution were common, and where services and justice were rare commodities, 'you would be mad if you were an average Afghan and you wouldn't side with the Taliban'.

* * *

During the war in Afghanistan, the SASR had one of the lowest, if not the lowest, official levels of PTSD, depression and mental-health disorders in the entire ADF. Mark Mathieson says this was in part a by-product of the SASR's selection criteria for stoics, soldiers who would be reluctant to look for mental-health help.

'Part of what we're looking for in operators is the ability to park shit,' he explains. 'To compartmentalise. And to continue to function at an extremely high level for a very long period of time. That's very useful in an operator.'

The rest, he says, is because both the SASR and the commando regiments made a conscious decision not to engage with any of the mental-health strategies being used by most of Defence, which meant they hugely under-reported their instances of mental-health injury.

'We know that 2 to 8 per cent of soldiers will suffer a mental-health issue after an operation,' Mathieson says. 'We know that, and yet the political vibe we were getting was that the only acceptable rate was zero. [Joint Health Command] had all these processes and training [that were becoming mandatory], and [SOCOMD] was saying: "How the fuck are we going to do that?"'

Mathieson says he was in meetings with SASR senior officers in which they discussed how they could avoid having to fully meet Joint Health Command's policies on PTSD.

'[SASR command decided,] "We're not doing it. If we do any of it, we have to do all of it, and we're not doing that. Then we're fucked,"' Mathieson reports. And this avoidance was possible with the flick of a pen. 'Just about everything can be vetoed by the CO [commanding officer]. If there's an operational imperative not to do it, that's what happens. It's a "get out of jail" card.'

The real level of PTSD and mental-health problems within the SASR during the war in Afghanistan will now never be known, but Mathieson suspects the decision not to engage with Joint Health Command was made because if that true level was revealed, the entire regiment might have been deemed combat-ineffective.

'Would you want to be the commanding officer who has to explain that you couldn't muster enough soldiers to keep the war going?' Mathieson asks.

He believes everyone at a certain level of seniority knew that, as a result of combat, some operators' lives would end or be ruined due to the psychological trauma they were left with after combat. The likelihood of injury, wounding, or death in combat or by accident was usually a consideration in military operational planning, and at the very least, Mark Mathieson says, an estimate of the resulting suicides or extreme mental-health disorders should have been factored in each time the SASR deployed a force element – regardless of whether the deaths or disorders came during or after the war.

'In officer training, you're trained to calculate the death rate of an operation or action, and weigh that against the action's objectives,' he explains. 'We should have been doing that as we went along, but no one ever did.'

According to Mathieson, after operators had experienced multiple SOTG rotations, 'red flags were popping up all over the place'. At the weekly welfare meeting with the commanding officer, Mathison saw an increase in instances of 'marital difficulties, domestic violence, kids struggling, kids acting out and being violent at school, low-level misdemeanours, speeding, getting mega-fucking-blind at the pub and fighting.'

While this type of behaviour was not uncommon in regular army units, which were full of teens and post-teens, it was unusual in the SASR, which was mostly staffed with intelligent family men aged in their thirties and forties.

Mathieson also increasingly noticed 'the jump' from Afghan veterans – meaning they had a physical response to noise or sudden movements. He also saw an obsession with managing a room while in Perth – for instance, ensuring you didn't have your back to a door or window. 'That stuff's perfectly normal and useful when on deployment,' he notes. 'If you're hypervigilant, that keeps you alive. It's not very functional long-term.'

Many of the soldiers who had deployed to Afghanistan were in a state of constant anxiety, and Mathieson says this was often leveraged by officers and NCOs to ensure extra drive and focus at work. Rather than recognising or acknowledging that constant anxiety could be a medical issue, Mathieson says, energy was often directed towards getting men back to Afghanistan, where it was accepted and useful.

'The organisation was structured like that. "You're having marital difficulties? Just move into the mess, mate. Problem solved. You're with your brothers full-time now." Deploy again after two months, sign a waiver, ignore an injury,' says Mathieson. 'That's what the army wants, by the way. They don't want people to say no.'

Also ignored in the regiment, Mathieson says, was an unhealthy creeping obsession with death, exhibited in the 'iconography, the slogans and music and the porn' that was being consumed and shared.

'All humans have a fascination with death, but civilians tend to overestimate military's cold professionalism around that subject. Doing your homework on killing people – what a dead body looks like when it's been hit by an airburst round – it's preparing yourself. It's part of the training. It used to be called "blooding",' says Mathieson. 'If it's done in an unmanaged, unprofessional way, it's a recipe for disaster.'

Helmet-cam footage, videos and photographs of dead Afghans were being spread within and among the patrols, as were gruesome stories of kill counts. Mathieson says the culture of death at the regiment became dangerous, and might also have changed the cultural and moral composition of the regiment.

'We had a lot of guys apply ... who had started to see that the SAS were operating as hunter/killers in Afghanistan, and they wanted that. They wanted to join the unit so they could do just that – hunt people and kill them,' Mathieson says.

'There were a lot of operators who took great pleasure from hunting and killing people, both professionally and personally. We gave them moral and political and legal permission to do it. We *asked* them to do it. Is it unrealistic for us to think that none of them might take great fucking pleasure in it?'

21

'He has my greatest sympathy ... it will not assuage his guilty conscience. I wish him well in what must be a difficult time for him'

IN THE WINTER OF 2009, two concurrent events of Australian military historical interest occurred in Uruzgan. The first was that a company of soldiers from the 1st Commando Regiment (1CDO), the part-time reserve element of the special forces, replaced what Chief of Defence Angus Houston described as 'exhausted' full-time special forces units. This was the first time since World War II that an Australian military reserve unit was deployed into a war zone. The second event was that two of those commandos were indicted for unlawful killings, the first and (at the time of writing) only time Australian soldiers deployed to Afghanistan were so charged.

1CDO is the oldest of the units in SOCOMD, having been raised in the 1950s, but it was also the least respected, as it was manned primarily by part-time soldiers. They were sometimes derisively tagged by the full-time operators as 'chocos', or chocolate soldiers – the suggestion being that they would melt when things got hot.

The reservists transitioned to full-time service for the six to eight months leading up to their deployment, and in that period they were trained by experienced full-time commandos and SASR operators. Even so, as Chief of Army Lieutenant General Ken Gillespie told the ABC later, 'There were some shortcomings in how we'd prepared this force for operations. There was a concern about leadership.'

The first SOTG that was constituted primarily of reservist shooters arrived in Afghanistan at the beginning of November 2008, with 1CDO designated as Force Element Charlie, or FE Charlie. Before the end of their first month in country, they had suffered their first casualty.

The reservists were to provide continuation in the hunting of JPEL targets, and they had been sent out to the Mehrabad Valley on a kill/capture mission. While on approach to the assault, 25-year-old Lieutenant Michael Fussell, a full time commando deployed with 1CDO, stepped on a pressure-plate IED and was killed instantly. A few weeks later, in the Baluchi Valley, another IED was triggered, but without loss of life.

Shortly after that, Force Element Charlie suffered another fatality. They had been sent out on a week-long vehicle patrol in search of a JPEL target, and while staying overnight at a patrol base just north of Dorafshan, they experienced an indirect rocket attack. These were common and usually ineffective, but on this occasion a rocket punched through the thin skin of a shipping container where some of the commandos were sleeping and smashed into 30-year-old Private Greg Sher.

In the immediate aftermath of Sher's death, a mortar and missile attack was ordered in the Baluchi Valley, ostensibly against JPEL target Objective Flambard, believed to be involved in the rocket attack. Flambard was reported killed, as were a number of other Afghans. There were suggestions that this was a reckless retaliatory attack for the Australians' deaths.

The ADF has stressed that it has never conducted revenge attacks, but some land and air assaults were authorised directly in the wake of Australian deaths. Some Afghan families claimed they'd inadvertently been targeted after Sher's death, and payments were made to a number of families by the ADF, with no admission of culpability. Then, on 11 February 2009, the raid from which allegations of unlawful killing resulted was undertaken.

Hunting a medium-value target named Mullah Noorallah, the Australians were to conduct a night 'hard-knock' visit to a compound of interest in the village of Sorkh Morghab, on the eastern bank of the Dorafshan River, close to where Objective Nile had been killed some years earlier. But this raid was to be drastically different from the Objective Nile raid; indeed, it would be defined by a lack of combatants, not a surplus.

In the dead of the night, the commandos approached a rural home in which a large extended family of wheat and corn farmers were sleeping. They included a man named Zahir and his brother Amrullah; Zakera, a teenager; Elsanulah, ten years old; Nawab, 11; Shuri Noor, aged four; Gutima, a toddler; and Esmatulah, a baby. The family lived in a traditional mud-brick compound. There were four external walls with no windows, while the living areas were a number of simple rooms built around an internal courtyard.

Between 20 and 30 soldiers – mostly Australian commandos, with some Afghan interpreters and a handful of Afghan National Army soldiers – broke the lock on the compound gates and entered the courtyard at about 2 am, splitting into two groups to clear the compound's rooms to the left and right. Through his night-vision goggles, an Australian lance corporal named David Millar peered into a room and saw a man with an AK-47 to his shoulder only a couple of metres away, covering a door about to be breached. This was Amrullah, ready to confront what he perhaps thought were thieves or tribal enemies.

Millar shot at Amrullah through the window, and Amrullah spun and returned fire. Millar then pulled out an F1 grenade – a fragmentation grenade built in the Victorian high-country town of Benalla – and posted it. When it exploded, the 4000 tiny steel ball bearings wrapped around the charge smashed through the room in a 'uniform distribution of lethal fragments through 360°', as the manufacturer, Thales, boasts in its marketing material. The ball bearings shredded sheets, clothing and skin, embedding deeply into flesh, organs and plaster. Women and children screamed.

Another burst of fire from Amrullah's AK-47 could be heard, and a sergeant ordered that another grenade be posted into the room. He also ordered for a machine gun to be fired into the room. It's believed the machine gun was not fired, perhaps because of a countermanding order. David Millar heeded the order to post another grenade in. Thousands more searing ball bearings blasted to all corners of the room.

There was a moment of silence, except for the ringing in the ears of the soldiers and survivors. The AK-47 had been silenced and, for the Australians, the shimmering green in the scene became opaque and unreal as dust and debris caught in the air and was illuminated in their NVGs.

When the Australian soldiers entered the room in which the grenades had been posted, they saw a scene of horror. There was some movement, some figures rolling in their own blood, but they also saw punctured death. Shuri Noor was still moving, injured. The babies, Gutima and Esmatulah, were still alive but barely. Nawab and Zakera were dead. Amrullah himself was wounded and later died.

The Australians were horrified and tried to treat the wounded children. Four-year-old Shuri Noor survived her wounds but the babies, Gutima and Esmatulah, died that night.

'This is what happens in war. Extremes happen. We had to grenade a room to try and save our lives. And this was the result,' one of the commandos said.

The next day, Lieutenant General Mark Evans, Chief of Joint Operations, made an official statement: 'During the conduct of this operation there was an exchange of fire between our forces and the Taliban. Tragically a number of people were killed and wounded during this incident.'

The matter went into an internal review process, and no further information was made available to the public. This review, conducted by the Chief of Joint Operations, found no major fault in the conduct of the soldiers or officers. This was not the end of the story, however.

The inaccessibility of the victims and locations in such investigations usually meant the Afghan side of the story was rarely heard, but in this instance Farid Popal, an Afghan man living in Perth, and SBS journalist Sophie McNeill worked with the bereaved family to shed light on the raid. Popal travelled to Kandahar and spoke to some of the surviving family members. He also sent a camera into Uruzgan, and at the compound where the massacre had happened, the family members' graves and the survivors' grief was recorded. SBS's *Dateline* aired a special about the raid, stressing that Australia's commandos had attacked not the Taliban but a family of farmers.

In a turn of events that shocked SOCOMD, a brief of evidence was developed by the Australian Defence Force Investigative Service (ADFIS), an independent ADF body often despised for its work, after it conducted investigations into potentially illegal actions by ADF members. That brief of evidence made its way to the desk of the ADF's first ever Director of Military Prosecutions, Brigadier Lyn McDade. She was a 23-year veteran of the ADF, having often served as a reservist while working in the Northern Territory as a civil and police prosecutor, the deputy coroner and a relieving magistrate For decades, there had been prosecutorial powers within each of the individual ADF commands, but in 2006 a single authority was empowered for prosecution across all commands, including SOCOMD.

Brigadier McDade read through the evidence presented by ADFIS, and concluded that three people should be charged: two soldiers and also the lieutenant colonel, referred to only as 'M', who ordered the raid, which Brigadier McDade believed was in contravention of a classified ISAF standing order. This ISAF order had been negotiated with the Afghan government and President Karzai, who was concerned about the number of civilians who were being killed in JPEL night raids and at vehicle checkpoints. ('We have shot an amazing number of people, but to my knowledge, none has ever proven to be a threat,' General McChrystal once said of the vehicle checkpoint deaths.)

It's believed the charge recommended against Lieutenant Colonel M was for breaking ISAF SOP 309, which prohibited commanders from assaulting nearby compounds after not finding their target in their target compound, unless that adjacent compound was already approved in advance for assault.

Brigadier McDade believed that the sergeant who ordered the second grenade to be thrown should be charged, as in her view the evidence showed that he knew there were women and children in the room when he gave the order. McDade also recommended charges against David Millar, who threw both grenades, as she believed the evidence suggested he too knew there were women and children in the room. Decades earlier, the Nuremberg trials against Nazi war criminals had established the international legal norm that military orders do not supersede legal obligations.

Brigadier McDade was advised by the Chief of Army, Lieutenant General Ken Gillespie, to think deeply about the ramifications of such a prosecution, but she felt obliged to proceed. And since the Director of Military Prosecutions sat outside the normal chain of command, she was able to do so.

There was outrage throughout much of the army when the charges were announced. A very public political storm emerged. Broadcaster Alan Jones championed the cause of the soldiers, saying: 'This is another consequence of the Rudd government. This woman was given untrammelled power, greater power than the military command, by the Rudd Government ... This is where it has brought us.' The new federal opposition leader, Liberal MP Tony Abbott, was also vocal, saying he thought the soldiers were being 'stabbed in the back' by their own government.

A group of former Australian generals – including Mark Smethurst's father, Major General Neville Smethurst – together petitioned for the charges to be dropped, saying: 'We must give our soldiers the confidence to undertake the difficult, bloody and unsavoury job with which they have been tasked.' Online abuse of Brigadier McDade piled up, and she received a number of physical threats.

The charge against the lieutenant colonel was the first to be dropped. Senior officers within SOCOMD gave statements to Brigadier McDade explaining how ISAF standard operating procedures were enacted in practice, which was not always in line with the theory or intent of the orders.

'The application in practice of ISAF SOP 309 involved a significant departure from what would be required from a plain reading of its terms,' Brigadier McDade wrote later in a submission to Defence Minister Stephen Smith. 'I considered that there was no reasonable prospect that a panel of military officers would find Lieutenant Colonel M guilty.'

The prosecutions of David Millar and his sergeant were also later thrown out – but not by Brigadier McDade. At a pre-trial hearing, held by Chief Judge Advocate Brigadier Ian Westwood, the second-most senior officer working in the military justice service after the Judge Advocate General (a position held, until 2007, by Ben Roberts-Smith's father, Len Roberts-Smith), ruled that regardless of the evidence, the soldiers could not be liable for the deaths because they owed no legal duty of care to the Afghans. Before the commandos could be convicted of manslaughter, it had to be established that they owed a duty of care to the family sleeping in their home. Of course, they were not permitted to breach the rules of armed conflict, but in the absence of a duty of care, negligent deaths were legally permissible. The Chief Judge Advocate ruled that, in a combat environment, a duty of care simply couldn't arise, and he cited legal precedent established during World War II.

In her letter to the defence minister, Brigadier McDade said she did 'not accept that [the Chief Judge Advocate's] decision is correct in law', and that she believed he had created 'new law' with his ruling. New law or old, this was how it would henceforth be within the ADF justice system: when Australian soldiers assaulted compounds during night raids, the civilians in those compounds were owed no duty of care by the assaulting soldiers.

This ruling was a relief for many SOCOMD soldiers, including David Millar, but he said it did not bring complete relief to him and the other commandos. Millar maintained that he'd done nothing wrong. It was true that he'd heard screaming from women and children after posting the first grenade into the room in front of him, he said, but it was never established that he knew where that screaming was coming from.

Millar later brought legal action against Lyn McDade for malicious prosecution and for making a false claim when saying in her ministerial submission that he 'knew for certain that there were women and children in the room'. On hearing about this legal action, McDade issued a statement to the ABC regarding David Millar: 'He has my greatest sympathy. However this litigation, if he has commenced it, will not assuage his guilty conscience. I wish him well in what must be a difficult time for him.' When McDade's statement was published, Millar's lawyer filed a motion to amend the claim of damages in order to include it.

There's no evidence to suggest the case went any further in court after this amendment. David Millar went back to Afghanistan as a private military contractor, but says he was too wary when conducting his duties, especially when children were around, to be effective. He was eventually medically discharged from the ADF after he exhibited symptoms consistent with PTSD.

Immediately after the killings, a payment was arranged by the ADF to be sent to a Sorkh Morghab village elder, with the intent that the money be handed over to the bereaved family. This was standard procedure for the ADF after the killing of children, women or non-combatants in Afghanistan; the accepted rate was $1500 for a death and $800 for a significant injury. The family say they have never received any compensation.

Those who served on that rotation still believe they were not afforded the organisational protection that that a full-time unit like the SASR would have been given.

'We did exactly our job, exactly as we're meant to do it,' David Millar told the ABC.

22

'He was lifting his trousers, pointing to the prosthetic
leg, expecting some sympathy from the troops'

AS FORCE ELEMENT CHARLIE reserve force rotated out of
Afghanistan in 2009, an SOTG replaced them, including Force
Element Bravo from 1CDO and the 2nd Squadron from the SASR,
for what would be an eventful tour.

The commandos would be tasked with a long and action-
packed job in Helmand Province supporting the British, who were
trying to install a turbine at a key hydroelectric dam (the turbine
was transferred but never installed). This job would result in some
significant battles, horrific injuries and the death of Australian
special forces engineer Sergeant Brett Till.

It was the SASR element that would make the headlines
however, generating perhaps Australia's most notorious piece
of wartime ephemera of the modern era: the prosthetic leg of a
man killed by Ben Roberts-Smith, which was then used, both in
Afghanistan and in Perth, as a drinking vessel, troop mascot and
key element of Robert-Smith's defamation suit.

When the SASR arrived back in Uruzgan in 2009, they had a
number of JPEL target packages ready to go. Shortly after coming
online in Uruzgan, the SASR element started a mission titled
Operation Harpoon, the aim of which was to prosecute a number
of JPEL targets across the province. The first target scratched off
was Objective Depth Charger, a bombmaker believed to have
been involved in the death of Michael Fussell.

Two patrols drove to Mehrabad, dropped off the vehicles then walked over a mountain through the night to the site of the ambush, which was the compound of an Afghan human source. The JPEL target was killed at a motorbike repair store adjacent to the garrisoned compound, with an electronic warfare operator monitoring the target as he moved closer to the ambush.

Before Objective Depth Charger arrived at the ambush site, according to an SASR soldier who gave testimony in the Ben Roberts-Smith defamation trial, a dispatch came through to the SASR element's radio from one of the patrol commanders that everyone in the killing field could be considered to be directly participating in hostilities – the legal threshold for lethal targeting – and that once the shooting started, everyone should be killed. It's not known how these other Afghans were legally designated as being able to be lethally engaged.

At the ambush site, an unknown number of Afghans were killed at close range. At least five Australians engaged the Afghans, including two men who were on telescopic ladders behind a wall.

The targeting eye then fell on a man named Mullah Ismail, elevated on the JPEL as Objective Sabre, a 'medium-value target'. After intelligence suggested that he and some bodyguards were bedded down in the village of Jalbay, in the Chenartu district, a raid was planned. The SASR element came back empty-handed and an after-action report was generated: '[R]eliable intelligence indicated a senior insurgent, who was identified for deliberate targeting, was at a compound. Afghan National Security Force (ANSF) led mission with SOTG to clear the compound. Senior insurgent not found.'

It was an ISAF requirement that night raids be led by an Afghan force, but as the Afghans lacked training and equipment, and were often not considered trustworthy, they probably would not have 'led' a mission with the Australian SASR then. It's true that the raid didn't locate Mullah Ismail – but three other men were found and killed: Muhammad Mussa, Janan Mussa and Taza Khan. One was killed, according to Defence's investigating officer's report, while he was 'observing courtyard though window', another while 'attempting to conceal himself in hay' and the third while 'moving tactically'. No weapons were found on these men, nor were they identified by Defence (the ABC's *Four Corners* program later identified them), yet the killings were cleared as legal, as 'each soldier who fired decided their target was a threat', according to internal reporting. Furthermore, the report said, the 'identities of the deceased were unlikely ever to be known with certainty; on the balance of probability, they were likely to have been associates of the senior insurgent leader and acted in a manner consistent with taking a direct part in hostilities'.

This type of reporting was done by military legal officers, who were tasked with ensuring that soldiers and officers adhered to Australian and international law while on deployment. A lawyer with experience of special forces targeting and investigation in Afghanistan says that without access to full internal reporting and the intelligence briefs, it's difficult to know exactly what the true story of these three killings is, but he found the reporting that was available to be unusual, lacking and inconsistent with what's typically required to use legal lethal force.

The official reporting found that these men were unarmed, and all appeared to be hiding or attempting to hide. Further reporting done by *Four Corners* said the family in the home that was targeted was hosting a wake for a child who had died recently. The family admitted that Mullah Ismail had come to the house to pay his respects to the dead and the family, but said that two of the men who were killed were family members and farmers uninvolved with the insurgency. The third, they said, was a peasant labourer who worked for them and was also not part of the insurgency.

The legal source says that he doesn't understand how the men who were killed could simultaneously have been unidentified, unarmed, not known to be connected to an armed force (except as 'associates' of a JPEL target) and yet considered to be acting 'in a manner consistent with taking direct part in hostilities'. Furthermore, he says, mixing the balance of probability and likelihood in the reporting creates a strange and confused legal standard. In a legal sense, 'on the balance of probability' means simply that there was more than a 50 per cent chance that they were associates of the insurgent; but 'likely' is a much higher threshold of probability.

Another legal officer interviewed says that the reporting was done in a very 'high-tempo environment', and that the reported circumstances around a killing were usually just the story of the people who pulled the trigger. 'When I wrote my reports, I had to rely on what I was told,' he says. 'Whether that was right or wrong, there was no way of validating what happened.'

There is undoubtedly more to this story, and further release of military reporting and intelligence ephemera would create more context, but this was all the information that was released to the public at the request of the Australian Senate. The family of the two men who were killed by the Australians wanted to get away from the war after the raid, and relocated their 35 family members from Chenartu closer to Tarin Kot, where they thought they would be less likely to be subjected to night raids or airstrikes. A report by Dutch NGO The Liaison Office estimated that more than half of the population of Chenartu fled the district between 2008 and 2011.

* * *

Before and after the mission hunting Mullah Ismail, the SASR were in the problem area around Dorafshan, doing 'strike to develop' missions that involved assaulting quiet compounds and villages in an attempt to agitate a SIGINT response or an attack from JPEL targets, and supporting the Australian Mentoring Task Force One (MTF-1), the conventional force that replaced the Australian reconstruction task forces, reflecting a strategic change from rebuilding Afghanistan's infrastructure to building its security forces.

When Dutch ethnographers arrived in Uruzgan, they found that the 70 or so villages in Dorafshan represented a patchwork of different clans and tribes. Most of the occupants were farmers, many of them subsistence farmers, and the Dutch found that the area had been suffering through drought conditions. Violence, often deadly, was common in the area, as residents fought over water, land or honour. The violence had only been exacerbated when Jan Mohammad came to power, as many of his tribal enemies lived in that area.

When the Dutch and Australian forces came into Uruzgan, efforts to pacify Dorafshan were a priority. The area was the entrance to the Baluchi and Chora valleys, and only 10 to 15 kilometres from Tarin Kot. With few bridges crossing the river, it had been primarily the eastern bank villages, which could be reached by road from Tarin Kot, that had benefited from the early reconstruction largesse. Many of those villages, even though not tribally disposed to do so, had engaged with the government. It was on the western bank that the bulk of the resentment against the government was felt: many of those villages had embraced the insurgency and the Taliban.

By 2009, two Australian patrol bases, Qudus and Buman, were situated east and west of the area, on the elevated edges of the green belt. At those bases, the 70-strong Australian mentoring element was attempting to stand up Afghan recruits. These recruits, far from their tribal lands, often did not have the fight in them.

One of the Australians mentoring at FOB Buman was 21-year-old Matthew Hopkins who, on 16 March, was shot and killed close to a western bank village called Kakarak, while on patrol with the Afghan soldiers he was mentoring. This was a place where, only a few weeks earlier, two other Australian soldiers who were part of the mentoring force had been injured as they supported Afghan recruits. It was also where Mark Donaldson had been injured in an IED strike in August 2008.

As the SASR arrived in Dorafshan, having been JPEL hunting in the Baluchi Valley, the Australian mentoring force and their Afghan partners were, again, fighting. A clearance mission named Operation Shak Hawel (meaning 'mysterious area') had been mounted and, in the village of Kakarak, fierce resistance had been experienced. As what became known as the Second Battle of Kakarak raged, with the Australian troops covered by Australian ASLAV cannons and machine guns, an SASR troop was watching the fighting from an elevated and defensible position they had established with their vehicles.

An SASR patrol commander testified that, the night before, an Afghan had been killed in the green belt, and in the morning a group of locals had massed towards the SASR element, complaining that an innocent man had been murdered. An undisclosed amount of reparation money was paid to the family in the morning, and the element then moved through western Dorafshan, hoping to join the fight with the MTF. A fight they found.

After the Australian infantry were repelled from Kakarak, a Navy SEAL JTAC attached to the troop directed bombs to a Kakarak compound from which the Australians had been receiving fire. The SASR were then tasked with assaulting the bombed compound, designated by the Australians as 'Whiskey 108'.

'That day particularly, a lot of people admit they thought they were going into a big battle,' Ben Roberts-Smith said in court in 2021. 'They thought they were going to lose their lives and it was a big battle.'

It was during this action that Roberts-Smith was alleged to have committed his first known murder.

* * *

The assault on Whiskey 108 was a whole-troop action, involving all five patrols. Under a slate-grey sky, with drizzle falling, the patrols crossed aqueducts and muddy fields of tall poppies, arriving in and around Whiskey 108 wet. At least one Afghan had been killed during the infiltration, but it seemed most insurgents nearby either weren't alert to the SASR infiltration or chose not to engage them. Two of the patrols were sent in to clear Whiskey 108, which according to one of the soldiers giving evidence in the defamation trial, was 'destroyed … pretty much rubble'.

In court, two very different versions of the assault of Whiskey 108 emerged.

Ben Roberts-Smith's testimony was that a man with a prosthetic leg was spotted running from the bombed compound, with a bolt-action rifle in his hands. Roberts-Smith said that, without any doubt, the man was directly participating in hostilities, so he raised his weapon and killed the man. Furthermore, Roberts-Smith testified that he knew that the man used 'the leg to conceal explosives'.

Ben Roberts-Smith's patrol commander, anonymised as Person 5, said there was a JPEL target they'd been hunting for some years named Objective Xiphoid, who 'was known to carry initiation sets for IEDs in his prosthetic limb', but that the killed man 'didn't appear to be [Xiphoid]'.

After he killed that man, Roberts-Smith said, another armed insurgent appeared and Roberts-Smith raised his rifle to shoot him, but his weapon experienced a stoppage. Roberts-Smith said he knelt to resolve the stoppage, and as he did so, another soldier shot and killed the man. Roberts-Smith assumed the second man was killed by one of the operators in his team, and he suggested two people. Both those men denied in court that either killing happened in the way Roberts-Smith testified. It was alleged in court that both Afghans were murdered.

'To have somebody tell you that is somehow a criminal act or war crime makes me angry. Makes me really angry,' Roberts-Smith said in court.

It's agreed that SASR patrols entered the courtyard of Whiskey 108, and testimony given at the defamation trial said that there were a number of women and children in the courtyard who were agitated and animated. After a cursory search of the courtyard, one of the Australians testified he found a 'battle bra' (chest webbing that can hold ammunition clips) as well as ammunition and an old Russian grenade in a bucket. After that discovery, he said the Australians decided to do a more comprehensive search of the compound, and there, covered by a mat and some grass, they found entrance to a small tunnel. Testimony was given that

Ben Roberts-Smith offered to clear the tunnel, but that suggestion that the huge soldier would attempt to clear the small tunnel was laughable. The job was given to a much shorter and slighter SASR operator, formerly of the NZSAS, designated in court as Person 35.

Person 5, testified that it was an Afghan soldier with his team who noticed the entrance to the tunnel, and that he sent Person 35 into the tunnel without his helmet, armour or rifle, who cleared the tunnel with his pistol and emerged saying the tunnel was clear.

Person 5 and Ben Roberts-Smith testified that a weapons cache was found in the tunnel, but no men.

After that tunnel clearance, Person 5 said, he called 'compound secure' and most of the troop started a 'rummage', looking for weapons and ammunition.

Five current or former SASR soldiers testified that two men came out of the tunnel, unarmed and compliant: one an old man and the other man disabled, with a prosthetic leg. One soldier – now a warrant officer in the SASR – says he patted down one of the men himself, and that both Afghans were processed as PUCs, or 'persons under control'.

'Once they came out, they were obviously very frightened. One had a distinctive limp, that's the person with the prosthetic leg,' said another soldier, anonymised as Person 40, in his evidence. He too is still serving in the SASR. 'Immediately [upon] coming out of his tunnel he was lifting his trousers, pointing to the prosthetic leg, expecting some sympathy from the troops,' he said. Person 40 said that a number of patrol commanders and even a troop commander – then a captain and now the SASR's most senior officer – were present when the two men were pulled from the tunnel.

This man, now a colonel, testified that he didn't personally see men come out of the tunnel, but was vague in his testimony and said he couldn't comprehensively say either way whether there may have been murders committed by his soldiers at Whiskey 108.

Another soldier, anonymised as Person 41, gave evidence that the two men who had emerged from the tunnel were in fact murdered: one was killed by Ben Roberts-Smith himself, and the other was killed under orders from the patrol second-in-command, Roberts-Smith, and the patrol commander, Person 5.

Person 41 said Roberts-Smith grabbed the old man who had just emerged from the tunnel 'by the scruff of his shirt' and dragged him in front of a soldier anonymised in court as Person 4, who has become one of the most integral parts of the defamation trial.

Person 4 was known within the patrol as 'the rookie' – a reference to a joke in the movie *Super Troopers*. He had joined the military almost 20 years earlier, in 1990, but had only passed SASR selection four years before this deployment. He was thus both a rookie and also more than 15 years older than some of the other operators in the patrol. Previously, testimony had been heard from an SASR operator that, prior to the Whiskey 108 mission, the patrol commander, Person 5, was 'in a jovial manner dancing a bit of a jig' and saying that 'we are going to blood the rookie'.

A number of soldiers testified that Person 4 was told by Ben Roberts-Smith and Person 5 to execute the Afghan in what Nine Media, defending its publications on the grounds of truth, claims was an instance of 'blooding' – where a junior soldier is ordered to achieve their first kill by executing a prisoner.

Person 41 testified that Ben Roberts-Smith 'kicked [the old Afghan man] in the back of the legs behind the knees until he was kneeling down'. The soldier said Roberts-Smith then 'pointed to the Afghan and said to Person 4 "shoot him"'. Person 41 said he left the courtyard then as he didn't want to see what would happen next. A few seconds later, he testified, he heard a suppressed gunshot, and when he came back into the courtyard he saw the Afghan dead, with blood flowing from a single gunshot wound to the head. Person 41 said that Person 4 looked to be 'in a bit of shock'.

Another soldier, anonymised as Person 18, gave evidence that after that mission, he heard Ben Roberts-Smith say to another man that he had 'blooded the rookie'.

When asked whether he was aware that it had been alleged that he murdered an unarmed Afghan on April 12, 2009, Person 4 said: 'Your honour, I object on grounds of self-incrimination.' He was compelled to answer and said he was aware of the allegation. He was asked whether he was anxious about this allegation and replied: 'My only hesitation is in fear of incriminating myself.'

Ben Roberts-Smith denies the allegation that he ordered the murder, or any wrongdoing. On the stand, he said he had never even heard the term 'blooding' until after he'd left the army and the war crimes allegations were published in the media. Person 5 testified similarly.

A number of soldiers identified the man whom Ben Roberts-Smith allegedly murdered as the man with the prosthetic leg. Person 41 gave evidence that he saw the murder personally, from a distance.

'[Ben Roberts-Smith] had his machine gun in his right arm, holding it up, and sort of frog-marching the Afghan by the scruff of the neck with his left arm,' Person 41 said. 'I turned to face [Roberts-Smith] to see what was happening. He then proceeded to throw the Afghan male down onto the ground. The Afghan male landed on his back. RS [Roberts-Smith] then reached down and grabbed him by the shoulder and flipped him onto his stomach. Then I observed him lower his machine gun and shoot approximately three to five rounds into the back of the Afghan male. After he'd done that, he looked up and saw me standing there, and looked at me and said, "Are we all cool, we good?" And I just replied, "Yeah mate, no worries."'

Another SASR operator, anonymised as Person 14, gave evidence in the trial that he saw one of the operators carrying a 'human shaped object', and that he then observed the operator throw the object on the ground and fire into it using an F89 Minimi machine gun. He said he saw Ben Roberts-Smith carrying the same weapon later, but couldn't, with absolute certainty, identify the soldier who killed the Afghan. This soldier also gave evidence that the dead man had a prosthetic leg.

Another soldier, anonymised as Person 24, said he personally witnessed the killing. '[Ben Roberts-Smith] was holding a man in his hand, it appeared he'd come off his feet and he was being held parallel to the ground,' he told the court. '[Roberts-Smith] marched approximately 15 metres, directly out from that entrance, dropped the man on the ground and immediately began with a machine gun burst into his back. I recall saying to Person 14 at the time, "Did we just witness an execution?"'

Person 24 admitted that he didn't see the shooter's face, but said he could tell it was Ben Roberts-Smith. Ben Roberts-Smith denies this allegation of murder, or any wrongdoing.

Person 24 called the killing an 'exhibition execution', but said that he wasn't happy that he had to testify against his comrade after being subpoenaed. He broke down as he gave his evidence. 'I still don't agree with the fact [Roberts-Smith] is here, under extreme duress, for killing bad dudes we went there to kill,' he said, but he also testified that the toll 'blooding' had taken on the mental health of some of his friends was extreme.

Person 18 said he heard a soldier say to Ben Roberts-Smith: 'You've just done this and the ISR [intelligence, surveillance and reconnaissance aircraft, likely a drone] is still flying above you and may be recording you.' Person 18 said a message was posted on the troop's internal chat asking where the ISR was, and another message claimed that it had been pushed off to another location.

Ben Roberts-Smith's barrister at the trial, Arthur Moses, claimed that all testimony of alleged criminality by his client at Whiskey 108 was fabricated. In cross-examination, he asked soldiers why their accounts were not offered to their superiors or investigators after the raid. One soldier said he feared that if he made a complaint, he might be seen as not 'willing to conduct the tasks of an SAS trooper'. The repercussions he feared if he reported an execution were 'removal from my patrol and [being] given a mundane job like possibly looking after the Afghan nationals [ANA soldiers] or even [being] sent back to HQ or worst case deemed unsuitable to be an SAS soldier and sent back to Australia.

'Word would have gotten back before I would have gotten back if I had made anything of the events and possibly bounced around back at the barracks with everyone knowing you dobbed in, so to speak, not wanting to work with you and effectively the career you'd worked, sort of, so hard for could possibly be over just like that,' he continued.

During the cross-examination of Person 5, who has a unique history of service, having served with the UK special forces, before spending 16 years in the SASR and then becoming part of DEVGRU's Red Squadron in a permanent SOCOMD/JSOC personnel exchange, it was revealed that Australian war crimes investigators investigating him and Roberts-Smith over three other alleged blooding murders in 2010 in western Dorafshan, with all of the alleged victims being detained prisoners.

The allegations are that two SASR personnel, newly minted into Person 5's patrol, were given orders by Person 5 and Ben Roberts-Smith to each execute a prisoner who was captured at a compound designated as Whiskey 591 on 14 May 2010. Investigators have also told Ben Roberts-Smith and Person 5 that they are investigating the alleged murder of a prisoner they believed may have been committed by Ben Roberts-Smith himself.

After Person 5 denied that he ever ordered a blooding – he claimed, as Roberts-Smith had, that he had never heard the term until it was used in the media – and that he was ever involved in any murders, Nine Media's barrister put it to Person 5 that he and Ben Roberts-Smith had colluded in creating coordinated false evidence in this trial. The barrister also asked Person 5 whether he and Ben Roberts-Smith had colluded to give false evidence to the IGADF. Person 5, who still maintained a Glaswegian burr, said this was a 'witch hunt', adding: 'There's been collusion, just not from our side. Your witnesses have been colluding for the last 12 years.'

After finishing his testimony, Person 5 was approached, outside his hotel room, by Australian Federal Police officers investigating war crimes. They had a warrant for the seizure of his phone. It's alleged the former soldier refused to comply with police order to hand over his phone and was physical with officers. The man was arrested and two charges were levelled against him: obstructing, hindering, intimidating or resisting a Commonwealth official, and causing harm to a Commonwealth judicial or law officer. The man was released on a $10,000 bond and was allowed to leave the country under the promise he would appear to face charges in court at a later date.

Following Person 5's testimony, Person 35 testified that he cleared the tunnel at Whiskey 108 and said no men came out of the tunnel. He says all killings at Whiskey 108 were lawful.

It was revealed, during cross-examination, that Person 35 is also being investigated for war crimes by the Office of the Special Investigator. It has been alleged that Person 35 murdered a man named Haji Nazar Gul on 11 September 2012 – the same day and in the same village that Ben Roberts-Smith is alleged to have kicked a man off a cliff and ordered him to be murdered. Another Australian soldier is being investigated for a third murder that was alleged to have been committed in the village that day. Person 35 says the allegation against him is baseless and that he has been falsely accused.

Alongside Ben Roberts-Smith, Person 5 and Person 35, two SASR operators who were part of the Whiskey 108 mission testified that no men were found in the tunnel, and that there were no murders committed during that mission.

Ben Roberts-Smith's lawyers, led by barrister Arthur Moses SC, claim that these men are bravely telling the truth in the face of a vast conspiracy of former and currently serving SASR members due to their jealousy of Ben Roberts-Smith's Victoria Cross and his successful post-military career in the media and beyond. There were no murders at Whiskey 108,' Moses said stating that the case against his client was, 'more like a Walter Mitty production,' citing the famous fictional fantasist, and who is often referenced within the Australian military when accusing individuals of lying and stealing unearned valour.

The Nine Media lawyers, led by barrister Nicholas Owens SC, claim that Ben Roberts-Smith and the men who said no men were found in the tunnel are perjuring themselves, in some instances to protect themselves from potential criminal prosecution and in others to protect their friend Ben Roberts-Smith.

It's an unavoidable truth that a dangerous conspiracy of collusion and perjury emerged out of the SASR during and after the Afghan war, regardless of which account Justice Anthony Besanko believes (a decision on this case is expected after the printing of this book). Another unavoidable truth is that allowing this allegation to fester untested within the SASR for more than a decade is not only a moral outrage, but a potential breach of national security.

Witnesses on both sides of this case are currently serving SASR operators working as part of the SASR's undeclared 4 Squadron, the most sensitive part of the regiment, which often works with ASIS, the ASD and international intelligence services in its mission of international intelligence gathering.

At least one of those witnesses currently serving within 4 Squadron must be lying to the court, war crimes investigators and, presumably, superiors within the regiment. This is an unacceptable threat to national security due to the potential for blackmail, and must be having a corrosive effect on the cohesion and efficacy of the squadron and the regiment.

* * *

The prosthetic leg of the Afghan man killed at Whiskey 108 made its way back to Tarin Kot strapped to the pack of an SASR soldier. It was hung, alongside collected enemy weapons and other trophies, at the makeshift SASR bar, the Fat Lady's Arms.

There it became a drinking vessel and something of totem for the troop, with many of the soldiers from G Troop taking home leg-shaped glasses after their deployment. The leg even took on its own moniker, 'Das Boot', a reference to the German film about a Nazi U-boat. The leg was mounted on a black board with the words 'DAS BOOT' written in a white gothic script above. Below the 'T' hung a German Iron Cross, the highest military honour awarded to soldiers in Nazi Germany.

Everyone who was in the SASR circle of trust drank at the Fat Lady's Arms, including US and UK special forces, selected support staff and even Australian generals. Many drank from Das Boot, and many who drank from Das Boot were photographed doing so.

There were articulated rules within SOCOMD about taking and disseminating photography and video from Afghanistan, but those rules were uniformly ignored. The SASR were often filming and photographing in and out of the base, and this material was liberally shared within patrols, troops, squadrons and rotations. It was rarely shared beyond the regiment, but after 2018, photographs of Das Boot started appearing in the media.

First, Fairfax newspapers (now part of Nine Media) published an image of the leg at the Fat Lady's Arms, and also a blurred image of the leg's former owner lying dead on the ground. Then, two years later, a photograph emerged of Warrant Officer John Letch drinking from the leg. Letch was, at the time of the photograph, still a serving member of the SASR, and someone who had expressed support for the IGADF report about alleged war crimes in Afghanistan. He was also known to have disagreed with at least one of the awards or honours given to Ben Roberts-Smith.

Letch was the Command Sergeant Major of the SASR when the image was published, but stood down from his position after the media exposure. Speculation was rife that the images of Das Boot were being used as leverage and ammunition in a simmering civil war within the SASR serving and veterans community.

Then, some months later, another image of Das Boot appeared in the media. This time the photograph was of a fist-pumping, grinning Ben Roberts-Smith, holding two Heineken beer cans as an American special forces soldier in a cowboy hat, pressed up against him, drank from the leg.

Roberts-Smith's barrister Bruce McClintock said of drinking from the dead man's leg, that: 'in the scheme of human wickedness it does not, in my submission, rate very high'.

'Allowances should be made ... for men who have engaged in the extremity of armed combat to relax and decompress,' he added.

23

'Are you trying to lose this war?'

IN 2009, KABUL LOOKED very much like half a dozen reconstruction capitals around the world. Sleek four-wheel drives cruised alongside armoured personnel carriers and ancient taxis, past barricaded four-star hotels and freezing beggars, and through a constant pall of dust, smog and, according to local legend, atomised human shit. Kidnaps sometimes happened, so too bomb and gun atrocities, but they were rare.

Kabul seemed to be a city external to Afghanistan, incomparable in any way with the villages of Dorafshan. One could usually drive the capital in a thin-skinned vehicle and walk unarmed, without a plate carrier, and usually one would observe a city that did not seem to be at war. One of the reasons for this was that Kabul was preserved as a safe place in which to do deals.

Every armed actor in Afghanistan benefited from the billions of dollars that flowed into Afghanistan, and Lieutenant General Raymond 'Tony' Thomas (ret.), commander of US Special Operations Command, said that the Taliban extracted a cut from every US dollar spent in Afghanistan; according to the Taliban finance minister, he said, many Taliban 'hope you never leave'.

One of the places where deals could be done in Kabul was Cedar House, a shabby restaurant attached to an ageing guesthouse in the city centre. It backed onto a park, allowing unseen exit and entrance, and was within walking distance of the International Zone and the Afghan palace. On 1 December

2009, three men met at Cedar House for a furtive meeting: one an Australian representing the US military, and two Afghan businessmen representing the Taliban.

The Australian was David Kilcullen, then an insurgency adviser to NATO and ISAF, and also a personal adviser to General McChrystal. Backchannel conversations were sought between ISAF and elements of the Taliban, but impediments existed on both sides. With the Taliban designated a terrorist organisation by the US government, no member of its military was permitted meet with a Taliban member – nor would any Taliban meet a uniformed member of the US military. Technically a civilian, Kilcullen was a 'carve-out' for off-the-book meetings.

The two Afghan businessmen he was meeting at Cedar were from Kandahar, not part of the military structure either but sympathetic to and supportive of the Taliban. They were likely in contact with the Quetta Shura, and were in Kabul as part of the Taliban team that was negotiating with representatives of President Karzai's government. (The terms they were presenting in 2009 were considered unacceptable by the United States at that time, but were accepted by President Donald Trump in 2020.)

Outside the restaurant, the bodyguards of the Afghans and the Australian shared kebabs in the carpark. Inside, Kilcullen spoke with the businessmen, trying to gauge the aims and goals of the Taliban, and to establish further backchannels with the enemy that, at some point, might be used to end the war.

As was the case with many of the places where deals were done in Kabul, Cedar House had a flatscreen television. It often showed international sport, but that night all in the restaurant were glued to the television for what was anticipated to be a landmark speech about the war.

President Barack Obama, less than a year into the job, was expected to detail how the US military would prosecute the war in Afghanistan from now on. It was to be the announcement of a new strategy generated after months of horse-trading, negotiations and expert input (including from research conducted by Kilcullen). Young and with dark hair and bright eyes, President Obama took to the lectern at the US Military Academy at West Point and gave a speech titled 'The New Way Forward in Afghanistan and Pakistan'.

'As cadets, you volunteered for service during this time of danger,' President Obama said. 'Some of you fought in Afghanistan. Some of you will deploy there. As your Commander in Chief, I owe you a mission that is clearly defined, and worthy of your service. And that's why, after the Afghan voting was completed, I insisted on a thorough review of our strategy ... the review has allowed me to ask the hard questions, and to explore all the different options, along with my national security team, our military and civilian leadership in Afghanistan, and our key partners. This review is now complete. And as Commander in Chief, I have determined that it is in our vital national interest to send an additional 30,000 US troops to Afghanistan.'

This was a significant surge of troops, nearly doubling the number of foreign troops in the country. President Obama continued: 'After 18 months, our troops will begin to come home. These are the resources that we need to seize the initiative, while building the Afghan capacity that can allow for a responsible transition of our forces out of Afghanistan.'

The two Kandahari businessmen dining with Kilcullen started to laugh, and the Australian asked why.

'Are you trying to lose this war?' one asked. 'Tomorrow the Taliban are going to go out on the street and they're going to say to everyone, "Hey, you may like the Americans, but did you just hear their president saying they're leaving in July?"' one said. '"So what will you do in August?"'

The calculus of the war had changed for the Taliban. The timeline might slip – as it did – but there was now a deadline from which the Taliban could work. An oft-repeated maxim in Afghanistan was that the Americans had watches, but the Taliban had time.

'The Taliban now knew what they needed to do, just to stay in the public eye and maintain some leverage in Afghanistan, but no more than that,' says Kilcullen. 'This is what military guys call "economy of force".'

The Taliban war objective was to have Afghans, especially rural Afghans, prefer their form of governance, justice and security to any other form being offered. And with large swathes of the country enraged by the mismanagement of the government and the heavy-handed behaviour of the occupying force, the Taliban rightly judged that aim would not require absolute military commitment.

* * *

The clock was now running for ISAF and for Afghanistan. An effective government and strong security forces had to be established in Afghanistan before Western forces left the country or it would surely fall into civil war, and likely Taliban ascendency. In 2009, the Afghan National Army had, on paper, roughly 90,000 troops. The plan was to stand up another 40,000 to 50,000 soldiers in 2010, and then another 100,000 in 2011. Australia's commitment to that was a brigade of soldiers who would assume complete security responsibility in Uruzgan Province.

In 2009, Kevin Rudd announced that Australia would have to 'significantly increase the "through-put" of Afghan National Army trainees. The aim is to deliver an ANA, that's Afghan National Army 4th Brigade in Oruzgan [Uruzgan], ready to provide security in the province as soon as they are able to assume those responsibilities.'

Australia was trying to stand up about 3300 soldiers in Uruzgan. The Afghan National Army's 4th Brigade would consist of a brigade headquarters, three infantry *kandaks*, a combat support *kandak*, a combat service support and a garrison *kandak*. They were also training and planning for a highway security *kandak* – that was Matiullah Khan's force.

Matiullah's men were local and loyal to him, and they were some of the more effective fighters, but elsewhere drug use was high and motivation was low. Desertion was a constant issue, with Afghan soldiers in Uruzgan earning about US$25 a week in cash and often fleeing their patrol base when their family needed that money or when the fighting in places where they had no familial or tribal stake was too extreme. In short, the Afghan security force presence was weak across the country, but especially so in Uruzgan – except for Matiullah's men.

When President Obama gave his speech at West Point, faith in the Afghan government was low. In fact, it was perhaps close to a nadir. Just a month before Obama's speech, Afghanistan had voted Hamid Karzai back into the highest office, but his re-election was tainted by violence, corruption, mistrust and disinterest.

The Taliban and Taliban-aligned candidates were not included in the election process, so the group boycotted the election and said they would violently disrupt both the campaign and election day. Furthermore, after nearly eight years of misrule, Karzai was no longer the international community's preferred candidate. Two other candidates were gaining help from the United States. Enter, once again, the Afghan warlords.

Hamid Karzai did a number of deals with Afghanistan's warlords to deliver him to power, most notably with alleged war criminal Abdul Rashid Dostum, who returned from Dubai three days before the election to help shore up the Karzai vote. Warlords were also engaged by ISAF and the United States to help bring security to election day. In 21 of the country's 34 provinces, ISAF paid for armed militia to provide election security – which did not help the perception of this as a free and fair election.

In Uruzgan, Australians troops manned 12 polling stations on election day, and they logged more than a dozen stand-off attacks – from 107mm rockets, 82mm mortars, small-arms fire and rocket-propelled grenades. No Australian soldiers were killed or wounded, but only about 150 voters went through each station. Voter turnout was very poor across the country, but in Uruzgan it was significantly lower than the national average.

With Hamid Karzai returned as president thanks in no small part to warlord horse-trading, a minority engaging in the political process and the Taliban playing a violent, destructive and obstructive role, it was business as usual in Afghanistan. For all international forces, the reality on the ground and the desired end state were a long way apart, and now, with the military forces scheduled to leave, there was a rush towards stability and reconstruction efforts.

Kevin Rudd announced a 'whole-of-government' commitment in Uruzgan, with the military, the AFP and diplomatic and aid efforts working cooperatively. (It was not mentioned, but Australia's special forces largely remained outside this attempted whole-of-government coordination.) Part of these efforts would be the first deployment of the Australian Civilian Corps (ACC), a new deployable arm of the Australian Public Service championed by Kevin Rudd. This element would be tasked with deploying technical government experts into disaster areas and war zones so that they might help with reconstruction.

One of the jobs of the ACC was to stabilise Chora Valley, the area north of Tarin Kot where billions of dollars and dozens of lives had been spent in pacification. This effort would later result in Australia's first civilian casualty of the war.

* * *

Throughout the day and night of 19 February 2010, Dutch prime minister Jan Peter Balkenende tried to keep his government together. Arguing in the cabinet room with the leaders of the other parties in the ruling coalition was a common task for Prime Minister Balkenende, and these arguments had sometimes gone through the night, but the dawn had always brought compromise. Until February 2010.

For 16 hours, Balkenende and his foreign minister, Maxime Verhagen, both from the Christian Democratic Appeal Party, had argued that the Dutch should continue their mission in Uruzgan for at least two more years. They cited the success of the mission so far: patrol bases had been built and more than 1600 police had been trained in Uruzgan, and any members of the government who had been regularly visiting Tarin Kot would have seen a provincial capital remade, with an increase of produce in the markets and wealth on the streets. The deputy prime minister and leader of the Labour Party, Wouter Bos, drew a line in the sand, however: there were no circumstances in which he and his party would approve an extension.

Bos argued that Tarin Kot was not Uruzgan, and that from what he'd been told, there was simply no winning in Afghanistan at this point. The Dutch mission had always been time-limited, and that limit had been reached. The commitment to the United States had been fulfilled.

The impasse could not be resolved. On 20 February, Prime Minister Balkenende contacted the Dutch monarch, Queen Beatrix, to inform her that his government would soon fall.

Wouter Bos's position was bolstered the next day when reports emerged that a NATO airstrike had killed a number of civilians in Uruzgan. In time it emerged that this attack did not involve Dutch forces but the operators of US Little Bird helicopters, who had engaged a convoy of minibuses they believed contained insurgents. They had killed 27 people, including women and children.

The Netherlands' combat mission to Afghanistan would conclude in August 2010, making it the first NATO country engaged in Afghanistan to end its participation. Task Force Uruzgan became the US-led Combined Team Uruzgan.

Under Prime Minister Rudd, the number of Australian soldiers in Afghanistan had grown from roughly 1000 to 1550, but requests for additional Australian troops were denied. Instead, some Slovakian and Singaporean soldiers were committed to Uruzgan, and there was also a recommitment by the United States.

For the Australian special forces, the removal of the Dutch forces from Uruzgan changed little, except that Matiullah Khan would now hold even more power in the province, and assume official positions. Colonel James Creighton, the commander of Combined Team Uruzgan, said this of Matiullah in a piece he wrote for *The Diplomat*: 'I recognized that although his suspect past and current dealings were not acceptable according to official Western practices, they fell under the tacit moral aegis of the Afghan National Police, provincial governor and Afghan president.' In 2011, Matiullah became the Chief of Police in Uruzgan Province, a position he would hold until his death.

In September 2011, the ABC asked the Department of Defence to explain the relationship between the Australian forces in Uruzgan and the warlord after he became the Chief of Police, and their response was this:

> As part of ISAF efforts to help stabilise Afghanistan, Australian forces regularly engage with a wide range of tribal and community leaders in Uruzgan in an inclusive and impartial way. In this setting, Matiullah Khan is one of many influential figures that Australians have engaged. Australia works with such individuals in a way to ensure that their influence is used positively, in support of governance and security in Uruzgan. As the Uruzgan Chief of Police, our expectation is that Matiullah Khan acts in an impartial and professional manner and continues to be a positive influence for security in the province.

This statement seriously understates and indeed misrepresents the relationship between the Australian special forces and Matiullah Khan.

Putting aside the operational relationship, Matiullah was the only 'community leader' from Uruzgan who had his representatives, including his second-in-command, Midoh Khan, visit Australia on Defence's tab, where Midoh was gifted a boozy harbour trip with Australian soldiers and a visit to Taronga Park Zoo. He was also the only community leader who had given dozens of gold watches to SOTG officers, and at least one Australian general.

In the months between the fall of the Dutch government and the removal of Dutch forces from Uruzgan, Australia also experienced a period of political turmoil. Kevin Rudd's popularity was waning; polling suggested that if he led the party into the next election, Labor would lose. This created concern within the government, and in June a spill motion was called. When Rudd realised that he would lose the motion, Julia Gillard won the spill unopposed and became the new prime minister. In July, Prime Minister Gillard announced a snap federal election to be held in August.

Leaked US State Department emails from Australia back to Washington explained that a change in government was unlikely to change the Australian commitment to Afghanistan. 'Labor Party officials have told us that one lesson Gillard took from the 2004 elections was that Australians will not elect a PM who is perceived to be anti-American,' one email read. 'Continuing to look into this, but from what I can tell it won't make too much of a difference. Both Labor and the opposition support Afghanistan, so that won't change,' read another.

Although Australia suffered a series of deaths in Afghanistan in June, July and August 2010 (it had taken eight years for the first 11 Australian soldiers to be killed in Afghanistan but it took only 80 days for the next ten), the war in Afghanistan was never a significant election issue. On 21 August, both the Labor Party and the Liberal Party won 72 seats in the House of Representatives, but Labor assumed minority government after being assured of the support of independents and the Greens. The Greens insisted on a number of concessions from Labor, including a parliamentary debate on Australia's involvement in the war. And so it was that in October 2010, nine years after Australian troops were committed to Afghanistan, the first parliamentary debate on the war was forced upon the major parties.

There were 28 speeches given in the House of Representatives, filled with talk about the September 11 attacks, the Bali bombings and Australia's ANZUS Treaty obligations, but few seemed to be born of any close understanding of what Australia was actually doing in Uruzgan. In that debate, the Greens argued that Australian forces should return home, but both Prime Minister Gillard and the opposition leader, Tony Abbott, voiced strong support for a continuation. So too did most of their colleagues.

'I believe we now have the right strategy, an experienced commander in General Petraeus [General David Petraeus had assumed control of ISAF after Stanley McChrystal had badmouthed President Obama in a *Rolling Stone* article] and the resources needed to deliver the strategy,' said Gillard.

One outlying speech was given by Dr Mal Washer, a Liberal MP from a Perth seat where many SASR soldiers lived, some of whom were Washer's friends. His speech argued that the battalion Australia was training was 'the most hopeless bunch of critters that God ever put on the planet', and that the Karzai government was the 'most corrupt government on the face of the planet'.

Washer's was one of very few speeches that advocated the removal of Australian forces, and the only one specifically calling for the removal of Australia's special forces from Afghanistan. '[W]hen you cross towards those areas where our boys [the SASR] are trying to stop these people building the IEDs ... you see no fathers,' he said. 'You do not see any brothers. It is obvious why not. We have the best professional teams in history in there, but we are not winning hearts and minds ... let us come home and try not to leave a bloodbath behind.'

24

'It is common knowledge that a Victoria Cross is a
political statement used by the government for a
good news story'

JOHN CANTWELL BECAME THE commander of all Australian
forces in Afghanistan in 2010 after significant combat experience,
not in Afghanistan but Iraq. The son of a Queensland peanut
farmer, Cantwell was born into a large Catholic family, five of
whose eight children joined the Australian Army. He joined as a
private soldier, but in his early twenties transitioned to the officer's
path and worked hard to become a tank commander.

As a 34-year-old major on exchange with the British Army,
Cantwell found himself in command of a British armoured
squadron for the invasion of Iraq in 1991. He saw combat and
watched as dozens of Iraqis were buried alive by American
bulldozers during the initial assault, a persistent image in his
mind to this day. As a 50-year-old brigadier, Cantwell served as
the Director of Strategic Operations in Iraq for all Multinational
Forces. More horrors attended this posting: one came when he
was in a Baghdad neighbourhood as a car bomb exploded nearby.
The blood-slicked road and scattered children's shoes dogged his
memory afterwards.

For the burden of his service, Cantwell was compensated with
rank and titles, including the US Order of the Legion of Merit,
Member of the Order of Australia, and Officer of the Order of
Australia. He also attained the rank of major general and was

given the most significant overseas command the ADF could confer: Commander Joint Task Force 633 (JTF 633).

All Australian forces in the Middle East Area of Operations, or MEAO (although the nomenclature was muddled, this included Australian forces in Afghanistan), worked as a large, regional task force named Joint Task Force 633. The commander of that task force was atop the command structure of all ADF task forces in the region, including the SOTG. Cantwell's office was Al Minhad Air Base, 20 kilometres south of Dubai in the United Arab Emirates, where Australia maintained a large military base for all operations in the region, but since Afghanistan was easily the largest and most kinetic area of operations, his office was also Tarin Kot and the patrol bases beyond, where the most active group under his command was the SOTG.

When Cantwell assumed command of JTF 633, he asked SOCOMD how he might help special forces operations, and two primary concerns emerged. One was the geographical limits being placed on the special forces – the provincial borders of Uruzgan – and the other was the lack of helicopters and ISR they needed on their operations. Cantwell says he attempted to solve those problems best he could.

Australia had helicopters operating in Afghanistan – two Chinooks from the 5th Aviation Regiment – but they were primarily working around Kandahar, according to Major General Cantwell, doing mail and garbage runs to remote US patrol bases. The already fractured SOTG was having to work a staggered operational cycle dictated by US helicopter availability. This meant the SASR worked some days and the commandos others, which caused further tension between the two force elements.

Cantwell contacted Chief of Defence Angus Houston, requesting that some of Australia's 30-plus Blackhawks and perhaps other Australian airframes be deployed to Tarin Kot, not only for the SOTG but for the Mentoring Task Force, who wanted to avoid the IED-laden roads. Cantwell says the CDF agreed that Australian helicopters were sorely needed, but 'within days I got a call from Bungendore CJOPS [Chief of Joint Operations] to give me a kick in the arse for speaking out of line. It was basically "pull your bloody head in",' says Cantwell.

The parameters of the mission were set: exactly 1550 Australian servicepeople, and no dedicated Australian helicopters. Both Force Element Alpha and Force Element Bravo became masters at finding their own rides.

For Force Element Bravo, the aircraft problem was partially resolved when it developed a relationship with the US Drug Enforcement Administration (DEA). The DEA had deployed paramilitary teams to Afghanistan with a controversial remit: to destroy Afghanistan's primary agricultural crop, the opium poppy. There were fears that this effort at eradication might kill agricultural workers, destroy their livelihood and ultimately stoke the insurgency.

The DEA paramilitary teams, known as Foreign-deployed Advisory Support Teams, or FAST teams, could not operate in the most dangerous areas of Afghanistan without military assistance, so Force Element Bravo agitated to partner with the DEA, who had their own rented fleet of US and Russian-built military helicopters. Australia's special forces had no authorisation from the Australian government to conduct drug-interdiction missions, nor could they be easily deployed to Helmand, where the bulk of these missions were being undertaken, but the rationale was that the opium poppy was funding the insurgency in Uruzgan, so 'counter-nexus operations' (with the 'nexus' being the point where the insurgency met drug production) were technically authorised.

The mission set was approved, and these operations became some of the most violent undertaken by the SOTG, with many hundreds and maybe thousands of Afghans protecting or working these poppy fields or processing plants killed by Force Element Bravo and the FAST teams.

For Force Element Alpha, it was established way back on rotation three that one way to get the use of American helicopters and ISR was by prosecuting national-level or regional-level JPEL targets. Many of these were outside Uruzgan, however. With the flick of a pen or a word over the phone, Major General Cantwell could approve missions beyond Australia's defined operational areas, and he did so regularly. The insurgents were not beholden to geographic boundaries, so it made no sense to him that the men hunting them should be.

In 2010, the SASR was involved in two large and well-publicised actions that happened outside the normal Australian areas of operations. In April, SOTG supported a popular uprising in Gizab, a district in northern Uruzgan that had been held for some time by insurgents. The Australians flew in to support what the US press characterised as the 'Gizab Good Guys', inserting with a group of Matiullah's men thanks to Blackhawks from the US 101st Airborne Division's Task Force No Mercy.

They cleared the district centre easily, and the uprising was characterised as a good news story across the United States. According to a US commander quoted in *The Washington Post*, this was 'perhaps the most important thing that has happened in southern Afghanistan this year'. But the action was seen differently by independent analysts, who said it was largely internecine family fighting.

Martine van Bijlert, an anthropological expert in tribal dynamics in Uruzgan, says the uprising was 'part of the regular ebb and flow of power relations – not necessarily good or bad, mainly ambiguous, highly fragile and utterly reversible'. She says the Taliban left the area during the 'uprising', but it wasn't the first time they'd been uninvited by families in the district centre, and their influence returned quickly.

The other and most notable Australian special forces action was the Shah Wali Kot offensive, an Australian-led assault on the northern area in Kandahar Province that the Taliban had attempted to surrender to Jason Amerine's force and Hamid Karzai back in 2002. The area had been established as a significant insurgent 'rat line' (a supply and movement corridor) from Kandahar into Uruzgan, and this June offensive was to be the seventh mission the SOTG would launch there, but there had been a deliberate pause between the sixth and seventh operations to allow the insurgents to build up, so they might later be killed en masse.

This seventh mission started with Australian commandos coming into the area with a number of Matiullah's men, and as soon as they did they were in a gunfight. Almost a hundred commandos would be involved in this battle on what was one of the hottest days of the year in the province. With the mercury hitting 45 degrees, sweat poured into Australian uniforms, with scorching waves of heat hitting them as machine guns and heavy weapons fired.

As that fight was happening, an SASR element was waiting in full battle kit in Tarin Kot, ready to hit any JPEL target that might be flushed out on the SIGINT net. After considerable political pressure had been exerted from Kabul to stop the night raids (pressure that would grow further after Hamid Karzai's ageing cousin was executed in a night raid in an instance of either mistaken identity or false denunciation), many special forces were not allowed to operate at night. It's believed the SASR could still prosecute night raids but chose to operate during the day to maximise their targeting opportunities.

As the commandos were fighting, a national-level JPEL target – reportedly Objective Slayer, who was being hunted by a JSOC element in Kandahar – was discovered on the SIGINT net in a nearby village called Tizak. The SASR launched in four Blackhawks from Task Force No Mercy, with support from an Apache, and in Tizak they found a much larger force than they'd expected. It was one of the few occasions in which outnumbered Australian forces were fighting an entrenched enemy in a full-frontal, close-quarters battle. There were moments of extreme peril for the SASR, especially when two or three PKM machine-gun positions were set up defensively against them.

As the battle raged, John Cantwell listened to radio transmissions from soldiers on the ground. Hearing the loud, chattering guns through the radio, he feared Australian dead, and was ecstatic to hear that at the resolution of the battle, no Australians had been killed, and only two friendlies had been wounded. Ultimately, the battle had been a rout. An estimated 76 Afghans were killed – most by the SASR, but some by the accompanying Apache. Only two Afghans were reported as captured.

A number of SASR operators and commandos were identified as having made significant contributions to the Australian forces prevailing in the battles, and they were duly awarded medals. One of those medals was another Victoria Cross, the highest honour in the Australian defence honours and awards system. The soldier receiving the Victoria Cross was Ben Roberts-Smith.

His citation read:

> Upon commencement of the assault, the patrol drew very heavy, intense, effective and sustained fire from the enemy position. Corporal Roberts-Smith and his patrol members fought towards the enemy position until, at a range of 40 metres, the weight of fire prevented further movement forward. At this point, he identified the opportunity to exploit some cover provided by a small structure.
>
> As he approached the structure, Corporal Roberts-Smith identified an insurgent grenadier in the throes of engaging his patrol. Corporal Roberts-Smith instinctively engaged the insurgent at point-blank range resulting in the death of the insurgent. With the members of his patrol still pinned down by the three enemy machine gun positions, he exposed his own position in order to draw fire away from his patrol, which enabled them to bring fire to bear against the enemy. His actions enabled his Patrol Commander to throw a grenade and silence one of the machine guns.
>
> Seizing the advantage, and demonstrating extreme devotion to duty and the most conspicuous gallantry, Corporal Roberts-Smith, with a total disregard for his own safety, stormed the enemy position killing the two remaining machine gunners.

The JPEL target the SASR was hunting in Tizak escaped the battle, but it was later reported that he had been wounded and had since died. Ten of those killed on site were later designated as medium-value targets. Speaking to a researcher at the Australian War Memorial, Ben Roberts-Smith said, 'The American command responsible for southern Afghanistan was ecstatic.'

* * *

Although all Australian command authority in Afghanistan flowed through Major General John Cantwell, he says his visibility of special forces operations was not complete. 'I was still always a non-SF guy,' he says. 'I didn't have free run of their compound. I absolutely didn't have run of their compound.'

As the ranking officer in the field, and with only four generals outranking him in Australia Army, Cantwell decided that he needed to know more about what the SOTG was doing, so he 'demanded to see it'.

'I was allowed extraordinary access to the special forces guys, significantly more than my predecessors,' says Cantwell, who shared meals with some operators, went shooting with them and drank at the Fat Lady's Arms. (He says he never saw 'Das Boot' and never drank from it; he was more surprised, he recalls, to see a motorbike doing donuts in the bar.)

At Camp Russell, Cantwell attempted to gain a better understanding of JPEL and what the SASR were doing in Afghanistan. He says he did authorise some JPEL missions and sign off on some JPEL targets, but also that there were American authorisations and ISAF authorisations running concurrently, so he didn't have a complete picture of what the Australian special forces were doing. From the knowledge he did have, however, Cantwell says he believed the targeting missions and how they related to the overall war strategy was flawed.

'That was a sense I entertained: that we were killing people ... great, but within hours and certainly within weeks there was a replacement,' says Cantwell. 'The insurgents were remarkably resilient in regenerating new players. It was whack-a-mole.

'The means of effectiveness was how many strikes we had and who we knocked off and how many crosses were on the big chart of known bad guys. That was the measure of effectiveness. What [were] we doing to prevent the populace from further being influenced by the Taliban and other insurgent groups?'

Patrol bases built north towards Chora and east through the Mehrabad Valley projected influence beyond Tarin Kot, but the projection from those bases was limited. So too was the coordination between Australian and coalition special forces, the conventional forces holding these bases and the Afghan government and military. After a battle like Tizak, there was usually neither effort nor capacity to bring in Afghan governmental elements to shore up the military gains.

'We never followed up on the [special forces'] actions to degrade the ability of the enemy. There was no coherent picture to emerge,' says Cantwell.

As he moved around Camp Russell, another concern about JPEL targeting arose in Cantwell's mind: the potential for, and evidence of, moral injury.

'We were just lining [the SASR] up and throwing them at targets, and because of the complexity of the situations, the number of weapons around [and] the inclination of Afghans to defend their home, especially after hours, it was such an obvious recipe for emotional trauma.'

As a human being, Cantwell was concerned that the people under his command might be suffering. As a senior officer, he was concerned that the war in Afghanistan might actually be degrading the capacity and capability of Australia's special forces.

'I did get a sense they were moving backwards,' he acknowledges. 'Towards the end of my tour, I was seeing many parts of the force in mental anguish. I was feeling it myself.'

After Iraq, John Cantwell had started to experience symptoms of PTSD and had been treated by a psychologist. In Afghanistan, he realised that his symptoms were returning.

'Because I was sensitive to it myself … I was watching for it, and I saw a lot of evidence within the special forces,' he says.

Cantwell asked a number of people, including the SASR's regimental sergeant major, about instances of PTSD at Camp

Russell, and he was told uniformly that there were none within Australia's special forces. 'I spoke to Ben Roberts-Smith about it,' he recalls. 'I spoke to him and his mates about it, and they said, "Shit no, sir, no one in the SAS has mental-health issues,"' Cantwell says, with emphasis denoting a nod and a wink. '"We're not allowed to have them."'

* * *

One of the people Ben Roberts-Smith killed in Tizak was a 15-year-old boy, who was reported to have been manning a machine gun when he was killed. The death of the boy was a good kill, one that was within the rules of engagement, but Roberts-Smith, while on the stand in courtroom 18D in 2021, said he struggled with it. This was one of many emotional and sometimes tearful moments in court as the hulking former soldier gave evidence.

There had been no media reports accusing Ben Roberts-Smith of any wrongdoing in Tizak before the trial, and therefore that engagement was not part of the defamation complaint filed by Roberts-Smith's legal team. But the former soldier's barrister Bruce McClintock SC questioned Roberts-Smith about the battle in the courtroom, describing it as a 'high water mark' for the regiment.

McClintock likely had two aims in mind when he introduced the Battle of Tizak into the defamation proceedings. The first was to establish the high reputational cliff from which Ben Roberts-Smith fell as articles emerged alleging that he was a war criminal. The second was an attempt to establish malicious motivations to the sources of those stories, many of whom were SASR operators themselves and, Ben Roberts-Smith claimed, were jealous of the Victoria Cross he was awarded.

'For all the good it has brought me and enabled me to do, it is unfortunately the case, in my instance particularly, that it has also brought me a lot of misfortune and pain,' Roberts-Smith said of his Victoria Cross investiture. 'It put a target on my back.' Roberts-Smith claimed that he was subsequently 'white-anted' by people within the SASR.

The claim that SASR soldiers would approach the media, lie and potentially implicate themselves in war crimes is one that Nine Media's barrister, Nicholas Owens SC, said was unlikely. In his opening address, Owens argued that the idea that 21 soldiers and former soldiers – the number then expected to give evidence against Ben Roberts-Smith – would perjure themselves simply because of jealousy was 'inherently implausible'.

'Some of these witnesses were involved in crimes themselves. Is it really to be supposed that a man, himself, would confess to murder just so as to give vent to some jealousy over a medal?' Owens asked.

Arthur Moses SC said that this is exactly what some of the witnesses did, stating that one witness, who he said is obsessed with Ben Roberts-Smith, 'heard rumours ... and because of the Victoria Cross he starts hunting for war crimes.' He also said that another witness lied to the court about a story that 'flip-flopped' on numerous occasions and that 'lies drip from this man's evidence.'

Person 4, the former 'rookie' who, it was alleged in court, executed an Afghan under the orders of Ben Roberts-Smith at Whiskey 108, gave evidence about his role in the Battle of Tizak, saying that he and Roberts-Smith had fought shoulder to shoulder. He told the court about being fired upon by three men while his patrol was still in their helicopter, and feeling heat as an RPG exploded. He told the court about landing and killing one of those men as Ben Roberts-Smith killed two others. He told the court that he and Roberts-Smith were directed to support the medical evacuation of an injured Australian soldier and an Afghan soldier. He spoke about the medevac helicopter receiving a large volume of small-arms fire, and of close air support being called in. Person 4 then detailed his memories of the action for which Ben Roberts-Smith was awarded the Victoria Cross.

Person 4, Ben Roberts-Smith and their patrol were told to move to where the rest of the troop was, he recalled. As they did so, they were pinned down by fire and took cover behind a wall. They tried to get a visual on the guns – by poking holes in the wall and peeking through them – but while they could be seen by the enemy and were being shot at when they presented, the Australians couldn't see the enemy. They decided to jump over the wall and advance, and as they did they were engaged. An SASR soldier found and killed one of the enemy in open ground, but more fire came in from unseen positions.

Person 4 said he vividly recalls machine-gun fire roaring between himself and Ben Roberts-Smith. In a grove of small and sparse trees, the Australians took any cover they could find.

'I distinctly remember lying there and looking towards [Roberts-Smith] and he was ashen in [the] face ... I remember thinking I would be looking exactly the same because I had an absolute feeling of absolute dread and fear due to the amount of fire we were receiving ... not only accurate fire but sustained, effective fire,' Person 4 said.

Person 4 testified that another soldier decided to try to flank the position, and that he and Roberts-Smith decided to assault forward and try to close with the enemy. They pushed forward, firing as they moved. They could see people ahead, but hadn't identified the enemy firing positions yet. Roberts-Smith moved towards a potential enemy position, a window in a compound through which an RPG could be seen resting on the wall. Person 4 said that he gave cover, and that as he did so he saw two machine-gun barrels and swirling exhaust gases in a compound about ten metres away. Ben Roberts-Smith had charged towards the window where the RPG was seen, and yelled back: 'One dead enemy!'

Another witness, currently serving in the SASR as a warrant officer, testified that Ben Roberts-Smith later told him that this man was unarmed and trying to hide. Ben Roberts-Smith denies this categorically.

Person 4 said that after this killing, he showed Ben Roberts-Smith hand signals that meant 'Two machine guns, ten metres slight right of an iron bark'. Person 4 said Roberts-Smith then showed him a grenade.

'Okay, on the count of three!' Person 4 yelled over the sound of machine guns. After the count, Person 4 popped out of cover and fired as Roberts-Smith threw the grenade. He and Roberts-

Smith ducked back behind cover and waited for an explosion, but none came. Person 4's evidence was that the weight of fire had by then lessened significantly anyway.

Person 4 testified that their patrol commander was then yelling at them, asking where the gunners were. Person 4 used field signals to explain where he'd seen them. Person 4 said that the patrol commander, Person 5, identified the position, and then Person 4 and Roberts-Smith gave covering fire so Person 5 could post the grenade. According to Person 4, he and Roberts-Smith heard the explosive report of the grenade and broke cover, as they were trained to do, sprinting towards the enemy position.

After the grenade blast, Person 4 testified, they were no longer receiving effective fire. He believed the now lone gunner had been stunned by the grenade and was firing off the vertical and into the trees. Person 4 said that Ben Roberts-Smith was the first to reach the wall where the guns had been firing, and shot both machine gunners, while Person 4 arrived two second later, also firing.

Person 4 said that both he and Roberts-Smith turned towards an open door from which they had seen movement, and each killed another man. They cleared and secured the compound, and that was the end of the action.

Another witness said the wounds sustained by one of the machine gunners were consistent with him having been killed by Person 4's suppressing fire. The witness also said that Ben Roberts-Smith and he, in a later conversation, agreed that Person 4 had killed one of the machine gunners – but this point was disputed by Ben Roberts-Smith's barrister.

'That action was the highlight of my professional career because I didn't let [Ben Roberts-Smith] down and we both supported each other and we overcame overwhelming odds together,' Person 4 said.

Person 4 said that, after he returned to Perth, he started to hear from people that he was to be awarded a Victoria Cross. He thought the timing made sense. 'It is common knowledge [within Defence] that a Victoria Cross is a political statement used by the government for a good news story,' he said. '[The government and heads of Defence] wanted a good news story. 2010 was the most violent period in Afghanistan and we lost a lot of people and they wanted a good news story.' Three days later, Person 4 testified, he was told it wasn't to be him receiving a Victoria Cross, but the judge's son, Ben Roberts-Smith.

The citation for that award, which was endowed in 2011, includes some significant departures from the testimony Person 4 offered. Person 4 was not recognised for his actions in the engagement until 2013, when he was awarded the Medal for Gallantry; he testified that he believed the delay was because 'there's a medal allocation for each rotation'.

This is a view with which most sources agree. Ben Roberts-Smith's patrol commander, Person 5, the former SBS and DEVGRU operator who is also being investigated for allegedly murdering PUCs, was awarded a Star of Gallantry for his actions at the Battle of Tizak. It is a medal second only to the Victoria Cross in the Australian honours and awards system.

In cross-examination, Arthur Moses SC asked Person 4 whether he was jealous of Ben Roberts-Smith being awarded the Victoria Cross, and Moses listed the accolades and blessings Roberts-Smith had subsequently enjoyed: he became a senior Channel Seven executive, Australian Father of the Year and the chair of the National Australia Day Council.

'Believe me, I'm not jealous of him,' Person 4 said.

The barrister went further, suggesting that Person 4 was obsessed with Ben Roberts-Smith and wanted to tear him down. Moses also discussed Person 4's various post-combat mental-health issues, and his 2021 medical discharge from the SASR due to a psychiatric disorder.

Person 4 vigorously denied the suggestion that his evidence was false. 'I loved [Ben Roberts-Smith] as a brother,' he stated. He told the court that he hadn't wanted anything to do with the defamation case, and that he'd been compelled to give evidence by subpoena.

* * *

An ADF officer who was in the SASR in 2010 but doesn't wish to be named says that the Battle of Tizak brought pride to the regiment, but also left it riven. He says that much conduct in Tizak was exemplary and, as Ben Roberts-Smith's Victoria Cross citation says, 'in keeping with the finest traditions of the Australian Army and the Australian Defence Force'. But some conduct in Tizak, the officer says, was not as exemplary.

He also claims that after the action, some medals were given to soldiers whom he believed already had an oversized and negative influence within the regiment, and who were being protected by a handful of influential officers. Another former SASR officer said that after Tizak, medals were given to 'big personalities with big egos who were bullies and just wanted to kill as many people as they could'.

A former SASR officer said Tizak, 'was basically the moment that [the officers] lost control of the regiment'.

In court, Andrew Hastie, formerly an SASR captain and until May 2022 Australia's assistant defence minister, testified that, after Tizak and the VC endowment, Ben Roberts-Smith was 'at the apex of the SAS power structure'.

* * *

Major General John Cantwell says a 'drumbeat of death' started in Uruzgan on 27 June 2010, when sappers Jacob Moerland and Darren Smith, 21 and 25 years old respectively, were killed while investigating a suspected IED in the Mehrabad Valley. Also killed was Herbie, their explosive-detection dog.

After those deaths came the devastating crash of a US Blackhawk carrying Australian commandos who were conducting a follow-up mission after Tizak. One American crew member died, as well as Australian commandos Private Scott Palmer, 27, Private Timothy Aplin, 38, and Private Benjamin Chuck, 27. Seven other commandos suffered serious injuries, including brain injuries.

Days later, a dismounted Australian mentoring patrol, returning to Combat Outpost Mashal in the Baluchi Valley, triggered an IED. It killed 23-year-old Private Nathan Bewes and seriously injured a number of people, including another Australian soldier and an eight-year-old girl.

In August, there was another SASR death. While conducting a mission in Kandahar with American forces, an SASR patrol was engaged at very close range. Trooper Jason Brown, 29, suffered fatal gunshot wounds. His patrol commander was hit six times in the helmet, trousers and body armour while trying to drag the man under his command to safety.

A week after that, two Australian privates, Grant Kirby, 35, and Tomas Dale, 21, were killed by an IED, again in the Baluchi Valley on the approach to Chora.

Four days after those deaths, an element of Australian soldiers from the Mentoring Task Force were patrolling with ANA troops in Deh Rawood, a district east of Tarin Kot that the Dutch had controlled and that had since been handed over to the Australians. The Dutch had put significant reconstruction resources into this district, and it was considered one of the safest in the province, but Deh Rawood was also known for shifting allegiances.

On 24 August 2010, the Australian and Afghan patrol was close to the village of Derapet when they were engaged by up to 100 insurgents. During the battle, Lance Corporal Jared MacKinney, 28, of the Mentoring Task Force, was killed. Later, another soldier, Corporal Daniel Keighran, was awarded Australia's third Victoria Cross of the war for his actions in the Battle of Derapet.

Time and time and time again, it fell to Major General Cantwell to stand in front of bereaved troops and tell them to keep going. This was not easy, because by now he had little faith that the war could be won.

'Everyone who looked at the picture I was seeing was feeling the same,' Cantwell says. 'My role became to bolster morale and tell them what they needed to hear, [so] they would keep going, keep fighting, keep sacrificing and do the things we ask them to do. I particularly played to the heritage we carried as Australians, the absolute criticality of looking after your mates. What I didn't say was that this was all going to go to shit in a couple of years. That was in my head all the time. I had no doubt, absolutely no doubt, it would all come apart the minute we stopped looking.'

Cantwell's deputy commander once asked his commanding officer why they were in Afghanistan – what it was all for. Together, the pair attempted a justification, which focused on all the Australian blood and treasure being expended. But they came to no reckoning.

'We're here because we're freaking here,' Cantwell told the officer. 'We're doing it because we've been told to do it.'

At the start of 2011, John Cantwell completed his posting and returned to Australia. There, his mental health deteriorated significantly and he was diagnosed with acute PTSD. He was medicated and eventually admitted into full-time psychiatric care. The treatment he received has been largely successful, Cantwell says, and he now manages his PTSD capably.

Major General Angus Campbell, formerly a troop and squadron commander in the SASR, replaced Cantwell as the commander of JTF 633. General Campbell is now the Chief of the Defence Force.

25

'Killing became incentivised ... It was absurd'

WHEN MARK WALES RETURNED for his second full combat tour to Uruzgan in mid-2010, he did so already depleted. In 2008 and 2009, the SASR officer had spent more days overseas than he had in Australia, with enough of those days being in Kabul that he managed to maintain a romantic relationship with an MI6 agent stationed there. His duties in 2008 and 2009 mostly took him to Kabul and also Kandahar, but sometimes also to Tarin Kot, which gave him the opportunity to check in with the SASR element that was fulfilling SOTG responsibilities.

In one instance in 2009, a friend pulled Wales into one of the SASR team rooms at Camp Russell, where the patrols slept and relaxed. It was midday and he was handed a strong Johnnie Walker and dry, and a laptop that was displaying a carousel of gruesome imagery.

'Check out the photos of this fuckin' ambush,' a soldier said.

The team was one that had been involved in the Battle of Khas Uruzgan, the action for which Mark Donaldson had been awarded the Victoria Cross. The images were from the mission the day before the battle, when the Australian snipers had drawn wave after wave of Afghans into their rifles' scopes.

'We smashed these cunts,' one of the soldiers said to Wales.

These people had indeed been smashed. The images on the computer screen were of a punctured Hilux and piles of dead bodies; whole limbs had been blown off by rounds, such was the power of some of the weapons used. In one image, brain and cerebrospinal fluid was still dripping from a large forehead wound. In another, half a man's head had been clean removed.

Wales knew that dissociation – something often lapping on the shores of hatred – was required in the field to be effective, and this looked like dissociation to him. He tried to engage with the images and the bravado and the midday drinking, but already he was battling with alcohol addiction and the effects of PTSD. One minute, one hour, one day at a time – that was how he was getting through this war.

'I was just sweeping it under the carpet,' Wales says of his PTSD. 'And concentrating on surviving this part of the war. Everyone was doing that.'

When Mark Wales came back to Uruzgan for his second SOTG rotation in mid-2010, he assumed responsibilities as the executive officer, or XO, of the incoming sabre squadron, 1 Squadron. During the handover, the outgoing squadron commander joked with Wales that he hoped they'd left some targets for the new guys. They had scratched nine men off the JPEL during the rotation, not to mention dozens upon dozens of others killed in the raids in Tizak and around Shah Wali Kot.

Officially, the mission for the SOTG was to make preparations to hand over to the Afghan lead, but unofficially, according to Wales, the job was 'industrialised killing in the hope of weakening the enemy'.

JPEL and high-value targeting was now the primary focus for the SASR, and on this rotation a long list of JPEL targets, new and old, were available: Objective Mace, Objective Nunchuck, Objective Torpedo, Objective Hyacinth, as well as elusive legacy targets like Objective Rapier. It was also on this rotation that Wales and a group of other special forces officers came to believe that the Afghanistan mission simply wasn't working.

Wales had spent about as much time in Afghanistan as just about anyone since 2007, and had seen the mission from every level. In Canberra and in Kabul, he thought, perhaps the facts could be arranged in such a way that there was justification for the idea that the war could still be won, but in the field things seemed different.

'There were macro issues that were so large, no amount of kill/capture missions were going to fix it,' says Wales.

The Pakistani border was open to the Taliban, and the tribal hatred of the Afghan government and what were seen as occupying forces was only growing. Other issues included the coalition's inability to build a faithful and effective local security force, and the fact that despite having operated continuously in Afghanistan for five years, the coalition forces had little understanding of the local tribal dynamics.

'We would try and study the human terrain there, but it was such a shitshow all you could only look at was the peaking features,' Wales says. 'Matiullah Khan was one, and his small coalition, there were the other police chiefs, but it was hard to know what was going on. Even [the Afghans] didn't even know. They were just there to make some money, establish their powerbase and use us to settle scores, so we were being used by some of these guys, no doubt. There was no real effective police force and army, and we knew that.'

After clearances, JPEL prosecutions and battles like the one in Tizak, there was no way for the Australians to secure and hold ground on which so much blood had been spilled, so they seceded territory to the insurgents as soon as they captured it. Much of the Australian mission had been dedicated to the building of the Afghan police and army, but there were myriad persistent issues with both the police and the army that were never resolved.

'It doesn't matter what valley you go into and who you kill, if there's no tail end built into the strategy, you're not helping the war effort,' says Wales. 'We could be as good as we wanted, it made no difference.'

Wales says another problem was that a dangerous incentive structure problem developed at the heart of Australia's special forces.

'They say it all the time in business. "You show me the incentive and I'll show you the behaviour." Jackpots, JPEL targets, medals for achieving kills on JPEL targets, all of this became built into SOTG,' says Wales, who, after leaving the military, completed an MBA at an Ivy League college in the United States.

Should a JPEL target be found and prosecuted, reporting would reflect that a high-value target had been eliminated and the mission had been a success. Should the JPEL target not be found but a gunfight ensue with insurgents being killed, that was a success too, regardless of the potential long-term effect of the killings.

'Killing became incentivised,' Wales says. 'We're not talking about securing the population or incremental effects, it was just a body count. It was absurd. There was no measuring impact when you're just measuring killing.'

On his second SOTG rotation, Wales says, the quality of JPEL targets was not what it had been. 'Me and [another officer] were laughing because there was a guy on the JPEL who was in charge of four guys. This guy's the equivalent of a lance corporal in the Australian Army. We now have lance corporals on our fucking JPEL.'

To launch a JPEL mission required hundreds of man hours in Afghanistan and Canberra, millions of dollars' worth of equipment, not to mention the exposure of Australian and Afghan soldiers and local civilians to large amounts of risk. A persistent thought in Wales's mind on this rotation was: 'This is a fucking joke – we're fighting dirt farmers.'

Another realisation Wales had was that each SOTG rotation was now potentially degrading the capacity of the SASR.

'We couldn't move forward because we were getting good experience in fighting – but it's not a state-on-state conflict, they're insurgents,' he says. 'After a few years we'd learned everything we were going to learn, and instead of going forward we were going backwards. We were burning everyone out; we were getting too stuck in an operational method.'

Wales wasn't alone in holding this opinion. A group of officers at the captain and major level believed the strategy of the war was fundamentally compromised, and perhaps detrimental to the regiment's ongoing warfighting capability. According to Wales, this was one of two schools of thought within the SASR's officer ranks.

'There were officers who … wanted to be associated with the soldiers who wanted to keep doing what they were doing, and there were the others who were like, "This clearly isn't working,"' says Wales. He says the dissenters were a 'quieter' group, because 'it's not what the regiment wants to hear when we're sending soldiers off to fight and potentially die'.

Wales says that the 'status quo' group of officers were often supported by patrol commanders and senior shooters who had earned status above their rank. These shooters, Wales says, garnered respect as they were the ones who assumed all the bodily (and, it seems now, legal) risk on behalf of the regiment. According to Wales, they developed a compact, spoken or unspoken, with the officers that essentially boiled down to: 'You guys let us do what we want and you'll get medals. Just stay the fuck out of our way.'

Successfully facilitating the prosecution of JPEL targets was one of the criteria for a class of medal that included the Distinguished Service Medal and the Distinguished Service Cross. These were often awarded to senior officers, and represented a significant boost to their careers. Twenty-seven Distinguished Service Cross and Bars (meaning the recipient was receiving a second or even third Distinguished Service Medal) were awarded during the Afghan conflict, along with 65 Distinguished Service Medals and Bars.

I asked Major General Cantwell (who received the Distinguished Service Cross for his command of JTF 633) whether he believed a dangerous incentive structure had emerged within the SOTG.

He hadn't thought about it, he replied. 'Maybe I was more naive than I thought I was,' he says.

* * *

Matthew Bouillaut, who rotated into Afghanistan in 2010 with Mark Wales as the squadron sergeant major, didn't care about the quality of the JPEL targets. It wasn't his job to care about that. As Bouillaut says, you could end up just as dead prosecuting a bad target as you could a good target. His job was to keep good order within the squadron, and to create a bridge between the soldiers and the officers.

Bouillaut had other concerns, though. He believed that some soldiers, part of a generation of SASR operators under him, were able and willing to perform some of the more glamorous and violent aspects of the job, but weren't as enthusiastic about fulfilling other obligations.

'I don't know if I'd call it weakness, but they weren't as hard as they should be,' he says.

Bouillaut is fully aware that there's a long tradition of senior soldiers thinking the junior soldiers under their command were too soft, but he was worried that this wasn't a generational issue but one caused by the long tail of this long war. There were structural concerns at the patrol level, he felt, and in the control the men exhibited on the patrols. The countenance and attitude of some of the shooters was changing, he says. Even the physical shape of these soldiers was changing: where once they were rangy and wiry like endurance athletes, now they were broad, musclebound powerlifters.

'I think that whole toughness and resilience thing was eroded with the way we operated,' Bouillaut says. 'Helicopter ops, shoot a couple of bad guys in the morning, you're in the gym in the afternoon.' He also believes that soldiers became too fixated on Afghanistan. 'We were on ops, but the world still turns. In a few months, we're going to be doing something else.'

Having a capability set like a Swiss Army knife was built into the foundations of the SASR. They were a 'break in case of emergency' force, a 'last line of defence' force, a 'solve the unsolvable problem' force, endlessly current in the desert, in the jungle, on the ocean, in the air and in any type of city. It was believed that these other capabilities should not be blunted, or the regiment's best soldiers might be caught doing endless raiding against targets that might or might not have related meaningfully to the aims of the conflict.

One of Bouillaut's jobs as the squadron sergeant major was to keep his soldiers current in their training and progressing through their careers, but he found that a certain group of soldiers and patrol commanders – men with a large amount of combat experience – were refusing courses and refusing to progress through their careers.

'There was a cartel of guys who wanted to be gunfighters, be patrol commanders and not go above that rank,' he explains. 'They didn't want the responsibility of running courses and running ranges, doing all the hard work behind the scenes that gets people on operations in the first place.'

Some courses, like those for soldiers preparing for rank advancement, were conducted by the regular army, not SOCOMD, and only rarely. If one of these courses coincided with a deployment, an SASR operator due for rank advancement was obliged to leave Afghanistan and return to Australia. Bouillaut says some shooters were refusing to do such courses, and were able to do so because of the reputational power they held over some SASR officers. Going back to Australia while on ops to do a course conducted by senior infantry soldiers – a class of soldier who, regardless of their position and experience, would be considered 'basically a piece of shit' – was unconscionable, and so often they didn't.

'There was a lot of blind eyes turned because everyone wanted to be good blokes,' Bouillaut says. And the only good blokes who existed in the world were operators in the regiment.

A culture of vicious exclusivity had emerged within the SASR. Described by some as 'the brotherhood' and others as like a 'motorcycle gang', a core of soldiers with extensive combat experience, who were often at corporal or sergeant level, exerted significant power over many in the regiment and the SOTG, even including support staff and SASR officers, who rotated in and out of the regiment and so were often eager to be accepted by the senior operators.

'It was a very arrogant, sheltered organisation to be in,' says Bouillaut. 'I noticed that in the regiment – and I was part of this – everyone who was out of the regiment was not worthy.'

Matthew Bouillaut left Afghanistan for the last time in 2011. He now lives in Tasmania and runs a business offering treks through the island's wilderness. He says he still loves the SASR: he appreciates every moment he spent serving in it, and would still be in the regiment if Campbell Barracks were in Tasmania. 'It is a special regiment, with exceptional people doing things no one else in the Australian military can do,' he says.

But he also notes that there is no point to the regiment if they're not accountable, subordinate to government and part of the rest of the military. 'At the end of the day we're in the army,' he says. 'You have to do what you're told, and some people couldn't accept that.'

Bouillaut was part of Task Force Black, one of the prototypical and most clandestine post-9/11 raiding forces, but even that force, he says, was strictly subordinate to the larger command structure and civilian political authority.

'At no stage was there a lack of chain of command, and at no stage would they get away with any of shit [some of the SASR patrols] were getting away with [in Afghanistan],' he explains. 'We weren't going to be fucking shooting anyone in the back of the head, that's for sure.'

26

'Our strategy is well-defined, our strategy is constant'

DURING 2011, A HANDFUL of targeted killings were conducted that affected the strategic situation in Afghanistan. One was executed by the United States, and the other by the Taliban and Taliban-aligned forces.

The first targeted killing was a pretty standard raid from a tactical perspective: a direct assault on a compound of interest where, intelligence suggested, a high-value target would be found. At this point, there were at least a dozen coalition elements in the region that could have conducted the assault – Australia alone had two – but the mission was handed to JSOC, with DEVGRU given the green light. The prosecuting force found limited resistance and the target was killed easily.

Three aspects of the raid made it different from the thousands that had preceded it. The first was that a new stealth variant of the UH-60 Blackhawk helicopter (quieter and with a smaller radar profile) was used to insert the soldiers. The second was that the raid was conducted into Pakistan, and not Afghanistan. And the third was that the target was Osama bin Laden.

Since the Battle of Tora Bora, the CIA and JSOC had dedicated huge amounts of resources to the hunt for Osama bin Laden, but for years there had been no solid leads. The torture conducted by the CIA, for instance, did not contribute to locating Bin Laden, nor to any good, actionable intelligence leading to the kill or capture of other al-Qaeda leaders. Then, in 2011, two men known to be al-Qaeda couriers were followed to a compound in the Pakistani town of Abbottabad, a few hundred kilometres from Afghanistan's eastern border. It was a place where, only a few months earlier, one of the Bali bombers, Umar Patek, had been arrested.

The location became one of extreme interest to the CIA when they found that the large and expensive compound had no phone or internet connection, and, according to drone imagery, hosted a tall, older, bearded man who like to walk the grounds of the compound but who never ventured into the streets or nearby park. The US intelligence agencies waited and watched and hoped for a revelatory moment, but none came. The decision to move on the compound was left to President Obama, who approved the raid in April 2011.

In the early morning of 2 May 2011, two squads of DEVGRU operators disgorged from prototype helicopters inside the compound. One of the helicopters partially crashed on entry due to a planning failure; while no one was injured, the helicopter had to be destroyed on the ground before exfiltration. The operators swept through the compound, killing five people, including Osama bin Laden, left with a trove of computers, hard drives and documents, boarded one of the stealth helicopters and a Chinook called up from a QRF position and sped back towards Jalalabad, where the mission had been launched.

Although Bin Laden was not personally involved in the territorial war across the border in Afghanistan, his killing did change the strategic picture for both the United States and the Taliban. For the United States, the killing of Bin Laden represented the achievement of a significant war aim and, unlike other goals claimed by the United States – such as women's education and the expansion of democracy – it was irreversible. The elimination of Bin Laden made it easier for the United States to negotiate their way out of Afghanistan – and it made it easier for the Taliban too.

Many of the older and more senior Taliban had pledged a *bay'ah*, or oath of personal fealty, to Bin Laden before the 9/11 attacks. These were sacred contracts under *sharia* law, and these bound men, who were positioning themselves as the keepers of *sharia* in Afghanistan, couldn't easily change their position on al-Qaeda while Bin Laden was alive. With his death, however, they were freed from their *bay'ahs*, and suddenly had more flexibility.

* * *

Five weeks after the killing of Osama bin Laden, President Obama gave a speech looking at 'the way forward in Afghanistan'. The US president explained to the United States, Afghanistan, Pakistan and the world that US forces would start withdrawing the next month. By the end of the year, some 10,000 US troops would be back at home.

'We're starting this drawdown from a position of strength ... We'll have to do the hard work of keeping the gains that we've made, while we draw down our forces and transition responsibility for security to the Afghan government,' Obama said. 'And next May, in Chicago, we will host a summit with our NATO allies and partners to shape the next phase of this transition.'

In the lead-up to that Chicago meeting, Prime Minister Julia Gillard gave a key speech at a luncheon sponsored by Boeing, explaining the timeline to which the Australian military was working.

'We have entered the final process, the process of transition, we know that that process will be 12 to 18 months long, and we know that at the end of that, the bulk of our forces will be able to return home,' Gillard said. 'So our strategy is well-defined, our strategy is constant, and we cannot allow even the most grievous of losses to change our strategy. We cannot have a circumstance where loss dictate how we will engage in this war and see our mission through. In my view, that wouldn't be appropriately honouring the men we have lost. In my view, it would be letting our nation down. We went there for a purpose and we will see that purpose through.'

Almost all of Australia's forces would be out of Uruzgan in 2013; so too most of the United States' forces. The dates of withdrawal were solidifying. The endgame was coming.

* * *

A month after Barack Obama's 'way forward' speech, the Taliban executed a devastating targeted killing campaign that meaningfully changed the political dynamics of southern Afghanistan. The first significant attack was against Ahmed Wali Karzai, the half-brother of Hamid Karzai and one of the most influential crime bosses, drug runners and, indeed, people in that part of the country.

On 12 July 2011, Ahmed Wali Karzai had been holding court in front of a large group of associates, underbosses and invitees at his home in Kandahar. Outside, layers of security surrounded his house, and a large cadre of bodyguards was present too. One of these was Sardar Mohammad, a sadistic but effective capo of Karzai's organisation who had run a private police force that murdered and tortured. Sardar was also well known to the CIA, feeding them information and sending requests from his boss.

It's not known why Sardar flipped or how the Taliban got to him, but that day Sardar pestered his boss for a private audience. As he and Karzai moved into an anteroom, Sardar raised his rifle and shot Karzai. Immediately, Karzai's loyal bodyguards ran into the room and killed Sardar, whose mutilated body was placed in the middle of a roundabout in central Kandahar.

Two days later, at a memorial for Karzai attended by many senior governmental officials and Popalzai leadership, a Taliban suicide bomber struck. The bomber evaded security by using an explosive device hidden under his turban. Four people were killed and 15 wounded. Later in the month, another turban bomb was used in Kandahar to kill Ghulam Haider Hamidi, the mayor of the city.

Two days after the deadly funeral of Ahmed Wali Karzai, one of his closest associates was killed in Kabul. Jan Mohammad had been meeting with an Uruzgani member of parliament in his house in Kabul, when a suicide bomber ran at his guards and detonated himself. That bomber cleared the way for two other gunmen to storm the house. A pitched battle ensued, first with

Jan Mohammad's guards and then with Afghan forces who were nearby. When the smoke cleared, the two gunmen were dead, as was the MP and Jan Mohammad and a number of bodyguards. The Taliban claimed responsibility, but others said it was a tribal revenge attack, emanating from the Chora Valley.

Later in the month, the Taliban's targeted violence made its way to Tarin Kot. On 28 July a car appeared to break down in front of the governor's compound. The driver called to some children nearby to help him move the car off the road, and as they flocked to him, he detonated the explosives in his chassis. This explosion was the trigger for a complex attack against the governor, Mohammad Omar Shirzad, and also Matiullah Khan.

After the car bomb was detonated at the governor's compound, another car bomb went off at Matiullah's compound, which was stormed by men carrying AK-47s and RPGs. The seven attackers were all killed before they could succeed in their mission. Australian soldiers rushed in to assist the wounded, bringing them into their base for emergency treatment and surgery. At least 22 Afghan civilians died in the attacks, roughly half of them children. A BBC journalist was also killed, mistakenly shot by a US soldier while hiding in a bathroom.

Matiullah Khan had not been physically injured in the attacks, but throughout this fighting season his influence, power and prospects had taken hit after hit. Matiullah's power had been derived from his tribal brother Ahmed Wali Karzai as much as it had from Ahmed Wali's blood brother Hamid Karzai. The Americans were leaving. Their allies were being killed. The post-Taliban systems of power were being disassembled. It was clear that the south of Afghanistan was again up for grabs.

* * *

When Dr Abdul Ghafar Stanikzai moved to Uruzgan in 2009, he knew he had his work cut out for him. He was to establish in Tarin Kot an office of the Afghan Independent Human Rights Commission (AIHRC), a body created and funded by the Afghan government, and from that office he was to investigate any violations of human rights by any actors. Like most Afghans, he had a fairly dim view of Uruzgan and those who lived there. He expected illiteracy, conservatism, dust, tribal violence and tribal law. He was not disappointed.

Although he'd not been to Uruzgan before 2009, Dr Stanikzai was familiar with many of the main actors there. Born in Logar Province, and part of the Ghilzai tribe, he shared tribal heritage with some insurgents. Dr Stanikzai had started his medical studies in Kandahar while the Taliban were in power, constantly fearing jail or beatings for possessing medical textbooks that featured drawings of genitalia. He was familiar with the warlords too, having travelled to Helmand Province in 2004 after the completion of his studies, where a warlord and narco-baron kept the streets and highways safe.

Dr Stanikzai knew an Australian, a kind and hardworking doctor from Brisbane named Neil, whom he worked alongside when he took a job as a field medical officer for the United Nations. Together, Dr Stanikzai says, he and Neil watched, throughout 2005 and 2006, the insurgency take hold. The patients they treated migrated from illness to gunshot and blast wounds. Many roads became impassable. The threat of suicide bombings and car bombings increased monthly.

As a field medical officer, Dr Stanikzai helped the AIHRC log injuries and deaths for its human rights reports. With a keen mind, a medical degree and great cultural appreciation of the fighting, Dr Stanikzai had an aptitude for human rights reporting and was asked to head the AIHRC office in Tarin Kot. His arrival there, however, was greeted by a wild and overstated expectation of what the commission could do. Since 2001, the people of Uruzgan had been consistently told that a mythical form of absolute justice called 'human rights' was one day coming to them. They initially thought that the AIHRC was the home of this justice.

'Their expectation was that we were very powerful. People were thinking that human rights could do everything, but it couldn't do anything,' says Dr Stanikzai.

People were travelling for days to reach Tarin Kot in order to receive justice from the AIHRC, and usually they were sorely disappointed. The AIHRC had nominal power under the Afghan constitution, but that power had to be expressed through the Afghan police, who had little ability to project authority in much of much of the province – and in the places where they did have any, their understanding of justice was filtered through one man, Matiullah Khan, and his family.

Matiullah was an Afghan warlord, a position that could only be attained through violence. Human rights and the absolute application of the law were far distant from the paradigm from which Matiullah had emerged. In fact, Dr Stanikzai says, in 2012 Matiullah's forces were committing torture and summary executions under the warlord's orders, in areas where Australian soldiers were working.

'Matiullah had his own [trucking] containers. They take people [to these containers], torture people, kill people or release people,' says Dr Stanikzai. Some Australian soldiers have acknowledged that they knew about these torture cells; they sometimes heard the screams.

Dr Stanikzai says he was also party to considerable Australian and international efforts to bring good governance and a modicum of lawfulness to Matiullah and the province. He says Matiullah's attitude and behaviour did change somewhat from 2009 until the withdrawal of the Australian military: he made some efforts to spread his wealth throughout the areas where he and his police maintained control. In part, Dr Stanikzai says, this change was because Matiullah literally didn't know what else to do with his money.

'He find too much money,' says Dr Stanikzai. 'It's unimaginable the amount of money he get from Australia and from the United States. Securing the road from Kandahar to [Tarin Kot], he was getting in one day $100,000 or $200,000.' Dr Stanikzai says this money was augmented by the proceeds of opium shipments from Helmand to Kandahar.

Efforts were made to shore up a legal system that might endure after the withdrawal of Western forces, but they were complicated by local systems of justice, compromised courts and vested interests. In 2011, there were multiple concurrent justice systems working in Uruzgan. There were the Taliban courts, with which the AIHRC had nothing to do, as well as the official federal and district court systems, which were often ignored. And then there were the Ulemi Shura (a religious leaders' council) and the Eslahi Shura (a reform council), informal justice councils based on traditional law.

The first set of *shura*, which were religious courts attended by religious leaders, should have held the most sway of the two councils, but Dr Stanikzai explains that the second *shura*, the Eslahi Shura, was by far the more powerful, as it had been started and was controlled by Matiullah.

'Every crime: robbery, killing, things like that was done by [the Eslahi] *shura*,' says Dr Stanikzai. 'Even domestic violence, women escape from house, everything. They make the decision, and sometimes send the decision to the [official federal] court. Because of the power of [Matiullah Khan]. The judge could not refuse because he would give money to everyone too.'

Dr Stanikzai says that while attending the Eslahi Shura in 2011 with Australian Department of Foreign Affairs and Trade and US State Department representatives, he confronted Matiullah about his subversion of the justice system. The prosecutors of the federal court hadn't had a case in three months, he said; did this mean there was no crime in Uruzgan?

'[Matiullah] jumped from his chair [and said], "The police are arresting people and sometimes dying as they do. We hand the people over to the prosecutor and they release the person so we can't do that,"' Dr Stanikzai says.

According to Dr Stanikzai, these national security and defence prosecutors often had a contentious relationship with Matiullah, sometimes over questions of justice and sometimes over access to and fraternity with Australian and US special forces.

Dr Stanikzai says that after Matiullah's outburst, he uttered a local saying that roughly translates as 'I wipe my dick with the constitution'.

In a number of instances, the AIHRC was asked to investigate killings likely undertaken by Matiullah or his men, but Dr Stanikzai says they were impossible to investigate. Some of these allegations came out of the Mehrabad Valley, the green belt east of Tarin Kot that connected the provincial capital with Popalzai enclaves in Chenartu. One of Matiullah's commanders was accused of at least one massacre in the clearance of Mehrabad, an area primarily populated by Ghilzai tribespeople.

The clearance of Mehrabad, conducted by Matiullah's men and also Australian forces, was considered a great anti-insurgent success, but a report from the Dutch ethnographic group The Liaison Office, looking into the stability of Uruzgan 18 months after the Dutch military withdrawal, said that this success was somewhat offset by the fact that insurgents from the area had not been reintegrated and that many were fighting elsewhere.

'Several former insurgents are rumoured to have asked to be reintegrated, yet no process seemed to exist, leaving the individuals at the mercy of [Matiullah], who, counter to government policy, threatened to kill them,' the report read. 'These potential reintegratees instead left the area out of fear and some re-joined the insurgency.'

According to Dr Stanikzai, a large number of Ghilzai people who were not involved in the insurgency also fled Mehrabad during the fighting, never to return.

* * *

As a program attempting to facilitate a working and effective judiciary in Tarin Kot, the Rule of Law Cell was one of the most admirable and ambitious elements of the SOTG. It was the brainchild of an SOTG commanding officer, a 1CDO corporal who was an architect by trade, and a legal officer named Brett Sangster.

The Rule of Law Cell was Sangster's passion, but as was also the case for the others working on it, it was his second job. In his role as an SOTG legal officer, Sangster's primary clients were the force elements that were prosecuting the war outside the wire. He was tasked with making sure the soldiers understood their legal obligations under the Laws of Armed Conflict and, more tangibly, that they adhered to what were increasingly complicated and expansive rules of engagement.

Not only were there separate and distinct Australian RoE for the SOTG and conventional forces, there were ISAF RoE that sometimes applied, as well as US RoE that had to be considered when working alongside US forces. Furthermore, some of the mission sets like the Tevara Sin/JPEL missions within the commandos' counter-nexus mission had their own distinct RoE. There was a lot to consider, and a lot for Sangster to impart – and that was before he took on the job of creating the Rule of Law Cell.

The Rule of Law Cell attempted the paradigmatic change that the war needed. Justice was at the heart of the war in Uruzgan: it was and would continue to be. Justice is what people in Uruzgan yearned for and craved, and, as much as any physical territory, something they would fight for. But any system of justice offered in Uruzgan must be compatible with local realities and understood on local terms. It could not apply only to some in the province, or be at odds with the behaviour of government and Western forces. It must also be pragmatically available. Tribal forms of justice, which were brutal and unforgiving but available, were preferred to the government's constitutional law, which was nice in principle, but for most people in Uruzgan seemed only to exist on paper.

The Rule of Law Cell, something of a pilot program, attempted to utilise existing but underused prosecutors, magistrates and laws in prosecuting insurgent crime, so that the Australians and their partners in the government of Afghanistan would be seen as purveyors of justice that was even-handed and fair. It would also attempt to stop Australian soldiers from shooting so many Afghans.

In the provincial capital, there were prosecutors, magistrates and laws – what was lacking were evidence, suspects and a mandate; something the Rule of Law Cell would attempt to provide. When raiding, the Rule of Law Cell asked the Australian force elements to fight to create an environment in which it was safe to gather evidence and suspects. They would carry with them evidence bags, cameras and equipment for bio-enrolment (retina and fingerprint scanners that could cross-check insurgent databases), and had procedures for PUC transfer back to Camp Russell. From there, the Australians had a detention facility in which they conducted 'tactical questioning', and where suspects could be held by military police before they were transferred to the Afghan justice system. With an uncorrupted chain of evidence, insurgents could be charged, convicted and sentenced, either to a jail term or maybe just a fine.

Eventually, the Rule of Law Cell procedures were built into SOTG concept of operations (CONOPS), meaning all deployed Australian soldiers knew of the program's existence and the Rule of Law Cell procedures became embedded in standard operating procedure. Sangster says the program was a success, primarily because many Australian soldiers wanted to engage with it: after years spent on multiple rotations, they wanted their mission to be going somewhere. They needed to see that they were fighting for a reason.

'The guys are highly intelligent on the whole,' Sangster says. '[For some soldiers] their frustration was that the job was just kinetic. They wanted to see gains, especially gains in the Tarin Kot township.'

Like many admirable Dutch and Australian state-building enterprises, the Rule of Law Cell under Brett Sangster only operated in Tarin Kot, where security had largely been established. Sangster says he knew the program was working when soldiers going on operations in Tarin Kot were 'became less focused on targeting and neutralising targets and they were bringing people in – people they would have killed usually under the rules of engagement'.

The system was, of course, imperfect. Matiullah's enemies were to be taken to him instead of being processed through the Afghan justice system, and the principles and practices of the Rule of Law Cell only applied to Tarin Kot township. After being sentenced, offending insurgents were often supposed to be transferred to Afghan prisons, but in many instances illegal deals were made to free them.

'[Some of the Australians] would really complain that we'd put them through this process and the [offenders] would end up back out, sometimes the next day, but they missed the point really,' Sangster remarks. 'The fact was we were building up some credibility, some goodwill and some semblance of rule of law in Tarin Kot, and I knew it was cutting through.'

The penal system was one of dozens of governmental systems that were corrupt in Uruzgan, but the knowledge that Australian soldiers and their partners were bringing detainees to an Afghan court, and that these suspects were then either convicted or released, depending on the evidence collected, became increasingly known in Tarin Kot. These efforts were also noticed in Kabul, where ISAF commander General David Petraeus asked to be briefed about the program.

* * *

As well as investigating human rights abuses, the AIHRC and Dr Stanikzai were tasked with training Afghan government forces in the theory and practice of human rights. They held weekly meetings with Afghan police, training them in how suspects and civilians should be treated in accordance with Afghan law. Dr Stanikzai would visit the multinational base to conduct these sessions; on one occasion he was invited to conduct training within Camp Russell.

On one occasion Dr Stanikzai held a session with the Wakunish, the SASR's partner force of primarily Hazaras and Uzbeks. In these special forces soldiers, he says, he found a willing audience.

'They had no idea [about] human rights or laws, they just know how to fight,' says Dr Stanikzai. 'I told them very basic things. How to approach people, telling the consequences of doing bad things, stopping them [from] torturing. They were all very carefully listening.'

During a break, the commanding officer of the men he was teaching, a man named Maidur who was later killed in a suicide attack, took Dr Stanikzai aside. 'We are having some tea and he says ... "We will try our best, but you are talking to us ... why are you not talking to the Australians? Because they are doing more than us."'

* * *

It was possible for two parallel evidence chains against a JPEL target to exist simultaneously. One was internal, used by Australians and Americans in condemning a target to the JPEL through intelligence and intercepts. This evidence was secret, as was the evidentiary standard that had to be reached. The other was the evidentiary standard of the Afghan courts, with intelligence and intercepts largely unable to be used in court either because the intelligence was classified or the Afghan court might not recognise it.

It's believed that, with their procedures and equipment, some Australian and American soldiers preferred to kill suspected insurgents rather than gather physical evidence that might be used in possibly corrupt Afghan judicial proceedings.

This potential preference for killing over capture was exacerbated when the right of habeas corpus was applied to Australian operations later in the war, meaning, in most cases that, for Afghans captured during missions, it had to be proven that they had broken an Afghan law, or they must be released after four days of detention.

Former SASR captain Andrew Hastie testified about this preference for killing during the Ben Roberts-Smith defamation trial. He gave evidence that, back in 2012, he had said to the

SASR's commanding officer: 'We have some issues that we need to look at, specifically this "catch and release" policy where you capture an insurgent and if you don't have evidence to put into the Afghan judicial system, they get released after three [sic] days. This system incentivises killing rather than capturing.'

The first suspected Afghan insurgent to have a warrant issued for his arrest courtesy of the work being done in the Rule of Law Cell was Hayat Ustad, a Tarin Kot logistician elevated on the JPEL as Objective Heggitt. His targeted killing by the SASR may have been undertaken because of the assurance of a 'jackpot' after his death (but not assured with an arrest), or perhaps because the prosecuting force was bored, as suggested, or it may have been simply a reflection of the nature of the prosecuting force and of the SOTG, which was not commanded by police or civilians but by military officers, who reported only to other military officers.

As Alexander Downer noted: 'Don't send the SAS in if you're worried they're going to kill someone. Of course they're going to kill someone.'

* * *

As well as conducting 'counter-leadership' JPEL missions, the SASR was increasingly engaged with Australian force protection JPEL missions. This meant raising on the JPEL those who might be considering or facilitating attacks against Australians.

JPEL wasn't the only way force protection was enabled by the SOTG, however. Operation Moon was a psychological operation to confuse and discredit the insurgency. This sometimes coincided with the Special Operation Engineering Regiment's Operation Iron Maiden, which entailed finding enemy weapons caches and either putting tracking devices on them or sabotaging them, sometimes by putting 'zero-fuses' in mortar or RPG rounds that would kill the user as soon as he tried to fire.

Also useful was the development of human sources: these were usually men who were compelled to betray the insurgents by way of leverage, internecine competition or money. ASIS efforts to recruit senior Taliban had limited success, but the Australian Army Intelligence Corps managed to develop a number of significant sources. Often this was accomplished after the source had been detained and taken to Tarin Kot, where they were turned during questioning by qualified Field HUMINT Team (FHT) professionals.

One such source was a point of immense pride to the small circle who knew about him. This man was inside the very heart of the insurgency not only in Uruzgan, but in all Afghanistan – indeed, he sat as part of the Quetta Shura in Pakistan. This source was a major asset in the Australian war effort, and was used sparingly, for fear he would be exposed. But when, in 2011, the source reported to his Australian handler that a team of child suicide bombers was being sent from Pakistan into Uruzgan, the intelligence had to be actioned.

Using the source's information and satellite imagery, the compound where the children were being held was identified. An SASR element – not part of the SOTG but in Tarin Kot as part of a secret intelligence cooperative – was sent on a clandestine surveillance mission to observe the location. Tracking the children's movements after they left this location, in order to find their local handlers and enablers, was considered, but it was decided that it was too risky. So a pretext was established for Afghan forces to raid the compound, and the children were brought back to Tarin Kot and questioned by Australian intelligence officers.

Then, on 29 October 2011, the Australians in Uruzgan were introduced to a new type of attack, one the SOTG could do nothing to pre-empt.

Inside the hessian confines of Patrol Base Sorkh Bed, a small outpost close to the Tarin Kot–Kandahar road, morning parade had just been dismissed. A *kandak* of Afghan National Army recruits were milling around, waiting for their working day to begin in earnest.

One of the soldiers on the base was an Alakozai sergeant named Darwesh, who had bragged to some of the other Afghan soldiers that he would one day change his allegiance and turn his weapon on the 40 Australian soldiers from the Mentoring Task Force who lived with him on the base.

The other Afghan soldiers later said they thought Darwesh had been all bark and no bite, but under a crisp, blue morning sky, with a shaved body and wearing white, like so many suicide bombers, he strode towards the Australians with murderous intent, in his hands a light machine gun. The Australian soldiers were talking to each other and the interpreters about what the day might bring, when Darwesh started to fire.

The engagement only lasted a few seconds. The Afghan fired in bursts at centre masses, as the Australians had trained him to do. He felled one target and then the next. Darwesh expended 44 of the 200 rounds in his weapon before the Australian soldiers could return fire and kill him.

In the moments of fear and shock afterwards, the Australians and Afghans saw more than a dozen people on the ground, shot: Australian soldiers and their Afghan interpreters. Three Australians lay dead: 26-year-old Captain Bryce Duffy, 22-year-old Corporal Ashley Birt and 29-year-old Lance Corporal Luke Gavin.

Ten days later, an ANA soldier named Mohammad Roozi walked up to an overwatch position at a patrol base 40 kilometres east of Tarin Kot and turned his machine gun on his Australian trainers. The Australians were in a partitioned part of the base, preparing a barbecue dinner, but from his elevated position Roozi had direct line of sight to them. He fired the machine gun at the Australians, and when that gun jammed, he used his M16 rifle. Three Australians and two Afghan interpreters were shot, but all men survived their wounds. Roozi escaped into the desert in an ANA Humvee loaded with weapons and supplies.

These attacks came in the wake of the killing of Lance Corporal Andrew Jones, an Australian cook, by ANA soldier Shafidullah Guhlamon at a combat outpost in the Chora Valley. After the murder, Guhlamon disappeared into Chora's green belt.

In all three of these 'green on blue' attacks, there were no glaring motivational factors, but they were part of a nationwide trend of Afghan soldiers turning their weapons on their trainers. These killings were a nightmare for Australia, not only from humanitarian perspective, but also tactically and politically. None of the Afghan soldiers who attacked Australians were in contact with the Taliban before their attack.

The Australians couldn't train Afghans without arming them, and Australia's entire exit strategy was built around standing up the ANA's 4th Brigade. The work had to continue, and the Australian troops had to be protected as well as possible, but it was not apparent how those two goals could be concurrently achieved.

There didn't seem to be a way of adequately predicting the behaviour of tens of the thousands of Afghans being trained; all that could be done was to ensure that every potential green-on-blue attacker must know that the Australians would not rest in their efforts to find him and kill him, should he betray them.

Both surviving attackers were raised on the JPEL, with Shafidullah Guhlamon designated Objective Morningstar and Mohammad Roozi Objective Shady Igloo. Guhlamon was easily found. A native of Khost, he returned to his home village, where he was killed by US Rangers in a night raid. Mohammad Roozi, who was not Pashtun but of Uzbek descent, was embraced by the Taliban when he escaped to Pakistan, and appeared in a propaganda video claiming to have killed 12 Australians.

A little later, the United States discovered Roozi back in Afghanistan, in Takhar Province abutting Tajikistan. The Americans invited the SASR to do the trigger-pulling on what was essentially a Delta mission with Australian augmented shooters. Roozi was killed by the SASR in 2013. This was a rare JPEL mission conducted by Australia in the north of the country.

* * *

The killing of Mohammad Roozi came in the endgame of Australia's war, a period of capacity realisation and also dark ignominy. This was a phase in which Australia's special forces operated in a way that they could have only dreamed about in 2001. After initially conducting long vehicle patrols, essentially waiting to be shot at, the SASR was now equipped and trained to do complex helicopter targeting ops, using very modern intelligence cycles.

During the early stages of the war, Australia's special forces had applied the 'F3' targeting cycle to their operations – 'Find, fix, finish'. This cycle later became 'F3EA', with 'exploit' and 'analyse' added to the cycle. This meant that during the 'fix' phase, the prosecuting force would also seek out intelligence – be it signals, hard material or intelligence born of interrogation. That intelligence might then lead to the creation of a new target.

Near the end of the war, the targeting cycle became 'F3EAD', adding 'disseminate' to the acronym. Ideally, this meant dissemination in real time, adding to the intelligence picture and creating new targets as the prosecuting force was in the field, so that they might stay in the field for another 'finish' (and perhaps another, and another), or another prosecuting force might attack a different target before it was able to disappear.

Each cycle pushed intelligence and approvals further away from Canberra and closer to Tarin Kot, and eventually even closer to the ground than that, with SASR patrol commanders becoming increasingly empowered throughout the war to mark Afghans for death. These changes in targeting procedures were part of the continuous parry and thrust in which insurgents and counterinsurgents had engaged throughout the war. Vehicle patrols and conventional battles gave way to IED strikes and suicide bombings, creating an era of helicopter operations and the JPEL prosecution that potentially ceded to the insurgency huge swathes of ground between population centres.

An intricate and expensive apparatus of surveillance, drones, signals, satellites and other intelligence was constructed, as was a system of swift approvals and prosecutions. And then the insider attacks started – a very effective foil to high-tech targeting. These attacks were devastating, and they didn't require advance coordination, expertise or equipment – just the will to execute.

Javid Ahmad, a senior intelligence manager and fellow at West Point's Modern War Institute, issued a report analysing insider attacks and made two major claims. The first was that these attacks were, to a certain extent, 'an outcome of cultural friction', with Western forces often misunderstanding their local partners and creating grievances over honour, culture, religion or justice, sometimes without knowing it. The second claim was that these attacks were, after 2011, the 'preferred warfighting tactic of the Taliban, a 'cultural weapon' that targeted two weakness in the US and Australian civil–military apparatus: 'a deep aversion to casualties' and 'the need to believe in benevolent narratives about why [we] fight'.

The insider attacks amplified the general sense of the aimlessness of the war in Afghanistan, highlighting the cultural differences between Western and Afghan soldiers and the chasm between their ideal outcomes. They were thus the perfect Taliban weapon and, according to Mullah Omar, were developed and promoted by the 'Call and Guidance, Luring and Integration Department', which Omar claimed was active across Afghanistan.

Some insider attacks were perpetrated by soldiers recruited by the Taliban in advance, some by insurgents in stolen Afghan security forces uniforms, but the majority by Afghans who simply flipped their allegiance, killed and fled, often hoping to find and join the Taliban. The international forces were leaving Afghanistan – everyone knew that – and as the withdrawal date came closer, some pragmatic Afghans perhaps saw an affiliation with international forces as being to their detriment.

All the attacks were in a way sponsored by the Taliban, which compelled mullahs to issue a series of fatwas or religious edicts calling for such killings, as well as creating and sharing propaganda and media that would inspire Afghan soldiers to make attacks. The only conceivable tactical response was revenge. For Australia, the endgame of the war was to be a perilous period, bodily and morally.

The SFTG/SOTG conducted 20 rotations into Afghanistan, but two near the end of the war would provide the vast majority of alleged crimes for which the IGADF's report into war crimes in Afghanistan found credible evidence. This report – which only investigated killings that were undeniably murder, and not those that were possibly the result of a heat-of-battle lethal action – found credible evidence of one instance of alleged murder by Australia's special forces (potentially with multiple victims) in each of the years 2007, 2009, 2010 and 2013, as the SOTG wound down.

For the year 2012, the report found credible evidence for 17 instances of alleged murder, many of which involved multiple victims. The report also noted that these rotations suffered from 'a wavering moral compass, and … declining psychological health'.

The Endgame

27

'General terms, as a monarch she was very happy
with our progress'

THE BOREDOM OF CANBERRA nearly killed David Savage. One
minute he was in the Department of Foreign Affairs and Trade
headquarters agreeing to a posting in Afghanistan, the next he
was in Chora being approached by a child in a suicide bomber's
vest. Those moments were months apart, but they were a one-two
punch for Savage and, one way or another, it was Canberra's fault.

When DFAT's First Assistant Secretary asked David Savage
whether he'd like to post to Afghanistan, he replied instantly: yes.

'You don't want to think about it?' the First Assistant Secretary
asked.

Savage didn't. Reports, commutes, meetings, lift passes, coffee
breaks – this was a drudgery to which he found himself allergic.

Savage was in his late forties, but this was his first office job,
having previously worked for the Australian Federal Police's
Special Operations Unit, and for the United Nations as a war
crimes investigator in Afghanistan. He'd had desks before, but he
hadn't had to spend much time behind them. Now he was finding
the groundhog days of office life mind-numbing and soul-crushing.
So when he was asked to take on a civilian reconstruction role in
Afghanistan, he said yes before his bored mind had even properly
registered the request.

He and two other public servants, both of whom had
experience in Afghanistan, were to report for initial general

Australian Civilian Corps training, which, Savage says, he was surprised to find was to be conducted by Defence personnel. Savage had a strong suspicion that the course was at least partially a recruitment tool for the Defence Intelligence Organisation, and was disappointed to find that he wouldn't to be taught much that would useful in the field.

After that initial training, the men conducted country-specific training, but there was no one to train them except one 'subject matter expert', who had spent only four days in Afghanistan, and all of them in Tarin Kot. Combined, the three public servants heading to Afghanistan had years of on-the-ground experience in the country, and fluency in at least two of Afghanistan's languages, so they excused themselves from their subject matter briefings and 'ended up having three weeks of sitting around, drinking coffee and reading [diplomatic] cables with no context'.

The three men flew to Al Minhad Air Base, Australia's permanent staging base into Afghanistan and the Middle East, and from there to Tarin Kot as 'stabilisation advisers'. None of the men knew exactly what that job entailed, but hoped someone would enlighten them before they were sent out into the field.

In Tarin Kot, they found they were, by and large, the oldest people on a base full of development and political advisers just out of university, many of whom were on their first posting; some had never even left Australia before. On the afternoon they arrived in Tarin Kot, the stabilisation advisers were given their one and only specific briefing – by a man in his early twenties who was on his first posting.

'He stood in front of a map of Uruzgan with a pointer, saying, "These are the Barakzai and this is the Popalzai, and these guys hate these guys, and these guys hate these guys, and this and this, and … you got that?"' says Savage.

The briefing went for about half an hour, and the stabilisation advisers were given no materials to take away and no direction to a place to access further information. After the briefing, the men were told to prepare to move into their bases early the next morning. One man was staying in Tarin Kot and one was off to

Patrol Base Razaq in Deh Rawood. David Savage was going to
FOB Mirwais in the Chora Valley.

A dozen hours later, Savage, with all of his gear, armour and
helmet, scrambled into an American Chinook helicopter that
was doing a mail run. 'Mirwais?' he yelled at the loadmaster. A
thumbs-up followed.

The helicopter landed and took off and landed and took off,
pepper-potting across Uruzgan, until finally Savage was the only
passenger left. They flew north and descended towards a remote,
rocky outcrop near a tiny base.

The US loadmaster yelled into Savage's ear: 'When we land,
you grab your gear and run like fuck. You're in "Injun country"
now!'

The helicopter touched down, and as the spitting dust settled,
David Savage struggled and strained, with all of his equipment,
towards a large and foreboding steel gate.

'Who the fuck are you?' was his greeting from the Green Beret
who opened the gate.

This was not FOB Mirwais but FOB Anaconda, the base
from with the SASR had launched their 2008 missions in Khas
Uruzgan. The magnitude of the fuck-up was reflected in how
quickly a helicopter and a section of Australian soldiers arrived.

Savage was then ferried on to FOB Mirwais, a small forward
base just above the Chora green belt, only a few hundred metres
from the base of Koran Ghar, where, just a few years earlier,
Ben Roberts-Smith, Matthew Locke and Kilo-2 had nearly
been overrun. Savage was to be the only civilian in a military
compound that was a world away from Camp Russell, where
SASR operators ate steak and lobster at dinner and drank frothies
at the Fat Lady's Arms.

Mirwais, like most of the forward bases, was spartan. The
Australian soldiers lived with Afghan recruits, sometimes
surviving on cold ready-to-eat meals (MREs) and sleeping on
the ground. Mirwais sometimes experienced indirect attacks,
but Chora was not what it had been five years earlier. Gone were
the insurgents manning fixed fighting positions and trenches in

open daylight. This was, in no small part, due to the district of an estimated 50,000 people – roughly the population of Queanbeyan – being lavished with money, a lot of it Australian taxpayers' money. Much of it was spent on unsustainable projects that benefited the insurgency, but as long as the money flowed, some level of stability could be maintained.

Savage says he learned how to be a stabilisation adviser by picking up the reconstruction ventures already in progress, which he describes as 'all kinds of fucked-up projects'.

One was a dam that had been commissioned between two nearby villages, neither of which wanted it, as they both had access to a permanent water source that had to be diverted to fill the dam. The villagers were blocking the filling of the dam, and Savage found that the local contractor who had built the dam couldn't be paid until it had been filled. The contractor told him he had offered a $20,000 bribe to the police chief so that he could complete his work, and he was desperate to pay off his bribe debt before he felt the ire of the police chief.

Until the dam was completed, there were all kinds of potentially violent flashpoints for which the Australian forces might be blamed, so more money was found to give to the obstinate villagers so the dam could be filled, the contractor compensated and the bribe to the police chief paid. Today, Savage says he is sure that the dam was emptied immediately after it was filled, and was likely never used.

There was also a nearby health centre, paid for by the Australian government, that was collapsing. David Savage found the contractor who had built the centre, and the man said he wasn't surprised that the building was collapsing as he was a well-digger and had never built a building before. The contractor said he had stressed this fact often as he was being commissioned.

Also in progress was the construction of a two-storey market building called the Caravanserai, paid for primarily by the German government, which, at the opening of the project, said it would be 'built with materials like clay, based on engineering principles that mean it will last 20 years. It's very well built.' That too was already collapsing before it was finished.

Savage was tasked with moving local shopkeepers from shops they owned and into the Caravanserai, where they would have to pay rent, but it was already starting to look like an ice-cream cake in the sun. 'They'd ask why they would want to move in, and I had no answer,' Savage says. 'I don't know why they would.'

There was an answer, however: give them money to move in. Money, during this phase of the war, was the answer to everything.

'How much money can I spend?' Savage says he would ask Canberra. 'And on what?'

'As much as you need,' they'd answer, according to Savage. 'Millions, whatever you need. Just spend.' He says there were no KPIs, no specific goals and no strategy – just spend.

And spending money liberally, Savage found, was one of the two primary jobs of a stabilisation adviser. The other was reporting – every day to Tarin Kot, and every week, fortnight and month to Canberra – on the great successes of the Australian Civilian Corps.

'Everything had to be positive,' he recalls. 'Everything. Every activity was a winner; that was clearly the environment they wanted to foster.'

The biggest winner was the US$32 million road that had been constructed between Tarin Kot and Chora. This had been the signature project for the Dutch, and was opened by their State Secretary for Foreign Affairs, Ben Knapen, who came to Uruzgan for the launch. 'I came here to see how the local population is building on the foundations put in place with Dutch development assistance,' he said. 'What I have seen gives me every confidence.' The road was ceremonially opened and then, within the hour, closed again.

In the original plans for the road, a series of dips and washaways for drainage were to be installed, with the planners knowing culverts would be used by insurgents to plant IEDs. These plans were changed in a rush to finish the road and eventually 120 culverts were built in. At the opening ceremony, an IED was detonated in one of these culverts, and the officials, such as the Dutch minister, had to be helicoptered back to Tarin Kot rather than taking the road. The road attack was blamed publicly on the Taliban, but many believe it was ordered by Matiullah, who was being paid to secure the road and had tried to renegotiate his agreement just before the opening.

Savage says Matiullah loomed large over the Chora Valley, ruling in the day as the Taliban ruled at night. Caught in the crushing twilight were a number of villages in the area. Not much more than a kilometre from FOB Mirwais was Niazi, a compound cluster of mostly Ghilzai tribal occupants. This was a village to which the governor had asked Savage to give particular attention.

Some locals in Niazi told Savage that the young men and boys could not be controlled due to, they say, the village elder having been targeted by coalition special forces. It's not known whether this elder had been targeted by Australian special forces, or if anyone from that village was on the JPEL, but Savage says that while he was at FOB Mirwais, there were a number of raids on Niazi. Its people were visited by the Taliban too, often in the form of *shabnameh*, or threatening night letters, in which they were warned not to engage with the government or the foreigners.

When a new Afghan National Police post to be staffed with Matiullah's men was built close to Niazi, Matiullah, who had come to Chora for the opening, was outraged that no one from the village had come to celebrate. David Savage watched as Matiullah sent his men into Niazi to drag the villagers to the ceremony. He saw the villagers being lined up in front of Matiullah, who was shaking with fury.

'He told them that if anyone didn't do what he told them to do, he was going to cut all their heads off,' says Savage. 'He meant it, and I think we all thought he was going to do it now.'

Afterwards, more *shabnameh* came, and not only saying they would kill the people of Niazi should they engage further with the government, but also that they might kill the Australian who visits their village. Savage says the insurgents were well aware of him as the only Australian civilian in the valley: he was out beyond the wire six days a week with his military escorts, two days with Australian diggers and four days with US National Guardsmen.

Many of the locals believed the Australian civilians who came to the Chora Valley were spies, and this assumption was not completely unfounded. Both ASIS and the Defence Intelligence Organisation had used aid organisations, governmental and non-governmental, as cover for their agents in Uruzgan. Savage says he was accepted by most families and tribes; in fact, he was welcomed as he was the faucet from which the money had been flowing into the valley with haphazard verve. He was visible, however, notable, symbolic. Killing him would change the valley, politically and financially. His killing would be disadvantageous for many, but it only had to be advantageous for one group, or one powerful man, for his life to be potentially forfeit.

Savage believes he was targeted by a local tribal leader known as 'brown eyes', who was working with the government but also with the insurgency. It was also possible (albeit unlikely) that someone may have learned that Paul Symon, head of the Defence Intelligence Organisation (now the director-general of ASIS); Peter Baxter, the director-general of AusAID; and one of the AFP's deputy commissioners were due to visit the White Compound in Chora the next day.

Savage was attacked as he and his American bodyguards were returning from the governor's compound, where he'd been preparing for the visit of the Australian dignitaries. On their way back to Mirwais, the Americans wanted to stop at a local bakery and buy Afghan bread. As they waited, Savage took photographs of reconstruction projects with a digital camera. The Americans joked and talked about their lives. These men were not like the Australian special forces: they were National Guardsmen, part-timers, with a fraction of the training of the special forces men, and earning a fraction of their money. They had only a fraction of the fight in them, too. Savage liked them, but he considered them boys who had just come into the area. They were not very good at their jobs.

Their forward scout reported that some labourers had fled a building site ahead, leaving their tools behind. This should have created alarm, but the Americans didn't know what it meant. Savage's personal bodyguard wandered 20 metres from his client, and another soldier actually watched the child who was to blow Savage up make his final approach for half a minute, not knowing what he was seeing.

What the soldier saw was also seen by his GoPro camera: a prepubescent boy, dressed in a hat and tunic of brilliant white – clothes that denoted the purity needed to enter the green fields of *el jannah* after martyrdom.

Savage was talking to a US intelligence officer when he was attacked, but was facing away from his assailant. The American saw the bomber, though, just for a moment before the detonation. Savage saw the man's expression change from mild interest to pure horror. David Savage experienced, doctors later said, the equivalent of taking eight shotgun blasts at close range. The pellets in the suicide vest smashed into his back, buttocks and legs, knocking him unconscious.

Savage was evacuated to Tarin Kot for surgery he wasn't expected to survive. Today he has lost the use of his legs and suffers from a mild brain injury. He also suffers psychological trauma and experiences regular nightmares.

A report about the attack prepared by the Australian Defence Force, which had responsibility for David Savage's read:

> The attack was an unexpected event … the patrol did
> not detect any threat prior to the PBIED [person-borne
> improvised explosive device] detonation. More broadly,
> there had been no intelligence warnings of such a threat.
>
> There were no shortfalls in the analysis or provision of
> intelligence advice or products to the PRT. There had been
> no credible or specific reporting to indicate any likelihood
> of a [suicide bomb] attack in the Chora district against
> such a target as the PRT.

Multiple military sources say there were specific warnings about an infiltration of child suicide bombers from Pakistan, but that these warnings were not relayed to Savage, or to DFAT.

* * *

Two months after David Savage was blown up, and barely two kilometres west of the attack, the SASR lost its last man in combat. As 3 Squadron was leaving the country and handing over to Ben Roberts-Smith's 2 Squadron in July 2012, a kill/capture mission was spooled up in a Chora Valley village. It's believed the target was a local insurgent named Najibullah Haibat, designated on the JPEL as Objective Koala Handy.

Haibat was designated as JPEL green, meaning he could be targeted by the SASR without any further command approval, and when signals intelligence geolocated him in Qala-i-Naw, the village area where Matthew Locke had been killed in October 2007, they were launching almost within the hour, hoping to rack up one more score on the jackpot leaderboard before heading home.

The SASR were to insert with their partner force, the National Directorate of Security Wakunish – or as the Australians often called them, the 'Wakkas'. Ostensibly, one of the primary roles of the SASR in Afghanistan at that time was to train the Wakunish, as they would be tasked with counterinsurgency responsibility in the province once the Australian special forces. The force was made up of soldiers from outside the province, and most of these men were not ethnic Pashtuns, meaning they could not integrate with the local community even if they wanted to. The Wakunish were not particularly effective, and only a dozen or so were being trained on the Australian base, with the rest of force being sent elsewhere and going unused on most missions.

Reports had emerged that local security forces had started working in concert with the Taliban, and that truces had emerged in which the Afghan National Army would not be attacked, but that the foreign forces would still be fair game. With the SASR and

Wakunish in the air, Haibat and his men were already in fighting positions, waiting not for the special forces but for a conventional army patrol that was moving out of FOB Mirwais.

Haibat's cousin, who lived close to Mirwais, had alerted the JPEL target that the Australians were coming his way. Haibat and his men ran to set an ambush. The call between the cousins was most likely intercepted by the SOTG or the US, which raised Haibat above the 'detection profile' and allowed a mission to be launched against him.

In preparation for their assault, an 'ops box' had been ordered – essentially, an area in which the SASR could work exclusively. The location of ops boxes would be sent to anyone who might be working in the area, and when the conventional forces at FOB Mirwais were told that an exclusion area had been set up in an area they were just about to move through, they were surprised and confused. With a little more time, the conventional forces and the SOTG would have figured out what had happened, but instead the two SASR patrols and the Wakunish flew into a hornets' nest of manned and prepared insurgent fighting positions.

The patrols landed and a gunfight ensued immediately. One local was attacked by an Australian combat dog, a Belgian Malinois named Devil, and the local shot and gravely wounded the dog. The affinity between the Australian operators and their working dogs was significant, and when Devil was shot, one of the patrol commanders broke cover and advanced towards where the injured dog lay. As he did, an insurgent in a tree fired at the patrol commander, hitting him above his chest plate. The bullet hit the Australian's collarbone and fragments smashed into his heart, killing him.

This patrol commander was 40-year-old father of two Blaine Diddams, Matthew Bouillaut's second-in-command during Operation Anaconda, and the man who first saw Afghan combat on television in 2001 as he smoked cigarettes and drank coffee in Perth with his patrol commander.

When the Australians left the Chora Valley, 12 Afghans lay dead, including the JPEL target. Diddams was posthumously awarded a Medal for Gallantry.

* * *

The loss of Blaine Diddams wasn't the only highly publicised death that happened on this rotation. Two whistleblowers emerged, Braden Chapman and Dusty Miller, alleging that some 3 Squadron operators had committed a series of crimes, including murder. Both men were support staff, meaning they had been posted into the unit and so were often not considered part of the 'brotherhood' of SASR operators.

Braden Chapman, an electronic warfare operator, told the ABC that the intelligence for kill/capture missions was vague, small caches of weapons would result in entire Afghan compounds being damaged or destroyed, property was destroyed wantonly and locals were sometimes beaten for little apparent reason. He also said that he had observed multiple murders during his 2012 rotation.

Dusty Miller, a medic on the same rotation working with Chapman, said that he also witnessed murders. He described to the ABC an incident in which an Afghan man, Haji Sadr, was shot in the leg; Miller treated his wound, but was told later that 'he didn't make it'. Miller said there was no way the wound could have killed Haji Sadr. Dr Stanikzai says this killing was investigated by his organisation, and they found that Haji Sadr had been kicked and beaten to death.

After Dr Stanikzai brought his AIHRC investigation finding to the Australian special forces in Tarin Kot, he was told that the Australians had conducted their own investigation and found the killing to be justified.

It was during this rotation that one of the most notorious alleged SASR murders occurred. Patrols from 3 Squadron were inserted into the Dorafshan village of Deh Jowz-e Hasanzai, about a kilometre north of Kakarak and a kilometre or so west of Sorkh Morghab.

In footage captured by helmet cam and broadcast by the ABC, an Australian SASR soldier stands over a cowering, unarmed youth, perhaps a teenager, who has been attacked by an Australian combat dog named Quake. Sources say this vision was taken minutes after the Australians had landed, and that the cowering youth had been carrying an ICOM radio, which he had thrown away as the Australians approached. The youth was *hors de combat*, a legal term meaning out of the battle or out of combat, and therefore was unable to be targeted legally.

'Want me to drop this cunt?' the soldier asks the dog handler, who says he doesn't know. The soldier then asks the same question of a patrol commander.

'Do it,' the patrol commander replies.

Three shots are fired into the Afghan, killing him.

This death was investigated by the ADF and was deemed to be a legal killing – but it's likely a weapon or a radio was dropped on the youth before Sensitive Site Exploitation (SSE) photographs were taken to justify the killing.

* * *

In November 2011, Ben Roberts-Smith accepted an offer from Queen Elizabeth II to visit Buckingham Palace. In Her Royal Highness's grand receiving room, with her corgis watching on, the huge soldier and tiny monarch exchanged pleasantries.

'She obviously recognises that Australian soldiers are very good at what they do and we've made great progress in Uruzgan,' Roberts-Smith told Channel Ten News on the grounds of Buckingham Palace after the meeting. 'So, general terms, as a monarch she was very happy with our progress, and that's something I'll pass on to the lads when I get home,' he continued.

Directly after the visit, Roberts-Smith toured France and Belgium, where he was scheduled to visit Australian World War I graves and speak to school students about the Anzacs, then he returned to Western Australia to prepare for what he likely expected to be the peak of his military career. Even though Roberts-Smith was still a corporal, he would be fulfilling a sergeant's task. He would command his own patrol in Afghanistan.

'[O]nce you reach patrol commander, that is the pinnacle for an SAS operator. You are now the man,' Roberts-Smith told *The Australian* newspaper in 2011.

This 2012 rotation would be Ben Roberts-Smith's last tour. Afterwards, he would begin a meteoric and very lucrative retirement as Australia's best known and most decorated soldier. (Roberts-Smith says he was earning $320,000 a year from speaking engagements alone before the war crime allegations against him were made public.)

When Roberts-Smith was in Europe, his troop was doing training in preparation for what was, for most of the soldiers, to be their final deployment to Afghanistan. But this European trip wasn't the only Victoria Cross engagement Roberts-Smith would undertake while the rest of his patrol was training.

'I was quite angry about that,' a soldier who was a more senior patrol commander in the same troop testified in the defamation case. That soldier says he raised concerns about Roberts-Smith's absence, highlighting the fact that Roberts-Smith's patrol included inexperienced soldiers, one of whom was deploying to Afghanistan for the first time.

As well as at Campbell Barracks, the troop trained at the Bindoon Training Area, an hour to the north, and at the coastal Lancelin Defence Training Area. Just before the troop took their final pre-deployment leave, a live-fire exercise was conducted on the sand dunes of Lancelin so that, according to testimony, the troop commander and troop sergeant – two men who were taking on those roles for the time in Afghanistan – could learn the detention process.

This exercise was conducted in an area with some shipping containers mocked up to serve as an Afghan compound, with steel-head targets in the compound serving as the enemy. Also on the site were SASR soldiers playing the role of Afghan villagers, one of whom was wearing a bite-proof suit – he was to be attacked by a combat dog during the assault.

A soldier anonymised in the defamation trial as Person 7, who did 11 tours of Afghanistan and still serves in the SASR as one of the most senior soldiers at 4 Squadron, gave evidence about this exercise. Person 7, then a senior patrol commander, says that for this exercise he was commanding a roof team, with Ben Roberts-Smith's team serving as an assault or clearance team. After the clearance, he testified, Ben Roberts-Smith led an operator – a man who was about to be deployed to Afghanistan with the SASR for the first time – up to one of the faux detainees, who was facing a wall, kneeling and bound. Person 7 said that Ben Roberts-Smith ordered a mock execution.

'Fucking kill him,' Person 7 testified that Roberts-Smith said to the junior operator.

According to Person 7, the soldier looked confused.

'Kill him,' Person 7 said Ben Roberts-Smith ordered.

Another soldier who saw this part of the exercise, anonymised as Person 19, testified that he too heard Ben Roberts-Smith order a mock execution.

'I remember that distinctly,' Person 19 said. 'It was unusual. I remember seeing the look on [the kneeling soldier's] face.'

Both the soldiers testified that the junior soldier said, 'Bang,' simulating an execution.

Person 7 said Ben Roberts-Smith put his hand on the soldier who had just conducted the mock execution and said, 'Are you good with that? Because that's how it's going to be over there.'

After hearing that, Person 7 said, he turned to another soldier who was standing on the shipping container and said, 'Geez, he's a fucking idiot.'

The junior soldier, anonymised as Person 10, confirmed this story in court.

After the exercise, Person 7 testified, he asked to have a moment with Ben Roberts-Smith, and they had this conversation (or words to this effect):

Person 7: 'What was that shit all about?'

Ben Roberts-Smith: 'What shit?'

Person 7: 'You know what shit I'm talking about. Pull your head in, grow up and wake up to yourself.'

According to the testimony of Person 7, Ben Roberts-Smith turned away mumbling. The only words Person 7 could decipher were 'fucking war'.

According to Person 19, Ben Roberts-Smith also told his patrol that drones should be 'pushed off to observe another area so they weren't observing what was happening in the compound' after an assault and during the sensitive site exploitation period. Person 19 also said that Roberts-Smith told his patrol that the officers should be kept outside the compound until the troop was ready to receive them.

"'That's when any people that we suspect of being enemy combatants, we take them into a room and shoot the cunts,'" he testified that Ben Roberts-Smith said.

Person 7 also testified that, during this rotation, Ben Roberts Smith told him: 'Before this trip's over, I'm going to choke a man to death with my bare hands, I'm going to look him in the eyes and I'm going to watch the life drain out of his eyes.' According to Person 7, Roberts-Smith made accompanying choking motions with his hands.

The choking claim mirrors reporting in the US media that DEVGRU operators who were well practised in the Brazilian martial art of jujitsu challenged prisoners at the location they were captured in Iraq or Afghanistan and were then choked to death.

Ben Roberts-Smith has denied all these allegations of illegality; of the choking allegation, he said: 'That is not how I speak. I never have and I never will.' Ben Roberts-Smith's lawyers have denied that their client made these comments, and have claimed that Person 19, Person 10 and Person 7 are not reliable or honest witnesses.

28

'It feels like you're in a bloody nightmare'

29 AUGUST 2012 WAS a blisteringly hot day at Patrol Base Wahab, an Afghan National Army base in the Baluchi Valley. At the height of the day, the temperature had been recorded as 50 degrees, and when the sun went down only minor respite was offered from the heat to India 21, a platoon of Australian soldiers from the Mentoring Task Force visiting the base.

Throughout the day, India 21 had been mentoring ANA recruits, and when their day ended, they were allowed to swap their multi-cam uniforms for personal training shorts and T-shirts. At nearly 10 pm, the temperature was still sitting at about 40 degrees and the platoon of Australian soldiers were gathered at one side of the base, sipping from water bottles, playing cards and board games. The off-duty Afghan soldiers were mostly at the other side of the small base, but there was interaction between the Afghans and the Australians, with a number of the ANA recruits coming over to chat with Australians, and even work out on the makeshift Australian gym.

There didn't appear to be tensions between the Australians and Afghans, but recently there were elevated concerns across the country about insider attacks after the end of the holy month of Ramadan, two weeks earlier. New nationwide orders had been issued, increasing force protection in the spaces where Afghans and ISAF soldiers cohabitated.

A 19-year-old Afghan *zabet* (roughly a sergeant) named Hekmatullah was one of the Afghans nearby the unarmed Australian soldiers, as one armed Australian soldier, also in T-shirt and shorts, wandered around as a 'guardian angel'. Hekmatullah bid the Australians goodbye, claiming it was time for him to assume guard duty. He asked for a light machine gun from the armoury, but instead was given a standard M16A2 assault rifle.

He walked back to the part of the base where the Australians were, and opened up on the men of India 21 at a distance of about five metres. He fired every bullet in the 30-round clip, injuring two Australians and killing 40-year-old Lance Corporal Stjepan (Rick) Milosevic, 23-year-old Private Robert Poate and 21-year-old sapper James Martin. After finishing his rampage, Hekmatullah jumped the fence of the base; witnesses saw him run towards a nearby compound. The teenage murderer was not in contact with the Taliban before the killings, but now he was desperate for them to grant him his duly earned recognition, and also shelter.

* * *

Shane Healey was sleeping. For the targeting analyst, it had been a relatively quiet day in the FATC. Force Element Alpha had been rotating in and out of air windows, meaning they had four days with helicopters that they could use to go hunting, and then four days without; 28 August had been a day without. It was Healey's birthday, so, with Force Element Bravo out of province, off in Helmand doing counter-nexus drug jobs, and Alpha grounded, he had managed to truncate his working day. Knocking off after 12 hours instead of the normal 15, he had a bottle of Corona and then went to sleep.

At about 1 am, there was a hammering on his door. It was another member of the FATC, calling him to his station. Something was happening. All hands were to stand to. When Healey arrived, it was controlled mayhem. He'd not seen the FATC like this before.

'What's going on?' Healey asked.

'Green on blue,' someone hollered.

Healey sat at his terminal and got to work. He plugged himself into the huge intelligence-gathering apparatus that had been developed, sending RFIs (requests for information) across the Australian and international network. Telephones and ICOM radios of known insurgents near Wahab had to be monitored too. They had to figure out if this attacker was part of the insurgency and, if so, which group he belonged to and whether there were going to be other attacks. Healey also had to positively identify who this killer was, so that he could be raised on the JPEL and legally targeted.

Helicopters had to be found too. The SASR would be going to Patrol Base Wahab that night. If there was intelligence they could act on, they were going to want to kill this attacker tonight.

'You don't get to kill Australian soldiers and get away with it,' Healey says.

At the Chora Valley base, the Afghans had been separated from the Australians, who were in a safe harbour created by their armoured and armed vehicles, but the situation was chaotic and intense there and in Tarin Kot.

A chat box popped up on Healey's computer screen from the Force Element Bravo Special Operations Command Centre (SOCC): 'FALLEN ANGEL.'

Healey couldn't quite fathom what he was seeing. In the chat box, callsigns started appearing. They denoted the commandos Private Nathanael 'Nate' Galagher, 23, and Lance Corporal Mervyn 'Merv' McDonald, 30, both reported dead. Four other commandos were seriously injured.

Just after the attack at Patrol Base Wahab, the commandos had been approaching a poppy farm in the Kajaki Fan area in Helmand. As a Vietnam-era Bell UH-1 Iroquois helicopter attempted to execute a night landing, dust blew up, obscuring the pilot's vision. He lost his horizon, started to flip the helicopter and then smashed it into the ground.

'Bravo has a fallen angel,' Healey announced to the FATC.

The buzz of activity stopped. The scant details available were devoured by all his colleagues. They now had two large, concurrent problems. In insurgent territory in Helmand Province, killed and injured soldiers (not to mention a helicopter) had to be secured and evacuated; and in the Baluchi Valley, a group of predominantly young and inexperienced Australian soldiers were caring for their dead and injured mates, while staring at a large group of Afghan soldiers of whom they had just become rightly suspicious.

A 'cease ops' was ordered – no new offensive missions. Despite this, the SASR were able to be sent to Wahab, not to hunt but to resolve the stand-off at the patrol base, and to show the diggers that big brother was there and, as Healey says, 'give them a hug'.

After both situations were resolved, and the dead and injured retrieved, the top priority of the SOTG became the hunt for the Wahab killer. Hekmatullah had now been identified and raised on the JPEL as Objective Jungle Effect. He was designated as the new 'national priority target' and marked as green, meaning missions could be launched against him, and assets such as helicopters would be made available for his prosecution.

The ADF had stressed multiple times throughout the war in Afghanistan that it did not conduct missions of retribution – and yet, in the wake of the Wahab killing, all SASR patrols were taken off their targets and retasked with hunting Objective Jungle Effect. A series of missions were launched, some using good intelligence and some, according to a soldier giving evidence in the Ben Roberts-Smith defamation trial, 'not the best'. Testimony was offered that at least one mission was conducted in the hunt for Hekmatullah without 'very reliable intelligence', or VRI, the evidentiary standard expected for many missions.

That mission was conducted in the Khod Valley, in Shahidi Hassas, in the village of Darwan, and it would produce perhaps the most iconic image of the Australian war: an Australian soldier, first described in the Fairfax newspapers as 'Leonidas' and later named as Ben Roberts-Smith, kicking an Afghan man off a cliff, emulating the actions of the fictionalised Leonidas, the Spartan warrior king in the film *300*.

The image of the alleged murder exists not in a photograph or video but in one's mind, after one reads the Nine Media reports of the incident. The image is shocking and insistent – but is it real, as the Nine Media organisations who published the claim say, or it is a fabrication created from malicious and fictional testimony, as Ben Roberts-Smith submitted at the trial?

* * *

The SASR, with elements of the commando regiment and accompanying Wakkas, was tasked with assaulting Darwan on 11 September 2012. Four US Blackhawk helicopters, accompanied by two Apache gunships, were used to insert the force, and accompanying the element was a Heron ISR drone, leased by the ADF from Israel for use in Afghanistan.

After a cordon was established at two compounds, a 'call out' was ordered, in which any occupants were told to present themselves, unarmed and with their hands up. In one compound, three people complied, but in the second compound, according to official internal SOTG reporting, the Australians saw two men 'rapidly withdraw into a darkened room'. The SASR entered that compound and killed the two men, one of whom, according the official reporting, was carrying a rifle, while the other was wearing a chest rig containing ammunition.

The report says that as the Australian force cleared the compounds, 'an FE member PID [positively identified] 1 X INS [one insurgent] armed with a Chicom type 56 [a Chinese-made AK-47 variant]'. The report says the man was killed, and an ICOM radio found.

After sensitive site exploitation had been conducted in the village, and the local males of fighting age had been detained and questioned, helicopters were approaching to remove the force. This was when, according to the report, 'an FE member observed an individual ... moving through a thickly vegetated cornfield and using an ICOM'. The report says the man ignored 'clear and repeated warnings from the FE', and that the Australians would 'not be able to apprehend the individual before he reached a potential weapons cache' – so he was shot and killed.

In its summary of the mission, the report says that before extraction, a KLE (key leadership engagement) was conducted with local elders, communicating 'themes that it was in LN [local nationals'] best interests to support GIROA [the government of the Islamic Republic of Afghanistan] and that Taliban influence would be negative for the region'.

The report notes that 'it is likely that associates of OBJ Jungle Effect were in the target area', but that the prosecuting force found no evidence of Hekmatullah having been in the village.

Internally, it was reported that the killed men had been identified as an insurgent commander known as Mullah Ghafor and another insurgent named Amir Jan, both from a village just north of Darwan called Ruyan, as well as a man named Nazir Guil and his nephew Uim.

* * *

'It feels like you're in a bloody nightmare. Every time they write it, I wonder: "How am I in this position?"' Ben Roberts-Smith responded in court 18D after Bruce McClintock SC asked his client what it was like to read in the press that you are accused of being a war criminal. McClintock also investigated what was perhaps the central allegation of murder: the allegation that Ben Roberts-Smith had kicked a man off a cliff in Darwan on 11 September 2012 and ordered another man execute the now seriously injured Afghan.

'The allegation is actually ludicrous, that my client killed an unarmed man outside in full view. It did not happen,' McClintock told the court.

Ben Roberts-Smith gave testimony in court about the mission in Darwan, explaining his role in the killing of two men. The first killing, Ben Roberts-Smith said, was of an Afghan who had been observed by soldiers in an overwatch position above the valley.

That man had run from the green belt into the barren, rocky hills above and couldn't be seen by the overwatch position. Ben Roberts-Smith says he spotted the man across the Helmand River, and saw that he was armed with an AK-47 variant.

Roberts-Smith testified that he removed his body armour, swam across the river and, after a short gun battle, killed this man. On the body, he said, were detonators the likes of which he and his soldiers had not seen before, indicating that this man might have been an insurgent commander.

The second killing, Ben Roberts-Smith said, happened just before the helicopter extraction. He gave evidence that he and a soldier anonymised as Person 11 were walking through a dry creek bed to the helicopter extraction point, and that Person 11 climbed a small embankment. Seeing what he thought was an insurgent, Person 11 shot and killed a man a few metres away. Roberts-Smith said he saw an ICOM radio on the Afghan man, and therefore considered it to have been a 'good kill'.

It's believed that there is no ISR drone footage of this kill; records of the internal SOTG chat that was taking place during the mission, tendered as evidence, show that the Heron drone was pushed off-target just before the killing occurred.

'ISR manager ... conserve hrs for more viable targeting period, pls stand down,' read a message from 'SOTG FE A OPS' as the US Blackhawks were inbound. Then, fewer than 15 minutes later, another message from 'SOTG FE A OPS' popped up: 'FE reporting additional 1 X EKIA [enemy killed in action].'

Person 4, the soldier who was alleged in court to have been known as 'the rookie', and who, it was alleged, had been ordered by Ben Roberts-Smith to execute a prisoner at Whiskey 108, gave contrary evidence about this killing. His testimony was that the killed man was a PUC collected during the mission, and that this man was first kicked off a cliff and then shot dead by another SASR member.

Person 4 testified that he saw Person 11 holding an Afghan prisoner – claimed in the media to be named Ali Jan – next to a small cliff.

'[Ben Roberts-Smith] had walked to a position maybe three or four metres away,' Person 4 told the court. 'As I was trying to understand ... he turned around and walked forward and kicked the individual in the chest.'

Person 4 said he saw the detainee – who, Person 4 claimed, had bound hands – fall from the cliff and smash his face on the rocks below. Person 4 said he saw teeth explode from the Afghan man's mouth. After the fall, he continued, the man was still alive but seriously injured.

'The individual was quite dusty and had sustained a serious facial injury,' Person 4 testified. 'As we were approaching that individual, he attempted to sit up and then fell back down again.'

Person 4 said that Roberts-Smith ordered him and Person 11 to drag the man to a tree. He did so, and then, as he was walking away, the detainee was shot and killed, either by Person 11 or by Ben Roberts-Smith. The court was shown a photograph of the killed man with an ICOM radio; the witness said he believed the radio had been taken from the body of the man whom Roberts-Smith had killed earlier and was waterlogged.

Two Afghan men also testified about this incident. One, Mohammed Hanifa Fatih, said that 'a big soldier who was wet up to here', gesturing to his stomach, 'and with sand from the river on his uniform' punched and kicked him numerous times as he was handcuffed. Fatih said that he knew Ali Jan, and that he wasn't a spotter or aligned with the Taliban.

'By God, he had nothing with him. He had no equipment with him ... They put those things with his body,' Fatih said.

The Afghan said that the villagers did have recent interactions with the Taliban, because they had been using the Taliban justice system to mediate a property matter.

Person 4 told the court that when the patrol returned to Tarin Kot, Ben Roberts-Smith gathered his patrol members so they could align their stories.

'The story is we engaged a spotter whilst moving to our HLZ [helicopter landing zone],' Person 4 testified that Ben Roberts-

Smith said. 'He was a VC winner at this time,' he also noted. 'He was running by his own narrative.'

'The only person who is running by their own narrative is you, Person 4,' replied Arthur Moses SC during cross-examination.

'That's incorrect,' said Person 4.

'You are making up stories, aren't you?'

'Absolutely not.'

At the time of writing, two other murders alleged to have been undertaken by SASR operators on that raid are being investigated. The deaths of the two men who 'rapidly [withdrew] into a darkened room' are now being investigated by the Office of the Special Investigator as murders. One of the alleged murderers is a close friend of Ben Roberts-Smith who testified in support of the VC recipient that no men were found in the tunnel at Whiskey 108. This soldier, anonymised in the defamation trial as Person 35, testified that the man he killed in Darwan, Nazir Guil, was armed, and that a false allegation has been made against him.

The hunt for Hekmatullah continued, and yet, despite numerous raids, the murderer managed to disappear. He likely reached Pakistan through the Khod Valley, in the northern part of Uruzgan, with the help of the insurgency and, it's rumoured, some elements of the Afghan National Army and/or the Afghan National Police.

* * *

In October 2012, Australian colonel Simon Stuart assumed control of Combined Team Uruzgan, and in November 2012 the Mentoring Task Force was replaced by the Australian Advisory Task Force, withdrawing the bulk of Australian forces from the patrol bases that had been established at the cost of blood and billions of dollars. The deconstruction and deconfliction of Australia's war in Afghanistan had already started. Autumn 2012 was the last high-intensity period of JPEL hunting, before winter and the waning of Australia's offensive mission in Uruzgan.

In this endeavour, the four SASR combat patrols were given an area of responsibility, meaning Australia's hunting grounds were roughly quartered. Each patrol commander was afforded a certain amount of latitude in the decision-making and analysis of the JPEL targets in their area, and the patrol commanders were considered subject matter experts on their area. One of these patrols was commanded by Ben Roberts-Smith, who was given the south-east quarter of Uruzgan. This included the Langar Valley and the essential approaches between Uruzgan and Kandahar.

Person 7, a senior patrol commander on this rotation, testified that it involved unnecessary killings, including murders, and that Ben Roberts-Smith was 'out of his depth' as a patrol commander.

One of the missions planned by Roberts-Smith was to Qala-i-Naw, where Matthew Locke and Blaine Diddams had been killed in what Person 7 described as a 'tethered goat mission'.

'That particular mission was based primarily on revenge,' he testified. 'If we didn't do it, it wouldn't have mattered whatsoever. We weren't up there targeting, we had no intelligence except the fact that there had been a battle the week before [the one in which Diddams had been killed].'

Person 7 earlier testified that Ben Roberts-Smith said to him of that mission: 'If those fuckers [the militia who were part of the battle in which Blaine Diddams had been killed] are up there, we're going to kill every one of those fuckers.'

Person 10, who was part of Ben Roberts-Smith's patrol, testified that his patrol commander was going to 'find fighting-aged males and kill them' on that mission. Person 7 testified that his view was that 'planning for [the mission] was certainly lacking', and that this resulted in a 'blue on blue' incident, in which the SASR patrol fired at a woman and a child and also at each other.

Person 7 also described a kill/capture mission over the border in Kandahar, close to Tizak, the plan for which required clearing a compound cluster so that an electronic signature could be generated that another hidden SASR element, with direction finding (DF) technology, could use to identify their target. Person 7 testified that 'loose intelligence' came through to the secreted element, with DF indicators suggesting a target was 10 kilometres to the west. Person 7 claimed that he sent the intelligence through with the DF indicators, and that the patrol inserted on the correct vector but 8 kilometres short of their target. According to Person 7, they conducted a clearance 'basically of rocks' and one empty compound.

'I asked him: "Do you understand how the equipment works, RS?"' Person 7 testified, suggesting that Ben Roberts-Smith did not have the technical understanding of electronic warfare capabilities that was needed to plan missions effectively.

Person 7 further claimed that Roberts-Smith planned a mission in Shahidi Hassas, which the 'whole troop' believed was conducted with the aim of being shot at, so that he could get another 'gong' (award). Person 7 testified that this mission created animus within the troop, because a JPEL target that presented in Tarin Kot couldn't be prosecuted because the patrols that would have attacked that target were being held in reserve as a QRF for the Shahidi Hassas mission.

Person 7 also gave evidence that this mission was planned as a clandestine special reconnaissance mission, but it went kinetic after Ben Roberts-Smith's patrol unnecessarily exploded a slab of dynamite and fired two 40mm bombs in an effort to elicit a response. In cross-examination, Arthur Moses SC claimed that all these allegations were untrue, and had been fabricated by Person 7 because he was racked with jealousy over Tizak, a battle in which he had been involved but for which he was awarded no medals.

'You still hold it as an issue, don't you?' said Moses.

'We're talking about it, Mr Moses, so I'll talk about it,' said Person 7.

'Something you've never put to bed, have you?'

'I have put it to bed as an issue, but I've said, as I said yesterday, I'm happy to talk about it.'

The previous day, Person 7 had been asked exhaustively about Tizak, and he had admitted that he didn't believe Ben Roberts-Smith deserved the Victoria Cross. But he also testified that it was not something he cared about when compared to the alleged murder in Darwan.

'You said yesterday that you put it to bed when the allegation arose concerning the cliff kick, correct?' Moses said.

'Yes, I did say that because it's a fair way more serious.'

'The reason you put it to bed, so you say, is because you latched onto that allegation to try and damage Mr Roberts-Smith's reputation, correct?'

'Mr Moses, I am a senior warrant officer in the army. I was told about an allegation of an egregious nature. I am not walking away from that. I'm not walking past that,' Person 7 testified.

* * *

On 12 October 2012, Ben Roberts-Smith's patrol was tasked with supporting another patrol in a kill/capture JPEL mission in the north-east of the province. An SASR soldier who gave evidence in the defamation trial said he was added to Roberts-Smith's patrol for this mission, and that the patrol was tasked with creating a cordon, stopping enemy fighters from coming into the target location or from leaving as the lead assault force prosecuted the target.

This soldier, anonymised in court as Person 14, said that as they were approaching the compounds to be assaulted, Ben Roberts-Smith said to his patrol: 'Fuck the cordon, we'll head for the [target].'

After the Blackhawks were exfiltrating, Person 14 said, he saw his patrol sprint for the target, forgetting the cordon. As he was trying to catch up with them, he saw two fighting-age males, so he and another soldier detained them, missing the assault.

Person 14 reassembled with the patrol in preparation for exfiltration at a compound just above the valley floor, where Ben Roberts-Smith, with a clutch of Afghan and Australian soldiers, was interrogating a slender middle-aged man with a beard.

According to Person 14, a call had come in over the radio that the helicopters were inbound, and that the element was to collapse, with the patrols folding in towards the landing zone. While waiting to head to the landing zone, Person 14 says he saw a discoloured patch on the bottom of a wall of the compound. After he kicked it twice, the wall crumbled, revealing a cache of weapons including binoculars, RPG tubes, rifles and rice sacks full of 5.56mm rounds.

With helicopters inbound, Person 14 said, Ben Roberts-Smith addressed their interpreter: 'Tell him [the commander of the Afghan soldiers] to shoot him [the local man] or I will.'

Person 14 claimed that Ben Roberts-Smith repeated the order after the interpreter demurred. He said there was also a conversation between the Afghan soldiers after the order had been relayed.

After that discussion, Person 14 said, one of the Afghans stepped forward with a suppressed M4 and fired a burst of rounds into the prisoner's chest, and then, after the prisoner was on the ground, two more shots into the man's head. Person 14 testified that as they were moving towards the landing zone, he bumped into the troop sergeant, the commander of all the patrol commanders.

'"What happened to the fucking PUC?"' the troop sergeant asked of the allegedly murdered detainee, according to Person 14.

Person 14 testified that he relayed to the troop sergeant what had happened, and that the troop sergeant was not happy.

'"The PUC count has already gone in and the helos are coming in,"' the troop sergeant allegedly said. Under cross examination, Person 14's character, testimony, trustworthiness and abilities of a soldier were tested. He admitted that he missed out on a 2010 deployment after losing a hard drive containing sensitive imagery, but denied drunkenly punching a female US soldier at a 2012 party on base in Tarin Kot. He was accused of knocking the woman unconscious into a pool but he says she 'jumped' into the pool after attacking him and grabbing his testicles. Person 14 strongly denied 'making up' his evidence. Ben Roberts-Smith denied allegations made by Person 14, and maintained that he acted lawfully throughout this rotation and on all rotations.

* * *

In October 2012, Ben Roberts-Smith and Andrew Hastie were both part of a mission to Syachow, in Kandahar just south of the Langar Valley. Hastie gave testimony about the assault, which, he said, involved a 'time-sensitive target' who was an 'individual matched against a handset' – most likely someone who had been raised as a JPEL target and was using their mobile phone.

Hastie's role in this mission was essentially as a 'shooter', he explained, as he was in Afghanistan to gather situational awareness in preparation for reinsertion on a later rotation in which he would serve as a troop commander. In the ready room in Camp Russell in preparation for the mission, Hastie noticed a friend from the 'married patch' in Shenton Park, Perth, where some of the SASR soldiers with families lived. Hastie tried to catch the eye of the man, anonymised in court as Person 66, but couldn't.

Person 66, a soldier working briefly in a patrol commanded by Ben Roberts-Smith, was a relatively recently qualified operator with little SOTG experience. He had come to Tarin Kot from another part of the country (where he was likely working with ASIS) to take part in his first SOTG out-of-the-wire mission.

Hastie testified that he came into Syachow in 'turn two' – referring to the second group of Blackhawks that landed in the village. When he arrived, he saw that 10 to 15 men had been detained and were being tactically questioned by Ben Roberts-Smith and his patrol. After walking away from that compound, Hastie testified, he heard two dispatches from the troop radio.

First: 'Shots fired.'

Hastie says he was confused, as he hadn't heard any unsuppressed gunfire.

Then: 'Two EKIA [enemies killed in action].'

Hastie testified that Ben Roberts-Smith later 'looked me in the eye and said, "Just a couple more dead cunts."'

A large cache of weapons were found in Syachow and destroyed in place before the SASR exfiltrated. Hastie testified that after he assessed a 'mosaic' of circumstantial evidence, including reporting from Ben Roberts-Smith (which Hastie characterised as being from an 'alternate universe'), he believed that at least one Afghan had been murdered in Syachow.

After the mission, Hastie said, Person 66 was 'not the person I know: happy go lucky kind of classic country Aussie'. Of the alleged murder, Hastie said: '[I]n my view Person 66 was blooded.'

Person 66 was subpoenaed to give evidence in the defamation trial, but Justice Besanko gave him leave to refuse questions about the alleged Syachow killing on the grounds that he might incriminate himself. Ben Roberts-Smith testified that two insurgents were killed legally during that mission, and categorically denied ordering Person 66 to commit murder.

Of the killing, one of Ben Roberts-Smith's lawyers said: '[The newspapers] have proffered no detail of the supposed crime, such as the identity of the victim, the time during the mission when it took place other than – or the place other than – a nearby field; nor, for that matter, is any motive identified.'

* * *

Ben Roberts-Smith's last mission in Afghanistan was conducted in November 2012, near a village known as Faisal, in the Langar Valley. This was a mission before which a senior soldier had specifically told Ben Roberts-Smith not to kill anyone wantonly, according to an SASR soldier anonymised as Person 16.

Person 16 testified that he was part of the cordon force in this mission, and in this capacity he stopped an approaching Hilux by levelling his rifle at it. Two men were found in the vehicle: one was an older male in traditional garb and quite 'staunch', while the other was a teenager, chubby and unable yet to grow a full beard. According to Person 16, this youth appeared 'extremely nervous' and was 'trembling uncontrollably'.

Neither man was armed, Person 16 testified, but when the vehicle was searched, components for IEDs were discovered.

Both men were handcuffed and processed as PUCs, with, according to Person 16, Ben Roberts-Smith receiving them for interrogation. Person 16 gave evidence that he was surprised, 15 minutes later, to hear a message from Ben Roberts-Smith: 'Two EKIA.'

Person 16 testified that he bumped into Ben Roberts-Smith in the Camp Russell lines a few days later, as the rotation was preparing to leave Afghanistan for good.

'What happened to that young fella who was shaking like a leaf?' Person 16 says he asked Roberts-Smith.

'I shot that cunt in the head. [The senior soldier] told me not to kill anyone on the last job. So I pulled out my 9mm, shot the cunt in the side of the head, blew his brains out. It was the most beautiful thing I've ever seen,' Person 16 testified that Ben Roberts-Smith said.

Person 16 was shown pictures in court of a dead Afghan youth, and he identified the dead youth as the teen he had detained. In the images, an AK-47 is visible on his body, but Person 16 reiterated that the youth had not been armed when he was searched, cuffed and sent for interrogation. Under cross-examination, Person 16 was asked why he made no further inquiries about whether a murder had taken place.

'Cause there was a code of silence within the regiment as to these things occurring,' Person 16 testified. 'The fear of retribution would have been a career-ending move. I would have been ostracised, and I also think my personal safety ... I would have been in danger, making such allegations against someone so influential.'

Under cross examination, Arthur Moses put it to Person 16 that there was a camp within the SASR attempting to discredit Ben Roberts-Smith and that the after-mission conversation between Person 16 and Ben Roberts-Smith about the alleged murder was 'something you have imagined.' Person 16 said that: 'His reply shocked me to the core, and that's why I remembered it.'

Ben Roberts-Smith has denied that this youth was killed unlawfully, and has stated that he never used his pistol in Afghanistan.

* * *

On Australia Day in 2013, Ben Roberts-Smith was awarded the Commendation for Distinguished Service – a decoration usually reserved for officers (often senior officers) – for his 'leadership and command' during his final rotation in Afghanistan. This made him the most highly decorated Australian soldier of the war.

The commendation detailed that Roberts-Smith had conducted more than 50 kill/capture missions during his 2012 rotation, and also five special reconnaissance missions. His citation reads: 'Corporal Roberts-Smith took responsibility for mentoring and developing both his own patrol and the personnel of the wider Special Operations Task Group ... His efforts ensured the effective transfer of his professional knowledge and experience to a new generation of special forces soldiers.'

The citation made specific mention of one mission:

On 21 October 2012, Corporal Roberts-Smith led a lone special reconnaissance patrol deep into the insurgent stronghold of Char-Chineh [Shahidi Hassas], Afghanistan, to gain intelligence for future operations. The patrol remained clandestine through the night but was contacted during the day, coming under intense enemy small arms and rocket fire. Corporal Roberts-Smith ordered the establishment of a defensive position and coordinated ground and aerial fire support to break contact and marry up with the extraction agency.

This was the mission that Person 7 said the 'whole troop' believed was only conducted to draw fire from the enemy, so that Roberts-Smith could get another 'gong'.

After hearing about the conferral of the Commendation for Distinguished Service on Ben Roberts-Smith, a group of SASR sergeants and patrol commanders signed a letter of complaint, saying that he was undeserving of the award, and sent it up the chain of command. Person 7, who was one of the signatories, testified in court that Ben Roberts-Smith had planned and led only five missions on that deployment, and that 'none of these jobs achieved any objective'.

* * *

Andrew Hastie's only full SOTG deployment was as a troop commander during rotation 19, the last for the Australian special forces in Afghanistan, before complete retrograde and deconfliction. After what he perceived to have happened in Syachow, and hearing rumours about places like Darwan, he and other men in positions of command looked to ensure that their rotation fulfilled their obligations but stayed as free as possible of legal and moral hazards.

One senior NCO addressed the incoming soldiers, saying: 'People are doing stupid shit overseas. Don't do it, don't ruin your life.'

When Hastie arrived at Camp Russell, he says he was relieved to find that his troop sergeant was also of the opinion that they should stay away from criminality. '"I didn't come to Afghanistan to put a dirt farmer on his knees and shoot him in the back of the head,"' Hastie testified that his troop sergeant told him.

Hastie's Troop B wasn't accused of any executions, but they didn't manage to stay completely away from death, controversy and criminality. On his first job, working with the Provincial Police Response Company – ostensibly Matiullah's SWAT team but in reality 'violent thugs in uniform' says Hastie – Hastie's troop was being supported by an Apache gunship. Under Hastie's battlefield command, the helicopter targeted what were thought to be a pair of insurgents but were actually two small boys, aged six and eight, pastoral nomads collecting firewood. Both were killed. There's no suggestion that this was an instance of criminality or wrongdoing, just more accidental death.

Then, on 28 April 2013, Hastie's troop was part of a 120-soldier element sent to Zabul Province, directly east of

Uruzgan, to attempt to kill or capture Objective Rapier, Abdul Hai, who had been hunted by the SASR since Mark Wales and his troop attempted to 'process' him. During the mission, the troop killed four men. A corporal was tasked with collecting biometric information about the killed men and testing for explosive residue, but, feeling time pressure, he produced a scalpel and severed the hands of three Afghan men.

Nine days earlier, the troop had been part of an information session conducted by ADFIS, with a civilian fingerprint and crime scene expert in attendance. An internal report says that the following exchange happened between a Defence scientist and one of the SASR soldiers.

'So you're sweet with us bringing back a hand?' the soldier asked.

'Yes ... you've got to do what you've got to do on the ground,' replied the scientist.

The report says an ADFIS sergeant was asked whether severing hands was a good method of securing fingerprint evidence, but claims that he told the soldier to ask his officers whether it was permissible. The sergeant said that after the session, the severance of hands was 'all they were focused on'.

The mutilation of a corpse is illegal, and in direct contravention of the Law of Armed Conflict.

Andrew Hastie was interviewed for the internal report. He said: '[M]y gut instinct was okay, that's a strange practice,' but that he had no recognition that it contravened the law. On his return to Tarin Kot, Hastie discussed the incident with his troop sergeant, who said: 'There's no uncertainty, I wouldn't cut people's fucking hands off, sir.'

Hastie reported the incident to his commanding officer, and a 'cease ops' was called, meaning all missions planned by Force Element Alpha and Force Element Bravo were paused. A source within SOCOMD says that some within the command believed it would have been preferable for Hastie not to a report the incident so that the 'cease ops', investigation and eventual media reporting would not have happened.

An internal report found the soldier who mutilated the corpse had 'failed to adequately appreciate the possible strategic consequences of those actions, in particular the potential responses from ... the Australian public and the media'.

The mission did not find Objective Rapier, nor did it discover any leads as to his whereabouts.

* * *

Some mark 22 June 2013 as the date that Australia's special forces' war in Afghanistan ended. This was the date of the last large gun battle the SOTG was involved in. It was also the date of Australia's last combat death, and of the final action in Afghanistan that resulted in a Victoria Cross.

Most of the commandos from Force Element Bravo can't remember why a clearance mission of a village in the Khod Valley had been ordered on that day, but they almost appreciated the opportunity for one last gunfight.

In the ISR footage of the infiltration on that raid, one soldier can be seen sprinting from the Chinook helicopter as it landed. Anyone who knew the platoon involved would already have known who the sprinting soldier was: Cameron Baird, the former AFL prospect and commando team leader and the man who charged into a Chenartu home after Luke Worsley was killed, posting grenades and firing his rifle, an action for which he was awarded the Medal for Gallantry. Baird always charged into battle. He was loved for it, although one of his commanding officer says he had always feared that it would one day get Baird killed.

A number of Afghans were killed as the Australians moved up through the valley, and the clearance was proceeding as planned until another team leader – one of Baird's closest friends – bypassed an Afghan, who shot him, rounds smashing into the Australian's plate armour but also his leg. The offending Afghan was shot and killed, but the clearance was halted as the injured commando required immediate medical assistance.

Baird's team was called to support the medical extraction, and as they did, they passed an entrenched insurgent position stacked with weaponry and ammunition. The Afghan and Australian elements exchanged gunfire at very close range. The Australians posted grenades though a doorway, creating a wall of dust between the two groups, who were shooting at a distance of only three or four metres.

Cameron Baird led the fight, charging many times to the door to fire and killing at least two men – before he collected a packet of rounds and was killed by the last living insurgent. After that insurgent was killed, Baird's body was taken back to Tarin Kot, as was the injured team leader, who continues his service within the Australian special forces.

I wrote a biography of Cameron Baird, which was published as *The Commando: The Life and Death of Cameron Baird VC, MG*. In 2016 I began work on the book by going to Holsworthy Barracks, the home of the full-time commando regiment, where I interviewed many of the men involved in that gunfight. I learned more from them about Australia's war that afternoon than I had in the decade before, which included time I'd spent in Afghanistan.

The men had been so wholly crafted by their experiences in Afghanistan, and deeply lamented that there would never be another war like this. One man told me he knew he would never feel as good as he had when he was in combat with his brothers. Another said that Bairdy was the lucky one: he had died charging at a machine gun, as this man now told me he would have liked to. One spoke about how impossible he felt it now was for him to live a normal life, applying himself to a normal morality. Another said he had lost his own emotional life: his father was about to undergo heart surgery, but he felt nothing.

All these men were still serving, but some showed obvious symptoms of post-combat stress as I interviewed them. One of the interviewees would take his own life while still in service fewer than two years later. According to his to psychiatrist, he was 'guilt ridden' because he had 'killed so many people'.

Cameron Baird had died no more than a kilometre from Bagh Khoshak, where the SASR had experienced its first gunfight in Uruzgan. No significant government presence was ever established in the area.

* * *

Even before Cameron Baird was killed, the SASR was winding down its operations in Afghanistan.

'I was actively saying to my boss: "Hey, we could fly on this target but it's June 2013. Do we really want to go out there and lose a bloke?"' Andrew Hastie says.

The morning Baird was killed, Hastie ran into the commando. They exchanged pleasantries, having worked together in the preceding weeks.

'I had his commando section attached to my troop, and I got to know him a bit,' Hastie recalls. 'I saw him at the DFAC [dining facility] the morning of the day he got killed. I said, "Hey, how you going, mate?" He said, "We're going out on some bullshit." Sure, they wanted to get into it, but was it worth dying for?'

* * *

On 28 October 2013, Tony Abbott, the new prime minister of Australia, and Bill Shorten, the new opposition leader, travelled to Tarin Kot for a ceremony marking the end of Australia's combat in Afghanistan.

'Australians have re-found a martial tradition that might have faded away with our parents and grandparents,' Abbott said. 'We have found new heroes like Mark Donaldson, Ben Roberts-Smith and Daniel Keighran [Prime Minister Abbott would announce Cameron Baird's Victoria Cross a year later] ... we have learnt that all the fierce and indomitable people of this beautiful but forbidding land are worthy of respect.'

Prime Minister Abbott unveiled a memorial at the base honouring the Australians who died in Uruzgan. The inscription read: 'Only the dead have seen the end of war.'

Those words were eternally true, but they were especially true for SOCOMD members. In just a few months' time, Prime Minister Abbott would send Australia's special forces back into battle, this time against ISIS and the Australian violent *jihadis* who had flown from their suburban homes and joined the death-obsessed wannabe theocracy.

The bulk of the Australian intelligence officers, analysts and shooters who would be sent to Iraq for the highly secretive mission would be SOTG veterans, but the force would be largely bereft of SASR operators. They were about to be placed firmly on the bench.

29

'Special forces, love them like brothers, watch them like children'

'BRO, BRO. I DON'T WANT anything to do with this, I want to be left alone.'

So said Person 4, according to the testimony of Person 7, when Person 7 approached him in 2014 to detail his experiences in Darwan to a superior. According to Person 7, this was the second time the allegation of murder in Darwan had gone up the chain of command, it having gone nowhere the first time.

Person 7 testified in court that in mid-2013 he became aware of the allegation that an Afghan had been kicked off a cliff and murdered. He said he convened a meeting with four SASR patrol commanders to talk about how to proceed. According to Person 7, he and the other sergeants met with the SASR's regimental sergeant major (RSM), the most senior soldier in the regiment and the figure tasked with keeping good order and discipline across the regiment. They explained what they knew of what had happened in Darwan.

'What are you hoping to get out of this?' the RSM said to Person 7 at the end of the meeting, according to Person 7's testimony.

'It's not about what I can get out of this, it's about what needs to be done,' Person 7 testified that he replied.

Another soldier who said he had a meeting with the RSM about the alleged killing in Darwan testified that the RSM 'wasn't receptive'. 'The RSM said, words to the effect of, "it was out of his hands, it was way over his head, he honestly didn't know what to do with it",' that soldier said.

Person 7 testified that when a new RSM was installed in 2014, he once again attempted to bring the allegations to light. He claimed that he did so after a soldier whom both he and Ben Roberts-Smith knew well was about to be removed from the regiment because of Ben Roberts-Smith's dislike of him; that soldier was considering contacting the media about Ben Roberts-Smith's conduct.

Person 7 said he asked the soldier not to speak to the media, and instead said he would raise the matter with the new RSM.

Person 7 said he approached Person 4 and asked him to talk to the RSM and give his own first-hand account of Darwan. But Person 4 didn't want anything to do with this – he wanted to be left alone. Person 7 says he reminded Person 4 of his legal and moral obligations, and then, according to Person 7, meetings were arranged with the new RSM.

Another soldier, anonymised as Person 18, testified that he was in one of these meetings, which he said ranged widely. 'It was the allegations that something had happened during [the] 2012 rotation; allegations of things that had happened in 2009; discrepancies between people in regards to Tizak; allegations of bullying; he went through each one of these, asking what we knew,' he testified.

Person 18 said he was in a meeting with Person 4, and the thing he most strongly remembered was Person 4 – the older rookie who was allegedly ordered to execute a man at Whiskey 108 – breaking down and crying as he relayed his memories of what had happened in Darwan. Andrew Hastie testified that he also took part in a meeting where the alleged murder was discussed and says that by 2013, multiple soldiers were claiming that Ben Roberts-Smith had kicked a man off a cliff.

The former RSM, now a major and senior leader within the SASR, was subpoenaed to appear at the trial, and on the stand he denied that he had been approached about the alleged murder in

Darwan, testifying that Person 7 approached him saying: 'I have concerns about Mr Roberts-Smith being a fit and proper person to be given the Victoria Cross, he had bullied [Person 7] and others and he had also claimed to have carried out actions that others believed they'd carried out.'

'Did any of the sergeants at that meeting raise concerns that Mr Roberts-Smith had broken the rules of engagement while serving in Afghanistan?' Arthur Moses SC asked the man designated as Person 100. "There was no mention of that and no hint of it mentioned either," Person 100 said.

Person 100 testified that he met with four corporals days later and that once again, the conversation was about bullying, lying with regard to kills and Ben Roberts-Smith's Victoria Cross. Person 100 says the conversation was not, however, about allegations of murder. This testimony lies in stark contrast to the accounts of Person 4 and Person 18 given in court.

Under cross-examination, Nine Media's lawyer suggested that Person 100 'didn't report [allegations of war crimes] because you wanted those allegations to be swept under the rug.'

'I could not report allegations that I was not aware of, sir.' Person 100 replied.

* * *

In making final submissions, Nine barrister Nicholas Owens laid out, over three days, the evidence he says had been collected for their truth defence, including each of the alleged murders that Nine claimed Ben Roberts-Smith was involved in. Owens did concede, however, that without being able to compel Person 66 to give evidence about the murder Nine alleges was committed in Syachow in 2012, it is unlikely the court will substantiate that allegation. The allegation was not, however, retracted.

Owens accused seven current and former SASR soldiers of collusion and perjury, including Ben Roberts-Smith, claiming a number of motivations but primarily the witnesses own potential legal exposure. He also alleged that some of these witnesses and

Ben Roberts-Smith attempted to subvert the course of justice. 'Efforts to suborn, intimidate or otherwise tamper with a witness are among the most forcible of presumptive indicators of consciousness of guilt,' Owens said.

Nicholas Owens also claimed that Ben Roberts-Smith mounted a secretive campaign against Person 6, a patrol commander who was alleged to have bought the prosthetic leg back to Tarin Kot after the killing at Whiskey 108 and was characterised as someone who hated Roberts-Smith.

Retired policeman John McLeod had given evidence about this allegation saying that, under instruction from his sometime employee Ben Roberts-Smith, he contacted journalists, the AFP commissioner and a serving member of parliament, Nick Xenophon, indicating that Person 6 had smuggled weapons into Afghanistan (to be used as drop weapons) and that he had illegal weapons at his home that may be used for a massacre. Person 6's home was raided by police, but no weapons were found.

Owens read from a text message that was alleged to have been sent by Ben Roberts-Smith to his then wife Emma Roberts reading: 'What happened to (Person 6) will scare the others.'

Arthur Moses noted that the context in which this message was sent was not in evidence and that the message was sent a full month after media reports about Person 6, saying this wasn't damning evidence but 'an invitation to conjecture and speculation'.

Owens alleged that threatening letters were sent to a number of soldiers and former soldiers with one letter, sent to a then serving member and was submitted as evidence that the recipient and other had been 'spreading lies' to the media and IGADF inquiry.

'You have one chance to save yourself,' the letter read, forcefully suggesting that he should recant his testimony. The letter stated that: 'We are very aware of your murderous actions over many tours in Afghanistan and we have specific mission details, dates and witnesses who are now willing to expose you to the authorities so you are criminally investigated. Just like when you participated in the execution of 2 PUCs from the Taliban's makeshift medical compound following the battle of Tizak.' It was signed: 'A friend of the regiment.'

Ben Roberts-Smith's ex-wife testified in court that her then husband had told her he had written the letters and printed them off at the Channel Seven offices where he worked. She says Ben Roberts-Smith told her that John McLeod had posted the letters.

John McLeod gave evidence saying he did send the letters, but that he didn't know their contents. When the media revealed what the contents of the letters were, McLeod testified that Ben Roberts-Smith asked him to say that he, McLeod, had written them. McLeod testified that he responded: 'Fuck that you weak dog' and says after that utterance he never spoke to Roberts-Smith again.

Arthur Moses alleged some of what McLeod says he was asked to do, he did on his own initiative and not under orders from Ben Roberts-Smith.

Throughout the trial, Ben Roberts-Smith maintained he has never sought to influence criminal proceedings or investigations, nor intimidate witnesses and, in his final submissions, Arthur Moses says that these allegations sit alongside all others that had not been established.

Moses said that the case presented by Nine ridiculously represented Roberts-Smith, a highly credentialed soldier, as a 'homicidal psychopath. Seriously?'

Moses spent some time making the distinction between very serious allegations, like murder, and lesser imputations, citing case law he believes establishes a higher burden of proof required to claim truth over very serious allegations.

He says a lack of ballistics and forensics evidence is something that should be considered and that, in all instances, Nine's case 'just didn't come up to proof' presenting a 'fanciful and salacious case theory, based on conjecture, speculation and imprecise testimony which they propound in this case'.

He further said that Nine media 'jumped on the rumours like salmon on a hook' and illegally published them as fact, accusing a number of Nine's witnesses of lying, perjury and collusion, reserving particular ire for Person 14 and Person 7. He said the Afghan witnesses in the case should all be discounted also as they are 'hardly impartial.'

The testimony of some soldiers like Person 4, the older rookie soldier who was shoulder to shoulder with Ben Roberts-Smith during the battle of Tizak, Moses said, was not a liar but confused about the facts.

'(Nine) failed to establish any motive, the case is a nonsense and, frankly, an embarrassment,' says Moses in closing.

A ruling on this case is expected after publication.

* * *

In late 2014, when a new commander, Major General Jeff Sengelman, was appointed as SOCAUST, he found myriad post-Afghanistan problems in his regiments, and especially in his premier regiment, the SASR. Many of these issues related to future capability, which had been neglected in the high-intensity period of warfare. The SASR needed to better integrate with land forces, build the capacity and legal framework for clandestine intelligence gathering, and re-engage with friendly forces in the region. But above all, it needed to continue to be a deployable and desirable option when political decisions were being made. Sengelman believed that this last issue was perhaps the most immediate.

Allegations of wrongdoing and internal fractures were rampant, and not only within the SASR. External agencies, including ASIS, had made complaints about the conduct of the SASR in Afghanistan. One complainant (who doesn't wish to be named), a man who worked outside of Tarin Kot with tribal leaders and the SASR, says that eventually he hated having to work with those 'fucking psychopaths', as you 'never knew who they were going to kill'.

There were allegations that an SASR soldier drunkenly threatened a female ASIS agent with his pistol in Kabul, and that the SASR killed wantonly, sometimes even killing ASIS sources.

This echoed an incident that took place on the border between Afghanistan and Pakistan. A CIA agent working as part of an Omega Team sent a DEVGRU element out to bring back two Afghan men, possibly sources. The DEVGRU operators instead chose to 'canoe' those two men in their sleep, as well as four other men sleeping nearby.

Sengelman informally surveyed his senior NCOs and officers, and asked his soldiers to (anonymously) write him letters about any alleged war crimes committed. He received more than 200 letters, and they spoke of executions and wanton killing, as well as drug and steroid abuse, domestic violence, weapon loss and potential theft, as well as bullying and a culture of silence.

Sengelman then commissioned a study from a sociologist and organisational expert named Dr Samantha Crompvoets, looking the 'culture and interactions' in SOCOMD. She would interview dozens of internal and external stakeholders. Dr Crompvoets had been tasked with conducting an investigation of culture, and not of murder and illegality, but she found that the insular nature of the command and the SASR contributed to criminality, and that SOCOMD had failed in its obligation to correct that nature.

One anonymous insider interviewed by Dr Crompvoets said, of the SASR soldiers: 'They cannot help themselves, they're not content with being given a role, go off and just do that role.' Another said: 'Special forces, love them like brothers, watch them like children.' Yet another believed that parochialism was wrecking Australia's special forces capability, and said the 'leaders were borderline criminal in their approach'.

After the release of Dr Crompvoets' report, the Chief of the Defence Force directed the Inspector-General of the ADF to investigate 'unsubstantiated stories' of possible crimes – illegal killings, and inhumane and unlawful treatment of detainees – over a lengthy period of time in the course of the SFTG/SOTG deployments in Afghanistan. Meanwhile, the SASR was placed under direct command of SOCAUST, meaning the regiment no longer had its own commanding officer. An operational pause was also placed on the regiment, so it could not be deployed on operations (with a few exceptions, such as counterterrorism operations).

In April 2014, the Australian Strategic Policy Institute issued a White Paper on the future of Australia's special forces post-Afghanistan. It recognised that the unidimensional warfare of the previous decade in Afghanistan had created 'operational fatigue', but also noted that a key job of SOCOMD was still 'maintaining and strengthening SOF cooperation with our US ally', and that this had been done in Afghanistan.

* * *

Three months after the White Paper was issued, a radical Sunni organisation – constituted of former Iraqi Ba'athists, Zarqawi loyalists and sectarian agitators and purists – exploited the weakness of the Iraqi state and attacked and occupied a series of cities and towns, from without and within, the largest of which was Mosul, Iraq's second city. Baghdad was also threatened, and the multibillion-dollar Iraqi military, paid for and trained by the United States and its allies, including Australia, showed little capacity to repel the attacks.

In August 2014, the Australian government announced that the ADF was supporting a humanitarian mission to relieve and support Yazidi minorities besieged by Islamic State in an area of Iraq called Sinjar, where the Sunni militia force planned to slaughter Yazidi men and sell the women into sex slavery. What wasn't announced was that some Australian special forces soldiers and intelligence analysts were already engaged in the conflict. An SASR element from the shadowy 4 Squadron had already been deployed in Jordan, where, alongside US, British, French and other intelligence services and special forces, they were tracking foreign fighters coming into the region in an operation named Gallant Phoenix.

On 26 August, a larger Australian special forces element was ordered to meet at Sydney airport for deployment, without any information as to where they were going or for how long. On

30 August they flew into the permanent Australian base at Al Minhad, in the UAE.

During the Sinjar siege, the Abbott government said it was not currently looking to put 'boots on the ground' in Iraq. When the Australian special forces element who were about to insert into Iraq were met by Major General Craig Orme of JTF 633 at Al Minhad, he said: 'They've said no boots on the ground, so it's just as well you blokes wear Merrells' – referring to the non-uniform hiking shoes preferred by Australian special forces.

This new SOTG was to be inserted into Iraq for six months. Again, there was no parliamentary debate or visibility, and the soldiers travelled on hastily generated diplomatic passports. This was to be rotation 1 of Operation Okra, a new Australian mission to Iraq. Targeted killing was again to be a major element of the deployment.

* * *

For the Australian special forces in this war against Islamic State, the key unit of operations was not the patrol or team, troop or platoon, but the strike cell.

On the ground in the fight against ISIS in Iraq, a number of reinvigorated, reorganised and rearmed Iraqi special forces elements (some rebranded Shi'ite death squads, some local militias loyal to Iran, some upskilled police units) were doing most of the fighting on the ground, with Australia's special forces there to 'advise and assist' them. One of the most significant ways Australia advised and assisted was via the strike cells, where intelligence was gathered, tactical plans were developed and migrated, aerial platforms were managed, and strikes were approved – all in one room.

The strike cell wasn't a place where the 'kill chain' would meander over hours or days, and across cities or perhaps continents. In the strike cell, approvals happened in one room, and bombs went on heads quickly, all day, every day. The strike cells in Iraq and Syria authorised more than 110,000 airstrikes against Islamic State, some in support of Iraq offensives and others targeted against individuals.

I wrote the book *Mosul: Australia's Secret War inside the ISIS Caliphate* about this deployment, and while Australians were generally not kicking in doors and clearing compounds as they had in Afghanistan, they were undoubtedly fighting a violent war.

While some Australian soldiers were deployed to Baghdad – where they worked at a secure air base, or at the massive strike cell at the multibillion-dollar US Embassy fortress, marking ISIS fighters for death while wearing civilian clothes and thongs – there were also many in the field. The Australians at Al Asad Air Base in Anbar Province were surrounded by ISIS-occupied territory, and experienced both direct and indirect attacks. They worked in Fallujah, a city that was destroyed so it might be saved. Australians also fought in two locations in Mosul, a *Mad Max*–style hellscape where they were attacked by ISIS drones and chemical weapons, and felt the shattering reports of car bombs sent to annihilate them. Death was everywhere.

The 4 Squadron SASR element, part of Gallant Phoenix, crossed a new martial bridge in the fight against ISIS. Very few Australian men who joined Islamic State survived the war, and it was generally reported that they were 'killed in the fighting', but some were tracked (very easily, in some cases, as they had brought their Australian mobile phones with them to Iraq and Syria) by Gallant Phoenix and killed in targeted airstrikes. This is believed to be the first known instance of Australian nationals being targeted and killed by their own government without any attempt at due process.

It was reported that Jake Bilardi, a confused 18-year-old from Melbourne who was radicalised online, was killed in a suicide car bombing in Ramadi, but it's believed he was targeted by Gallant Phoenix before he could complete his suicide strike. Tony Abbott also confirmed to me that, as prime minister, he approved a strike in Syria against an ISIS recruiter named Mohammad Ali Baryalei, a former Kings Cross bouncer and *Underbelly* actor. He was recruiting new Australian violent *jihadis* and, under pressure from his ISIS superiors, attempting to instigate an atrocity in Sydney.

Most of the Australian men who joined ISIS as violent *jihadis* were killed, many in targeted airstrikes. It's not known how or whether Australian intelligence services and 4 Squadron were involved in these killings but it's possible men like violent Sydney *jihadi* Khaled Sharrouf, killed in an airstrike as the Syrian city of Raqqa started to fall, were being tracked and by Gallant Phoenix and that Australian military or governmental officials were part of the kill chain. The strike that killed Sharrouf also killed two of his Australian children, boys aged 11 and 12.

* * *

Shane Healey was part of the first element that inserted into Baghdad during Operation Okra. There he fulfilled a significant intelligence function, briefed the Australian and US commanders regularly, and returned to Australia a wreck.

When he arrived home in Sydney, he was greeted by his former partner and their two-year-old son, who ran to him, yelling, 'Daddy!' As the boy jumped into Healey's arms, the soldier broke down and, for the first and only time, cried with his colleagues around him.

Here was the end of Healey's war. Only after the cessation of the fighting did he get a feel for the hectic pace of his post-9/11 life.

After multiple private military deployments to Iraq, where he had killed and seen friends killed; after domestic work as part of the SOCOMD Tactical Assault Group (which included attending the Derrinallum siege and lethal bomb blast in Victoria, and the suspected attempted bombing of Sydney schoolgirl Madeleine Pulver); after working on Operation Hawick, dedicated to recovering the bodies of the Australians killed in the MH17 attack in Ukraine; and after responding to chemical attacks in Syria – after all of that, as well as SOTG deployments to Afghanistan and Iraq, Healey was done.

As the tears fell, he thought not of what had been done, but what had been lost. He thought about the birth of his middle son, who came into the world less than three weeks after Hekmatullah went on his shooting rampage, and three days after the Darwan mission. Healey was planning, and was authorised, to return home for the birth, but had stayed at his post for the hunt. The hunt had been paramount. The war had been paramount. War is always paramount for those fighting it.

Alongside Healey arriving back to Sydney was Ian Langford, a small, quiet but fierce special forces officer who had deployed to Afghanistan as a commando major in 2006, and whose star within Defence had not stopped rising since then. Langford had assumed SOCOMD battlefield command in Afghanistan and Iraq, commanded 2CDO and was almost universally respected by those who had served under him. Now a brigadier, he is known as one of Australia's sharpest military minds.

'You're done, aren't you?' Langford asked Healey, who had been briefing the officer in Iraq only a few weeks earlier, as he had daily in Afghanistan in 2012.

Healey says that before his 2015 briefings, he had been vomiting with anxiety. He had only respect and appreciation for Langford, but the environment outside his commander's sphere had become poisonous and overwhelming. The allostatic load, or cumulative stress, had become too much for Healey. The pain of injuries that had not been properly attended to – including to his shoulders that meant he could no longer raise a weapon – was just too much. All the death, all the action. It was all too much.

'Yep, I'm done,' Healey replied.

Healey started transitioning out of the military. The anxiety and hyper-functioning fostered in a SOCOMD member remained, but not the circumstances that required them. Healey had surgeries on both shoulders, which requiring painkillers and long periods of rehab. His relationship with his partner was dissolving. Like so many Afghan veterans, Healey's transition from the painful twilight of his military career to a fully realised civilian life involved time in hospital for full-time psychiatric care.

In 2020, Healey requested that Joint Health Command retrospectively consider him to be 'treated as medically unfit'. The command reviewed his records. '[R]egarding PTSD ... the member has multiple entries from [Health Services] from service in Afghanistan in 2010 and 2012 and Iraq,' Healey was notified. '[M]ember was clearly described as a "psychological wreck".'

Healey had never known about these PTSD diagnoses, nor was he aware that he should have been considered unfit for deployment due to PTSD-related issues. He was given a retrospective diagnosis of PTSD in 2020, and a retrospective medical discharge from the ADF.

* * *

Of the SASR operators with whom he deployed, Mark Wales estimates that roughly 80 per cent have some sort of ongoing serious mental-health issue caused, or seriously exacerbated, by their service in Afghanistan. A few, he says, have diagnosed maladies and are being treated. This is the case for Wales himself. The vast bulk of those suffering, however, are not being treated, nor are their mental-health injuries captured by statistics. According to Wales, these men simply left the unit after Afghanistan, 'walked off into the shadows and took [their PTSD] with them'.

In many instances, he says, these suffering former operators would find it profoundly difficult to reintegrate into a normal civilian life even if they did find treatment; the best course of action would be to help them transition into a lifestyle that fits with their ongoing mental-health issues, including jobs where they may be able to work independently or from home.

There is only limited understanding of PTSD and its relationship with common comorbidities such as depression, hypervigilance, anxiety disorders, and drug and alcohol addiction, in Australia and elsewhere. Even more poorly understood is how post-combat mental-health issues relate to physiological changes that are commonly experienced by special forces soldiers, like traumatic brain injury caused by weapon blasts or explosive entry, impact or overpressure injuries, possible instances of chronic traumatic encephalopathy (CTE), hearing loss and chronic pain, often back pain.

There has been an attempt to capture the post-combat experience of the large cohort of special forces created following 9/11 in the catch-all diagnosis of 'operator syndrome', but studies of this syndrome are new and few.

What is known is that blind eyes were turned to PTSD and other mental-health issues by commanders, in favour of capability in overstressed regiments that were asked to deploy endlessly. This was true of the SASR, but also across SOCOMD.

* * *

Opportunities to ask questions of special forces commanders about their failed mental-health obligations have been limited, as most are still serving and may not be approached, except through the near impenetrable iron curtain of Defence media. Recently, however, two such commanders were compelled to answer questions after being subpoenaed to appear at the coronial inquest of the self-harm death of a commando sergeant who had multiple combat tours of Afghanistan and Iraq.

Counsel assisting the coroner, Kristina Stern SC (who later acted for Defence interests in the Ben Roberts-Smith trial) asked questions of a lieutenant colonel still serving in SOCOMD and who cannot be named.

The commando sergeant was sent to Iraq as part of Operation Okra after being diagnosed with severe PTSD and related alcohol abuse issues. He had been hospitalised with PTSD, and SOCOMD had known about these and his other mental-health symptoms before they deployed him. Joint Health Command had ruled that the sergeant was undeployable as he had 'extensive psychological and alcohol dependence history [and that] ongoing stressors ... [place him] at high risk of deterioration while deployed'.

The lieutenant colonel admitted that he personally exercised command authority to overrule the medical ruling and send the sergeant back to a war zone. Evidence was offered that, when this lieutenant colonel heard that one of his sergeants was undeployable due to severe PTSD, he said: 'What the fuck? [He] must deploy with us. No one can replace him or his knowledge of the team this close to deployment.'

'It was one of the lowest risk of trauma of any of his deployments,' the lieutenant colonel testified of Operation Okra. 'You can find trauma in Sydney.'

The commando was stationed for part of his deployment at Al-Taqaddum Air Base, between Ramadi and Fallujah, two cities that had to be violently liberated from ISIS. The inquest learned, from my book *Mosul: Australia's Secret War inside the ISIS Caliphate*, that the commando had conducted an out-of-the-wire mission with US special forces to retrieve the body of a killed US pilot from enemy territory. The lieutenant colonel was asked about this mission, and its potential to exacerbate the commando's PTSD.

Initially, the ADF position was to categorically deny that the commando had been involved in this mission. Later, that position changed.

'The amount of things that he had gone through in his time in the regiment, and also as a private security contractor ... it would be surprising to me that a relatively benign activity like this triggers a relapse of PTSD,' the lieutenant colonel said of the body-retrieval mission. 'We're talking about a guy [who] carried Luke Worsley, he applied a tourniquet to a bloke who had lost his leg, he had been there when Cam [Baird] won his VC.'

'Did it not occur to you that the events involving Luke Worsley and Cameron Baird were precisely the events that may have given rise to his PTSD?' Stern responded. Was it not 'entirely foreseeable to you ... that if [the commando] was involved in any way in the mission to recover [the] body, that could cause an exacerbation of his PTSD?'

The lieutenant colonel agreed, in retrospect, that it could have.

Next, Brigadier Ian Langford was questioned about his decision to sign the first waiver for deployment the commando received, which was issued after the commando had been diagnosed with severe PTSD and was suffering from 'impulsive aggressive acts, emotional disregulation, moderate psych distress and harmful use of alcohol'. Langford responded that he wasn't given a full picture of the mental health of the soldier under his command when he signed the waiver.

Brigadier Langford and the lieutenant colonel were asked about the extensive training modules they were required to undertake before assuming command, and then about how many modules they had been ordered to do, or had sought to undertake themselves, that focused on PTSD, post-combat stress or mental health. The answer was none.

Mark Smethurst, formerly a commanding officer of the SOTG and of 2CDO, and now the chair of the Commando Welfare Trust, says the mental-health weight of the Afghanistan War is only beginning to be understood. In 2021, it was believed that that 464 currently serving and former soldiers had taken their own lives since the invasion of Afghanistan, but a 2022 study by the Australian Institute of Health and Welfare found that 1273 soldiers and former soldiers had died by self-harm since 2001.

'It's such a small number of people we lost in combat, but look at the damage we've done to those individuals,' says Smethurst of the suicides. 'You look at Vietnam vets, Korean vets – they talk about the value of their fight. Our veterans are now are asking themselves: "Is what I did worthwhile?"'

30

'We were just killing so many people and it didn't make any difference at all'

IN FEBRUARY 2015, MATIULLAH KHAN visited Kabul, and there, as he was leaving a hotel with some friends, he saw the last thing he ever would: a woman wearing a full-body burqa. Only it wasn't a woman but a man wearing a suicide vest under his blue robes. Matiullah was killed instantly in the blast.

A few months after the killing, the Taliban launched a successful offensive against Kunduz, a northern city of roughly 300,000 people. For the first time since the US invasion in 2001, an Afghan city was held by the Taliban, and fear ran through the country. There was deep scepticism about the ability of the Afghan security forces, but almost no observers or commentators had thought Afghanistan's cities would be under threat so soon after the US troop withdrawal. It was a relatively small Taliban force that had taken the city, and a series of airstrikes from US planes eventually drove them out.

One of the air attacks was conducted by a US AC-130 gunship on a building that, it was later revealed, was a Médecins Sans Frontières trauma centre. The attack killed 42 people: patients, some injured Taliban, and medical staff. The doctors who attempted to flee the hospital were tracked by the AC-130 guns and killed, in some instances blown apart or decapitated.

Meanwhile, in the United States, the Special Inspector General for Afghanistan Reconstruction (SIGAR) was secretly investigating the failures of America's war in the country, and interviewing key actors.

In an interview on 25 August 2015, Douglas Lute, former White House 'czar' for Afghanistan, said:

> [W]e were devoid of a fundamental understanding of Afghanistan – we didn't know what we were doing ... for example, the economy: we stated our goal was to establish a 'flourishing market economy'. I thought we should specify a flourishing drug trade – that is the only part of the market that's working. It's really much worse than you think. There is a fundamental gap of understanding on the front end, overstated objectives, an overreliance on the military, and a lack of understanding of the resources necessary ... If the American public knew the dysfunction.

These interviews were conducted for internal review only, and were not expected to be published. They were made public after *The Washington Post* persisted through years of legal injunction.

Jeff Eggers, a National Security Council staffer and former Navy SEAL, was interviewed by SIGAR about the troop surge and said: '[O]verall it was our assumption that security would improve from 2008 to 2012 as we increased resources and that we would see a return on our investment. Generals Petraeus and Allen had faith that what happened in Iraq would happen in Afghanistan, but that never materialized.' Eggers said this was likely due to the Afghan military and police remaining corrupt 'down to patrol level'. 'After the killing of Osama bin Laden, I said that Osama was probably laughing in his watery grave considering how much we have spent on Afghanistan,' said Eggers.

Brown University's Costs of War project found in 2019 that the United States' bill for the war in Afghanistan, including interest and ongoing veteran care, is US$2.27 trillion, and rising. This is more than 100 times the gross domestic product of Afghanistan, and ten times the cost of the Apollo and Gemini spaceflight programs combined, adjusted for inflation.

An unnamed former adviser to a US Army special command force told SIGAR in 2017, 'They thought I was going to come to them with a map to show them where the good guys and bad guys live. It took several conversations for them to understand that I did not have that information in my hands. At first, they just kept asking: "But who are the bad guys, where are they?"'

Ryan Crocker, the US ambassador to Afghanistan, spoke to SIGAR about the central issue of the war: the 'over-aggregation of the enemy to include the Taliban as part of our response to al Qaeda. Why, if we were focused on al Qaeda, were we talking about the Taliban? Why were we talking about the Taliban all the time instead of focusing our strategy on al Qaeda?'

Al-Qaeda was an organisation with malignant and expansionist aims. The Taliban are ideologically malignant also, but with few aims outside Afghanistan. They were also largely indistinct from much of the population in those provinces of Afghanistan where the guns were loudest.

In September 2017, the Taliban seized a number of facilities in Uruzgan, including health centres, some of which had been built and paid for by the Australian government. After the seizures, comments from a Taliban spokesman reflected the nature of the cooperative relationship between the Taliban and the Afghan government: the Taliban had closed the centres not because they were run by the government, he said, but because the centres were performing so poorly. The Taliban could no longer allow them to run.

'In most of these centres there was no proper medication. There were no doctors or healthcare personnel,' the spokesman said. 'We asked repeatedly for better services but no one cared. Now if the local administration do not provide basics, we will.'

* * *

Regardless of the public-facing rhetoric, Australia's only significant war aim in Afghanistan was to maintain its alliance with the United States – an objective that significantly hindered our ability to make independent decisions, such as when to leave the war and the composition of our forces.

'I've likened it to this: you don't want to be the first guy that stops clapping at the end of Stalin's speech,' says David Kilcullen.

Australia's primary war aim was achieved after the initial 2001 and 2002 deployments of the SASR, but it was then put in peril after Australia reinserted in 2005. With US allies in provinces across the country, Australia would have significantly undermined its war aim if it had left Afghanistan before the other major allies.

'When it turned out the Americans didn't have a plan, [Australia was] screwed,' says Kilcullen. 'We couldn't make them win and we couldn't win ourselves and we couldn't leave. Nobody in the war in Afghanistan, except for the Americans and the Taliban, can win or lose the war. No coalition player would win except the US, and if the Americans didn't have a strategy, we were all trapped.'

The Australian SASR was ensnared, happily in many instances, prosecuting endless kill/capture missions, with the regiment becoming, as Kilcullen describes it, 'fungible SOF' – meaning they were not fulfilling a role that was specific to their capabilities, but a generic raiding, direct-action role as part of a 'JPEL servicing machine'. The JPEL program, however, became something that not even JSOC believed was working in Afghanistan.

Michael Flynn, former JSOC deputy to General McChrystal and later Director of Intelligence in Afghanistan, was interviewed by SIGAR about the intelligence used in the war and the kill/capture program. He said this: 'I spent three years hunting human beings to kill them or capture them in Iraq, in Afghanistan and East Africa ... that was JSOC's missions.' And of the Afghanistan mission, he said: 'We were just killing so many people and it didn't make any difference at all ... we are participating in conflict, we are not really here to win.'

Mark Smethurst, who in 2012 was the commander of the combined ISAF special operations forces, says that there should have been recognition and understanding that counterinsurgencies can take decades to resolve, and the decision to telegraph the end of the Western war was a dangerous one.

'All I knew was that there would be no line drawn under the JPEL,' says former SASR captain Mark Wales. 'We would keep killing these leaders for generations, and new ones would continue to rise through the ranks.'

Wales also says that many of the missions the SASR were asked to do could and should have been carried out by conventional forces. A great number of Australia's JPEL missions were 'cordon and search' operations, meaning an external cordon was established at an area of interest to keep enemies out, while an internal cordon was created so that a force might search the area, often for a JPEL target. It has been noted by many, including in the IGADF report, that the bulk of this work could have been done by conventional infantry forces, spreading the workload.

'They would have taken more casualties and wouldn't have been as good at it, but they could have done it,' says Wales.

Speculation as to why conventional forces were not used for such missions centres on two hypotheses. One is that SOCOMD and the special forces regiments wanted to take as much of the combat pie as they could, to ingratiate themselves politically and gain further funding and facilitates. Another is that the national security veil that could be draped around the special forces was useful in creating an informational cordon around Australia's seemingly obligatory but politically unpalatable activities in Afghanistan.

All serving SOTG members have 'protected identity' status: they cannot be named in any public forum, nor are they allowed to speak to the media. Were conventional forces tasked with prosecution of JPEL targets, the Australian public and Australian lawmakers would have had a much greater understanding of the war, and therefore may have had a darker opinion of it.

The professionalism of SOCOMD members might thus have been abused in Afghanistan in the service of politically expedient secrecy.

* * *

'The thing that struck me when I went through Tarin Kot and Kandahar was how tired our guys looked,' says Kilcullen. 'Much more tired than, say, the Dutch, and certainly more tired than the British.'

'We [pushed] the SAS especially, but also 2 Commando, in this very soul-destroying form of warfare where all you're doing is hitting targets night after night after night. You're not achieving anything in terms of winning the war, because that's not why you're there. You're there to demonstrate that we can, and it became a self-licking ice-cream cone.'

The ice-cream cone metaphor describes a system that only affects itself – that exists only to exist. Kilcullen was not the only person I interviewed to describe elements of Australia's war in Afghanistan in this way.

The SOTG became incredibly effective at finding and hunting targets, and the SASR and commandos became known and feared across the province as '*quetalof*', or 'bearded devils', but there was no effective way of forcing fealty to a broken Afghan government. Kilcullen says the special forces war, as it was prosecuted, might have created a net-negative peace dividend in Uruzgan.

'Did [Australia] create more guerrillas by the way we operated? Absolutely. No doubt about that,' says Kilcullen. 'We did a lot of fighting in Chora, where our local ally was directing us, and when our ally is Matiullah Khan, obviously we're going to be fighting the enemies of Matiullah Khan.'

When speaking about the motivations and composition of the tribes, communities and militias of southern Afghanistan, three former SOTG veterans said the same thing to me: 'They're all Taliban.'

I asked Major General John Cantwell about the estimated 11,000 people killed legally by Australia's special forces, and whether he had an understanding of how many of these people were al-Qaeda fighters, how many were Taliban coming out of the province or country, and how many were locals who were the enemy of our tribal allies or locals who felt honour-bound to fight or were caught in the fighting.

There was a long pause before he answered. 'When people were killed by us, they were generally left on the battlefield for their families to collect.'

Epilogue

AFTER THE UNITED STATES unitarily signed a peace agreement with the Taliban in February 2020 and committed to removing all US assets, including intelligence and air support, from Afghanistan within 14 months, the government of Afghanistan was on borrowed time.

The Afghan National Army fought fiercely in many places, and tens of thousands of Afghan troops died in the protection of their cities, but in real terms the fight was already over. There were no US planes, no drones, no intelligence. Taliban forces were surrounding the capital. All that was left was either a negotiation or a massacre.

On 14 August 2021, with the Taliban in control of most of the country, a massive airlift of coalition staff, coalition partners and vulnerable people started at Kabul's Hamid Karzai International Airport. On 15 August, Abdul Ghani Baradar – the Uruzgani mullah who had attempted to negotiate with Jason Amerine's American element and Hamid Karzai 20 years earlier – entered Kabul to assume control of the city on behalf of the Taliban.

A number of international forces scrambled task forces to Kabul to aid the evacuation of their citizens, dual nationals and allies. Australia's mission airlifted 3200 people from Kabul who were Australian citizens or visa holders, and another 900 people at the behest of coalition partners. The Australian mission was admirable and difficult, but had little capacity to retrieve people from most of Kabul, let alone Uruzgan. The chaotic, embarrassing, violent and highly publicised withdrawal from Kabul was traumatising for many Australians who had served in Afghanistan.

Andrew Hastie says people approached him during this period asking if what was happening in Kabul was affecting his mental state. It wasn't. He had reconciled with the war years before the re-ascendency of the Taliban. Hastie had been mentally affected by his service, with a persistent nightmare in which he and Ben Roberts-Smith have killed an Australian soldier, but says it disappeared as soon as information about the alleged murders in Afghanistan conducted by the SASR stated to make its way into the public realm.

'When I came back from Afghanistan, I became more engaged in political questions. I read a biography of Churchill and was struck by his maiden speech to the UK parliament in 1901. Although a veteran and supporter of the Boer War, he was sympathetic to the Boer cause and even respected their struggle. he said: 'If I were a Boer I hope I should be fighting in the field,' says Hastie. 'I felt the same about the Afghan people: they were dirt poor, tough and willing to fight for their homes. If I was an Afghan, I'd probably be fighting too.' Hastie wasn't an Afghan, however, so he fought for Australia and supported the war.

From Hastie's perspective as a cavalry officer, which he was before his time in the SASR, and then as a troop commander, the war in Afghanistan did seem to him like big-government liberalism exported into Afghanistan at gunpoint.

The coalition's strategy, he explains, said to the Afghans, '"This is the way you should live. We're going to help you get there, never mind your culture, your geography, your traditions, your religion. This is how it should be." By the time I left, I thought, "This is crazy. You can't change people's hearts through coercion."'

Hastie was concerned not only about strategy, but also about the very necessity of the mission. 'These guys weren't al-Qaeda,' he says. 'They barely have 3G on their phones. They're using diesel generators for basic amenities, living in mud huts in almost biblical surroundings – it's not like they're going to get on a plane and attack us.'

The realisations he gained during and after the war were part of a political awakening and activation. In the first half of 2015, he fought Islamic State as part of the SASR's Gallant Phoenix contribution. In the second half, he fought the Labor Party in a federal by-election, an election that he won, making him, at age 32, the federal MP for the Western Australian seat of Canning. Hastie had to contest his seat again at the 2016 general election, and after winning again, he joined the Parliamentary Joint Committee on Intelligence and Security. Until the Liberal/National coalition's May 2022 election loss (Hastie retained his seat easily and is now shadow defence minister), he was the chair of that committee, and also the assistant defence minister.

In those roles, Hastie says, he tried to help amend the governmental framework that allowed the strategic failures and aimlessness of the war and the informational blockages, including the Department of Defence's ability to 'manage' ministers and apply what he calls an 'Orwellian attitude to media management'.

Currently, the Australian government has few ways to compel Defence to give information to the government, except by having ministers request information via their direct contacts (who themselves may not be able to extract information from their subordinates or contemporaries). There is currently a Joint Standing Committee on Foreign Affairs, Defence and Trade, but that committee has no mandate to summons Defence personnel and ask hard questions, so Defence engages with this committee on a somewhat voluntary basis.

Hastie says he has been agitating for a 'statutory defence committee where the major parties can work in a classified and open environment'. He says this could help create 'future defence ministers who know the environment, can ask the right questions and can do their job properly'.

Hastie says minor parties like the Greens would not be invited to join such a committee – which means that regardless of the committee's reports and recommendations, one of the principal issues of Australia's war would not be investigated: the tacit agreement that appeared to arise between the two major parties not to expose or embarrass each other over Australia's role in Iraq and Afghanistan.

I suggested to Hastie that the interlinked issues of war crimes in Afghanistan, veteran suicides and the strategic failures of the war might require a historical and statutory reckoning such as a royal commission – an inquiry process in which current and former Defence members, and also current and former government ministers, might be compelled to speak. Hastie doesn't agree, because of the low historical conversion rate from royal commission recommendations to actual change.

Mark Wales believes there must be some official and open investigation into the war, and specifically into the actions of the special forces, but he also thinks that attacking and de-fanging the special forces capability would be counterproductive, and might also assign blame incompletely.

'The whole idea [of the SASR] is that you have a group of people who are fucking vicious, highly lethal and very good at their job,' says Wales. 'You want them because the country needs it, but don't send them somewhere and say kill everyone but be nice about it. Clearly the government has made a huge mistake because they've left us there for ten years off the leash, and the unit needs a lot of blame, but the buck stops somewhere [else].

'Until we recognise all of our failures, how are we going to grow as a country and as a military? [The war in Afghanistan] was a huge fucking failure. But I'm also realistic. I know our government and military aren't stupid enough to come out and say "that was my fault". There's very little incentive to do that, [but] there should be blood over this one.'

* * *

After returning from Iraq, Brigadier Ian Langford, at the time a colonel, gave a series of talks in Canberra titled 'Ethics Under Fire: Issues and Challenges from Contemporary Conflict for the Australian Army'. His speeches looked at the ethics of the involvement of Australia's special forces in the post-9/11 wars.

Langford discussed the principles of *jus ad bellum* and *jus in bello*, the two foundations of 'just war theory', a branch of philosophy that looks at the conditions under which warfare can ethically be initiated and conducted. Just war theory is built on the foundational ideas that warfare is inherently bad, that protecting civilians is inherently good, and that the goal of a just war is to re-establish an acceptable and long-lasting peace, as quickly as possible and with the least amount of bloodshed.

According to just war theory, an ethical war can only be waged as a method of last resort. It should only be fought by (or for) an authority that is recognised as legitimate by the population in the area where the fighting is happening, and should only be fought if there is a reasonable chance of success. The theory also holds that the level of violence in a war must be proportional to the aims of the conflict.

Langford, however, noted that there is a difference between fixed ethics, or the 'difference between right and wrong', and situational ethics, which 'apply when we allow for the circumstances of the situation'. Both must be considered, he said, when looking at the actions of Australia's special forces.

The international laws of war and Australian law are immutable, but ethical theories and frameworks may be elastic, depending on the circumstances, as 'what is right and what is righteous [can be] very different'.

According to Langford, the ADF must ensure that 'when we depart from situational ethics, it's for an intended purpose and then [we have] the organisational leadership and the core leadership ability to be able to ... maintain a moral compass'. In short, without the appropriate leadership, the 'departure from situational ethics' may create a permanent moral drift, which a force may find difficult to rectify.

Brigadier Langford was the SOTG commander in 2012, receiving the Distinguished Service Cross for his service in that role. When the IGADF report found that most of the alleged murders by SOTG members took place in 2012, Langford attempted to hand back his DSC. General Angus Campbell, who also received medals for his command in Afghanistan, told his subordinate that he could not give the medal back, and must wait for 'a sensible reform plan to be developed', and 'give opportunity for me and others to be more systematic in the approach we take'.

It was revealed in April 2022 that no administrative action has been taken against any officer due to alleged murders in Afghanistan, no promotions have been blocked, and no medals have been revoked. Instead, General Campbell wrote, 19 officers who were commanding soldiers who may have committed murder must 'learn from this experience' as their careers progress unhindered, unless and until any charges from the Office of the Special Investigator arise.

Alongside the Office of the Special Investigator inquiries, the Morrison government committed to launching an oversight panel in the wake of the shocking release of the 2020 IGADF report on alleged war crimes in Afghanistan. The panel was tasked with identifying the cultural and structural issues within Defence and SOCOMD that may have contributed to illegality or wrongdoing in Afghanistan. They were also to make recommendations, that would be given to government and then defence. When announcing the oversight panel to the media, then defence minister Linda Reynolds strongly committed to a transparent process of reform, saying: 'I will get an official report every quarter from [the oversight panel] and I will be reporting regularly to the parliament on their reports to me.' She then added: 'Can I just stress [that] nothing will be out of bounds for this inquiry.'

To date, none of the panel's reports, issued to Peter Dutton, the defence minister replacing Reynolds, have been spoken of in parliament nor is it known whether any of their findings or recommendations have been acknowledged or actioned by government or defence.

I contacted the new Labor defence minister, Richard Marles, after the federal election in May 2022, in the hope of asking him about how the Albanese government plans to address military and special forces reform. At time of writing he has not replied.

However, it seems major changes are afoot at SOCOMD. In July 2022 the commanding officer of the SASR, Person 81 of the Ben Roberts-Smith trial, announced to his senior staff that a major training module would no longer be part of the SASR reinforcement cycle, changing the capability of the regiment. The module, titled Tactical Prosecution Continuum (TCP), is akin to the Close Quarter Battle module that Mark Smethurst introduced to the 2nd Commando Regiment, completely changing the capability set of the element.

Without a capability like TCP or CQB, a force like the SASR would be able to find and fix, but often not finish, as they would no longer be capable of direct-action missions and room to room, urban fighting. This would also mean that the SASR may not be able to fully fulfill their 'black' or counterterrorism role either. This likely means any direct action and counter terrorism missions that arise in the future may be handed over to the commandos.

This begs the questions of what the SASR's new capability is. Some have suggested that the SASR may be moving back to their long-range surveillance and reconnaissance role, but since 2001, massive improvements in drone, satellite and optic technology have made that role less desirable. It's possible the SASR may be attempting to pivot to a 'grey' or intelligence gathering capability, as desired while Mark Mathieson was unit psychologist. There is also a suggestion that the regiment may, in the future, be downsized or perhaps even gently disbanded, with an increasing number of capabilities being moved east, to the commandos and SOER.

* * *

In August 2022, Richard Marles and Prime Minister Albanese announced a major review of Australian Defence capabilities in what was described as 'much bigger than Dibb,' referring to the 1986 strategic review conducted by Paul Dibb and the ensuing ground breaking *The Defence of Australia* white paper, that recommended Australia's special forces largely concentrate on homeland operations.

The leadership pair also announced that two men who were deeply involved in the war in Afghanistan would be undertaking the review: Sir Angus Houston, Chief of Defence from 2005–2011, and Professor Stephen Smith, who was the Minister of Foreign Affairs and then Minister of Defence under Prime Ministers Rudd and Gillard.

Richard Males said that *The Defence of Australia* white paper's strategic updates have, 'established a strategic setting for this country for 35 years, and inherent in that was an idea that if any country meant to do us harm, we would be given a 10-year warning.

'In 2020, the Defence Strategic Update observed for the first time that we're within that 10-year window,' said Marles. The country that the leadership group feared may wish to do harm to Australia is China.

At the announcement, Sir Angus Houston said Australia's security situation was, 'the worst I've ever seen in my lifetime' and that recently Australia's defence circumstances have changed dramatically.

The review will consider all current and planned Australian capabilities and programs, including those relating to Australia's special forces who were expecting an expensive equipment and communications upgrade in line with the recommendations of a 2016 Defence White Paper.

Expected to be considered in the current review are disruptive technologies like cyberwarfare, hypersonic missiles, expanded drone and unmanned capabilities, with Richard Males announcing that it was important that the review would 'cross pollinate' with new capabilities offered by the AUKUS agreement. Prime Minister Albanese also noted that the review will look at interoperability with Australia's allies like the United States.

The review is expected to be delivered to the federal government in the first half of 2023.

* * *

I asked former defence ministers Joel Fitzgibbon and Brendan Nelson whether it would be appropriate now to release to the public all the secret information that exists about the scope of

Australia's war, including the number of Afghans who were killed, legally or illegally by Australia's special forces (thought to be about 11,000), how they were killed and the circumstances of their deaths. Fitzgibbon said that would not be appropriate, as such information might impact on Australia's national security and the government's ability to deploy the ADF in certain parts of the world. Nelson, on the other hand, said the information should be made available. 'I think Australians need to know just how brave and how professional and how effective these men, and they were men, were,' he argued.

I asked Mark Wales the same question. 'There should be public information,' he replied. 'That should be released to the public. You guys voted a government for this war to continue and this is the effect of it. This is what happens when you don't debate an involvement in a war until 2010. I think the public needs to have its face rubbed in the dogshit a little bit.'

I posed a slightly different question to Andrew Hastie, asking how the deaths in which Australia was involved during the war – Australians who died in combat or were psychologically wrecked, as well as Afghans who were killed illegally or accidentally, and those who were killed legally – might be incorporated into our understanding of ourselves as modern Australians.

In answer, Hastie recalled a homily given by Archbishop Peter Jensen at the funeral of an Australian commando killed by an IED in Afghanistan. The archbishop said the blood of this commando was on the hands of every person in the service, and every person in the country, as, in a democracy, we all participated in the decisions made regarding the war.

I asked how voters could have been responsible when there were massive and 'Orwellian' efforts by the ADF and the government to stop the public from knowing what was actually happening in Afghanistan, in the service of US–Australian diplomatic and military relations.

'Maybe we never will reconcile with it,' Hastie said. 'Maybe that's just one of the paradoxes of war.'

Acknowledgements

Most of those who agreed to be interviewed in this book did so with the knowledge that there may be a downside to doing so, be it the scratching of a scar or perhaps exposing or acknowledging a difficult truth or legacy. These people spoke to me anyway, because they believe in an obligation to transparency and truth, which I believe is a true ANZAC virtue.

On ANZAC Day and in other moments of commemoration we say the words 'lest we forget': a call not only to remember the dead, but to also think of a tomorrow that we hope may be better through knowledge of the mistakes of yesterday. It is impossible to consciously avoid a mistake unless we know what that mistake was. A great many thanks go to all of those who spoke.

Individual thanks go to Shane, who gave me insights infused throughout the book and ScoJo, who I owe a Milo to.

Thanks also go Jude and Col Evans, who generously gave me desk to write and help give me time to finish this book. Thanks also (and always) go to their daughter and granddaughter, Claire and Poppy, and also to my mum, who are the world's loveliest people.

Thanks also go to my publisher Helen, editor Lachlan, agent Jane and my friend Tim Concolo.